Open Resources for Community College Algebra (Part II)

Open Resources for Community College Algebra (Part II)

Portland Community College Faculty

August 10, 2019

Project Leads: Ann Cary, Alex Jordan, Ross Kouzes
Technology Engineer: Alex Jordan
Contributing Authors: Ann Cary, Alex Jordan, Ross Kouzes, Scot Leavitt, Cara Lee, Carl Yao, Ralf Youtz
WeBWorK Problem Coding: Chris Hughes, Alex Jordan, Carl Yao
Significant Contributors: Kara Colley, Wendy Lightheart
Cover Image: Ralf Youtz

Edition: 2.0

Website: pcc.edu/ORCCA

Acknowledgements

This book has been made possible through Portland Community College's Strategic Investment Funding, approved by PCC's Budget Planning Advisory Council and the Board of Directors. Without significant funding to provide the authors with the adequate time, an ambitious project such as this one would not be possible.

The technology that makes it possible to create integrated print, HTML eBook, and WeBWorK content is PreTeXt, created by Rob Beezer. David Farmer and the American Institute of Mathematics deserve credit for the PreTeXt HTML eBook layout being feature-rich, yet easy to navigate. A grant from OpenOregon funded the original bridge between WeBWorK and PreTeXt.

This book uses WeBWorK to provide most of its exercises, which may be used for online homework. WeBWorK was created by Mike Gage and Arnie Pizer, and has benefited from over 25 years of contributions from open source developers. In 2013, Chris Hughes, Alex Jordan, and Carl Yao programmed most of the WeBWorK questions in this book with a PCC curriculum development grant.

The javascript library MathJax, created and maintained by David Cervone, Volker Sorge, Christian Lawson-Perfect, and Peter Krautzberger allows math content to render nicely on screen in the HTML eBook. Additionally, MathJax makes web accessible mathematics possible.

The PDF versions are built using the typesetting software LaTeX, created by Donald Knuth and enhanced by Leslie Lamport.

Each of these open technologies, along with many that we use but have not listed here, has been enhanced by many additional contributors over the past 40 years. We are indebted to these contributors for their many contributions. By releasing this book with an open license, we honor their dedication to open software and open education.

vi

To All

HTML, PDF, and print.   This book is freely available as an HTML eBook, a PDF for reading on a screen, and a PDF intended for printing. Additionally, a printed and bound copy is available for purchase at low cost. All versions offer the same content and are synchronized such that cross-references match across versions. They can each be found at pcc.edu/orcca.

There are some differences between the HTML eBook, PDF screen version, and PDF-for-print version.

- The HTML eBook offers interactive elements, easier navigation than print, and its content is accessible in ways that a PDF cannot be. It has content (particularly in appendices) that is omitted from the PDF versions for the sake of economy. It requires no more software than a modern web browser with internet access.

- Two PDF versions can be downloaded and then accessed without the internet. One version is intended to be read on a screen with a PDF viewer. This version retains full color, has its text centered on the page, and includes hyperlinking. The other version is intended for printing on two-sided paper and then binding. Most of its color has been converted with care to gray scale. Text is positioned to the left or right of each page in a manner to support two-sided binding. Hyperlinks have been disabled.

- Printed and bound copies are available for purchase online. Up-to-date information about purchasing a copy should be available at pcc.edu/orcca. Contact orcca-group@pcc.edu if you have trouble finding the latest version online. Any royalties generated from these sales support OER development and maintenance at PCC and/or scholarships to PCC students.

Copying Content.   The source files for this book are available through pcc.edu/orca, and openly licensed for use. However, it may be more conveneient to copy certain things directly from the HTML eBook.

The graphs and other images that appear in this manual may be copied in various file formats using the HTML eBook version. Below each image are links to .png, .eps, .svg, .pdf, and .tex files for the image.

Mathematical content can be copied from the HTML eBook. To copy math content into *MS Word*, right-click or control-click over the math content, and click to Show Math As MathML Code. Copy the resulting code, and Paste Special into *Word*. In the Paste Special menu, paste it as Unformatted Text. To copy math content into LaTeX source, right-click or control-click over the math content, and click to Show Math As TeX Commands.

Tables can be copied from the HTML eBook version and pasted into applications like *MS Word*. However, mathematical content within tables will not always paste correctly without a little extra effort as described above.

Accessibility. The HTML eBook version is intended to meet or exceed web accessibility standards. If you encounter an accessibility issue, please report it.

- All graphs and images should have meaningful alt text that communicates what a sighted person would see, without necessarily giving away anything that is intended to be deduced from the image.

- All math content is rendered using MathJax. MathJax has a contextual menu that can be accessed in several ways, depending on what operating system and browser you are using. The most common way is to right-click or control-click on some piece of math content.

- In the MathJax contextual menu, you may set options for triggering a zoom effect on math content, and also by what factor the zoom will be. Also in the MathJax contextual menu, you can enable the Explorer, which allows for sophisticated navigation of the math content.

- A screen reader will generally have success verbalizing the math content from MathJax. With certain screen reader and browser combinations, you may need to set some configuration settings in the MathJax contextual menu.

Tablets and Smartphones. PreTeXt documents like this book are "mobile-friendly." When you view the HTML version, the display adapts to whatever screen size or window size you are using. A math teacher will usually recommend that you do not study from the small screen on a phone, but if it's necessary, the HTML eBook gives you that option.

WeBWorK for Online Homework. Most exercises are available in a ready-to-use collection of WeBWorK problem sets. Visit webwork.pcc.edu/webwork2/orcca-demonstration to see a demonstration WeBWorK course where guest login is enabled. Anyone interested in using these problem sets may contact the project leads. The WeBWorK set defintion files and supporting files should be available for download from pcc.edu/orcca.

Odd Answers. The answers to the odd homework exercises at the end of each section are not printed in the PDF versions for economy. Instead, a separate PDF with the odd answers is available through pcc.edu/orcca. Additionally, the odd answers are printed in an appendix in the HTML eBook.

Interactive and Static Examples. Traditionally, a math textbook has examples throughout each section. This textbook uses two types of "example":

Static These are labeled "Example." Static examples may or may not be subdivided into a "statement" followed by a walk-through solution. This is basically what traditional examples from math textbooks do.

Active These are labeled "Checkpoint." In the HTML version, active examples have WeBWorK answer blanks where a reader may try submitting an answer. In the PDF output, active examples are almost indistinguishable from static examples, but there is a WeBWorK icon indicating that a reader could interact more actively using the eBook. Generally, a walk-through solution is provided immediately following the answer blank.

Some readers using the HTML eBook will skip the opportunity to try an active example and go straight to its solution. That is OK. Some readers will try an active example once and then move on to just read the solution. That is also OK. Some readers will tough it out for a period of time and resist reading the solution until they answer the active example themselves.

For readers of the PDF, the expectation is to read the example and its solution just as they would read a static example.

A reader is *not* required to try submitting an answer to an active example before moving on. A reader *is* expected to read the solution to an active example, even if they succeed on their own at finding an answer.

Reading Questions.   Each section has a few "reading questions" immediately before the exercises. These may be treated as regular homework questions, but they are intended to be something more. The intention is that reading questions could be used in certain classroom models as a tool to encourage students to do their assigned reading, and as a tool to measure what basic concepts might have been misunderstood by students following the reading.

At some point it will be possible for students to log in to the HTML eBook and record answers to reading questions for an instructor to review. The infrastructure for that feature is not yet in place at the time of printing this edition, but please check pcc.edu/orcca for updates.

Alternative Video Lessons.   Most sections open with an alternative video lesson (that is only visible in the HTML eBook). These video play lists are managed through a YouTube account, and it is possible to swap videos out for better ones at any time, provided that does not disrupt courses at PCC. Please contact us if you would like to submit a different video into these video collections.

x

Pedagogical Decisions

The authors and the greater PCC faculty have taken various stances on certain pedagogical and notational questions that arise in basic algebra instruction. We attempt to catalog these decisions here, although this list is certainly incomplete. If you find something in the book that runs contrary to these decisions, please let us know.

- Basic math is addressed in an appendix. For the course sequence taught at PCC, this content is prerequisite and not within the scope of this book. However it is quite common for students in the basic algebra sequence to have skills deficiencies in these areas, so we include the basic math appendix. It should be understood that the content there does not attempt to teach basic math from first principles. It is itended to be more of a review.

- Interleaving is our preferred approach, compared to a proficiency-based approach. To us, this means that once the book covers a topic, that topic will be appear in subsequent sections and chapters in indirect ways.

- We round decimal results to four significant digits, or possibly fewer leaving out trailing zeros. We do this to maintain consistency with the most common level of precision that WeBWorK uses to assess decimal answers. We generally *round*, not *truncate*, and we use the $\approx$ symbol. For example, $\pi \approx 3.142$ and Portland's population is ≈ 609500. On rare occasions where it is the better option, we truncate and use an ellipsis. For example, $\pi = 3.141\ldots$.

- We offer *alternative* video lessons associated with each section, found at the top of most sections in the HTML eBook. We hope these videos provide readers with an alternative to whatever is in the reading, but there may be discrepancies here and there between the video content and reading content.

- We believe in opening a topic with some level of application rather than abstract examples, whenever that is possible. From applications and practical questions, we move to motivate more abstract definitions and notation. At first this may feel backwards to some instructors, with some easier examples *following* more difficult contextual examples.

- Linear inequalities are not strictly separated from linear equations. The section that teaches how to solve $2x + 3 = 8$ is immediately followed by the section teaching how to solve $2x + 3 < 8$. Our aim is to not treat inequalities as an add-on optional topic, but rather to show how intimately related they are to corresponding equations.

- When issues of "proper formatting" of student work arise, we value that the reader understand *why* such things help the reader to communicate outwardly. We believe that mathematics is about more than understanding a topic, but also about understanding it well enough to communicate results to others. For example we promote progression of equations like

$$1 + 1 + 1 = 2 + 1$$
$$= 3$$

instead of

$$1 + 1 + 1 = 2 + 1 = 3.$$

We want students to understand that the former method makes their work easier for a reader to read. It is not simply a matter of "this is the standard and this is how it's done."

- When solving equations (or systems of linear equations), most examples should come with a check, intended to communicate to students that checking is part of the process. In Chapters 1–4, these checks will be complete simplifications using order of operations one step at a time. The later sections may have more summary checks where steps are skipped or carried out together, or we promote entering expressions into a calculator to check.

- Within a section, any first context-free example of solving some equation (or system) should summarize with some variant of both "the solution is…" and "the solution set is…." Later examples can mix it up, but always offer at least one of these.

- With applications of linear equations (not including linear systems), we limit applications to situations where the setup will be in the form $x + \text{expression-in-}x = C$ and also to certain rate problems where the setup will be in the form $at + bt = C$. There are other classes of application problem (mixing problems, interest problems, …) which can be handled with a system of two equations, and we reserve these until linear systems are covered.

- With simplifications of rational expressions in one variable, we always include domain restrictions that are lost in the simplification. For example, we would write $\frac{x(x+1)}{x+1} = x$, for $x \neq -1$. With *multivariable* rational expressions, we are content to ignore domain restrictions lost during simplification.

Entering WeBWorK Answers

This preface offers some guidance with syntax for WeBWorK answers. WeBWorK answer blanks appear in the active reading examples (called "checkpoints") in the HTML eBook version of the book. If you are using WeBWorK for online homework, then you will also enter answers into WeBWorK answer blanks there.

Basic Arithmetic. The five basic arithmetic operations are: addition, subtraction, multiplication, and raising to a power. The symbols for addition and subtraction are $+$ and $-$, and both of these are directly avialable on most keyboards as + and -.

On paper, multiplication is sometimes written using $\times$ and sometimes written using $\cdot$ (a centered dot). Since these symbols are not available on most keyboards, WeBWorK uses * instead, which is often shift-8 on a full keyboard.

On paper, division is sometimes written using $\div$, sometimes written using a fraction layout like $\frac{4}{2}$, and sometimes written just using a slash, /. The slash is available on most full keyboards, near the question mark. WeBWorK uses / to indicate division.

On paper, raising to a power is written using a two-dimensional layout like 4^2. Since we don't have a way to directly type that with a simple keyboard, calculators and computers use the caret character, ^, as in 4^2. The character is usually shift-6.

Roots and Radicals. On paper, a square root is represented with a radical symbol like $\sqrt{}$. Since a keyboard does not usually have this symbol, WeBWorK and many computer applications use sqrt( ) instead. For example, to enter $\sqrt{17}$, type sqrt(17).

Higher-index radicals are written on paper like $\sqrt[4]{12}$. Again we have no direct way to write this using most keyboards. In *some* WeBWorK problems it is possible to type something like root(4, 12) for the fourth root of twelve. However this is not enabled for all WeBWorK problems.

As an alternative that you may learn about in a later chapter, $\sqrt[4]{12}$ is mathematically equal to $12^{1/4}$, so it can be typed as 12^(1/4). Take note of the parentheses, which very much matter.

Common Hiccups with Grouping Symbols. Suppose you wanted to enter $\frac{x+1}{2}$. You might type x+1/2, but this is not right. The computer will use the order of operations and do your division first, dividing 1 by 2. So the computer will see $x + \frac{1}{2}$. To address this, you would need to use grouping symbols like parentheses, and type something like (x+1)/2.

Suppose you wanted to enter $6^{1/4}$, and you typed 6^1/4. This is not right. The order of operations places a higher priority on exponentiation than division, so it calculates 6^1 first and then divides the result by 4. That is simply not the same as raising 6 to the $\frac{1}{4}$ power. Again the way to address this is to use grouping symbols, like 6^(1/4).

Entering Decimal Answers. Often you will find a decimal answer with decimal places that go on and on. You are allowed to round, but not by too much. WeBWorK generally looks at how many *significant digits* you use, and generally expects you to use **four or more** correct significant digits.

"Significant digits" and "places past the decimal" are not the same thing. To count significant digits, read the number left to right and look for the first nonzero digit. Then count all the digits to the right including that first one.

The number 102.3 has four significant digits, but only one place past the decimal. This number could be a correct answer to a WeBWorK question. The number 0.0003 has one significant digit and four places past the decimal. This number might cause you trouble if you enter it, because maybe the "real" answer was 0.0003091, and rounding to 0.0003 was too much rounding.

Special Symbols. There are a handful of special symbols that are easy to write on paper, but it's not clear how to type them. Here are WeBWorK's expectations.

Symbol	Name	How to Type
∞	infinity	infinity or inf
π	pi	pi
$\cup$	union	U
$\mathbb{R}$	the real numbers	R
$\vert$	such that	| (shift-\, where \ is above the enter key)
$\leq$	less than or equal to	<=
$\geq$	greater than or equal to	>=
$\neq$	not equal to	!=

Contents

Part II

Preparation for STEM

Chapter 5

Exponents and Polynomials

5.1 Adding and Subtracting Polynomials

A polynomial is a particular type of algebraic expression.

- A company's sales, s (in millions of dollars), can be modeled by $2.2t + 5.8$, where t stands for the number of years since 2010.

- The height of an object from the ground, h (in feet), launched upward from the top of a building can be modeled by $-16t^2 + 32t + 300$, where t represents the amount of time (in seconds) since the launch.

- The volume of an open-top box with a square base, V (in cubic inches), can be calculated by $30s^2 - \frac{1}{2}s^2$, where s stands for the length of the square base, and the box sides have to be cut from a certain square piece of metal.

All of the expressions above are polynomials. In this section, we will learn some basic vocabulary relating to polynomials and we'll then learn how to add and subtract polynomials.

5.1.1 Polynomial Vocabulary

There is a lot of vocabulary associated with polynomials. We start this section with a flood of vocabulary terms and some examples of how to use them.

Definition 5.1.2 A **polynomial** is an expression with one or more terms summed together. A term of a polynomial must either be a plain number or the product of a number and one or more variables raised to natural number powers. The expression 0 is also considered a polynomial, with zero terms. ◊

Example 5.1.3
- Here are three polynomials: $x^2 - 5x + 2$, $t^3 - 1$, $7y$.
- The expression $3x^4y^3 + 7xy^2 - 12xy$ is an example of a polynomial in more than one variable.
- The polynomial $x^2 - 5x + 3$ has three terms: x^2, $-5x$, and 3.
- The polynomial $3x^4 + 7xy^2 - 12xy$ also has three terms.

- The polynomial $t^3 - 1$ has two terms.

Remark 5.1.4 A polynomial will never have a variable in the denominator of a fraction or under a radical.

Definition 5.1.5 The **coefficient** (or numerical coefficient) of a term in a polynomial is the numerical factor in the term. ◊

Example 5.1.6

- The coefficient of the term $\frac{4}{3}x^6$ is $\frac{4}{3}$.

- The coefficient of the second term of the polynomial $x^2 - 5x + 3$ is -5.

- The coefficient of the term $\frac{y^7}{4}$ is $\frac{1}{4}$.

Checkpoint 5.1.7 Identify which of the following are polynomials and which are not.

   a. The expression $-2x^9 - \frac{7}{13}x^3 - 1$ ($\square$ is $\square$ is not) a polynomial.

   b. The expression $5x^{-2} - 5x^2 + 3$ ($\square$ is $\square$ is not) a polynomial.

   c. The expression $\sqrt{2}x - \frac{3}{5}$ ($\square$ is $\square$ is not) a polynomial.

   d. The expression $5x^3 - 5^{-5}x - x^4$ ($\square$ is $\square$ is not) a polynomial.

   e. The expression $\frac{25}{x^2} + 23 - x$ ($\square$ is $\square$ is not) a polynomial.

   f. The expression $37x^6 - x + 8^{\frac{4}{3}}$ ($\square$ is $\square$ is not) a polynomial.

   g. The expression $\sqrt{7x} - 4x^3$ ($\square$ is $\square$ is not) a polynomial.

   h. The expression $6x^{\frac{3}{2}} + 1$ ($\square$ is $\square$ is not) a polynomial.

   i. The expression $6^x - 3x^6$ ($\square$ is $\square$ is not) a polynomial.

Explanation.

   a. The expression $-2x^9 - \frac{7}{13}x^3 - 1$ is a polynomial.

   b. The expression $5x^{-2} - 5x^2 + 3$ is not a polynomial because it has a negative exponent on a variable.

   c. The expression $\sqrt{2}x - \frac{3}{5}$ is a polynomial. Note that *coefficients* can have radicals even though variables cannot, and the square root here is *only* applied to the 2.

   d. The expression $5x^3 - 5^{-5}x - x^4$ is a polynomial. Note that *coefficients* can have negative exponents even though variables cannot.

   e. The expression $\frac{25}{x^2} + 23 - x$ is not a polynomial because it has a variable in a denominator.

   f. The expression $37x^6 - x + 8^{\frac{4}{3}}$ is a polynomial. Note that *coefficients* can have fractional exponents even though variables cannot.

   g. The expression $\sqrt{7x} - 4x^3$ is not a polynomial because it has a variable inside a radical.

   h. The expression $6x^{\frac{3}{2}} + 1$ is not a polynomial because a variable has a fractional exponent.

   i. The expression $6^x - 3x^6$ is not a polynomial because it has a variable in an exponent.

Definition 5.1.8 A term in a polynomial with no variable factor is called a **constant term**. ◊

Example 5.1.9 The constant term of the polynomial $x^2 - 5x + 3$ is 3.

Definition 5.1.10 The **degree** of a term is one way to measure how "large" it is. When a term only has one variable, its degree is the exponent on that variable. When a term has more than on variable, its degree is the sum of the exponents on the variables. A constant term has degree 0. ◊

Example 5.1.11

- The degree of $5x^2$ is 2.

- The degree of $-\frac{4}{7}y^5$ is 5.

- The degree of $-4x^2y^3$ is 5.

- The degree of 17 is 0. Constant terms always have 0 degree.

Definition 5.1.12 The **degree of a nonzero polynomial** is the greatest degree that appears amongst its terms. ◊

Definition 5.1.13 The **leading term** of a polynomial is the term with the greatest degree (assuming there is no tie). The coefficient of a polynomial's leading term is called the polynomial's **leading coefficient**. ◊

Example 5.1.14 The degree of the polynomial $4x^2 - 5x + 3$ is 2 because the terms have degrees 2, 1, and 0, respectively, and 2 is the largest. Its leading term is $4x^2$, and its leading coefficient is 4.

Remark 5.1.15 To help us recognize a polynomial's degree, the standard convention at this level is to write a polynomial's terms in order from highest degree to lowest degree. When a polynomial is written in this order, it is written in **standard form**. For example, it is standard practice to write $7 - 4x - x^2$ as $-x^2 - 4x + 7$ since $-x^2$ is the leading term. By writing the polynomial in standard form, we can look at the first term to determine both the polynomial's degree and leading term.

There are special names for polynomials with a small number of terms, and for polynomials with certain degrees.

monomial A polynomial with one term, such as $3x^5$, is called a monomial.

binomial A polynomial with two terms, such as $3x^5 + 2x$, is called a binomial.

trinomial A polynomial with three terms, such as $x^2 - 5x + 3$, is called a trinomial.

constant polynomial A zeroth-degree polynomial is called a constant polynomial. An example is the polynomial 7, which has degree zero.

linear polynomial A first-degree polynomial is called a linear polynomial. An example is $-2x + 7$.

quadratic polynomial A second-degree polynomial is called a quadratic polynomial. An example is $4x^2 - 2x + 7$.

cubic polynomial A third-degree polynomial is called a cubic polynomial. An example is $x^3 + 4x^2 - 2x + 7$.

Fourth-degree and fifth-degree polynomials are called quartic and quintic polynomials, respectively. If the degree of the polynomial, n, is greater than five, we'll simply call it an nth-degree polynomial. For example, the polynomial $5x^8 - 4x^5 + 1$ is an 8th-degree polynomial.

5.1.2 Adding and Subtracting Polynomials

Example 5.1.16 Production Costs. Bayani started a company that makes one product: one-gallon ketchup jugs for industrial kitchens. The company's production expenses only come from two things: supplies and labor. The cost of supplies, S (in thousands of dollars), can be modeled by $S = 0.05x^2 + 2x + 30$, where x is number of thousands of jugs of ketchup produced. The labor cost for his employees, L (in thousands of dollars), can be modeled by $0.1x^2 + 4x$, where x again represents the number of jugs they produce (in thousands of jugs). Find a model for the company's total production costs.

Since Bayani's company only has these two costs, we can find a model for the total production costs, C (in thousands of dollars), by adding the supply costs and the labor costs:

$$C = \left(0.05x^2 + 2x + 30\right) + \left(0.1x^2 + 4x\right)$$

To finish simplifying our total production cost model, we'll combine the like terms:

$$C = 0.05x^2 + 0.1x^2 + 2x + 4x + 30$$
$$= 0.15x^2 + 6x + 30$$

This simplified model can now calculate Bayani's total production costs C (in thousands of dollars) when the company produces x thousand jugs of ketchup.

In short, the process of adding two or more polynomials involves recognizing and then combining the like terms.

Checkpoint 5.1.17 Add the polynomials.
$$\left(6x^2 + 4x\right) + \left(4x^2 - 5x\right)$$

Explanation.   We combine like terms as follows

$$\left(6x^2 + 4x\right) + \left(4x^2 - 5x\right) = \left(6x^2 + 4x^2\right) + (4x - 5x)$$
$$= 10x^2 - x$$

Example 5.1.18 Simplify the expression $\left(\frac{1}{2}x^2 - \frac{2}{3}x - \frac{3}{2}\right) + \left(\frac{3}{2}x^2 + \frac{7}{2}x - \frac{1}{4}\right)$.
Explanation.

$$\left(\frac{1}{2}x^2 - \frac{2}{3}x - \frac{3}{2}\right) + \left(\frac{3}{2}x^2 + \frac{7}{2}x - \frac{1}{4}\right)$$
$$= \left(\frac{1}{2}x^2 + \frac{3}{2}x^2\right) + \left(-\frac{2}{3}x + \frac{7}{2}x\right) + \left(-\frac{3}{2} + \left(-\frac{1}{4}\right)\right)$$
$$= \left(\frac{4}{2}x^2\right) + \left(-\frac{4}{6}x + \frac{21}{6}x\right) + \left(-\frac{6}{4} + \left(-\frac{1}{4}\right)\right)$$
$$= \left(2x^2\right) + \frac{17}{6}x + \left(-\frac{7}{4}\right)$$
$$= 2x^2 + \frac{17}{6}x - \frac{7}{4}$$

Example 5.1.19 Profit, Revenue, and Costs. From Example 5.1.16, we know Bayani's ketchup company's production costs, C (in thousands of dollars), for producing x thousand jugs of ketchup is modeled by $C = 0.15x^2 + 6x + 30$. The revenue, R (in thousands of dollars), from selling the ketchup can be modeled by

$R = 13x$, where x stands for the number of thousands of jugs of ketchup sold. The company's net profit can be calculated using the concept:

$$\text{net profit} = \text{revenue} - \text{costs}$$

Assuming all products produced will be sold, a polynomial to model the company's net profit, P (in thousands of dollars) is:

$$\begin{aligned} P &= R - C \\ &= (13x) - \left(0.15x^2 + 6x + 30\right) \\ &= 13x - 0.15x^2 - 6x - 30 \\ &= -0.15x^2 + (13x + (-6x)) - 30 \\ &= -0.15x^2 + 7x - 30 \end{aligned}$$

The key distinction between the addition and subtraction of polynomials is that when we subtract a polynomial, we must subtract each term in that polynomial.

Notice that our first step in simplifying the expression in Example 5.1.19 was to subtract *every* term in the second expression. We can also think of this as distributing a factor of -1 across the second polynomial, $0.15x^2 + 6x + 30$, and then adding these terms as follows:

$$\begin{aligned} P &= R - C \\ &= (13x) - \left(0.15x^2 + 6x + 30\right) \\ &= 13x + (-1)(0.15x^2) + (-1)(6x) + (-1)(30) \\ &= 13x - 0.15x^2 - 6x - 30 \\ &= -0.15x^2 + (13x + (-6x)) - 30 \\ &= -0.15x^2 + 7x - 30 \end{aligned}$$

Example 5.1.20 Subtract $\left(5x^3 + 4x^2 - 6x\right) - \left(-3x^2 + 9x - 2\right)$.

Explanation. We must first subtract every term in $\left(-3x^2 + 9x - 2\right)$ from $\left(5x^3 + 4x^2 - 6x\right)$. Then we can combine like terms.

$$\begin{aligned} \left(5x^3 + 4x^2 - 6x\right) &- \left(-3x^2 + 9x - 2\right) \\ &= 5x^3 + 4x^2 - 6x + 3x^2 - 9x + 2 \\ &= 5x^3 + \left(4x^2 + 3x^2\right) + (-6x + (-9x)) + 2 \\ &= 5x^3 + 7x^2 - 15x + 2 \end{aligned}$$

Checkpoint 5.1.21 Subtract the polynomials.

$$(3x - 10) - (-5x + 7)$$

Explanation. We combine like terms as follows

$$\begin{aligned} (3x - 10) - (-5x + 7) &= (3x - (-5x)) + (-10 - 7) \\ &= 8x - 17 \end{aligned}$$

Let's look at one last example where the polynomial has multiple variables. Remember that like terms must have the same variable(s) with the same exponent.

Example 5.1.22 Subtract $\left(3x^2y + 8xy^2 - 17y^3\right) - \left(2x^2y + 11xy^2 + 4y^2\right)$.

Explanation. Again, we'll begin by subtracting each term in $\left(2x^2y + 11xy^2 + 4y^2\right)$. Once we've done this, we'll need to identify and combine like terms.

$$\left(3x^2y + 8xy^2 - 17y^3\right) - \left(2x^2y + 11xy^2 + 4y^2\right)$$
$$= 3x^2y + 8xy^2 - 17y^3 - 2x^2y - 11xy^2 - 4y^2$$
$$= \left(3x^2y - 2x^2y\right) + \left(8xy^2 - 11xy^2\right) + \left(-17y^3 - 4y^2\right)$$
$$= x^2y - 3xy^2 - 17y^3 - 4y^2$$

5.1.3 Evaluating Polynomial Expressions

Evaluating expressions was introduced in Section 1.1, and involves replacing the variable(s) in an expression with specific numbers and calculating the result. Here, we will look at evaluating polynomial expressions.

Example 5.1.23 Evaluate the expression $-12y^3 + 4y^2 - 9y + 2$ for $y = -5$.

Explanation.   We will replace y with -5 and simplify the result:

$$-12y^3 + 4y^2 - 9y + 2 = -12(-5)^3 + 4(-5)^2 - 9(-5) + 2$$
$$= -12(-125) + 4(25) + 45 + 2$$
$$= 1647$$

Recall that in Subsection 1.1.4 and Example 1.1.15 we discussed how $(-5)^2$ and -5^2 are not the same expressions. The first expression, $(-5)^2$, represents the number -5 squared, and is $(-5)(-5) = 25$. The second expression, -5^2, is the *opposite* of the number that you get after you square 5, and is $-5^2 = -(5 \cdot 5) = -25$.

Example 5.1.24 Evaluate the expression $C = 0.15x^2 + 6x + 30$ from Example 5.1.16 for $x = 10$ and explain what this means in context.

Explanation.   We will replace x with 10:

$$C = 0.15x^2 + 6x + 30$$
$$= 0.15(10)^2 + 6(10) + 30$$
$$= 0.15(100) + 60 + 30$$
$$= 15 + 90$$
$$= 105$$

The context was that x represents so many thousands of jugs of ketchup, and C represents the total cost, in thousands of dollars, to produce that many jugs. So in context, we can interpret this as it costing $105,000 to produce 10,000 jugs of ketchup.

Checkpoint 5.1.25

    a. Evaluate $(-y)^2$ when $y = -2$.

    b. Evaluate $(-y)^3$ when $y = -2$.

Explanation.

    a. $(-y)^2 = \left(-1(-2)\right)^2$
$$= (2)^2$$
$$= 4$$

b. $(-y)^3 = (-1(-2))^3$
$$= (2)^3$$
$$= 8$$

5.1.4 Reading Questions

1. What are the names for a polynomial with one term? With two terms? With three terms? Care to take a guess at the name of a polynomial with four terms?

2. Adding and subtracting polynomials is mostly about combining ⬜ terms.

3. What should you be careful with when evaluating a polynomial for a negative number?

5.1.5 Exercises

Review and Warmup

1. List the terms in each expression.

a. $6s - 0.9z + 3.5$

b. $-y - 6.5z^2$

c. $1.6y^2 + 6.7z - 0.2x - 2.2t^2$

d. $-0.5x + 6.2z - 2 + 3.4y^2$

2. List the terms in each expression.

a. $7.6s^2 + 7.3s^2 + 1.5$

b. $-2.2z^2$

c. $-4.1x - 2.5t^2$

d. $-3.9t + 8.1z^2 + 6.7z^2 + 7.4x$

3. List the terms in each expression.

a. $-8.9s - 2.6 - 0.6x + 2.8y$

b. $-2.6t - 6.8x^2 + 6.4$

c. $5.8z^2 + 4.7s^2 + 3.4$

d. $-8.4y^2$

4. List the terms in each expression.

a. $-7.3t^2 + 5.6t - 2.5 - 4.7z^2$

b. $5.9y^2 + 3.1t^2$

c. $-8.5s^2$

d. $-6.8t^2 + 4.7t^2 + 6.4 + 3.6s^2$

Simplify each expression, if possible, by combining like terms.

5. a. $-6t - 5t - 5t - 6t$

b. $2t - 3t + 8s + 4t$

c. $9s^2 + 2s^2 + 7z^2$

d. $-4y^2 + 7y^2 - 5z$

6. a. $-4t^2 + 4y^2$

b. $-6s + 3 + 6s^2$

c. $5s^2 - 4t + 3s + 6$

d. $7z^2 + 5y^2 - 6x^2$

7. a. $-\frac{3}{8}t - \frac{1}{9}t$

b. $-\frac{2}{3}x + 7s - 2s$

c. $-\frac{7}{8}z - \frac{5}{7}z + \frac{7}{8}z$

d. $-\frac{6}{7}s^2 - \frac{1}{5}t^2$

8. a. $\frac{1}{3}t^2 - \frac{2}{3}y$

b. $-\frac{2}{9}s^2 + \frac{8}{9} - \frac{1}{9}z^2 + 2$

c. $-\frac{6}{5}z^2 - \frac{3}{8}s^2 - s^2$

d. $\frac{3}{5}s^2 + \frac{1}{2}y - \frac{1}{8}s^2 + \frac{1}{3}$

Vocabulary Questions Is the following expression a monomial, binomial, or trinomial?

9. $4y^{12} - 13y^3$ is a   ($\square$ monomial $\square$ binomial $\square$ trinomial) of degree [   ].

10. $-11r^7 + 4r^2$ is a   ($\square$ monomial $\square$ binomial $\square$ trinomial) of degree [   ].

11. 40 is a   ($\square$ monomial $\square$ binomial $\square$ trinomial) of degree [   ]

12. 5 is a   ($\square$ monomial $\square$ binomial $\square$ trinomial) of degree [   ]

13. $-18y^{11} - 9y^7 - 20y^6$ is a   ($\square$ monomial $\square$ binomial $\square$ trinomial) of degree [   ]

14. $-20r^{10} - 2r^9 - 10r^2$ is a   ($\square$ monomial $\square$ binomial $\square$ trinomial) of degree [   ]

15. $8x^3 + 17x^7 + 6x$ is a   ($\square$ monomial $\square$ binomial $\square$ trinomial) of degree [   ]

16. $-14x^7 - 16x^8 + 6x$ is a   ($\square$ monomial $\square$ binomial $\square$ trinomial) of degree [   ]

17. $13y^{11}$ is a   ($\square$ monomial $\square$ binomial $\square$ trinomial) of degree [   ]

18. $-2y^{19}$ is a   ($\square$ monomial $\square$ binomial $\square$ trinomial) of degree [   ]

Find the degree of the following polynomial.

19. $2x^8y^6 - 16x^2y^4 - 6x^2 + 13$

20. $6x^7y^9 + 11x^3y + 11x^2 + 1$

Simplifying Polynomials Add the polynomials.

21. $(6x - 2) + (-7x - 5)$

22. $(8x - 9) + (2x + 10)$

23. $(10x^2 + 5x) + (-10x^2 + 4x)$

24. $(-8x^2 - 3x) + (-x^2 - 2x)$

25. $(-3x^2 - 9x + 1) + (4x^2 - 7x + 3)$

26. $(4x^2 + 6x - 9) + (7x^2 + 8x + 2)$

27. $(4y^3 - 7y^2 - 4) + (-3y^3 - 4y^2 - 7)$

28. $(-10r^3 - 4r^2 + 6) + (-4r^3 + 7r^2 + 1)$

29. $(7r^6 - 2r^4 - 4r^2) + (4r^6 - 10r^4 - r^2)$

30. $(4t^6 - 8t^4 + 6t^2) + (-5t^6 + 3t^4 - 9t^2)$

Add the polynomials.

31. $(0.8t^5 - 0.3t^4 - 0.1t^2 - 0.4) + (0.4t^5 - 0.9t^3 + 0.4)$

32. $(0.2t^5 + 0.5t^4 - 0.6t^2 - 0.1) + (0.5t^5 + 0.2t^3 - 0.8)$

33. $\left(-2x^3 + 3x^2 - 5x + \dfrac{7}{6}\right) + \left(3x^3 - 10x^2 + 3x + \dfrac{5}{4}\right)$

34. $\left(3x^3 + 7x^2 + 5x + \dfrac{7}{10}\right) + \left(-5x^3 - 7x^2 + 2x + \dfrac{1}{4}\right)$

Subtract the polynomials.

35. $\left(-4x+1\right)-\left(-10x-3\right)$

36. $\left(-x-6\right)-\left(-x-8\right)$

37. $\left(x^2+7x\right)-\left(7x^2-3x\right)$

38. $\left(3x^2-5x\right)-\left(x^2-3x\right)$

39. $\left(-5x^9-3x^4\right)-\left(-5x^3-6\right)$

40. $\left(10x^{10}-4x^8\right)-\left(6x-4\right)$

41. $\left(-10x^2+6x-4\right)-\left(-4x^2+8x+2\right)$

42. $\left(-2x^2-10x-4\right)-\left(-8x^2+3x-10\right)$

43. $\left(-8x^6-3x^4-5x^2\right)-\left(7x^6-3x^4-5x^2\right)$

44. $\left(5y^6-9y^4+5y^2\right)-\left(7y^6+6y^4+8y^2\right)$

45. $\left(-5x^3+3x^2-5x-5\right)-\left(-8x^2-6x+7\right)$

46. $\left(6x^3-7x^2-5x+5\right)-\left(9x^2+2x-7\right)$

Add or subtract the given polynomials as indicated.

47. $\left[4r^{16}-10r^{15}+r^{14}-\left(-8r^{16}+3r^{15}-2r^{14}\right)\right]-\left(-9r^{16}-7r^{15}-8r^{14}\right)$

48. $\left[t^9+8t^8-\left(-8t^9-10t^8\right)\right]-\left(-5t^9-4t^8\right)$

49. $\left[7t^{13}+5t^{12}-\left(-9t^{13}-10t^{12}\right)\right]-\left[-10t^{13}+2t^{12}+\left(-10t^{13}-7t^{12}\right)\right]$

50. $\left[4t^{14}-8t^{13}+3t^5-\left(-9t^{14}+8t^{13}-9t^5\right)\right]-\left[-7t^{14}-8t^{13}+7t^5+\left(-4t^{14}-10t^{13}-8t^5\right)\right]$

Add or subtract the given polynomials as indicated.

51. $\left(2x^7y^3+8xy\right)+\left(-3x^7y^3+4xy\right)$

52. $\left(9x^4y^3-10xy\right)+\left(2x^4y^3+9xy\right)$

53. $\left(10x^9y^7+6xy+8\right)+\left(9x^9y^7+9xy+9\right)$

54. $\left(5x^8y^3-10xy-6\right)+\left(3x^8y^3-6xy+3\right)$

55. $\left(6x^8y^9+5x^5y^3+9xy\right)+\left(-3x^8y^9-7x^5y^3+8xy\right)$

56. $\left(-7x^7y^8+8x^3y^4+6xy\right)+\left(3x^7y^8-2x^3y^4+7xy\right)$

57. $\left(8x^6-3xy+5y^9\right)-\left(-2x^6-9xy+2y^9\right)$

58. $\left(9x^5+7xy-8y^6\right)-\left(2x^5+10xy-5y^6\right)$

59. $\left(-10x^7y^6+2x^2y^4+2xy\right)-\left(-2x^7y^6-10x^2y^4+5xy\right)$

60. $\left(2x^8y^9-6x^3y^4-3xy\right)-\left(-4x^8y^9+10x^3y^4-8xy\right)$

61. $\left(3x^4-9y^2\right)-\left(-2x^4+3x^2y^2+7x^4y^2-2y^2\right)$

62. $\left(-4x^9+4y^4\right)-\left(2x^9-10x^8y^4+4x^9y^4-10y^4\right)$

63. Subtract $-4y^{18}-8y^7-6y^5$ from the sum of $9y^{18}-4y^7+7y^5$ and $-10y^{18}+3y^7-7y^5$.

64. Subtract $-10r^{11}-6r^5-2r^3$ from the sum of $5r^{11}-9r^5+4r^3$ and $-10r^{11}+7r^5-7r^3$.

65. Subtract $-7x^3y^7-6xy$ from $-2x^3y^7-9xy$

66. Subtract $8x^3y^8+10xy$ from $10x^3y^8+7xy$

Evaluating Polynomials

67. Evaluate the expression t^2:

    a. For $t=5$.

    b. For $t=-4$.

68. Evaluate the expression t^2:

    a. For $t=2$.

    b. For $t=-8$.

69. Evaluate the expression $-x^2$:

    a. For $x = 4$.

    b. For $x = -2$.

71. Evaluate the expression y^3:

    a. For $y = 2$.

    b. For $y = -2$.

73.   a. Evaluate $(-2r)^2$ when $r = -1$.

    b. Evaluate $(-2r)^3$ when $r = -1$.

75. Evaluate the expression $\frac{1}{3}(x+3)^2 - 7$ when $x = -6$.

77. Evaluate the expression $\frac{1}{3}(x+4)^2 - 9$ when $x = -7$.

79. Evaluate the expression $-16t^2 + 64t + 128$ when $t = -3$.

81. Evaluate the expression $-16t^2 + 64t + 128$ when $t = -4$.

70. Evaluate the expression $-x^2$:

    a. For $x = 3$.

    b. For $x = -4$.

72. Evaluate the expression y^3:

    a. For $y = 4$.

    b. For $y = -3$.

74.   a. Evaluate $(-r)^2$ when $r = -3$.

    b. Evaluate $(-r)^3$ when $r = -3$.

76. Evaluate the expression $\frac{1}{5}(x+4)^2 - 4$ when $x = -9$.

78. Evaluate the expression $\frac{1}{4}(x+1)^2 - 6$ when $x = -5$.

80. Evaluate the expression $-16t^2 + 64t + 128$ when $t = -5$.

82. Evaluate the expression $-16t^2 + 64t + 128$ when $t = 2$.

Applications of Simplifying Polynomials The formula

$$y = \frac{1}{2}a t^2 + v_0 t + y_0$$

gives the vertical position of an object, at time t, thrown with an initial velocity v_0, from an initial position y_0 in a place where the acceleration of gravity is a. The acceleration of gravity on earth is $-9.8 \frac{m}{s^2}$. It is negative, because we consider the upward direction as positive in this situation, and gravity pulls down.

83. What is the height of a baseball thrown with an initial velocity of $v_0 = 82 \frac{m}{s}$, from an initial position of $y_0 = 94$ m, and at time $t = 1$ s?

One seconds after the baseball was thrown, it was [   ] high in the air.

84. What is the height of a baseball thrown with an initial velocity of $v_0 = 87 \frac{m}{s}$, from an initial position of $y_0 = 76$ m, and at time $t = 9$ s?

Nine seconds after the baseball was thrown, it was [   ] high in the air.

85. An auto company's sales volume can be modeled by $6.1x^2 + 6.9x + 4$, and its cost can be modeled by $4.6x^2 + 3.7x + 4$, where x represents the number of cars produced, and y stands for money in thousand dollars. We can calculate the company's net profit by subtracting cost from sales. Find the polynomial which models the company's sales in thousands of dollars.

The company's profit can be modeled by [   ] dollars.

86. An auto company's sales volume can be modeled by $8.4x^2 + 1.2x + 3.9$, and its cost can be modeled by $4.9x^2 - 2.2x + 3.9$, where x represents the number of cars produced, and y stands for money in thousand dollars. We can calculate the company's net profit by subtracting cost from sales. Find the polynomial which models the company's sales in thousands of dollars.

The company's profit can be modeled by [   ] dollars.

87. A handyman is building two pig pens sharing the same side. Assume the length of the shared side is x meters. The cost of building one pen would be $34x^2 - 4x + 22$ dollars, and the cost of building the other pen would be $22x^2 + 4x + 46.5$ dollars. What's the total cost of building those two pens?

A polynomial representing the total cost of building those two pens is [   ] dollars.

88. A handyman is building two pig pens sharing the same side. Assume the length of the shared side is x meters. The cost of building one pen would be $23.5x^2 + 8x + 20.5$ dollars, and the cost of building the other pen would be $25.5x^2 - 8x + 19$ dollars. What's the total cost of building those two pens?

A polynomial representing the total cost of building those two pens is [   ] dollars.

89. A farmer is building fence around a triangular area. The cost of building the shortest side is 35x dollars, where x stands for the length of the side in feet. The cost of building the other two sides can be modeled by $8x^2 + 0.5x + 40$ dollars and $4x^3 - 4x + 35$ dollars, respectively. What's the total cost of building fence for all three sides?

The cost of building fence for all three sides would be [   ] dollars.

90. A farmer is building fence around a triangular area. The cost of building the shortest side is 40x dollars, where x stands for the length of the side in feet. The cost of building the other two sides can be modeled by $5x^2 + 4.5x + 30$ dollars and $4x^3 + 1.5x + 35$ dollars, respectively. What's the total cost of building fence for all three sides?

The cost of building fence for all three sides would be [   ] dollars.

91. An architect is designing a house on an empty plot. The area of the plot can be modeled by the polynomial $4x^4 + 6x^2 - 2.5x$, and the area of the house's base can be modeled by $6x^3 - 2.5x + 15$. The rest of the plot is the yard. What's the yard's area?

The area of the yard can be modeled by the polynomial [   ].

92. An architect is designing a house on an empty plot. The area of the plot can be modeled by the polynomial $5x^4 + 16x^2 + 6x$, and the area of the house's base can be modeled by $4x^3 + 6x + 15$. The rest of the plot is the yard. What's the yard's area?

The area of the yard can be modeled by the polynomial [   ].

5.2 Introduction to Exponent Rules

In this section, we will look at some rules or properties we use when simplifying expressions that involve multiplication and exponents.

5.2.1 Exponent Basics

Before we discuss any exponent rules, we need to quickly remind ourselves of some important concepts and vocabulary.

When working with expressions with exponents, we have the following vocabulary:

$$\text{base}^{\text{exponent}} = \text{power}$$

For example, when we calculate $8^2 = 64$, the **base** is 8, the **exponent** is 2, and the expression 8^2 is called the 2nd **power** of 8.

The foundational understanding of exponents is that when the exponent is a positive integer, the power can be rewritten as repeated multiplication of the base. For example, the 4th power of 3 can be written as 4 factors of 3 like so:

$$3^4 = 3 \cdot 3 \cdot 3 \cdot 3$$

5.2.2 Exponent Rules

Product Rule.   If we write out $3^5 \cdot 3^2$ without using exponents, we'd have:

$$3^5 \cdot 3^2 = (3 \cdot 3 \cdot 3 \cdot 3 \cdot 3) \cdot (3 \cdot 3)$$

If we then count how many 3s are being multiplied together, we find we have $5 + 2 = 7$, a total of seven 3s. So $3^5 \cdot 3^2$ simplifies like this:

$$3^5 \cdot 3^2 = 3^{5+2}$$
$$= 3^7$$

Example 5.2.2 Simplify $x^2 \cdot x^3$.

To simplify $x^2 \cdot x^3$, we write this out in its expanded form, as a product of x's, we have

$$x^2 \cdot x^3 = (x \cdot x)(x \cdot x \cdot x)$$
$$= x \cdot x \cdot x \cdot x \cdot x$$
$$= x^5$$

Note that we obtained the exponent of 5 by adding 2 and 3.

This demonstrates our first exponent rule, the **Product Rule**: when multiplying two expressions that have the same base, we can simplify the product by adding the exponents.

$$x^m \cdot x^n = x^{m+n} \tag{5.2.1}$$

Checkpoint 5.2.3 Use the properties of exponents to simplify the expression.
$$x^{16} \cdot x^9$$

Explanation.   We *add* the exponents as follows:
$$x^{16} \cdot x^9 = x^{16+9}$$
$$= x^{25}$$

Recall that $x = x^1$. It helps to remember this when multiplying certain expressions together.

Example 5.2.4 Multiply $x(x^3 + 2)$ by using the distributive property.
According to the distributive property,
$$x(x^3 + 2) = x \cdot x^3 + x \cdot 2$$

How can we simplify that term $x \cdot x^3$? It's really the same as $x^1 \cdot x^3$, so according to the Product Rule, it is x^4. So we have:
$$x(x^3 + 2) = x \cdot x^3 + x \cdot 2$$
$$= x^4 + 2x$$

Power to a Power Rule.   If we write out $\left(3^5\right)^2$ without using exponents, we'd have 3^5 multiplied by itself:
$$\left(3^5\right)^2 = \left(3^5\right) \cdot \left(3^5\right)$$
$$= (3 \cdot 3 \cdot 3 \cdot 3 \cdot 3) \cdot (3 \cdot 3 \cdot 3 \cdot 3 \cdot 3)$$

If we again count how many 3s are being multiplied, we have a total of two groups each with five 3s. So we'd have $2 \cdot 5 = 10$ instances of a 3. So $\left(3^5\right)^2$ simplifies like this:
$$\left(3^5\right)^2 = 3^{2 \cdot 5}$$
$$= 3^{10}$$

Example 5.2.5 Simplify $\left(x^2\right)^3$.
To simplify $\left(x^2\right)^3$, we write this out in its expanded form, as a product of x's, we have
$$\left(x^2\right)^3 = \left(x^2\right) \cdot \left(x^2\right) \cdot \left(x^2\right)$$
$$= (x \cdot x) \cdot (x \cdot x) \cdot (x \cdot x)$$
$$= x^6$$

Note that we obtained the exponent of 6 by multiplying 2 and 3.

This demonstrates our second exponent rule, the **Power to a Power Rule**: when a base is raised to an exponent and that expression is raised to another exponent, we multiply the exponents.
$$(x^m)^n = x^{m \cdot n}$$

Checkpoint 5.2.6 Use the properties of exponents to simplify the expression.
$$\left(r^{11}\right)^2$$

Explanation.   We *multiply* the exponents as follows:

$$\left(r^{11}\right)^2 = r^{11\cdot 2}$$
$$= r^{22}$$

Product to a Power Rule.   The third exponent rule deals with having multiplication inside a set of parentheses and an exponent outside the parentheses. If we write out $(3t)^5$ without using an exponent, we'd have $3t$ multiplied by itself five times:

$$(3t)^5 = (3t)(3t)(3t)(3t)(3t)$$

Keeping in mind that there is multiplication between every 3 and t, and multiplication between all of the parentheses pairs, we can reorder and regroup the factors:

$$(3t)^5 = (3\cdot t)\cdot(3\cdot t)\cdot(3\cdot t)\cdot(3\cdot t)\cdot(3\cdot t)$$
$$= (3\cdot 3\cdot 3\cdot 3\cdot 3)\cdot(t\cdot t\cdot t\cdot t\cdot t)$$
$$= 3^5 t^5$$

We could leave it written this way if 3^5 feels especially large. But if you are able to evaluate $3^5 = 243$, then perhaps a better final version of this expression is $243t^5$.

We essentially applied the outer exponent to each factor inside the parentheses. It is important to see how the exponent 5 applied to *both* the 3 *and* the t, not just to the t.

Example 5.2.7 Simplify $(xy)^5$.

To simplify $(xy)^5$, we write this out in its expanded form, as a product of x's and y's, we have

$$(xy)^5 = (x\cdot y)\cdot(x\cdot y)\cdot(x\cdot y)\cdot(x\cdot y)\cdot(x\cdot y)$$
$$= (x\cdot x\cdot x\cdot x\cdot x)\cdot(y\cdot y\cdot y\cdot y\cdot y)$$
$$= x^5 y^5$$

Note that the exponent on xy can simply be applied to both x and y.

This demonstrates our third exponent rule, the **Product to a Power Rule**: when a product is raised to an exponent, we can apply the exponent to each factor in the product.

$$(x\cdot y)^n = x^n\cdot y^n$$

Checkpoint 5.2.8 Use the properties of exponents to simplify the expression.

$(4x)^4$

Explanation.   We *multiply* the exponents and apply the rule $(ab)^m = a^m\cdot b^m$ as follows:

$$(4x)^4 = (4)^4 x^4$$
$$= 256x^4$$

List 5.2.9: Summary of the Rules of Exponents for Multiplication

> If a and b are real numbers, and m and n are positive integers, then we have the following rules:
>
> **Product Rule** $a^m \cdot a^n = a^{m+n}$
>
> **Power to a Power Rule** $(a^m)^n = a^{m \cdot n}$
>
> **Product to a Power Rule** $(ab)^m = a^m \cdot b^m$

Many examples will make use of more than one exponent rule. In deciding which exponent rule to work with first, it's important to remember that the order of operations still applies.

Example 5.2.10 Simplify the following expressions.

a. $\left(3^7 r^5\right)^4$

b. $\left(t^3\right)^2 \cdot \left(t^4\right)^5$

Explanation.

a. Since we cannot simplify anything inside the parentheses, we'll begin simplifying this expression using the Product to a Power Rule. We'll apply the outer exponent of 4 to each factor inside the parentheses. Then we'll use the Power to a Power Rule to finish the simplification process.

$$\left(3^7 r^5\right)^4 = \left(3^7\right)^4 \cdot \left(r^5\right)^4$$
$$= 3^{7 \cdot 4} \cdot r^{5 \cdot 4}$$
$$= 3^{28} r^{20}$$

Note that 3^{28} is too large to actually compute, even with a calculator, so we leave it written as 3^{28}.

b. According to the order of operations, we should first simplify any exponents before carrying out any multiplication. Therefore, we'll begin simplifying this by applying the Power to a Power Rule and then finish using the Product Rule.

$$\left(t^3\right)^2 \cdot \left(t^4\right)^5 = t^{3 \cdot 2} \cdot t^{4 \cdot 5}$$
$$= t^6 \cdot t^{20}$$
$$= t^{6+20}$$
$$= t^{26}$$

Remark 5.2.11 We cannot simplify an expression like $x^2 y^3$ using the Product Rule, as the factors x^2 and y^3 do not have the same base.

5.2.3 Reading Questions

1. How many exponent rules are discussed in this section? Write an example of each rule in action.

2. The order of operations say that operations inside parentheses should get the highest priority. But with $(5x)^3$, you cannot actually do anything with the 5 and the x. Which exponent rule allows you to sidestep the order of operations and still simplify this expression a little?

5.2.4 Exercises

Review and Warmup

1. Evaluate the following.

  a. 2^2

  b. 3^3

  c. $(-4)^2$

  d. $(-3)^3$

2. Evaluate the following.

  a. 2^2

  b. 5^3

  c. $(-2)^2$

  d. $(-5)^3$

3. Evaluate the following.

  a. 1^6

  b. $(-1)^{13}$

  c. $(-1)^{14}$

  d. 0^{20}

4. Evaluate the following.

  a. 1^7

  b. $(-1)^{11}$

  c. $(-1)^{16}$

  d. 0^{19}

5. Evaluate the following.

  a. $(-5)^2$

  b. -2^2

6. Evaluate the following.

  a. $(-3)^2$

  b. -4^2

7. Evaluate the following.

  a. $(-2)^3$

  b. -4^3

8. Evaluate the following.

  a. $(-1)^3$

  b. -4^3

Exponent Rules Use the properties of exponents to simplify the expression.

9. $9 \cdot 9^7$

10. $2 \cdot 2^3$

11. $3^9 \cdot 3^7$

12. $4^6 \cdot 4^2$

13. $y^9 \cdot y^5$

14. $t^{11} \cdot t^{17}$

15. $r^{13} \cdot r^{11} \cdot r^7$

16. $y^{15} \cdot y^4 \cdot y^{15}$

17. $\left(18^9\right)^3$

18. $\left(20^5\right)^6$

19. $\left(t^2\right)^2$

20. $\left(y^3\right)^{10}$

21. $(3t)^2$

22. $(2x)^3$

23. $(4ry)^3$

24. $(3xy)^3$

25. $\left(3t^{10}\right)^2$

26. $\left(5r^{11}\right)^3$

27. $\left(-4r^{20}\right) \cdot (5r^7)$

28. $\left(8r^3\right) \cdot (-3r^{20})$

29. $\left(-9r^3\right)^3$

30. $\left(-6y^5\right)^2$

31. $(-2y^9) \cdot (7y^{19}) \cdot$ $(-2y^{10})$

32. $(-6r^{11}) \cdot$ $(-2r^{12}) \cdot (2r^5)$

33. a. $\left(-10t^3\right)^2$

   b. $-\left(10t^3\right)^2$

34. a. $\left(-8m^5\right)^2$

   b. $-\left(8m^5\right)^2$

Use the properties of exponents to simplify the expression.

35. $\left(-\dfrac{y^{17}}{7}\right) \cdot \left(\dfrac{y^{11}}{4}\right)$

36. $\left(\dfrac{y^{20}}{3}\right) \cdot \left(-\dfrac{y^5}{3}\right)$

37. Use the distributive property to write an equivalent expression to $-3x(6x-1)$ that has no grouping symbols.

38. Use the distributive property to write an equivalent expression to $-6r(3r+8)$ that has no grouping symbols.

39. Use the distributive property to write an equivalent expression to $-9t^4(t-4)$ that has no grouping symbols.

40. Use the distributive property to write an equivalent expression to $-3b^3(b+4)$ that has no grouping symbols.

41. Use the distributive property to simplify $3+5c(2+6c)$ completely.

42. Use the distributive property to simplify $6+2y(2+10y)$ completely.

43. Use the distributive property to simplify $8m-2m(7-9m^3)$ completely.

44. Use the distributive property to simplify $5n-7n(1-10n^4)$ completely.

45. Use the distributive property to simplify $2q^2-3q^2(-5-10q^3)$ completely.

46. Use the distributive property to simplify $8x^2-9x^2(-10-10x^4)$ completely.

47. Simplify the following expressions if possible.

   a. r^2+r^2

   b. $(r^2)(r^2)$

   c. r^2+r^3

   d. $(r^2)(r^3)$

48. Simplify the following expressions if possible.

   a. $t+t$

   b. $(t)(t)$

   c. $t+t^2$

   d. $(t)(t^2)$

49. Simplify the following expressions if possible.

   a. b^3+b^3

   b. $(b^3)(b^3)$

   c. b^3+b^2

   d. $(b^3)(b^2)$

50. Simplify the following expressions if possible.

   a. c^2+c^2

   b. $(c^2)(c^2)$

   c. c^2+c^4

   d. $(c^2)(c^4)$

51. Simplify the following expressions if possible.

   a. $-2q^2+q^2$

   b. $(-2q^2)(q^2)$

   c. $-2q^2+4q^3$

   d. $(-2q^2)(4q^3)$

52. Simplify the following expressions if possible.

   a. m^4+2m^4

   b. $(m^4)(2m^4)$

   c. m^4-m^3

   d. $(m^4)(-m^3)$

53. Simplify the following expressions if possible.

   a. $-2n^4-3n^4$

   b. $(-2n^4)(-3n^4)$

   c. $-2n^4-4n^2$

   d. $(-2n^4)(-4n^2)$

54. Simplify the following expressions if possible.

   a. $4q^4+3q^4$

   b. $(4q^4)(3q^4)$

   c. $4q^4+4q^3$

   d. $(4q^4)(4q^3)$

55. Simplify the following expressions if possible.

   a. $x^2+4x+4x^2$

   b. $(x^2)(4x)(4x^2)$

56. Simplify the following expressions if possible.

a. $-2r^4 - r - 2r^4$

b. $(-2r^4)(-r)(-2r^4)$

Simplify the following expression.

57. $-3t^5(-4t^5)^2$

58. $3b^3(-2b^2)^2$

59. $3c^4r^3(2c^2r^4)^3$

60. $5nx^2(-2n^5x)^2$

61. $(-3m^4)(5m^3) + (3m^4)(-3m^3)$

62. $(n^3)(3n^4) + (5n)(5n^6)$

63. $(-4q^4)(2q^4)^4 + (3q^2)(-2q^6)$

64. $(3x^2)(x^3)^2 + (5x^2)(-4x^3)$

65. $(2r^3)(r^2)^2 + (-5r)^2(4r^5)$

66. $(3t^5)(2t^3)^4 + (3t^2)^2(-t^{13})$

67. $(-2b)^4 q^{10} - 3(b^2q^5)^2$

68. $(4c^3)^2 x^{10} - 5(c^3x^5)^2$

Challenge

69.

a. Let $x^{11} \cdot x^a = x^{28}$. Let's say that a is a natural number. How many possibilities are there for a?

b. Let $x^b \cdot x^c = x^{90}$. Let's say that b and c are natural numbers. How many possibilities are there for b?

c. Let $x^d \cdot x^e = x^{1450}$. Let's say that d and e are natural numbers. How many possibilities are there for d?

70. Choose the correct inequality or equal sign to make the relation true.
3^{400} ($\square <$ $\square >$ $\square =$) 4^{300}

71. Fill in the blanks with algebraic expressions that make the equation true. You may not use 0 or 1 in any of the blank spaces.

Here is an example: $? + ? = 8x$.

One possible answer is: $3x + 5x = 8x$.

There are infinitely many correct answers to this problem. *Be creative.* After finding a correct answer, see if you can come up with a different answer that is also correct.

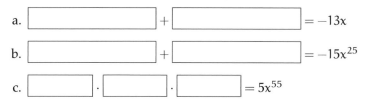

a. $\boxed{} + \boxed{} = -13x$

b. $\boxed{} + \boxed{} = -15x^{25}$

c. $\boxed{} \cdot \boxed{} \cdot \boxed{} = 5x^{55}$

5.3 Dividing by a Monomial

We learned how to *add* and *subtract* polynomials in Section 5.1. Then in Section 5.2, we learned how to *multiply* monomials together (but not yet how to multiply general polynomials together). In this section we learn how to *divide* a general polynomial by a monomial.

5.3.1 Quotient of Powers Rule

When we *multiply* the same base raised to powers, we *add* the exponents, as in $2^2 \cdot 2^3 = 2^5$. What happens when we *divide* the same base raised to powers?

Example 5.3.2 Simplify $\frac{x^5}{x^2}$ by first writing out what each power means.

Explanation. Without knowing a rule for simplifying this quotient of powers, we can write the expressions without exponents and simplify.

$$\begin{aligned}
\frac{x^5}{x^2} &= \frac{x \cdot x \cdot x \cdot x \cdot x}{x \cdot x} \\
&= \frac{\cancel{x} \cdot \cancel{x} \cdot x \cdot x \cdot x}{\cancel{x} \cdot \cancel{x} \cdot 1} \\
&= \frac{x \cdot x \cdot x}{1} \\
&= x^3
\end{aligned}$$

Notice that the difference of the exponents of the numerator and the denominator (5 and 2, respectively) is 3, which is the exponent of the simplified expression.

When we divide as we've just done, we end up canceling factors from the numerator and denominator one-for-one. These common factors cancel to give us factors of 1. The general rule for this is:

Fact 5.3.3 Quotient of Powers Rule. *For any non-zero real number a and integers m and n where $m > n$,*

$$\frac{a^m}{a^n} = a^{m-n}$$

This rule says that when you're dividing two expressions that have the same base, you can simplify the quotient by subtracting the exponents. In Example 5.3.2, this means that we can directly compute $\frac{x^5}{x^2}$:

$$\begin{aligned}
\frac{x^5}{x^2} &= x^{5-2} \\
&= x^3
\end{aligned}$$

Now we can update the list of exponent rules from Section 5.2.

List 5.3.4: Summary of the Rules of Exponents (Thus Far)

If a and b are real numbers, and m and n are positive integers, then we have the following rules:

Product Rule $a^m \cdot a^n = a^{m+n}$

Power to a Power Rule $(a^m)^n = a^{m \cdot n}$

Product to a Power Rule $(ab)^m = a^m \cdot b^m$

Quotient of Powers Rule $\frac{a^m}{a^n} = a^{m-n}$ (when $m > n$)

5.3.2 Dividing a Polynomial by a Monomial

Recall that dividing by a number c is the same as multiplying by the reciprocal $\frac{1}{c}$. For example, whether you divide 8 by 2 or multiply 8 by $\frac{1}{2}$, the result is 4 either way. In symbols,

$$\frac{8}{2} = \frac{1}{2} \cdot 8 \qquad \text{(both work out to 4)}$$

If we apply this idea to a polynomial being divided by a monomial, say with $\frac{a+b}{c}$, we can see that the distributive law works for this kind of division as well as with multiplciation:

$$\frac{a+b}{c} = \frac{1}{c} \cdot (a+b)$$
$$= \frac{1}{c} \cdot a + \frac{1}{2} \cdot b$$
$$= \frac{a}{c} + \frac{b}{c}$$

In the end, the c has been "distributed" into the a and the b. Once we recognize that division by a monomial is distributive, we are left with individual monomial pairs that we can divide.

Example 5.3.5 Simplify $\dfrac{2x^3 + 4x^2 - 10x}{2}$.

We recognize that the 2 we're dividing by can be divided into each and every term of the numerator. Once we recognize that, we will simply perform those divisions.

$$\frac{2x^3 + 4x^2 - 10x}{2} = \frac{2x^3}{2} + \frac{4x^2}{2} + \frac{-10x}{2}$$
$$= x^3 + 2x^2 - 5x$$

Example 5.3.6 Simplify $\dfrac{15x^4 - 9x^3 + 12x^2}{3x^2}$.

Explanation.   We recognize that each term in the numerator can be divided by $3x^2$. To actually carry out that division we'll need to use the Quotient of Powers Rule. This is going to cause a change in each coefficient and exponent.

$$\frac{15x^4 - 9x^3 + 12x^2}{3x^2} = \frac{15x^4}{3x^2} + \frac{-9x^3}{3x^2} + \frac{12x^2}{3x^2}$$
$$= 5x^2 - 3x + 4$$

Remark 5.3.7 Once you become comfortable with this process, you might leave out the step where we wrote out the distribution. You will do the distribution in your head and this will become a one-step exercise. Here's how Example 5.3.6 would be visualized:

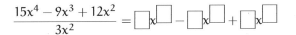

And when calculated, we'd get:

$$\frac{15x^4 - 9x^3 + 12x^2}{3x^2} = 5x^2 - 3x + 4$$

(With the last term, note that $\frac{x^2}{x^2}$ reduces to 1.)

Example 5.3.8 Simplify $\dfrac{20x^3y^4 + 30x^2y^3 - 5x^2y^2}{-5xy^2}$.

Explanation.

$$\frac{20x^3y^4 + 30x^2y^3 - 5x^2y^2}{-5xy^2} = \frac{20x^3y^4}{-5xy^2} + \frac{30x^2y^3}{-5xy^2} + \frac{-5x^2y^2}{-5xy^2}$$
$$= -4x^2y^2 - 6xy + x$$

Checkpoint 5.3.9 Simplify the following expression
$$\frac{18r^{20} + 18r^{16} - 54r^{14}}{-6r^2}$$

Explanation. We divide each term by $-6r^2$ as follows.

$$\frac{18r^{20} + 18r^{16} - 54r^{14}}{-6r^2} = \frac{18r^{20}}{-6r^2} + \frac{18r^{16}}{-6r^2} + \frac{-54r^{14}}{-6r^2}$$
$$= -\frac{18}{6}r^{18} - \frac{18}{6}r^{14} + \frac{54}{6}r^{12}$$
$$= -3r^{18} - 3r^{14} + 9r^{12}$$

Example 5.3.10 The density of an object, ρ (pronounced "rho"), can be calculated by the formula

$$\rho = \frac{m}{V}$$

where m is the object's mass, and V is its volume. The mass of a certain cancerous growth can be modeled by $4t^3 - 6t^2 + 8t$ grams, where t is the number of days since the growth began. If its volume is 2t cubic centimeters, find the growth's density.

Explanation.   We have:

$$\rho = \frac{m}{V}$$

$$= \frac{4t^3 - 6t^2 + 8t}{2t} \,\frac{g}{cm^3}$$

$$= \frac{4t^3}{2t} - \frac{6t^2}{2t} + \frac{8t}{2t} \,\frac{g}{cm^3}$$

$$= 2t^2 - 3t + 4 \;\frac{g}{cm^3}$$

The growth's density can be modeled by $2t^2 - 3t + 4\,\frac{g}{cm^3}$.

5.3.3 Reading Questions

1.   How is dividing a polynomial by a monomial similar to distributing multiplication over a polynomial? For example, how is the process of simplifying $\frac{15x^3 + 5x^2 + 10x}{5x}$ similar to simplifying $5x\left(15x^3 + 5x^2 + 10x\right)$?

5.3.4 Exercises

Quotient of Powers Rule   Use the properties of exponents to simplify the expression.

1. $\dfrac{y^3}{y}$
2. $\dfrac{t^5}{t^4}$
3. $\dfrac{-25y^{20}}{5y^{13}}$
4. $\dfrac{21t^{15}}{7t^9}$

5. $\dfrac{8r^5}{48r^2}$
6. $\dfrac{10r^{12}}{40r^2}$
7. $\dfrac{33y^{18}}{11y^{10}}$
8. $\dfrac{-78t^{13}}{13t^7}$

9. $\dfrac{15r^{17}}{60r^5}$
10. $\dfrac{2r^6}{4r}$
11. $\dfrac{r^5}{r^4}$
12. $\dfrac{x^7}{x^3}$

13. $\dfrac{13^{11}}{13^5}$
14. $\dfrac{14^{18}}{14^{15}}$
15. $\dfrac{16^{12} \cdot 14^{10}}{16^4 \cdot 14^8}$
16. $\dfrac{17^6 \cdot 13^{12}}{17^4 \cdot 13^9}$

17. $\dfrac{-85x^9y^{10}z^{18}}{17x^6y^3z^{17}}$
18. $\dfrac{76x^{18}y^8z^9}{19x^{10}y^4z^7}$
19. $\dfrac{4x^{12}y^9}{2x^6y^3}$
20. $\dfrac{-20x^7y^{18}}{4x^4y^7}$

Dividing Polynomials by Monomials   Simplify the following expression

21. $\dfrac{-20y^{17} + 65y^8}{5}$

22. $\dfrac{-117y^7 + 45y^4}{9}$

23. $\dfrac{16y^{14} + 16y^9 - 8y^7}{4y^3}$

24. $\dfrac{40r^{14} + 96r^{12} + 80r^{10}}{-8r^3}$

25. $\dfrac{65r^{13} + 50r^7}{5r}$

26. $\dfrac{27t^{20} + 18t^9}{9t}$

27. $\dfrac{54t^{15} - 117t^{11} - 99t^9 - 117t^8}{-9t^4}$

28. $\dfrac{-60x^{21} + 55x^{10} + 25x^9 + 30x^8}{-5x^4}$

29. $\dfrac{80x^2y^2 - 16xy + 80xy^2}{-8xy}$

30. $\dfrac{63x^2y^2 - 18xy + 54xy^2}{-9xy}$

31. $\dfrac{-28x^{14}y^{22} + 70x^{11}y^{17} + 91x^{12}y^{20}}{7x^5y^2}$

32. $\dfrac{-3x^{25}y^{14} + 3x^{14}y^{13} - 9x^{22}y^9}{3x^5y^2}$

33. $\dfrac{-40r^{19} - 25r^{14} + 5r^6}{5r^2}$

34. $\dfrac{-72r^9 - 64r^6 - 24r^4}{-8r^2}$

Application Problems

35. A rectangular prism's volume can be calculated by the formula $V = Bh$, where V stands for volume, B stands for base area, and h stands for height. A certain rectangular prism's volume can be modeled by $30x^5 - 35x^3 - 15x^2$ cubic units. If its height is $5x$ units, find the prism's base area.

     B = [_____] square units

36. A rectangular prism's volume can be calculated by the formula $V = Bh$, where V stands for volume, B stands for base area, and h stands for height. A certain rectangular prism's volume can be modeled by $35x^6 + 40x^4 + 15x$ cubic units. If its height is $5x$ units, find the prism's base area.

     B = [_____] square units

37. A cylinder's volume can be calculated by the formula $V = Bh$, where V stands for volume, B stands for base area, and h stands for height. A certain cylinder's volume can be modeled by $18\pi x^6 + 12\pi x^5 - 6\pi x^3$ cubic units. If its base area is $2\pi x^2$ square units, find the cylinder's height.

     h = [_____] units

38. A cylinder's volume can be calculated by the formula $V = Bh$, where V stands for volume, B stands for base area, and h stands for height. A certain cylinder's volume can be modeled by $12\pi x^5 - 20\pi x^4 + 6\pi x^3$ cubic units. If its base area is $2\pi x^2$ square units, find the cylinder's height.

     h = [_____] units

5.4 Multiplying Polynomials

Previously in Section 5.2, we learned to multiply two monomials together (such as $4xy \cdot 3x^2$). And in Section 5.1, we learned how to add and subtract polynomials even when there is more than one term (such as $(4x^2 - 3x) + (5x^2 + x - 2)$). In this section, we will learn how to multiply polynomials with more than one term.

Example 5.4.2 Revenue. Avery owns a local organic jam company that currently sells about 1500 jars a month at a price of $13 per jar. Avery has found that for each time they would raise the price of a jar by 25 cents, they will sell 50 fewer jars of jam per month.

In general, this company's revenue can be calculated by multiplying the cost per jar by the total number of jars of jam sold. If we let x represent the number of times the price was raised by 25 cents, then the price will be $13 + 0.25x$.

Conversely, the number of jars the company will sell will be the 1500 they currently sell each month, minus 50 times x. This gives us the expression $1500 - 50x$ to represent how many jars the company will sell after raising the price x times.

Combining these expressions, we can write a formula for the revenue model:

$$\text{revenue} = (\text{price per item}) \times (\text{number of items sold})$$
$$R = (13 + 0.25x)(1500 - 50x)$$

To simplify the expression $(13 + 0.25x)(1500 - 50x)$, we'll need to multiply $13 + 0.25x$ by $1500 - 50x$. In this section, we learn how to do that.

5.4.1 Review of the Distributive Property

Polynomial multiplication relies on the distributive property , and may also rely on the rules of exponents. When we multiply a monomial with a binomial, we apply this property by distributing the monomial to each term in the binomial. For example,

$$-4x(3x^2 + 5) = (-4x) \cdot (3x^2) + (-4x) \cdot (5)$$
$$= -12x^3 - 20x$$

Remark 5.4.3 We can use the distributive property when multiplying on either the left or the right. This means that $a(b + c) = ab + ac$, but also $(b + c)a = ba + ca$.

Example 5.4.4 A rectangle's length is 4 meters longer than its width. Assume its width is w meters. Use a simplified polynomial to model the rectangle's area in terms of w as the only variable.

Explanation.

Since the rectangle's length is 4 meters longer than its width, we can model its length by $w + 4$ meters.

The rectangle's area would be:

$$A = \ell w$$
$$= (w + 4)w$$
$$= w^2 + 4w$$

The rectangle's area can be modeled by $w^2 + 4w$ square meters.

In the second line of work above, we should recognize that $(w + 4)w$ is equivalent to $w(w + 4)$. Whether the w is written before or after the binomial, we are still able to use distribution to simplify the product.

Checkpoint 5.4.5 A rectangle's length is 3 feet shorter than twice its width. If we use w to represent the rectangle's width, use a polynomial to represent the rectangle's area in expanded form.

area = [　　　　　　　　　　　] square feet

Explanation. The rectangle's width is w feet. Since the rectangle's length is 3 feet shorter than twice its width, its length is $2w - 3$ feet. A rectangle's area formula is:

area = (length) · (width)

After substitution, we have:

area = (length) · (width)

$$= (2w - 3)w$$
$$= 2w^2 - 3w$$

The rectangle's area is $2w^2 - 3w$ square feet.

The distributive property can be understood visually with a **generic rectangle**.

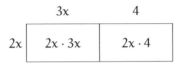

Figure 5.4.6: A Generic Rectangle Modeling $2x(3x + 4)$

The big rectangle consists of two smaller rectangles. The big rectangle's area is $2x(3x + 4)$, and the sum of those two smaller rectangles is $2x \cdot 3x + 2x \cdot 4$. Since the sum of the areas of those two smaller rectangles is the same as the bigger rectangle's area, we have:

$$2x(3x + 4) = 2x \cdot 3x + 2x \cdot 4$$
$$= 6x^2 + 8x$$

Generic rectangles can be used to visualize multiplying polynomials.

5.4.2 Multiplying Binomials

Multiplying Binomials Using Distribution. Whether we're multiplying a monomial with a polynomial or two larger polynomials together, the first step is still based on the distributive property . We'll start with multiplying two binomials and then move on to larger polynomials.

We know we can distribute the 3 in $(x + 2)3$ to obtain $(x + 2) \cdot 3 = x \cdot 3 + 2 \cdot 3$. We can actually distribute *anything* across $(x + 2)$ if it is multiplied. For example:

$$(x + 2)🐱 = x \cdot 🐱 + 2 \cdot 🐱$$

With this in mind, we can multiply $(x + 2)(x + 3)$ by distributing the $(x + 3)$ across $(x + 2)$:

$$(x + 2)(x + 3) = x(x + 3) + 2(x + 3)$$

To finish multiplying, we'll continue by distributing again, but this time across $(x + 3)$:

$$(x + 2)(x + 3) = x(x + 3) + 2(x + 3)$$

$$= x \cdot x + x \cdot 3 + 2 \cdot x + 2 \cdot 3$$
$$= x^2 + 3x + 2x + 6$$
$$= x^2 + 5x + 6$$

To multiply a binomial by another binomial, we simply had to repeat the step of distribution and simplify the resulting terms. In fact, multiplying any two polynomials will rely upon these same steps.

Multiplying Binomials Using FOIL.   While multiplying two binomials requires two applications of the distributive property, people often remember this distribution process using the acronym FOIL. FOIL refers to the pairs of terms from each binomial that end up distributed to each other.

If we take another look at the example we just completed, $(x + 2)(x + 3)$, we can highlight how the FOIL process works. FOIL is the acronym for "First, Outer, Inner, Last".

$$(x + 2)(x + 3) = \overbrace{(x \cdot x)}^{F} + \overbrace{(3 \cdot x)}^{O} + \overbrace{(2 \cdot x)}^{I} + \overbrace{(2 \cdot 3)}^{L}$$
$$= x^2 + 3x + 2x + 6$$
$$= x^2 + 5x + 6$$

F: x^2 The x^2 term was the result of the product of *first* terms from each binomial.

O: $3x$ The $3x$ was the result of the product of the *outer* terms from each binomial. This was from the x in the front of the first binomial and the 3 in the back of the second binomial.

I: $2x$ The $2x$ was the result of the product of the *inner* terms from each binomial. This was from the 2 in the back of the first binomial and the x in the front of the second binomial.

L: 6 The constant term 6 was the result of the product of the *last* terms of each binomial.

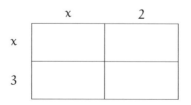

Figure 5.4.7: Using FOIL Method to multiply $(x + 2)(x + 3)$

Multiplying Binomials Using Generic Rectangles.   We can also approach this same example using the generic rectangle method. To use generic rectangles, we treat $x + 2$ as the base of a rectangle, and $x + 3$ as the height. Their product, $(x + 2)(x + 3)$, represents the rectangle's area. The next diagram shows how to set up generic rectangles to multiply $(x + 2)(x + 3)$.

Figure 5.4.8: Setting up Generic Rectangles to Multiply $(x + 2)(x + 3)$

The big rectangle consists of four smaller rectangles. We will find each small rectangle's area in the next diagram by the formula area = base · height.

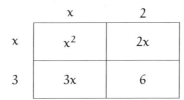

Figure 5.4.9: Using Generic Rectangles to Multiply $(x + 2)(x + 3)$

To finish finding this product, we need to add the areas of the four smaller rectangles:

$$(x + 2)(x + 3) = x^2 + 3x + 2x + 6$$
$$= x^2 + 5x + 6$$

Notice that the areas of the four smaller rectangles are exactly the same as the four terms we obtained using distribution, which are also the same four terms that came from the FOIL method. Both the FOIL method and generic rectangles approach are different ways to represent the distribution that is occurring.

Example 5.4.10 Multiply $(2x - 3y)(4x - 5y)$ using distribution.

Explanation. To use the distributive property to multiply those two binomials, we'll first distribute the second binomial across $(2x - 3y)$. Then we'll distribute again, and simplify the terms that result.

$$(2x - 3y)(4x - 5y) = 2x(4x - 5y) - 3y(4x - 5y)$$
$$= 8x^2 - 10xy - 12xy + 15y^2$$
$$= 8x^2 - 22xy + 15y^2$$

Example 5.4.11 Multiply $(2x - 3y)(4x - 5y)$ using FOIL.

Explanation. First, Outer, Inner, Last: Either with arrows on paper or mentally in our heads, we'll pair up the four pairs of monomials and multiply those pairs together.

$$(2x - 3y)(4x - 5y) = \overset{F}{(2x \cdot 4x)} + \overset{O}{(2x \cdot (-5y))} + \overset{I}{(-3y \cdot 4x)} + \overset{L}{(-3y \cdot (-5y))}$$
$$= 8x^2 - 10xy - 12xy + 15y^2$$
$$= 8x^2 - 22xy + 15y^2$$

Example 5.4.12 Multiply $(2x - 3y)(4x - 5y)$ using generic rectangles.

Explanation. We begin by drawing four rectangles and marking their bases and heights with terms in the given binomials:

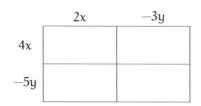

Figure 5.4.13: Setting up Generic Rectangles to Multiply $(2x - 3y)(4x - 5y)$

Next, we calculate each rectangle's area by multiplying its base with its height:

	2x	−3y
4x	$8x^2$	$-12xy$
−5y	$-10xy$	$15y^2$

Figure 5.4.14: Using Generic Rectangles to Multiply $(2x - 3y)(4x - 5y)$

Finally, we add up all rectangles' area to find the product:

$$(2x - 3y)(4x - 5y) = 8x^2 - 10xy - 12xy + 15y^2$$
$$= 8x^2 - 22xy + 15y^2$$

Example 5.4.15 Multiply and simplify the formula for Avery's organic jam revenue, R (in dollars), from Example 5.4.2 where $R = (13 + 0.25x)(1500 - 50x)$ and x represents the number of times they raised the price by 25 cents.

Explanation.   To multiply this, we'll use FOIL:

$$R = (13 + 0.25x)(1500 - 50x)$$
$$= (13 \cdot 1500) - (13 \cdot 50x) + (0.25x \cdot 1500) - (0.25x \cdot 50x)$$
$$= 19500 - 650x + 375x - 12.5x^2$$
$$= -12.5x^2 - 275x + 19500$$

Example 5.4.16 Tyrone is an artist and he sells each of his paintings for \$200. Currently, he can sell 100 paintings per year. So his annual revenue from selling paintings is $\$200 \cdot 100 = \$20000$. He plans to raise the price. However, for each \$20 price increase per painting, his customers will buy 5 fewer paintings annually.

Assume Tyrone would raise the price of his paintings x times, each time by \$20. Use an expanded polynomial to represent his new revenue per year.

Explanation.   Currently, each painting costs \$200. After raising the price x times, each time by \$20, each painting's new price would be $200 + 20x$ dollars.

Currently, Tyrone sells 100 paintings per year. After raising the price x times, each time selling 5 fewer paintings, he would sell $100 - 5x$ paintings per year.

His annual revenue can be calculated by multiplying each painting's price by the number of paintings he would sell:

$$\begin{aligned}
\text{annual revenue} &= (\text{price})(\text{number of sales}) \\
&= (200 + 20x)(100 - 5x) \\
&= 200(100) + 200(-5x) + 20x(100) + 20x(-5x) \\
&= 20000 - 1000x + 2000x - 100x^2 \\
&= -100x^2 + 1000x + 20000
\end{aligned}$$

After raising the price x times, each time by \$20, Tyrone's annual income from paintings would be $-100x^2 + 1000x + 20000$ dollars.

5.4.3 Multiplying Polynomials Larger Than Binomials

The foundation for multiplying any pair of polynomials is distribution and monomial multiplication. Whether we are working with binomials, trinomials, or larger polynomials, the process is fundamentally the same.

Example 5.4.17 Multiply $(x + 5)\left(x^2 - 4x + 6\right)$.

We can approach this product using either distribution generic rectangles. We cannot directly use the FOIL method, although it can be helpful to draw arrows to the six pairs of products that will occur.

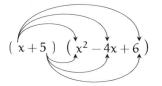

Figure 5.4.18: Multiply Each Term by Each Term

Using the distributive property, we begin by distributing across $\left(x^2 - 4x + 6\right)$, perform a second step of distribution, and then combine like terms.

$$\begin{aligned}
(x + 5)\left(x^2 - 4x + 6\right) &= x\left(x^2 - 4x + 6\right) + 5\left(x^2 - 4x + 6\right) \\
&= x \cdot x^2 - x \cdot 4x + x \cdot 6 + 5 \cdot x^2 - 5 \cdot 4x + 5 \cdot 6 \\
&= x^3 - 4x^2 + 6x + 5x^2 - 20x + 30 \\
&= x^3 + x^2 - 14x + 30
\end{aligned}$$

With the foundation of monomial multiplication and understanding how distribution applies in this context, we are able to find the product of any two polynomials.

Checkpoint 5.4.19 Multiply the polynomials.
$(a - 3b)(a^2 + 7ab + 9b^2)$

Explanation. We multiply the polynomials by using the terms from $a - 3b$ successively.

$$\begin{aligned}
(a - 3b)\left(a^2 + 7ab + 9b^2\right) &= aa^2 + a \cdot 7ab + a \cdot 9b^2 - 3ba^2 - 3b \cdot 7ab - 3b \cdot 9b^2 \\
&= a^3 + 4a^2b - 12ab^2 - 27b^3
\end{aligned}$$

5.4.4 Reading Questions

1.   Describe three ways you can go about multiplying $(x + 3)(2x + 5)$.

2.   If you multiplied out $(a + b + c)(d + e + f + g)$, how many terms would there be? (Try to answer without actually writing them all down.)

5.4.5 Exercises

Review and Warmup Use the properties of exponents to simplify the expression.

1. $x^{10} \cdot x^9$ **2.** $r^{13} \cdot r^3$ **3.** $(10y^{15}) \cdot (-2y^{15})$

4. $(6r^{17}) \cdot (3r^8)$ **5.** $(-3y^{12})^2$ **6.** $(-8x^2)^3$

7.   Count the number of terms in each expression.

    a. $5x$

    b. $-8x^2 - 3$

    c.
$-y^2 - 6x^2 + 8x - 7x^2$

    d. $y^2 - 8y + 3x^2 - 2$

8.   Count the number of terms in each expression.

    a. $7x^2 - 2z$

    b. $-9t + 8y^2 + x + 7t^2$

    c. x^2

    d. $t + 7 + 2y$

9.   List the terms in each expression.

    a. $8.2x + 6.3s^2$

    b. $7.9y + 6z - 3.4z^2$

    c. $-6.5y - 3.6t + 3.1$

    d. $2.8t$

10.   List the terms in each expression.

    a.
$-8.3x^2 - 3.6y^2 + 5.9s$

    b. $-6.7z^2 + 6.2$

    c.
$-4.7t + 7.1t + 4.9s - 6.3$

    d.
$-5.5s + 5.5t^2 - 6.2z - 3.3s$

11.   List the terms in each expression.

    a. $-6.7x + 4.6t + 3.9z$

    b.
$3.5z^2 + 6.5t + 6.5 - 5.5y$

    c. $-4.5z^2 + 8.9s^2$

    d. $8.6t - 3s^2 - 0.9s^2$

12.   List the terms in each expression.

    a. $-5.1s^2 - 5.3x + 1.9y$

    b. $2.3z + 2.5y^2 + 0.3s$

    c.
$-7.8z + 6.1x^2 + 7.9 - 0.9z$

    d. $4.5t^2 - 0.5s^2$

13.   Simplify each expression, if possible, by combining like terms.

    a. $-4s + 3x^2 + 2t + 6t$

    b. $-7x - 6x$

    c. $4s^2 - 6x^2$

    d. $8s^2 - 6y^2$

14.   Simplify each expression, if possible, by combining like terms.

    a.
$-2s^2 - 7s^2 - 2s^2 - 2x^2$

    b. $-9z + 3y^2 - 4z - 6z$

    c. $5y^2 - 3 - 4t^2$

    d. $9z + 6z - 5z$

15.   Simplify each expression, if possible, by combining like terms.

    a. $-4s - s$

    b. $\frac{4}{3}x - \frac{8}{5}s + 7t$

    c. $-\frac{2}{5}t - 1 - 7t^2 - \frac{5}{9}x^2$

    d. $-t - \frac{2}{3}t - \frac{8}{9}x$

16. Simplify each expression, if possible, by combining like terms.

   a. $\frac{1}{4}s^2 - \frac{5}{7}t^2$

   b. $-\frac{4}{3}x^2 - \frac{5}{7}y^2$

   c. $4z^2 + 2 - \frac{9}{2}x$

   d. $-4y^2 + \frac{1}{2}t + \frac{4}{3}t^2$

Multiplying Monomials with Binomials Multiply the polynomials.

17. $-5x\,(x + 9)$ 18. $-3x\,(x - 5)$ 19. $-6x\,(-7x - 10)$

20. $7x\,(-2x + 10)$ 21. $4x^2\,(x - 5)$ 22. $6x^2\,(x + 3)$

23. $-8t^2\,(5t^2 - 4t)$ 24. $5x^2\,(2x^2 - 8x)$ 25. $-2x^2\,(9x^2 - 3x + 5)$

26. $8x^2\,(6x^2 - 8x + 8)$ 27. $(-5x^{12}y^5)(-10x^5 - 9y^3)$ 28. $(-6x^{14}y^{13})(5x^{10} + 9y^{11})$

Multiply the polynomials.

29. $(7a^{16}b^{20})(9a^{16}b^{19} - 8a^{19}b^{18})$ 30. $(-8a^{17}b^9)(-4a^3b^9 + 8a^{13}b^{18})$

31. $(9a^5)(-7a^9 - 8a^4b^9 + 10b^7)$ 32. $(10a^8)(2a^5 + 8a^9b^6 - 10b^7)$

Applications of Multiplying Monomials with Binomials

33. A rectangle's length is 1 feet shorter than 3 times its width. If we use w to represent the rectangle's width, use a polynomial to represent the rectangle's area in expanded form.

   area = [   ]
   square feet

34. A rectangle's length is 2 feet shorter than 5 times its width. If we use w to represent the rectangle's width, use a polynomial to represent the rectangle's area in expanded form.

   area = [   ]
   square feet

35. A triangle's height is 4 feet longer than 4 times its base. If we use b to represent the triangle's base, use a polynomial to represent the triangle's area in expanded form. A triangle's area can be calculated by $A = \frac{1}{2}bh$, where b stands for base, and h stands for height.

   area = [   ]
   square feet

36. A triangle's height is 4 feet longer than twice its base. If we use b to represent the triangle's base, use a polynomial to represent the triangle's area in expanded form. A triangle's area can be calculated by $A = \frac{1}{2}bh$, where b stands for base, and h stands for height.

   area = [   ]
   square feet

37. A trapezoid's top base is 5 feet longer than its height, and its bottom base is 9 feet longer than its height. If we use h to represent the trapezoid's height, use a polynomial to represent the trapezoid's area in expanded form. A trapezoid's area can be calculated by $A = \frac{1}{2}(a + b)h$, where a stands for the top base, b stands for the bottom base, and h stands for height.

area = ☐
square feet

38. A trapezoid's top base is 6 feet longer than its height, and its bottom base is 2 feet longer than its height. If we use h to represent the trapezoid's height, use a polynomial to represent the trapezoid's area in expanded form. A trapezoid's area can be calculated by $A = \frac{1}{2}(a + b)h$, where a stands for the top base, b stands for the bottom base, and h stands for height.

area = ☐
square feet

Multiplying Binomials Multiply the polynomials.

39. $(r + 2)(r + 10)$

40. $(t + 9)(t + 5)$

41. $(6t + 9)(t + 4)$

42. $(3x + 1)(x + 7)$

43. $(x + 9)(x - 4)$

44. $(x + 5)(x - 10)$

45. $(y - 9)(y - 6)$

46. $(y - 3)(y - 1)$

47. $(4r + 7)(r + 4)$

48. $(2r + 8)(3r + 6)$

49. $(5t - 9)(t - 5)$

50. $(3t - 5)(6t - 5)$

51. $(2x - 1)(x - 5)$

52. $(8x - 6)(x - 7)$

53. $(4x - 2)(x + 1)$

54. $(10y - 8)(y + 5)$

55. $(5y - 4)(3y^2 - 6)$

56. $(3r - 10)(2r^2 - 6)$

57. $(10r^3 + 5)(r^2 + 10)$

58. $(7t^3 + 10)(t^2 + 7)$

59. $(3t^2 - 7)(t^2 - 7)$

60. $(6x^2 - 3)(x^2 - 7)$

61. $(a + 3b)(a + 3b)$

62. $(a - 4b)(a + 7b)$

63. $(a + 9b)(5a - 4b)$

64. $(a - 6b)(6a - 10b)$

65. $(7a + 9b)(3a - 4b)$

66. $(8a - 4b)(9a + 4b)$

67. $(9ab - 7)(6ab - 4)$

68. $(10ab + 2)(3ab + 4)$

69. $5(x + 2)(x - 5)$

70. $-3(x + 9)(x - 4)$

71. $x(x - 9)(x - 4)$

72. $2y(y + 5)(y - 6)$

73. $-(2y - 3)(y - 5)$

74. $-5(4r - 3)(r - 3)$

Applications of Multiplying Binomials

75. An artist sells his paintings at $17.00 per piece. Currently, he can sell 140 paintings per year. Thus, his annual income from paintings is $17 \cdot 140 = 2380$ dollars. He plans to raise the price. However, for each $5.00 of price increase per painting, his customers would buy 10 fewer paintings annually. Assume the artist would raise the price of his painting x times, each time by $5.00. Use an expanded polynomial to represent his new income per year.
new annual income =
☐ dollars

76. An artist sells his paintings at $18.00 per piece. Currently, he can sell 110 paintings per year. Thus, his annual income from paintings is $18 \cdot 110 = 1980$ dollars. He plans to raise the price. However, for each $3.00 of price increase per painting, his customers would buy 8 fewer paintings annually. Assume the artist would raise the price of his painting x times, each time by $3.00. Use an expanded polynomial to represent his new income per year.
new annual income =
☐ dollars

77. A rectangle's base can be modeled by $x + 9$ meters, and its height can be modeled by $x - 9$ meters. Use a polynomial to represent the rectangle's area in expanded form.

area $=$ [ ]

square meters

78. A rectangle's base can be modeled by $x + 10$ meters, and its height can be modeled by $x - 4$ meters. Use a polynomial to represent the rectangle's area in expanded form.

area $=$ [ ]

square meters

Multiplying Larger Polynomials Multiply the polynomials.

79. $(-2x + 4)\left(x^2 - 2x - 2\right)$

80. $(2x + 2)\left(x^2 + 2x + 3\right)$

81. $(3x - 3)\left(-2x^3 - 3x^2 - 4x + 4\right)$

82. $(-3x + 5)\left(2x^3 + 3x^2 + 5x + 3\right)$

83. $\left(x^2 - 4x + 3\right)\left(x^2 + 4x + 3\right)$

84. $\left(x^2 - 4x - 3\right)\left(x^2 - 4x - 5\right)$

85. $(a - 8b)(a^2 - 3ab - 2b^2)$

86. $(a + 9b)(a^2 + 7ab + 2b^2)$

87. $(a + b + 10)(a + b - 10)$

88. $(a + b - 2)(a + b + 2)$

Challenge

89. Fill in the blanks with algebraic expressions that make the equation true. You may not use 0 or 1 in any of the blank spaces. An example is $? + ? = 8x$, where one possible answer is $3x + 5x = 8x$. There are infinitely many correct answers to this problem. *Be creative.* After finding a correct answer, see if you can come up with a different answer that is also correct.

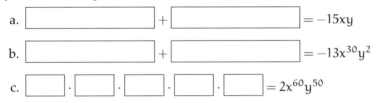

a. [ ] $+$ [ ] $= -15xy$

b. [ ] $+$ [ ] $= -13x^{30}y^2$

c. [ ] $\cdot$ [ ] $\cdot$ [ ] $\cdot$ [ ] $\cdot$ [ ] $= 2x^{60}y^{50}$

5.5 Special Cases of Multiplying Polynomials

Since we are now able to multiply polynomials together in general, we will look at a few special patterns with polynomial multiplication where there are some shortcuts worth knowing about.

5.5.1 Squaring a Binomial

Example 5.5.2 To "square a binomial" is to take a binomial and multiply it by itself. In the same way that $4^2 = 4 \cdot 4$, it's also true that $(x+4)^2 = (x+4)(x+4)$. To expand this expression, we'll simply distribute $(x+4)$ across $(x+4)$:

$$\begin{aligned} (x+4)^2 &= (x+4)(x+4) \\ &= x(x+4) + 4(x+4) \\ &= x^2 + 4x + 4x + 16 \\ &= x^2 + 8x + 16 \end{aligned}$$

Similarly, to expand $(y-7)^2$, we'll have:

$$\begin{aligned} (y-7)^2 &= (y-7)(y-7) \\ &= y(y-7) - 7(y-7) \\ &= y^2 - 7y - 7y + 49 \\ &= y^2 - 14y + 49 \end{aligned}$$

These two examples might look like any other example of multiplying binomials, but looking closely we can see that something *special* happened. Focusing on the original expression and the simplified one, we can see that a specific pattern occurred in each:

$$(x+4)^2 = x^2 + 2(4x) + 4^2$$

And:

$$(y-7)^2 = y^2 - 2(7y) + 7^2$$

Either way, we have:

$$(\text{first})^2 \pm 2(\text{first})(\text{second}) + (\text{second})^2$$

and the choice of $+$ or $-$ matches the original binomial.

What we're seeing is a pattern relating two things. The left side is the **square of a binomial**, and the result on the right is called a **perfect square trinomial**, a trinomial that was born from something getting squared.

The general way this pattern is established is by squaring each of the two most general binomials, $(a+b)$ and $(a-b)$. Once we have done so, we can substitute anything in place of a and b and rely upon the general pattern to simplify squared binomials.

We can write $(a+b)^2$ as $(a+b)(a+b)$ and then multiply those binomials:

$$\begin{aligned} (a+b)^2 &= (a+b)(a+b) \\ &= a^2 + ab + ba + b^2 \end{aligned}$$

$$= a^2 + 2ab + b^2$$

Notice the final simplification step was to add $ab + ba$. Since these are like terms, we can combine them into $2ab$.

Similarly, we can find a general formula for $(a - b)^2$:

$$(a - b)^2 = (a - b)(a - b)$$
$$= a^2 - ab - ba + b^2$$
$$= a^2 - 2ab + b^2$$

Fact 5.5.3 Binomial Squared Formulas. *If* a *and* b *are real numbers or variable expressions, then we have the following formulas:*

$$(a + b)^2 = a^2 + 2ab + b^2$$
$$(a - b)^2 = a^2 - 2ab + b^2$$

These formulas will allow us to multiply this type of special product more quickly.

Remark 5.5.4 Notice that when both $(a + b)^2$ and $(a - b)^2$ are expanded, the last term is *adding* b^2 either way. This is because any number or expression, regardless of its sign, is positive after it is squared.

Some students will prefer to memorize the Binomial Squared Formulas and apply them by substuting expressions in for a and b. An alternative visualization is presented in Figure 5.5.5.

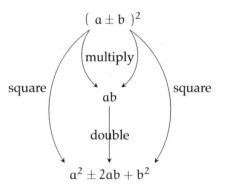

Figure 5.5.5: Visualizing the Squaring of a Binomial

Example 5.5.6 Expand $(2x - 3)^2$ using the Binomial Squared Formulas.

To apply the formula for squaring a binomial, we take $a = 2x$ and $b = 3$. Expanding this, we have:

$$(2x - 3)^2 = (2x)^2 - 2(2x)(3) + (3)^2$$
$$= 4x^2 \quad - 12x \quad + 9$$

Checkpoint 5.5.7 Expand the following using the Binomial Squared Formula.

    a. $(5xy + 1)^2$ b. $4(3x - 7)^2$

Explanation.

   a. $(5xy + 1)^2 = (5xy)^2 + 2(5xy)(1) + 1^2$
                   $= 25x^2y^2 + 10xy + 1$

   b. With this expression, we will first note that the factor of 4 is *outside* the portion of the expression that is squared. Using the order of operations, we will first expand $(3x-7)^2$ and then multiply that expression by 4:

$$4(3x - 7)^2 = 4\left((3x)^2 - 2(3x)(7) + 7^2\right)$$
$$= 4\left(9x^2 - 42x + 49\right)$$
$$= 36x^2 - 168x + 196$$

Example 5.5.8 Use the visualization in Figure 5.5.5 to expand these binomials squared.
   a. $(x + 8)^2$ b. $(2t - 7)^2$

Explanation.

   a. Diagramming the process: b. Diagramming the process:

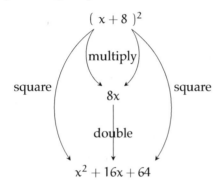 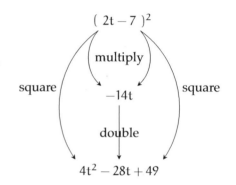

Example 5.5.9
A circle's area can be calculated using the formula

$$A = \pi r^2$$

where A stands for area, and r stands for radius. If a certain circle's radius can be modeled by $x - 5$ feet, use an expanded polynomial to model the circle's area.

Explanation.   The circle's area would be:

$$A = \pi r^2$$
$$= \pi(x - 5)^2 \qquad \text{Now use a method for squaring this binomial} \ldots$$
$$= \pi\left(x^2 - 10x + 25\right)$$
$$= \pi x^2 - 10\pi x + 25\pi$$

The circle's area can be modeled by $\pi x^2 - 10\pi x + 25\pi$ square feet.

Checkpoint 5.5.10 Expand $\left(y^3 - 12\right)^2$.
Explanation.

$$\left(y^3 - 12\right)^2 = \left(y^3\right)^2 - 2\left(y^3\right)(12) + 12^2$$
$$= y^6 - 24y^3 + 144$$

Warning 5.5.11 Common Mistakes. Now we know how to expand $(a + b)^2$ and $(a - b)^2$. It is a common mistake to think that these are equal to $a^2 + b^2$ and $a^2 - b^2$, respectively, as if you could just "distribute" the exponent. Now we know that actually you get $a^2 + 2ab + b^2$ and $a^2 - 2ab + b^2$.

5.5.2 The Product of the Sum and Difference of Two Terms

To motivate the next "special case" for multiplying polynomials, we'll look at a couple of examples.

Example 5.5.12 Multiply the following binomials:

    a. $(x + 5)(x - 5)$ b. $(y - 8)(y + 8)$

Explanation. We can approach these as using distribution, FOIL, or generic rectangles, and obtain the following:

    a. $(x + 5)(x - 5) = x^2 - 5x + 5x - 25$
$$= x^2 - 25$$

    b. $(y + 8)(y - 8) = y^2 - 8y + 8y - 64$
$$= y^2 - 64$$

Notice that for each of these products, we multiplied the sum of two terms by the difference of the *same* two terms. Notice also in these three examples that once these expressions were multiplied, the two middle terms were opposites and thus canceled to zero.

    These pairs, generally written as $(a+b)$ and $(a-b)$, are known as **conjugates**. If we multiply $(a+b)(a-b)$, we can see this general pattern more clearly:

$$(a + b)(a - b) = a^2 - ab + ab - b^2$$
$$= a^2 - b^2$$

As with the square of a binomial producing a perfect suqare trinomial, this pattern also has two things we can give a name to. The left side is the **product of a sum and its conjugate**, and the result on the right is a **difference of squares**.

Fact 5.5.13 The Product of a Sum and Its Conjugate Formula. *If a and b are real numbers or variable expressions, then we have the following formula:*
$$(a + b)(a - b) = a^2 - b^2$$

Example 5.5.14 Multiply the following using Fact 5.5.13.

    a. $(4x - 7y)(4x + 7y)$ b. $-2(3x + 1)(3x - 1)$

Explanation. The first step to using this method is to identify the values of a and b.

  a. In this instance, $a = 4x$ and $b = 7y$. Using the formula,

$$(4x - 7y)(4x + 7y) = (4x)^2 - (7y)^2$$
$$= 16x^2 - 49y^2$$

  b. In this instance, we have a constant factor as well as a product in the form $(a + b)(a - b)$. We will first expand $(3x+1)(3x-1)$ by identifying $a = 3x$ and $b = 1$ and using the formula. Then we will multiply the factor of -2 through this expression. So,

$$-2(3x+1)(3x-1) = -2\left((3x)^2 - 1^2\right)$$
$$= -2\left(9x^2 - 1\right)$$
$$= -18x^2 + 2$$

Checkpoint 5.5.15 Expand $(4x+2)(4x-2)$.

Explanation.

$$(4x+2)(4x-2) = (4x)^2 - 2^2$$
$$= 16x^2 - 4$$

Checkpoint 5.5.16 Expand $\left(x^7 + 9\right)\left(x^7 - 9\right)$.

Explanation.

$$\left(x^7 + 9\right)\left(x^7 - 9\right) = \left(x^7\right)^2 - 9^2$$
$$= x^{14} - 81$$

5.5.3 Binomials Raised to Other Powers

Example 5.5.17 Simplify the expression $(x+5)^3$ into an expanded polynomial.

Before we start expanding this expression, it is important to recognize that $(x+5)^3 \neq x^3 + 5^3$, similar to the message in Warning 5.5.11. To be sure, we can see that if we evaluate at $x = 1$, we get different results.

$$(1+5)^3 = 6^3 \qquad\qquad 1^3 + 5^3 = 1 + 125$$
$$= 216 \qquad\qquad\qquad = 126$$

We will need to rely on distribution to expand this expression. The first step in expanding $(x+5)^3$ is to remember that the exponent of 3 indicates that

$$(x+5)^3 = \overbrace{(x+5)(x+5)(x+5)}^{3\text{ times}}$$

Once we rewrite this in an expanded form, we next multiply the two binomials on the left and then finish by multiplying that result by the remaining binomial:

$$(x+5)^3 = \overbrace{(x+5)(x+5)}^{\text{a binomial squared}}(x+5)$$
$$= \left(x^2 + 10x + 25\right)(x+5)$$
$$= x^3 + 5x^2 + 10x^2 + 50x + 25x + 125$$
$$= x^3 + 15x^2 + 75x + 125$$

Checkpoint 5.5.18 Expand $(2y - 6)^3$.

Explanation.

$$\begin{array}{rl}
(2y - 6)^3 &= \overbrace{(2y - 6)(2y - 6)}^{\text{a binomial squared}}(2y - 6) \\
&= \left(4y^2 - 24y + 36\right)(2y - 6) \\
&= 8y^3 - 24y^2 - 48y^2 + 144y + 72y - 216 \\
&= 8y^3 - 72y^2 + 216y - 216
\end{array}$$

Generalizing, if we want to expand a binomial raised to a high whole number power, we can start by rewriting the expression without an exponent. Then it will help some to use the formula for the square of a binomial.

Example 5.5.19 To multiply $(x - 3)^4$, we'd start by rewriting $(x - 3)^4$ in expanded form as:

$$(x - 3)^4 = \overbrace{(x - 3)(x - 3)(x - 3)(x - 3)}^{\text{4 times}}$$

We will then multiply pairs of polynomials from the left to the right.

$$\begin{array}{rl}
(x - 3)^4 &= \overbrace{(x - 3)(x - 3)}^{\text{a perfect square}}\overbrace{(x - 3)(x - 3)}^{\text{a perfect square}} \\
&= \left(x^2 - 6x + 9\right)\left(x^2 - 6x + 9\right) \\
&= x^4 - 6x^3 + 9x^2 - 6x^3 + 36x^2 - 54x + 9x^2 - 54x + 81 \\
&= x^4 - 12x^3 + 54x^2 - 108x + 81
\end{array}$$

5.5.4 Reading Questions

1. How many special patterns should you be on the lookout for when multiplying and/or squaring binomials?

2. Do you prefer to memorize the formula for the square of a binomial or to visualize the process?

5.5.5 Exercises

Review and Warmup Use the properties of exponents to simplify the expression.

1. $\left(3y^{11}\right)^4$		**2.** $\left(5x^{12}\right)^3$		**3.** $(2x)^2$		**4.** $(4r)^2$	
5. $\left(-10y^5\right)^2$		**6.** $\left(-7x^6\right)^{3\cdot}$		**7.** $-3\left(-3t^8\right)^3$		**8.** $-4\left(-8t^9\right)^2$	

Simplify each expression, if possible, by combining like terms.

9.   a. $-9s + 2$

  b. $7x + 2$

  c. $9y^2 + 3y$

  d. $-x + 8s$

10.   a. $-2t + 7x$

  b. $-y - 2s$

  c. $-9x^2 + 5y$

  d. $t - 8y$

11.   a.
$7t^2 + 7 - 5t^2 - 4$

  b. $-t^2 - 2t^2$

  c. $3y + 6y - 2x$

  d. $-4s - 3z + 7z$

12.   a. $t + 6t$

  b.
$9z - 6t + 2 + 7z$

  c.
$6x - 5x - 4z + 2s^2$

  d. $3z^2 + 2$

Perfect Square Trinomial Formula Expand the square of a *bi*nomial.

13. $(x + 6)^2$

14. $(y + 3)^2$

15. $(9y + 2)^2$

16. $(6r + 3)^2$

17. $(r - 9)^2$

18. $(t - 2)^2$

19. $(6t - 2)^2$

20. $(3t - 8)^2$

21. $(8x^2 - 4)^2$

22. $(5x^2 - 10)^2$

23. $(y^7 - 11)^2$

24. $(y^{10} + 6)^2$

25. $(6a - 5b)^2$

26. $(7a + 2b)^2$

27. $(8ab - 8)^2$

28. $(9ab + 5)^2$

29. $(x^2 + 10y^2)^2$

30. $(x^2 + 2y^2)^2$

Difference of Squares Formula Multiply the polynomials.

31. $(x - 5)(x + 5)$

32. $(y + 12)(y - 12)$

33. $(5y + 4)(5y - 4)$

34. $(3r - 9)(3r + 9)$

35. $(10 + 6r)(10 - 6r)$

36. $(6 + 10t)(6 - 10t)$

37. $(t^5 - 8)(t^5 + 8)$

38. $(t^9 + 10)(t^9 - 10)$

39. $(4x^9 - 9)(4x^9 + 9)$

40. $(2x^7 + 3)(2x^7 - 3)$

41. $(1 - 12y^5)(1 + 12y^5)$

42. $(1 - 8y^3)(1 + 8y^3)$

43. $(6x + 3y)(6x - 3y)$

44. $(7x - 8y)(7x + 8y)$

45. $(ab - 8)(ab + 8)$

46. $(ab - 9)(ab + 9)$

47. $4(t + 6)(t - 6)$

48. $5(x - 3)(x + 3)$

49. $2(2x - 3)(2x + 3)$

50. $6(5y + 5)(5y - 5)$

51. $3(y + 4)^2$

52. $5(r + 10)^2$

53. $7(7r + 1)^2$

54. $6(4t + 5)^2$

Multiply the polynomials.

55. $(x^2 + 9y^2)(x^2 - 9y^2)$

56. $(x^2 + 10y^2)(x^2 - 10y^2)$

57. $(2x^8 + 4y^3)(2x^8 - 4y^3)$

58. $(3x^6 - 10y^3)(3x^6 + 10y^3)$

59. $(4x^4y^8 + 7y^3)(4x^4y^8 - 7y^3)$

60. $(5x^2y^4 + 3y^3)(5x^2y^4 - 3y^3)$

Binomials Raised to Other Powers Simplify the given expression into an expanded polynomial.

61. $(r + 6)^3$

62. $(r + 4)^3$

63. $(r - 2)^3$

64. $(t - 6)^3$

65. $(4t + 2)^3$

66. $(2x + 4)^3$

67. $(5x - 2)^3$

68. $(4y - 5)^3$

69. Determine if the following statements are true or false.

a. $(a - b)^2 = a^2 - b^2$

($\square$ True $\square$ False)

b. $(a + b)^2 = a^2 + b^2$

($\square$ True $\square$ False)

c. $(a + b)(a - b) = a^2 - b^2$

($\square$ True $\square$ False)

70. Determine if the following statements are true or false.

a. $(2(a - b))^2 = 4(a - b)^2$

($\square$ True $\square$ False)

b. $2(a + b)^2 = 2a^2 + 2b^2$

($\square$ True $\square$ False)

c. $2(a + b)(a - b) = 2a^2 - 2b^2$

($\square$ True $\square$ False)

5.6 More Exponent Rules

5.6.1 Review of Exponent Rules for Products and Exponents

In Section 5.2, we introduced three basic rules involving products and exponents. Then in Section 5.3, we introduced one more. We begin this section with a recap of these four exponent rules.

List 5.6.2: Summary of Exponent Rules (Thus Far)

Product Rule When multiplying two expressions that have the same base, simplify the product by adding the exponents.

$$x^m \cdot x^n = x^{m+n}$$

Power to a Power Rule When a base is raised to an exponent and that expression is raised to another exponent, multiply the exponents.

$$(x^m)^n = x^{m \cdot n}$$

Product to a Power Rule When a product is raised to an exponent, apply the exponent to each factor in the product.

$$(x \cdot y)^n = x^n \cdot y^n$$

Quotient of Powers Rule When dividing two expressions that have the same base, simplify the quotient by subtracting the exponents.

$$\frac{x^m}{x^n} = x^{m-n}$$

For now, we only know this rule when $m > n$.

Checkpoint 5.6.3

    a. Simplify $r^{16} \cdot r^5$.   b. Simplify $\left(x^{11}\right)^{10}$.   c. Simplify $(3r)^4$.   d. Simplify $\frac{3y^7}{y^3}$.

Explanation.

    a. We *add* the exponents because this is a product of powers with the same base:

$$r^{16} \cdot r^5 = r^{16+5}$$
$$= r^{21}$$

    b. We *multiply* the exponents because this is a power being raised to a power:

$$\left(x^{11}\right)^{10} = x^{11 \cdot 10}$$
$$= x^{110}$$

c. We apply the power to each factor in the product:

$$(3r)^4 = 3^4 r^4$$
$$= 81r^4$$

d. We *subtract* the exponents because this expression is dividing powers with the same base:

$$\frac{3y^7}{y^3} = \frac{3}{1}\frac{y^7}{y^3}$$
$$= 3y^{7-3}$$
$$= 3y^4$$

5.6.2 Quotient to a Power Rule

One rule we have learned is the product to a power rule, as in $(2x)^3 = 2^3 x^3$. When two factors are multiplied and the product is raised to a power, we may apply the exponent to each of those factors individually. We can use the rules of fractions to extend this property to a *quotient* raised to a power.

Example 5.6.4 Let y be a real number, where $y \neq 0$. Find another way to write $\left(\frac{5}{y}\right)^4$.

Explanation.   Writing the expression without an exponent and then simplifying, we have:

$$\left(\frac{5}{y}\right)^4 = \left(\frac{5}{y}\right)\left(\frac{5}{y}\right)\left(\frac{5}{y}\right)\left(\frac{7}{y}\right)$$
$$= \frac{5 \cdot 5 \cdot 5 \cdot 5}{y \cdot y \cdot y \cdot y}$$
$$= \frac{5^4}{y^4}$$
$$= \frac{625}{y^4}$$

Similar to the product to a power rule, we essentially applied the outer exponent to the "factors" inside the parentheses—to factors of the numerator *and* factors of the denominator. The general rule is:

Fact 5.6.5 Quotient to a Power Rule. *For real numbers a and b (with $b \neq 0$) and natural number m,*

$$\left(\frac{a}{b}\right)^m = \frac{a^m}{b^m}$$

This rule says that when you raise a fraction to a power, you may separately raise the numerator and denominator to that power. In Example 5.6.4, this means that we can directly calculate $\left(\frac{5}{y}\right)^4$:

$$\left(\frac{5}{y}\right)^4 = \frac{5^4}{y^4}$$
$$= \frac{625}{y^4}$$

Checkpoint 5.6.6

a. Simplify $\left(\dfrac{p}{2}\right)^6$.

b. Simplify $\left(\dfrac{5^6 w^7}{5^2 w^4}\right)^9$. If you end up with a large power of a specific number, leave it written that way.

c. Simplify $\dfrac{\left(2r^5\right)^7}{\left(2^2 r^8\right)^3}$. If you end up with a large power of a specific number, leave it written that way.

Explanation.

a. We can use the quotient to a power rule:

$$\left(\frac{p}{2}\right)^6 = \frac{p^6}{2^6}$$
$$= \frac{p^6}{64}$$

b. If we stick closely to the order of operations, we should first simplify inside the parentheses and then work with the outer exponent. Going this route, we will first use the quotient rule:

$$\left(\frac{5^6 w^7}{5^2 w^4}\right)^9 = \left(5^{6-2} w^{7-4}\right)^9$$
$$= \left(5^4 w^3\right)^9$$
$$= \left(5^4\right)^9 \cdot \left(w^3\right)^9$$
$$= 5^{4 \cdot 9} \cdot w^{3 \cdot 9}$$
$$= 5^{36} \cdot w^{27}$$

c. According to the order of operations, we should simplify inside parentheses first, then apply exponents, then divide. Since we cannot simplify inside the parentheses, we must apply the outer exponents to each factor inside the respective set of parentheses first:

$$\frac{\left(2r^5\right)^7}{\left(2^2 r^8\right)^3} = \frac{2^7 \left(r^5\right)^7}{\left(2^2\right)^3 \left(r^8\right)^3}$$
$$= \frac{2^7 r^{5 \cdot 7}}{2^{2 \cdot 3} r^{8 \cdot 3}}$$
$$= \frac{2^7 r^{35}}{2^6 r^{24}}$$
$$= 2^{7-6} r^{35-24}$$
$$= 2^1 r^{11}$$
$$= 2r^{11}$$

5.6.3 Zero as an Exponent

So far, we have been working with exponents that are natural numbers $(1, 2, 3, \ldots)$. By the end of this section, we will expand our understanding to include exponents that are any integer, as with 5^0 and 12^{-2}. As a first step, let's explore how 0 should behave as an exponent by considering the pattern of decreasing powers of 2 in Figure 5.6.7.

Power		Product		Result	
2^4	$=$	$2 \cdot 2 \cdot 2 \cdot 2$	$=$	16	
2^3	$=$	$2 \cdot 2 \cdot 2$	$=$	8	(divide by 2)
2^2	$=$	$2 \cdot 2$	$=$	4	(divide by 2)
2^1	$=$	2	$=$	2	(divide by 2)
2^0	$=$	?	$=$	?	

Figure 5.6.7: Descending Powers of 2

As we move down from one row to the row below it, we reduce the exponent in the power by 1 and we remove a factor of 2 from the product. The result in one row is half of the result of the previous row. The question is, what happens when the exponent gets down to 0 and you remove the last remaining factor of 2? Following that pattern with the final results, moving from 2^1 to 2^0 should meant the result of 2 is divided by 2, leaving 1. So we have:

$$2^0 = 1$$

Fact 5.6.8 The Zero Exponent Rule. *For any non-zero real number* a,

$$a^0 = 1$$

We exclude the case where $a = 0$ from this rule, because our reasoning for this rule with the table had us dividing by the base, and we cannot divide by 0.

Checkpoint 5.6.9 Simplify the following expressions. Assume all variables represent non-zero real numbers.

   a. $\left(173x^4y^{251}\right)^0$ b. $(-8)^0$ c. -8^0 d. $3x^0$

Explanation. To simplify any of these expressions, it is critical that we remember an exponent only applies to what it is touching or immediately next to.

   a. In the expression $\left(173x^4y^{251}\right)^0$, the exponent 0 applies to everything inside the parentheses.

$$\left(173x^4y^{251}\right)^0 = 1$$

   b. In the expression $(-8)^0$ the exponent applies to everything inside the parentheses, -8.

$$(-8)^0 = 1$$

   c. In contrast to the previous example, the exponent only applies to the 8. The exponent has a higher priority than negation in the order of operations. We should consider that $-8^0 = -\left(8^0\right)$, and so:

$$-8^0 = -\left(8^0\right)$$
$$= -1$$

d. In the expression $3x^0$, the exponent 0 only applies to the x:

$$3x^0 = 3 \cdot x^0$$
$$= 3 \cdot 1$$
$$= 3$$

5.6.4 Negative Exponents

We understand what it means for a variable to have a natural number exponent. For example, x^5 means
$\overbrace{x \cdot x \cdot x \cdot x \cdot x}^{\text{five times}}$. Now we will try to give meaning to an exponent that is a negative integer, like in x^{-5}.

To consider what it could possibly mean to have a negative integer exponent, let's extend the pattern we examined in Figure 5.6.7. In that table, each time we move down a row, we reduce the power by 1 and we divide the value by 2. We can continue this pattern in the power and value columns, going all the way down into when the exponent is negative.

Power	Result	
2^3	8	
2^2	4	(divide by 2)
2^1	2	(divide by 2)
2^0	1	(divide by 2)
2^{-1}	$1/2 = 1/2^1$	(divide by 2)
2^{-2}	$1/4 = 1/2^2$	(divide by 2)
2^{-3}	$1/8 = 1/2^3$	(divide by 2)

Figure 5.6.10: Negative Powers of 2

We are seeing a pattern where $2^{\text{negative number}}$ is equal to $\frac{1}{2^{\text{positive number}}}$. Note that the choice of base 2 was arbitrary, and this pattern works for all bases except 0, since we cannot divide by 0 in moving from one row to the next.

Fact 5.6.11 The Negative Exponent Rule. *For any non-zero real number* a *and any natural number* n,

$$a^{-n} = \frac{1}{a^n}$$

If we take reciprocals of both sides, we have another helpful fact:

$$\frac{1}{a^{-n}} = a^n.$$

Taken together, these facts tell us that a power in the numerator with a negative exponent belongs in the *denominator* (with a *positive* exponent). And similarly, a power in the denominator with a negative exponent belongs in the *numerator* (with a *positive* exponent). In other words, you can view a negative exponent as telling you to move something to/from the numerator/denominator of an expression, changing the sign of the exponent at the same time.

You may be expected to simplify expressions so that they do not have any negative exponents. This can always be accomplished using the negative exponent rule. Try it with these exercises.

Checkpoint 5.6.12

a. Write $4y^{-6}$ without using negative exponents.

b. Write $\dfrac{3x^{-4}}{yz^{-2}}$ without using negative exponents.

c. Simplify $\left(-5x^{-5}\right)\left(-8x^4\right)$ and write it without using negative exponents.

Explanation.

a. An exponent only applies to whatever it is "touching". In the expression $4y^{-6}$, only the y is affected by the exponent.

$$4y^{-6} = 4 \cdot \frac{1}{y^6}$$
$$= \frac{4}{y^6}$$

b. Negative exponents tell us to move some variables between the numerator and denominator to make the exponents positive. The x^{-4} in the numerator should become x^4 in the denominator. The z^{-2} in the denominator should become z^2 in the numerator.

$$\frac{3x^{-4}}{yz^{-2}} = \frac{3z^2}{yx^4}$$

Notice that the factors of 3 and y did not move, as both of those factors had positive exponents.

c. The product of powers rule still applies, and we can add exponents even when one or both are negative:

$$\left(-5x^{-5}\right)\left(-8x^4\right) = (-5)(-8)x^{-5}x^4$$
$$= 40x^{-1}$$
$$= \frac{40}{x}$$

5.6.5 Summary of Exponent Rules

Now that we have some new exponent rules beyond those from Section 5.2 and Section 5.3, let's summarize.

List 5.6.13: Summary of the Rules of Exponents for Multiplication and Division

> If a and b are real numbers, and m and n are integers, then we have the following rules:
>
> **Product Rule** $a^m \cdot a^n = a^{m+n}$
>
> **Power to a Power Rule** $(a^m)^n = a^{m \cdot n}$
>
> **Product to a Power Rule** $(ab)^m = a^m \cdot b^m$
>
> **Quotient Rule** $\dfrac{a^m}{a^m} = a^{m-n}$, as long as $a \neq 0$
>
> **Quotient to a Power Rule** $\left(\dfrac{a}{b}\right)^m = \dfrac{a^m}{b^m}$, as long as $b \neq 0$
>
> **Zero Exponent Rule** $a^0 = 1$ for $a \neq 0$
>
> **Negative Exponent Rule** $a^{-m} = \dfrac{1}{a^m}$
>
> **Negative Exponent Reciprocal Rule** $\dfrac{1}{a^{-m}} = a^m$

Remark 5.6.14 Why we have "$a \neq 0$" and "$b \neq 0$" for some rules. We have to be careful to make sure the rules we state don't suggest that it would ever be OK to divide by zero. Dividing by zero leads us to expressions that have no meaning. For example, both $\frac{2}{0}$ and $\frac{0}{0}$ are *undefined*, meaning no one has defined what it means to divide a number by 0. Also, we established that $a^0 = 1$ using repeated division by a in table rows, so that reasoning doesn't work if $a = 0$.

Warning 5.6.15 A Common Mistake. It may be tempting to apply the rules of exponents to expressions containing addition or subtraction. However, none of the Summary of the Rules of Exponents for Multiplication and Division involve addition or subtraction in the initial expression. Because whole number exponents mean repeated multiplication, not repeated addition or subtraction, trying to apply exponent rules in situations that do not use multiplication simply doesn't work.

Can we say something like $a^m + a^n = a^{m+n}$? How would that work out when $a = 2$, $m = 3$, and $n = 4$?

$$2^3 + 2^4 \overset{?}{=} 2^{3+4}$$

$$8 + 16 \overset{?}{=} 2^7$$

$$24 \overset{\text{no}}{=} 128$$

As we can see, that's not even close. This attempt at a "sum rule" falls apart. In fact, without knowing values for a, n, and m, there's no way to simplify the expression $a^n + a^m$.

Checkpoint 5.6.16 Decide whether each statements is true or false.

   a. $(7 + 8)^3 = 7^3 + 8^3$

      ($\square$ true $\square$ false)

   b. $(xy)^3 = x^3 y^3$

      ($\square$ true $\square$ false)

   c. $2x^3 \cdot 4x^2 \cdot 5x^6 = (2 \cdot 4 \cdot 5)x^{3+2+6}$

      ($\square$ true $\square$ false)

   d. $\left(x^3 y^5\right)^4 = x^{3+4} y^{5+4}$

      ($\square$ true $\square$ false)

   e. $2\left(x^2 y^5\right)^3 = 8x^6 y^{15}$

      ($\square$ true $\square$ false)

   f. $x^2 + x^3 = x^5$

      ($\square$ true $\square$ false)

   g. $x^3 + x^3 = 2x^3$

      ($\square$ true $\square$ false)

   h. $x^3 \cdot x^3 = 2x^6$

      ($\square$ true $\square$ false)

   i. $3^2 \cdot 2^3 = 6^5$

      ($\square$ true $\square$ false)

   j. $3^{-2} = -\frac{1}{9}$

      ($\square$ true $\square$ false)

Explanation.

   a. False, $(7 + 8)^3 \neq 7^3 + 8^3$. Following the order of operations, on the left $(7 + 8)^3$ would simplify as 15^3, which is 3375. However, on the right side, we have

$$7^3 + 8^3 = 343 + 512$$
$$= 855$$

   Since $3375 \neq 855$, the equation is false.

   b. True. As the cube applies to the product of x and y, $(xy)^3 = x^3 y^3$.

c. True. The coefficients do get multiplied together and the exponents added when the expressions are multiplied, so $2x^3 \cdot 4x^2 \cdot 5x^6 = (2 \cdot 4 \cdot 5)x^{3+2+6}$.

d. False, $\left(x^3 y^5\right)^4 \neq x^{3+4}y^{5+4}$. When we have a power to a power, we multiply the exponents rather than adding them. So
$$\left(x^3 y^5\right)^4 = x^{3 \cdot 4} y^{5 \cdot 4}$$

e. False, $2\left(x^2 y^5\right)^3 \neq 8x^6 y^{15}$. The exponent of 3 applies to x^2 and y^5, but does not apply to the 2. So
$$2\left(x^2 y^5\right)^3 = 2x^{2 \cdot 3} 6y^{5 \cdot 3}$$
$$= 2x^6 y^{15}$$

f. False, $x^2 + x^3 \neq x^5$. The two terms on the left hand side are not like terms and there is no way to combine them.

g. True. The terms x^3 and x^3 are like terms, so $x^3 + x^3 = 2x^3$.

h. False, $x^3 \cdot x^3 \neq 2x^6$. When x^3 and x^3 are multiplied, their coefficients are each 1. So the coefficient of their product is still 1, and we have $x^3 \cdot x^3 = x^6$.

i. False, $3^2 \cdot 2^3 \neq 6^5$. Note that neither the bases nor the exponents are the same. Following the order of operations, on the left $3^2 \cdot 2^3$ would simplify as $9 \cdot 8$, which is 72. However, on the right side, we have $6^5 = 7776$. Since $72 \neq 7776$, the equation is false.

j. False, $3^{-2} \neq -\frac{1}{9}$. The exponent of -2 on the number 3 does not result in a negative number. Instead, $3^{-2} = \frac{1}{3^2}$, which is $\frac{1}{9}$.

As we mentioned before, many situations we'll come across will require us to use more than one exponent rule. In these situations, we'll have to decide which rule to use first. There are often different, correct approaches we could take. But if we rely on order of operations, we will have a straightforward approach to simplify the expression correctly. To bring it all together, try these exercises.

Checkpoint 5.6.17

a. Simplify $\dfrac{6x^3}{2x^7}$ and write it without using negative exponents.

b. Simplify $4\left(\frac{1}{5}tv^{-4}\right)^2$ and write it without using negative exponents.

c. Simplify $\left(\dfrac{3^0 y^4 \cdot y^5}{6y^2}\right)^3$ and write it without using negative exponents.

d. Simplify $\left(7^4 x^{-6} t^2\right)^{-5} \left(7x^{-2} t^{-7}\right)^4$ and write it without using negative exponents. Leave larger numbers (such as 7^{10}) in exponent form.

Explanation.

a. In the expression $\frac{6x^3}{2x^7}$, the coefficients reduce using the properties of fractions. One way to simplify the variable powers is:

$$\begin{aligned}
\frac{6x^3}{2x^7} &= \frac{6}{2} \cdot \frac{x^3}{x^7} \\
&= 3 \cdot x^{3-7} \\
&= 3 \cdot x^{-4} \\
&= 3 \cdot \frac{1}{x^4} \\
&= \frac{3}{x^4}
\end{aligned}$$

b. In the expression $4\left(\frac{1}{5}tv^{-4}\right)^2$, the exponent 2 applies to each factor inside the parentheses.

$$\begin{aligned}
4\left(\frac{1}{5}tv^{-4}\right)^2 &= 4\left(\frac{1}{5}\right)^2 (t)^2 \left(v^{-4}\right)^2 \\
&= 4\left(\frac{1}{25}\right)(t^2)\left(v^{-4 \cdot 2}\right) \\
&= 4\left(\frac{1}{25}\right)(t^2)\left(v^{-8}\right) \\
&= 4\left(\frac{1}{25}\right)(t^2)\left(\frac{1}{v^8}\right) \\
&= \frac{4t^2}{25v^8}
\end{aligned}$$

c. To follow the order of operations in the expression $\left(\frac{3^0 y^4 \cdot y^5}{6y^2}\right)^3$, the numerator inside the parentheses should be dealt with first. After that, we'll simplify the quotient inside the parentheses. As a final step, we'll apply the exponent to that simplified expression:

$$\begin{aligned}
\left(\frac{3^0 y^4 \cdot y^5}{6y^2}\right)^3 &= \left(\frac{1 \cdot y^{4+5}}{6y^2}\right)^3 \\
&= \left(\frac{y^9}{6y^2}\right)^3 \\
&= \left(\frac{y^{9-2}}{6}\right)^3 \\
&= \left(\frac{y^7}{6}\right)^3 \\
&= \frac{\left(y^7\right)^3}{6^3} \\
&= \frac{y^{7 \cdot 3}}{216} \\
&= \frac{y^{21}}{216}
\end{aligned}$$

d. We'll again rely on the order of operations, and look to simplify anything inside parentheses first and then apply exponents. In this example, we will begin by applying the product to a power rule, followed by the power to a power rule.

$$\left(7^4x^{-6}t^2\right)^{-5}\left(7x^{-2}t^{-7}\right)^4 = \left(7^4\right)^{-5}\left(x^{-6}\right)^{-5}\left(t^2\right)^{-5}\cdot(7)^4\left(x^{-2}\right)^4\left(t^{-7}\right)^4$$
$$= 7^{-20}x^{30}t^{-10}\cdot 7^4x^{-8}t^{-28}$$
$$= 7^{-20+4}x^{30-8}t^{-10-28}$$
$$= 7^{-16}x^{22}t^{-38}$$
$$= \frac{x^{22}}{7^{16}t^{38}}$$

5.6.6 Reading Questions

1. When you are considering using the exponent rule $a^m\cdot a^n = a^{m+n}$, are m and n allowed to be negative integers?

2. What are the differences between these three expressions?

$$x+0 \qquad 0x \qquad x^0$$

3. If you rearrange $\frac{xy^{-3}}{a^2b^8c}$ so that it is written without negative exponents, how many factors will you have "moved?"

5.6.7 Exercises

Review and Warmup

1. Evaluate the following.

   a. 3^2

   b. 2^3

   c. $(-4)^2$

   d. $(-2)^3$

2. Evaluate the following.

   a. 3^2

   b. 5^3

   c. $(-4)^2$

   d. $(-5)^3$

Use the properties of exponents to simplify the expression.

3. $6\cdot 6^7$

4. $7\cdot 7^4$

5. $7^{10}\cdot 7^8$

6. $8^7\cdot 8^2$

Simplifying Products and Quotients Involving Exponents Use the properties of exponents to simplify the expression.

7. $r^{20}\cdot r^6$

8. $t^3\cdot t^{18}$

9. $\left(y^4\right)^7$

10. $\left(t^5\right)^3$

11. $\left(2r^6\right)^4$

12. $\left(4y^7\right)^3$

13. $\left(-2y^{13}\right)\cdot\left(9y^4\right)$

14. $\left(6r^{15}\right)\cdot\left(-8r^{16}\right)$

15. $\left(-\frac{r^{18}}{8}\right)\cdot\left(\frac{r^{10}}{8}\right)$

16. $\left(-\frac{r^{20}}{4}\right)\cdot\left(-\frac{r^3}{7}\right)$

17. $-2\left(-4r^2\right)^3$

18. $-3\left(-10r^3\right)^2$

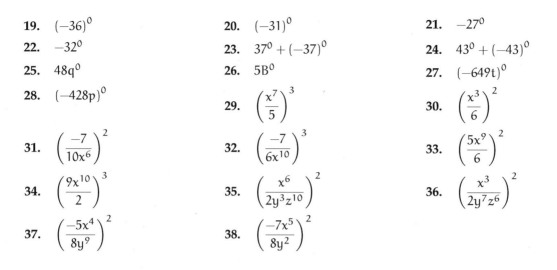

19. $(-36)^0$

20. $(-31)^0$

21. -27^0

22. -32^0

23. $37^0 + (-37)^0$

24. $43^0 + (-43)^0$

25. $48q^0$

26. $5B^0$

27. $(-649t)^0$

28. $(-428p)^0$

29. $\left(\dfrac{x^7}{5}\right)^3$

30. $\left(\dfrac{x^3}{6}\right)^2$

31. $\left(\dfrac{-7}{10x^6}\right)^2$

32. $\left(\dfrac{-7}{6x^{10}}\right)^3$

33. $\left(\dfrac{5x^9}{6}\right)^2$

34. $\left(\dfrac{9x^{10}}{2}\right)^3$

35. $\left(\dfrac{x^6}{2y^3z^{10}}\right)^2$

36. $\left(\dfrac{x^3}{2y^7z^6}\right)^2$

37. $\left(\dfrac{-5x^4}{8y^9}\right)^2$

38. $\left(\dfrac{-7x^5}{8y^2}\right)^2$

Rewrite the expression simplified and using only positive exponents.

39. $\left(\dfrac{1}{6}\right)^{-2}$

40. $\left(\dfrac{1}{7}\right)^{-3}$

41. $\dfrac{7^{-2}}{4^{-3}}$

42. $\dfrac{7^{-3}}{2^{-2}}$

43. $10^{-1} - 8^{-1}$

44. $2^{-1} - 5^{-1}$

45. $5x^{-4}$

46. $15x^{-5}$

47. $\dfrac{9}{x^{-6}}$

48. $\dfrac{20}{x^{-8}}$

49. $\dfrac{14x^{-9}}{x}$

50. $\dfrac{9x^{-10}}{x}$

51. $\dfrac{18x^{-17}}{x^{-35}}$

52. $\dfrac{9x^{-19}}{x^{-23}}$

53. $\dfrac{16x^{-4}}{17x^{-7}}$

54. $\dfrac{6x^{-7}}{7x^{-24}}$

55. $\dfrac{y^{-12}}{r^{-8}}$

56. $\dfrac{y^{-20}}{x^{-3}}$

57. $\dfrac{y^{-8}}{t^{17}}$

58. $\dfrac{r^{-16}}{y^{12}}$

59. $\dfrac{1}{8r^{-5}}$

60. $\dfrac{1}{40t^{-13}}$

61. $\dfrac{t^2}{t^{24}}$

62. $\dfrac{x^4}{x^7}$

63. $\dfrac{9x^{33}}{3x^{38}}$

64. $\dfrac{-18y^7}{9y^{22}}$

65. $\dfrac{-11y^4}{3y^5}$

66. $\dfrac{-7y^5}{3y^{36}}$

67. $\dfrac{r^4}{(r^6)^2}$

68. $\dfrac{r^2}{(r^3)^8}$

69. $\dfrac{t^{-4}}{(t^9)^6}$

70. $\dfrac{t^{-5}}{(t^6)^3}$

71. $x^{-20} \cdot x^5$

72. $x^{-14} \cdot x^9$

73. $(5y^{-7}) \cdot (7y^2)$

74. $(2y^{-19}) \cdot (2y^9)$

75. $\left(\dfrac{10}{9}\right)^{-2}$

76. $\left(\dfrac{3}{2}\right)^{-2}$

77. $(-8)^{-3}$

78. $(-9)^{-3}$

79. $\dfrac{1}{(-10)^{-2}}$

80. $\dfrac{1}{(-2)^{-3}}$

81. $\dfrac{-6}{(-2)^{-2}}$

82. $\dfrac{3}{(-2)^{-3}}$

83. 5^{-3}

84. 6^{-2}

85. $7^{-1} + 2^{-1}$

86. $8^{-1} + 6^{-1}$

87. $\dfrac{1}{9^{-2}}$

88. $\dfrac{1}{10^{-2}}$

89. -2^{-3}

90. -3^{-2}

91. $\dfrac{(5y^3)^3}{y^{22}}$

92. $\dfrac{(5y^9)^3}{y^{29}}$

93. $\dfrac{(5y^6)^2}{y^{-13}}$

94. $\dfrac{(5r^{12})^3}{r^{-9}}$

95. $\left(\dfrac{r^{14}}{r^4}\right)^{-3}$ **96.** $\left(\dfrac{t^7}{t^5}\right)^{-2}$ **97.** $\left(\dfrac{20t^{19}}{5t^2}\right)^{-4}$ **98.** $\left(\dfrac{10x^{13}}{5x^7}\right)^{-3}$

99. $\left(-5x^{-7}\right)^{-3}$ **100.** $\left(-2y^{-18}\right)^{-2}$ **101.** $\left(4y^{-12}\right)^{-3}$ **102.** $\left(3y^{-6}\right)^{-2}$

103. $\dfrac{7r^9 \cdot 6r^6}{5r^2}$ **104.** $\dfrac{5r^6 \cdot 5r^{10}}{7r^{13}}$ **105.** $\left(t^4\right)^3 \cdot t^{-7}$ **106.** $\left(t^{13}\right)^5 \cdot t^{-16}$

107. $\left(3x^8\right)^2 \cdot x^{-15}$ **108.** $\left(3x^4\right)^3 \cdot x^{-8}$ **109.** $\dfrac{\left(y^9\right)^2}{\left(y^8\right)^4}$ **110.** $\dfrac{\left(y^6\right)^3}{\left(y^{15}\right)^5}$

111. $\left(y^4\right)^{-5}$ **112.** $\left(r^{15}\right)^{-3}$ **113.** $\left(r^{12}y^6\right)^{-3}$ **114.** $\left(t^4x^3\right)^{-3}$

115. $\left(t^{-10}r^{12}\right)^{-3}$ **116.** $\left(x^{-15}y^8\right)^{-3}$ **117.** $\left(\dfrac{x^{15}}{2}\right)^{-3}$ **118.** $\left(\dfrac{y^{10}}{4}\right)^{-4}$

119. $\left(\dfrac{y^{11}}{x^7}\right)^{-3}$ **120.** $\left(\dfrac{y^{11}}{t^7}\right)^{-3}$ **121.** $\dfrac{\left(r^3x^{-5}\right)^{-3}}{\left(r^{-3}x^5\right)^{-2}}$ **122.** $\dfrac{\left(r^5x^{-7}\right)^{-3}}{\left(r^{-8}x^3\right)^{-4}}$

Rewrite the expression simplified and using only positive exponents.

123. $8x^{-5}y^3z^{-3}\left(3x^8\right)^{-3}$ **124.** $10x^{-4}y^4z^{-8}\left(3x^4\right)^{-4}$

125. $\left(\dfrac{x^4y^5z^4}{x^{-2}y^{-5}z^{-4}}\right)^{-3}$ **126.** $\left(\dfrac{x^4y^8z^5}{x^{-5}y^{-7}z^{-8}}\right)^{-2}$

Challenge

127. Consider the exponential expression $\dfrac{x^a \cdot x^b}{x^c}$ where $a > 0, b < 0$, and $c > 0$.

a. Are there values for a, b, and c so that the expression equals x^7? If so, fill in the blanks below with possible values for a, b, and c. If not, fill in the blanks below with the word none.

$a =$ [　　　], $b =$ [　　　], and $c =$ [　　　]

b. Are there values for a, b, and c so that the exponential expression equals $\dfrac{1}{x^6}$? If so, fill in the blanks below with possible values for a, b, and c. If not, fill in the blanks below with the word none.

$a =$ [　　　], $b =$ [　　　], and $c =$ [　　　]

128. Consider the exponential expression $\dfrac{x^a \cdot x^b}{x^c}$ where $a < 0, b < 0$, and $c > 0$.

a. Are there values for a, b, and c so that the expression equals x^6? If so, fill in the blanks below with possible values for a, b, and c. If not, fill in the blanks below with the word none.

$a =$ [　　　], $b =$ [　　　], and $c =$ [　　　]

b. Are there values for a, b, and c so that the expression equals $\dfrac{1}{x^7}$? If so, fill in the blanks below with possible values for a, b, and c. If not, fill in the blanks below with the word none.

$a =$ [　　　], $b =$ [　　　], and $c =$ [　　　]

129. Consider the exponential expression $\dfrac{x^a \cdot x^b}{x^c}$ where $a > 0, b > 0$, and $c < 0$.

    a. Are there values for a, b, and c so that the expression equals x^7? If so, fill in the blanks below with possible values for a, b, and c. If not, fill in the blanks below with the word none.

$a =$ [＿＿＿＿＿] , $b =$ [＿＿＿＿＿] , and $c =$ [＿＿＿＿＿]

    b. Are there values for a, b, and c so that the expression equals $\frac{1}{x^7}$? If so, fill in the blanks below with possible values for a, b, and c. If not, fill in the blanks below with the word none.

$a =$ [＿＿＿＿＿] , $b =$ [＿＿＿＿＿] , and $c =$ [＿＿＿＿＿]

5.7 Exponents and Polynomials Chapter Review

5.7.1 Adding and Subtracting Polynomials

In Section 5.1 we covered the definitions of a polynomial, a coefficient of a term, the degree of a term, the degree of a polynomial, theleading term of a polynomial, a constant term, monomials, binomials, and trinomials, and how to write a polynomial in standard form.

Example 5.7.1 Polynomial Vocabulary. Decide if the following statements are true or false.

  a. The expression $\frac{3}{5}x^2 - \frac{1}{5}x^7 + \frac{x}{2} - 4$ is a polynomial.

  b. The expression $4x^6 - 3x^{-2} - x + 1$ is a polynomial.

  c. The degree of the polynomial $\frac{3}{5}x^2 - \frac{1}{5}x^7 + \frac{x}{2} - 4$ is 10.

  d. The degree of the term $5x^2y^4$ is 6.

  e. The leading coefficient of $\frac{3}{5}x^2 - \frac{1}{5}x^7 + \frac{x}{2} - 4$ is $\frac{3}{5}$.

  f. There are 4 terms in the polynomial $\frac{3}{5}x^2 - \frac{1}{5}x^7 + \frac{x}{2} - 4$.

  g. The polynomial $\frac{3}{5}x^2 - \frac{1}{5}x^7 + \frac{x}{2} - 4$ is in standard form.

Explanation.

  a. True. The expression $\frac{3}{5}x^2 - \frac{1}{5}x^7 + \frac{x}{2} - 4$ is a polynomial.

  b. False. The expression $4x^6 - 3x^{-2} - x + 1$ is *not* a polynomial. Variables are only allowed to have whole number exponents in polynomials and the second term has a -2 exponent.

  c. False. The degree of the polynomial $\frac{3}{5}x^2 - \frac{1}{5}x^7 + \frac{x}{2} - 4$ is *not* 10. It is 7, which is the highest power of any variable in the expression.

  d. True. The degree of the term $5x^2y^4$ is 6.

  e. False. The leading coefficient of $\frac{3}{5}x^2 - \frac{1}{5}x^7 + \frac{x}{2} - 4$ is *not* $\frac{3}{5}$.The leading coefficient comes from the degree 7 term which is $-\frac{1}{5}$.

  f. True. There are 4 terms in the polynomial $\frac{3}{5}x^2 - \frac{1}{5}x^7 + \frac{x}{2} - 4$.

  g. False. The polynomial $\frac{3}{5}x^2 - \frac{1}{5}x^7 + \frac{x}{2} - 4$ is *not* in standard form. The exponents have to be written from highest to lowest, i.e. $-\frac{1}{5}x^7 + \frac{3}{5}x^2 + \frac{x}{2} - 4$.

Example 5.7.2 Adding and Subtracting Polynomials. Simplify the expression $\left(\frac{2}{9}x - 4x^2 - 5\right) + \left(6x^2 - \frac{1}{6}x - 3\right)$.

Explanation.   First identify like terms and group them either physically or mentally. Then we will look for common denominators for these like terms and combine appropriately.

$$\left(\frac{2}{9}x - 4x^2 - 5\right) + \left(6x^2 - \frac{1}{6}x - 3\right)$$
$$= \frac{2}{9}x - 4x^2 - 5 + 6x^2 - \frac{1}{6}x - 3$$

$$= \left(-4x^2 + 6x^2\right) + \left(\frac{2}{9}x - \frac{1}{6}x\right) + (-3 - 5)$$

$$= 2x^2 + \left(\frac{4}{18}x - \frac{3}{18}x\right) - 8$$

$$= 2x^2 + \frac{1}{18}x - 8$$

5.7.2 Introduction to Exponent Rules

In Section 5.2 we covered the rules of exponents for multiplication.

Rules of Exponents. Let x, and y represent real numbers, variables, or algebraic expressions, and let m and n represent positive integers . Then the following properties hold:

Product of Powers $x^m \cdot x^n = x^{m+n}$

Power to Power $(x^m)^n = x^{m \cdot n}$

Product to Power $(xy)^n = x^n \cdot y^n$

Example 5.7.3 Simplify the following expressions using the rules of exponents:
   a. $-2t^3 \cdot 4t^5$ b. $5\left(v^4\right)^2$ c. $-(3u)^2$ d. $(-3z)^2$

Explanation.

   a. $-2t^3 \cdot 4t^5 = -8t^8$ b. $5\left(v^4\right)^2 = 5v^8$ c. $-(3u)^2 = -9u^2$ d. $(-3z)^2 = 9z^2$

5.7.3 Dividing by a Monomial

In Section 5.3 we covered how you can split a fraction up into multiple terms if there is a sum or difference in the numerator. Mathematically, this happens using the rule $\frac{a+b}{c} = \frac{a}{c} + \frac{b}{c}$. This formula can be used for any number of terms in the numerator, and for both sums and differences.

Example 5.7.4 Simplify the expression $\frac{12x^5 + 2x^3 - 4x^2}{4x^2}$.
Explanation.

$$\frac{12x^5 + 2x^3 - 4x^2}{4x^2} = \frac{12x^5}{4x^2} + \frac{2x^3}{4x^2} - \frac{4x^2}{4x^2}$$

$$= 3x^3 + \frac{x}{2} - 1$$

5.7.4 Multiplying Polynomials

In Section 5.4 we covered how to multiply two polynomials together using distribution, FOIL, and generic rectangles.

Example 5.7.5 Multiplying Binomials. Expand the expression $(5x - 6)(3 + 2x)$ using the binomial multiplication method of your choice: distribution, FOIL, or generic rectangles.

Explanation. We will show work using the FOIL method.

$$(5x - 6)(3 - 2x) = (5x \cdot 3) + (5x \cdot (-2x)) + (-6 \cdot 3) + (-6 \cdot (-2x))$$
$$= 15x - 10x^2 - 18 + 12x$$
$$= -10x^2 + 27x - 18$$

Example 5.7.6 Multiplying Polynomials Larger than Binomials. Expand the expression $(3x-2)\left(4x^2 - 2x + 5\right)$ by multiplying every term in the first factor with every term in the second factor.

Explanation. $(3x - 2)\left(4x^2 - 2x + 5\right)$
$$= 3x \cdot 4x^2 + 3x \cdot (-2x) + 3x \cdot 5 + (-2) \cdot 4x^2 + (-2) \cdot (-2x) + (-2) \cdot 5$$
$$= 12x^3 - 6x^2 + 15x - 8x^2 + 4x - 10$$
$$= 12x^3 - 14x^2 + 19x - 10$$

5.7.5 Special Cases of Multiplying Polynomials

In Section 5.5 we covered how to square a binomial and how to find the product of the sum or difference of two terms.

Example 5.7.7 Squaring a Binomial. Recall that Fact 5.5.3 gives formulas that help square a binomial. Simplify the expression $(2x + 3)^2$.

Explanation. Remember that you *can* use FOIL to do these problems, but in the interest of understanding concepts at a higher level for use in later chapters, we will use the relevant formula from Fact 5.5.3. In this case, since we have a sum of two terms being squared, we will use $(a + b)^2 = a^2 + 2ab + b^2$.

First identify a and b. In this case, $a = 2x$ and $b = 3$. So, we have:

$$(a + b)^2 = (a)^2 + 2(a)(b) + (b)^2$$
$$(2x + 3)^2 = (2x)^2 + 2(2x)(3) + (3)^2$$
$$= 4x^2 + 12x + 9$$

Example 5.7.8 The Product of the Sum and Difference of Two Terms. Recall that Fact 5.5.13 gives a formula to help multiply things that look like $(a + b)(a - b)$.

Simplify the expression $(7x + 4)(7x - 4)$.

Explanation. Remember that you *can* use FOIL to do these problems, but in the interest of understanding concepts at a higher level for use in later chapters, we will use the formula from Fact 5.5.13. In this case, that means we will use $(a + b)(a - b) = a^2 - b^2$.

First identify a and b. In this case, $a = 7x$ and $b = 4$. So, we have:

$$(a + b)(a - b) = (a)^2 - (b)^2$$
$$(7x + 4)(7x - 4) = (7x)^2 - (4)^2$$
$$= 49x^2 - 16$$

Example 5.7.9 Binomials Raised to Other Powers. To raise binomials to powers higher than 2, we start by expanding the expression and multiplying all factors together from left to right.

Expand the expression $(2x - 5)^3$.

Explanation.

$$(2x - 5)^3$$
$$= (2x - 5)(2x - 5)(2x - 5)$$
$$= \left[(2x)^2 - 2(2x)(5) + 5^2\right](2x - 5)$$
$$= \left[4x^2 - 20x + 25\right](2x - 5)$$
$$= \left[4x^2\right](2x) + \left[4x^2\right](-5) + [-20x](2x) + [-20x](-5) + [25](2x) + [25](-5)$$
$$= 8x^3 - 20x^2 - 40x^2 + 100x + 50x - 125$$
$$= 8x^3 - 60x^2 + 150x - 125$$

5.7.6 More Exponent Rules

In Section 5.6 we covered the exponent rules and how to use them.

Example 5.7.10 Quotients and Exponents. Let t and q be real numbers, where $q \neq 0$ and $t \neq 0$. Find another way to write $\left(\frac{q^9}{t \cdot q^3}\right)^2$.

Explanation. We first use the Quotient Rule, then the Quotient to a Power Rule, then the Power to a Power Rule.

$$\left(\frac{q^9}{t \cdot q^3}\right)^2 = \left(\frac{q^{9-3}}{t}\right)^2$$
$$= \left(\frac{q^6}{t}\right)^2$$
$$= \frac{q^{6 \cdot 2}}{t^2}$$
$$= \frac{q^{12}}{t^2}$$

Example 5.7.11 The Zero Exponent. Recall that the Zero Exponent Rule says that any real number raised to the 0-power is 1. Using this, and the other exponent rules, find another way to write -9^0.

Explanation. Remember that in expressions like -9^0, the exponent only applies to what it is directly next to! In this case, the 0 only applies to the 9 and not the negative sign. So,

$$-9^0 = -1$$

Example 5.7.12 Negative Exponents. Write $5x^{-3}$ without any negative exponents.

Explanation. Recall that the Negative Exponent Rule says that a factor in the numerator with a negative exponent can be flipped into the denominator. So

$$5x^{-3} = \frac{5}{x^3}$$

Note that the 5 does not move to the denominator because the -3 exponent *only applies* to the x to which it is directly attached.

Example 5.7.13 Summary of Exponent Rules. Use the exponent rules in List 5.6.13 to write the expressions in a different way. Reduce and simplify when possible. Always find a way to write your final simplification without any negative exponents.

a. $\dfrac{24p^3}{20p^{12}}$
b. $\left(\dfrac{2v^5}{4g^{-2}}\right)^4$
c. $12n^7\left(m^0 \cdot n^2\right)^2$
d. $\dfrac{k^5}{k^{-4}}$

Explanation.

a.
$$\begin{aligned}
\frac{24p^3}{20p^{12}} &= \frac{24}{20} \cdot \frac{p^3}{p^{12}} \\
&= \frac{6}{5} \cdot p^{3-12} \\
&= \frac{6}{5} \cdot p^{-9} \\
&= \frac{6}{5} \cdot \frac{1}{p^9} \\
&= \frac{6}{5p^9}
\end{aligned}$$

b.
$$\begin{aligned}
\left(\frac{2v^5}{4g^{-2}}\right)^4 &= \left(\frac{v^5}{2g^{-2}}\right)^4 \\
&= \left(\frac{v^5g^2}{2}\right)^4 \\
&= \frac{v^{5\cdot4}g^{2\cdot4}}{2^4} \\
&= \frac{v^{20}g^8}{16}
\end{aligned}$$

c.
$$\begin{aligned}
12n^7\left(m^0 \cdot n^2\right)^2 &= 12n^7\left(1 \cdot n^2\right)^2 \\
&= 12n^7\left(n^2\right)^2 \\
&= 12n^7 n^{2\cdot2} \\
&= 12n^7 n^4 \\
&= 12n^{7+4} \\
&= 12n^{11}
\end{aligned}$$

d.
$$\begin{aligned}
\frac{k^5}{k^{-4}} &= k^5 \cdot k^4 \\
&= k^{5+4} \\
&= k^9
\end{aligned}$$

5.7.7 Exercises

Adding and Subtracting Polynomials Is the following expression a monomial, binomial, or trinomial?

1. $-2r^{12} + 12r^9$ is a (□ monomial □ binomial □ trinomial) of degree $\boxed{}$.

2. $-16r^7 - 8r^4 - 12r^3$ is a (□ monomial □ binomial □ trinomial) of degree $\boxed{}$

Find the degree of the following polynomial.

3. $12x^6y^9 + 11xy^4 + 5x^2 - 19$

4. $17x^6y^7 - 4xy^2 - 19x^2 + 10$

Add the polynomials.

5. $\left(-2x^2 - 6x - 7\right) + \left(-10x^2 - 8x - 4\right)$

6. $\left(3x^2 - 9x - 7\right) + \left(-5x^2 + 2x + 9\right)$

7. $\left(-5x^6 - 10x^4 + 9x^2\right) + \left(5x^6 - 9x^4 + x^2\right)$

8. $\left(2y^6 - 7y^4 - 2y^2\right) + \left(6y^6 + 3y^4 - 6y^2\right)$

Add the polynomials.

9. $\left(6x^3 - 3x^2 + 3x + \dfrac{5}{4}\right) + \left(-5x^3 + 9x^2 - 10x + \dfrac{1}{2}\right)$

10. $\left(-7x^3 - 6x^2 - 3x + \dfrac{7}{8}\right) + \left(8x^3 + 6x^2 - 9x + \dfrac{3}{2}\right)$

Subtract the polynomials.

11. $\left(4x^2 + 10x\right) - \left(10x^2 + 7x\right)$ **12.** $\left(6x^2 + 3x\right) - \left(-2x^2 + x\right)$

13. $\left(-10x^2 - 9x + 9\right) - \left(10x^2 - 7x - 3\right)$ **14.** $\left(2x^2 + 3x - 9\right) - \left(5x^2 + 7x - 1\right)$

15. $\left(7x^6 - 8x^4 + 8x^2\right) - \left(2x^6 - 4x^4 + 2x^2\right)$ **16.** $\left(-4x^6 - 5x^4 - 2x^2\right) - \left(-3x^6 - 7x^4 - 6x^2\right)$

Add or subtract the given polynomials as indicated.

17. $\left(5x^3 - 6xy + 9y^9\right) - \left(2x^3 + 4xy + 2y^9\right)$ **18.** $\left(6x^9 + 9xy - 3y^8\right) - \left(-2x^9 + 5xy - 6y^8\right)$

19. A handyman is building two pig pens sharing the same side. Assume the length of the shared side is x meters. The cost of building one pen would be $26x^2 + 4x - 49.5$ dollars, and the cost of building the other pen would be $37x^2 - 4x + 9.5$ dollars. What's the total cost of building those two pens?
A polynomial representing the total cost of building those two pens is

     dollars.

20. A handyman is building two pig pens sharing the same side. Assume the length of the shared side is x meters. The cost of building one pen would be $45.5x^2 - 4.5x + 49.5$ dollars, and the cost of building the other pen would be $40.5x^2 + 4.5x - 18.5$ dollars. What's the total cost of building those two pens?
A polynomial representing the total cost of building those two pens is

     dollars.

Introduction to Exponent Rules Use the properties of exponents to simplify the expression.

21. $8 \cdot 8^6$ **22.** $9 \cdot 9^3$ **23.** $t^2 \cdot t^{17}$ **24.** $y^4 \cdot y^{10}$

25. $t^6 \cdot t^4 \cdot t^{17}$ **26.** $r^8 \cdot r^{16} \cdot r^6$ **27.** $\left(10^5\right)^7$ **28.** $\left(12^2\right)^2$

29. $\left(y^9\right)^9$ **30.** $\left(t^{10}\right)^6$ **31.** $(2y)^4$ **32.** $(4r)^2$

33. $\left(4r^4\right) \cdot \left(9r^8\right)$ **34.** $\left(-6t^6\right) \cdot \left(-8t^{20}\right)$ **35.** $\left(-2x^5\right)^3$ **36.** $\left(-7t^7\right)^2$

Use the properties of exponents to simplify the expression.

37. $\left(\dfrac{t^{12}}{9}\right) \cdot \left(\dfrac{t^{19}}{3}\right)$ **38.** $\left(-\dfrac{x^{14}}{3}\right) \cdot \left(-\dfrac{x^{13}}{8}\right)$

Dividing by a Monomial Simplify the following expression

39. $\dfrac{-63t^{14} - 108t^{11}}{9}$ **40.** $\dfrac{55t^4 + 35t^3}{5}$ **41.** $\dfrac{3x^{21} - 3x^{12} + 18x^7}{3x^3}$

42. $\dfrac{64x^{19} - 88x^{10} + 64x^7}{-8x^3}$ **43.** $\dfrac{90x^{10} + 108x^8}{9x}$ **44.** $\dfrac{42y^{16} + 35y^7}{7y}$

Multiplying Polynomials Multiply the polynomials.

45. $-x(x - 3)$ **46.** $x(x + 9)$ **47.** $6r^2\left(9r^2 + 8r + 6\right)$

48. $-3t^2 \left(7t^2 - 4t - 3\right)$ **49.** $(8t + 9)(t + 3)$ **50.** $(5x + 3)(x + 1)$

51. $(x + 1)(x - 4)$ **52.** $(x + 8)(x - 10)$ **53.** $(3y - 6)(2y - 5)$

54. $(2y - 5)(4y - 9)$ **55.** $3(x + 2)(x + 3)$ **56.** $-3(x + 2)(x + 3)$

57. $x(x - 2)(x + 2)$ **58.** $-x(x + 2)(x + 3)$

Multiply the polynomials.

59. $(a - 2b)(a^2 + 10ab + 6b^2)$ **60.** $(a + 3b)(a^2 - 5ab - 6b^2)$

61. A rectangle's length is 3 feet shorter than 4 times its width. If we use w to represent the rectangle's width, use a polynomial to represent the rectangle's area in expanded form.

area = [＿＿＿＿＿＿＿＿＿]
square feet

62. A rectangle's length is 4 feet shorter than twice its width. If we use w to represent the rectangle's width, use a polynomial to represent the rectangle's area in expanded form.

area = [＿＿＿＿＿＿＿＿＿]
square feet

Special Cases of Multiplying Polynomials Expand the square of a *binomial*.

63. $(10y + 7)^2$ **64.** $(6r + 1)^2$ **65.** $(r - 8)^2$

66. $(t - 2)^2$ **67.** $(9a - 6b)^2$ **68.** $(10a + 3b)^2$

Multiply the polynomials.

69. $(x + 9)(x - 9)$ **70.** $(x - 1)(x + 1)$ **71.** $(2 - 10y)(2 + 10y)$

72. $(8 + 5y)(8 - 5y)$ **73.** $\left(4r^8 + 8\right)\left(4r^8 - 8\right)$ **74.** $\left(2r^5 - 7\right)\left(2r^5 + 7\right)$

Simplify the given expression into an expanded polynomial.

75. $(t + 5)^3$ **76.** $(t + 3)^3$

More Exponent Rules Use the properties of exponents to simplify the expression.

77. $\left(3r^{12}\right)^2$ **78.** $\left(5x^3\right)^4$ **79.** $\left(5t^6\right) \cdot \left(4t^8\right)$

80. $\left(8t^8\right) \cdot \left(-3t^{20}\right)$ **81.** $\left(-\dfrac{t^{10}}{3}\right) \cdot \left(\dfrac{t^{14}}{4}\right)$ **82.** $\left(-\dfrac{x^{12}}{6}\right) \cdot \left(-\dfrac{x^7}{3}\right)$

83. $(-18)^0$ **84.** $(-13)^0$ **85.** -45^0

86. -50^0 **87.** $\left(\dfrac{-3}{8x^8}\right)^2$ **88.** $\left(\dfrac{-3}{4x^2}\right)^2$

89. $\dfrac{6x^{11}}{36x^2}$ **90.** $\dfrac{8x^{19}}{32x^{17}}$ **91.** $\left(\dfrac{x^3}{2y^4z^7}\right)^2$

92. $\left(\dfrac{x^9}{2y^8z^5}\right)^2$

Rewrite the expression simplified and using only positive exponents.

93. $\left(\dfrac{1}{8}\right)^{-2}$

94. $\left(\dfrac{1}{9}\right)^{-2}$

95. $17x^{-12}$

96. $11x^{-3}$

97. $\dfrac{6}{x^{-5}}$

98. $\dfrac{16}{x^{-6}}$

99. $\dfrac{15x^{-10}}{x^{-13}}$

100. $\dfrac{6x^{-12}}{x^{-3}}$

101. $\dfrac{r^{-5}}{\left(r^9\right)^9}$

102. $\dfrac{t^{-5}}{\left(t^6\right)^7}$

103. $t^{-20} \cdot t^7$

104. $t^{-14} \cdot t^{10}$

105. $\left(8x^{-8}\right) \cdot \left(-7x^2\right)$

106. $\left(6x^{-20}\right) \cdot \left(-3x^{12}\right)$

107. $\left(-5y^{-13}\right)^{-3}$

108. $\left(-2y^{-7}\right)^{-2}$

109. $\left(3r^{14}\right)^4 \cdot r^{-37}$

110. $\left(4r^{10}\right)^2 \cdot r^{-8}$

111. $\left(t^{11}x^4\right)^{-5}$

112. $\left(t^{13}x^{13}\right)^{-2}$

113. $\left(t^{-9}r^{10}\right)^{-5}$

114. $\left(x^{-6}t^{12}\right)^{-2}$

115. $\left(\dfrac{x^{13}}{4}\right)^{-2}$

116. $\left(\dfrac{y^8}{4}\right)^{-4}$

Chapter 6

Radical Expressions and Equations

6.1 Square and nth Root Properties

In this section, we learn what expressions like $\sqrt{25}$ and $\sqrt[3]{27}$ mean, and some of the properties they have that allow for simplification.

6.1.1 Square Roots

Consider the non-negative number 25. You can ask the question "what number multiplies by itself to make 25?" We use the symbol $\sqrt{25}$ to represent the answer to this question, whether or not you know the "answer".

A geometric visualization of the same idea is to imagine a square with 25 units of area inside it. What would a side length have to be? We use $\sqrt{25}$ to represent that side length.

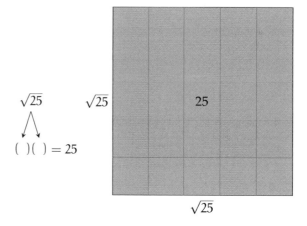

Definition 6.1.2 Square Root. Given a non-negative number x, if $r \cdot r = x$ for some positive number r, then r is called the **square root** of x, and we can write $\sqrt{x}$ instead of r. The $\sqrt{}$ symbol is called the **radical** or the **root**. We call expressions with the $\sqrt{}$ symbol **radical expressions**. The number inside the radical is called the **radicand**. ◇

For example, if you are confronted with the expression $\sqrt{16}$, you should think about the equation $r \cdot r = 16$ (or if you prefer, $r^2 = 16$) and ask yourself if you know a positive value for r that solves that equation. Of course, 4 is a non-negative solution. So we an say $\sqrt{16} = 4$.

65

To demonstrate more of the vocabulary, both $\sqrt{2}$ and $3\sqrt{2}$ are radical expressions. In both expressions, the number 2 is the radicand.

The word "radical" means something like "on the fringes" when used in politics, sports, and other places. It actually has that same meaning in math, when you consider a square with area A as in Figure 6.1.3.

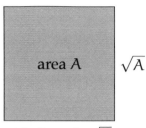

side length $\sqrt{A}$

Figure 6.1.3: "Radical" means "off to the side."

The one-digit multiplication times table has special numbers along the diagonal. They are known as **perfect squares**. And for working with square roots, it will be helpful if you can memorize these first few perfect square numbers. For example, the times table tells us that $7 \cdot 7 = 49$. Just knowing that fact from memory lets us know that $\sqrt{49} = 7$. It's advisable to memorize the following:

$$\sqrt{0} = 0 \qquad \sqrt{1} = 1 \qquad \sqrt{4} = 2$$
$$\sqrt{9} = 3 \qquad \sqrt{16} = 4 \qquad \sqrt{25} = 5$$
$$\sqrt{36} = 6 \qquad \sqrt{49} = 7 \qquad \sqrt{64} = 8$$
$$\sqrt{81} = 9 \qquad \sqrt{100} = 10 \qquad \sqrt{121} = 11$$
$$\sqrt{144} = 12 \qquad \sqrt{225} = 15 \qquad \sqrt{256} = 16$$

×	1	2	3	4	5	6	7	8	9
1	1	2	3	4	5	6	7	8	9
2	2	4	6	8	10	12	14	16	18
3	3	6	9	12	15	18	21	24	27
4	4	8	12	16	20	24	28	32	36
5	5	10	15	20	25	30	35	40	45
6	6	12	18	24	30	36	42	48	54
7	7	14	21	28	35	42	49	56	63
8	8	16	24	32	40	48	56	64	72
9	9	18	27	36	45	54	63	72	81

Figure 6.1.4: Multiplication table with squares

6.1.2 Square Root Decimal Values

Most square roots have decimal places that go on forever. Take $\sqrt{5}$ as an example. The number 5 is between two perfect squares, 4 and 9. Therefore, as demonstrated in Figure 6.1.5, $\sqrt{4} < \sqrt{5} < \sqrt{9}$. In other words,

$$2 < \sqrt{5} < 3$$

So $\sqrt{5}$ has a decimal value somewhere between 2 and 3.

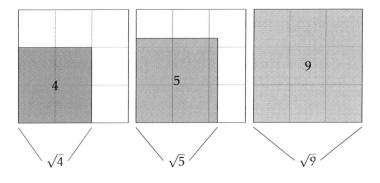

Figure 6.1.5: $2 < \sqrt{5} < 3$

With a calculator, we can see:

$$\sqrt{5} \approx 2.236$$

Actually the decimal will not terminate, and that is why we used the $\approx$ symbol instead of an equals sign. To get 2.236 we rounded down slightly from the true value of $\sqrt{5}$. With a calculator, we can check that $2.236^2 = 4.999696$, a little shy of 5.

When the radicand is a perfect square, its square root is a rational number. If the radicand is not a perfect square, the square root is irrational. (It has a decimal that goes on forever without any pattern that is easy to see.) We want to be able to estimate square roots without using a calculator.

Example 6.1.6 To estimate $\sqrt{10}$ without a calculator, we can find the nearest perfect squares that are whole numbers on either side of 10. Recall that the perfect squares are $1, 4, 9, 16, 25, 36, 49, 64, \ldots$ The perfect square that is just below 10 is 9 and the perfect square just above 10 is 16.

This tells us that $\sqrt{10}$ is between $\sqrt{9}$ and $\sqrt{16}$, or between 3 and 4. We can also say that $\sqrt{10}$ is much closer to 3 than 4 because 10 is closer to 9, so we think 3.1 or 3.2 would be a good estimate.

To check our estimates (3.1 or 3.2) we can square them and see if the result is close to 10. We find $3.1^2 = 9.61$ and $3.2^2 = 10.24$, so our estimates are pretty good.

Checkpoint 6.1.7 Estimate $\sqrt{19}$ without a calculator.

Explanation. The radicand, 19, is between 16 and 25, so $\sqrt{19}$ is between $\sqrt{16}$ and $\sqrt{25}$, or between 4 and 5. We notice that 19 is in the middle between 16 and 25 but closer to 16. We estimate $\sqrt{19}$ to be about 4.4.

We can check our estimate by calculating:

$$4.4^2 = 19.36$$

So 4.4^2 is close to 19, and 4.4 is close to $\sqrt{19}$.

6.1.3 Cube Root and Higher Order Roots

The concept behind a square root easily extends to a **cube root**. What if we have a number in mind, like 64, and we would like to know what number can be multiplied with itself *three* times to make 64? A geometric visualization of the same idea is to imagine a cube with 64 units of area inside it. What would an edge length have to be? We use $\sqrt[3]{64}$ to represent that edge length.

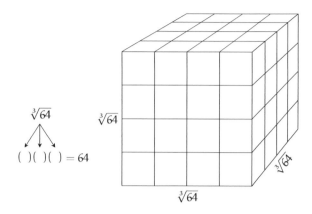

Definition 6.1.8 **nth Root.** Given a number x, if $\overbrace{r \cdot r \cdots \cdots r}^{\text{n times}} = x$ for some number r, then r is called an **nth root** of x. (Or if you prefer, when $r^n = x$.)

- When n is odd, there is always exactly one real number nth root for any x, and we can write $\sqrt[n]{x}$ to mean that one nth root.

- When n is even and x is positive, there are two real number nth roots, one of which is positive and the other of which is negative. We can write $\sqrt[n]{x}$ to mean the positive nth root.

- When n is even and x is negative, there aren't any real number nth roots, and we say that $\sqrt[n]{x}$ is "undefined" or "does not exist".

The $\sqrt[n]{}$ symbol is called the **nth radical** or the **nth root**. We call expressions with the $\sqrt[n]{}$ symbol **radical expressions**. The number inside the radical is called the **radicand**. The **index** of a radical is the number n in $\sqrt[n]{}$. ◊

As noted earlier, when we have $\sqrt[3]{}$, we can say "cube root" instead of "3rd root". Also, when we have $\sqrt[2]{}$, we can say "square root" instead of "2nd root" and we can simply write $\sqrt{x}$ instead.

For some examples of nth roots:

- $\sqrt[3]{8} = 2$, because $\overbrace{2 \cdot 2 \cdot 2}^{\text{3 instances}} = 8$.

- $\sqrt[4]{81} = 3$, because $\overbrace{3 \cdot 3 \cdot 3 \cdot 3}^{\text{4 instances}} = 81$.

- $\sqrt[5]{-32} = -2$, because $\overbrace{(-2) \cdot (-2) \cdot (-2) \cdot (-2) \cdot (-2)}^{\text{5 instances}} = -32$.

As with square roots, in general an nth root's decimal value is a decimal that goes on forever. For example, $\sqrt[3]{20} \approx 2.714\ldots$. For practical applications, we may want to use a calculator to find a decimal approximation to an nth root. Some calculators will do this for you directly, and some will not.

- Maybe your calculator has a button that looks like $\sqrt[x]{y}$. Then you should be able to type something like 3 $\sqrt[x]{y}$ 20 to get $\sqrt[3]{20} \approx 2.714\ldots$.

- Maybe your calculator has a button that looks like $\sqrt[n]{}$. Then you should be able to type something like 3 $\sqrt[n]{}$ 20 to get $\sqrt[3]{20} \approx 2.714\ldots$.

- Maybe your calculator allows you to type letters, parentheses, and commas, and you can type `root(3,20)` to get $\sqrt[3]{20} \approx 2.714\ldots$.

- Maybe your calculator allows you to type letters, parentheses, and commas, but the syntax for an nth root is reversed from the last example, and you can type `root(20,3)` to get $\sqrt[3]{20} \approx 2.714\ldots$.

- If your calculator has none of the above options, then you should be able to type `20^(1/3)` as a way to get $\sqrt[3]{20} \approx 2.714\ldots$. This is technically using mathematics we will learn in Section 6.3.

Try using your own calculator to calculate $\sqrt[3]{20}$ so that you can become familiar with whatever method it uses.

Example 6.1.9
A pyramid has a square base, and its height is equal to one side length of the square at its base. In this situation, the volume V of the pyramid, in in^3, is given by $V = \frac{1}{3}s^3$, where s is the pyramid's base side length in in. Archimedes droppped the pyramid in a bathtub, and judging by how high the water level rose, the volume of the pyramid is $243\,\text{in}^3$ (a little more than 1 gal). How tall is the pyramid?

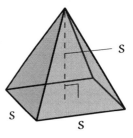

The equation tells us that:

$$243 = \frac{1}{3}s^3$$

We can multiply on both sides by 3 and:

$$729 = s^3$$

This means that s is $\sqrt[3]{729}$. A calculator tells us that this is 9. So the pyramid's height is 9 inches.

6.1.4 Roots of Negative Numbers

Can we find the square root of a negative number, such as $\sqrt{-64}$? How about its cube root, $\sqrt[3]{-64}$?

As noted in Defintion 6.1.8, when the index of an nth root is odd, there will always be a real number nth root even when the radicand is negative. For example, $\sqrt[3]{-64}$ is -4, because $(-4)(-4)(-4) = -64$.

When the index of an nth root is even, it is a problem to have a negative radicand. For example, to find $\sqrt{-64}$, you would need to find a value r so that $r \cdot r = -64$. But whether r is positive or negative, multiplying it by itself will give a positive result. It could never be -64. So there is no way to have a real number square root of a negative number. And the same thing is true for *any* even index nth root with a negative radicand, such as $\sqrt[4]{-64}$. An even-indexed root of a negative number is not a real number.

If you are confronted with an expression like $\sqrt{-25}$ or $\sqrt[4]{-16}$ (any square root or even-indexed root of a negative number), you can state that the expression "is not real" or that it is "not defined" (as a real number). Don't get carried away though. Expressions like $\sqrt[3]{-27}$ and $\sqrt[5]{-1}$ *are* defined, because the index is odd.

Imaginary Numbers. Mathematicians imagined a new type of number, neither positive nor negative, that would multiply by itself to make a negative result. But that is beyond the scope of this section.

6.1.5 Radical Rules and Exponent Rules

In an earlier chapter, we learned some algebra rules for exponents. A summary of these rules is in List 5.6.13. There are a couple of very similar rules for radicals, presented here without motivation. (These rules are easier to explain once we study Section 6.3.)

List 6.1.10: Rules of Radicals for Multiplication and Division

> If a and b are positive real numbers, and m is a positive integer , then we have the following rules:
>
> **Root of a Product Rule** $\sqrt[m]{a \cdot b} = \sqrt[m]{a} \cdot \sqrt[m]{b}$
>
> **Root of a Quotient Rule** $\sqrt[m]{\dfrac{a}{b}} = \dfrac{\sqrt[m]{a}}{\sqrt[m]{b}}$ as long as $b \neq 0$

Knowing these algebra rules helps to make complicated radical expressions look simpler.

Example 6.1.11 Simplify $\sqrt{18}$. Anything we can do to make the radicand a smaller simpler number is helpful. Note that $18 = 9 \cdot 2$, so we can write

$$
\begin{aligned}
\sqrt{18} &= \sqrt{9 \cdot 2} \\
&= \sqrt{9} \cdot \sqrt{2} \qquad \text{according to the Root of a Product Rule} \\
&= 3\sqrt{2}
\end{aligned}
$$

This expression $3\sqrt{2}$ is considered "simpler" than $\sqrt{18}$ because the radicand is so much smaller.

Checkpoint 6.1.12 Simplify $\sqrt{72}$.

Explanation.   As with the previous example, it will help if 72 can be written as a product of a perfect square. In this case, 4 divides 72, and $72 = 4 \cdot 18$. So

$$
\begin{aligned}
\sqrt{72} &= \sqrt{4 \cdot 18} \\
&= \sqrt{4} \cdot \sqrt{18} \\
&= 2\sqrt{18}
\end{aligned}
$$

But we aren't done. Can 18 can be written as a product of a perfect square? Yes, because $18 = 9 \cdot 2$. So

$$
\begin{aligned}
\sqrt{72} &= 2\sqrt{18} \\
&= 2\sqrt{9 \cdot 2} \\
&= 2\sqrt{9} \cdot \sqrt{2} \\
&= 2 \cdot 3\sqrt{2} \\
&= 6\sqrt{2}
\end{aligned}
$$

This is as simple as we can make this expression.

Example 6.1.13 Simplify $\sqrt[3]{80}$. Anything we can do to make the radicand a smaller simpler number is helpful. With lessons learned from the previous examples, maybe there is a way to rewrite 80 as the product of two numbers in a helpful way. Since we have a *cube* root, writing 80 as a product of a perfect *cube* would be helpful. We can write $80 = 8 \cdot 10$, where 8 is a perfect cube.

$$
\sqrt[3]{80} = \sqrt[3]{8 \cdot 10}
$$

$$= \sqrt[3]{8} \cdot \sqrt[3]{10} \qquad \text{according to the Root of a Product Rule}$$
$$= 2\sqrt[3]{10}$$

This expression $2\sqrt[3]{10}$ is considered "simpler" than $\sqrt[3]{80}$ because the radicand is so much smaller.

Checkpoint 6.1.14 Simplify $\sqrt[4]{48}$.

Explanation. As with the previous example, it will help if 48 can be written as a product of a 4th power. In this case, 16 divides 48, and $48 = 16 \cdot 3$. So

$$\sqrt[4]{48} = \sqrt[4]{16 \cdot 3}$$
$$= \sqrt[4]{16}\sqrt[4]{3}$$
$$= 2\sqrt[4]{3}$$

This is as simple as we can make this expression.

When a radical is applied to a fraction, the Root of a Quotient Rule is useful.

Example 6.1.15 Simplify $\sqrt{\frac{8}{25}}$. According to the Root of a Quotient Rule,

$$\sqrt{\frac{8}{25}} = \frac{\sqrt{8}}{\sqrt{25}}$$
$$= \frac{\sqrt{8}}{5}$$
$$= \frac{\sqrt{4 \cdot 2}}{5}$$
$$= \frac{\sqrt{4} \cdot \sqrt{2}}{5}$$
$$= \frac{2\sqrt{2}}{5}$$

This is as simple as we can make this expression, unless you prefer to write it as $\frac{2}{5}\sqrt{2}$.

Checkpoint 6.1.16

a. $\sqrt{\frac{1}{36}}$
b. $\sqrt[3]{\frac{8}{27}}$
c. $\sqrt[3]{\frac{81}{125}}$

Explanation.

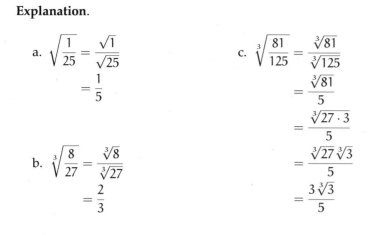

a. $\sqrt{\dfrac{1}{25}} = \dfrac{\sqrt{1}}{\sqrt{25}}$

$= \dfrac{1}{5}$

b. $\sqrt[3]{\dfrac{8}{27}} = \dfrac{\sqrt[3]{8}}{\sqrt[3]{27}}$

$= \dfrac{2}{3}$

c. $\sqrt[3]{\dfrac{81}{125}} = \dfrac{\sqrt[3]{81}}{\sqrt[3]{125}}$

$= \dfrac{\sqrt[3]{81}}{5}$

$= \dfrac{\sqrt[3]{27 \cdot 3}}{5}$

$= \dfrac{\sqrt[3]{27}\,\sqrt[3]{3}}{5}$

$= \dfrac{3\,\sqrt[3]{3}}{5}$

6.1.6 Multiplying Square Root Expressions

We can use the Root of a Product Rule and the Root of a Quotient Rule to multiply and divide square root expressions. We want to simplify each radical first to keep the radicands as small as possible.

Example 6.1.17 Multiply $\sqrt{8} \cdot \sqrt{54}$.

Explanation.   We will simplify each radical first, and then multiply them together. We do not want to multiply $8 \cdot 54$ because we will end up with a larger number that is harder to factor.

$$
\begin{aligned}
\sqrt{8} \cdot \sqrt{54} &= \sqrt{4 \cdot 2} \cdot \sqrt{9 \cdot 6} \\
&= \sqrt{4} \cdot \sqrt{2} \cdot \sqrt{9} \cdot \sqrt{6} \\
&= 2\sqrt{2} \cdot 3\sqrt{6} \\
&= 6\sqrt{2} \cdot \sqrt{6} \\
&= 6\sqrt{12} \\
&= 6\sqrt{4 \cdot 3} \\
&= 6\sqrt{4} \cdot \sqrt{3} \\
&= 6 \cdot 2\sqrt{3} \\
&= 12\sqrt{3}
\end{aligned}
$$

It is worth noting that this is considered as simple as we canmake it, because the radicand of 3 is so small.

Checkpoint 6.1.18 Multiply $2\sqrt{7} \cdot 3\sqrt{21}$.

Explanation.   First multiply the non-radical factors together and the radical factors together. Then look for further simplifications.

$$\begin{aligned}
2\sqrt{7} \cdot 3\sqrt{21} &= 2 \cdot 3 \cdot \sqrt{7} \cdot \sqrt{21} \\
&= 6 \cdot \sqrt{7} \cdot \sqrt{7 \cdot 3} \\
&= 6\sqrt{49 \cdot 3} \\
&= 6 \cdot 7 \cdot \sqrt{3} \\
&= 42\sqrt{3}
\end{aligned}$$

Example 6.1.19 Multiply $\sqrt{\frac{6}{5}} \cdot \sqrt{\frac{3}{5}}$.

Explanation. First multiply the fractions together under the radical. Then look for further simplifications.

$$\begin{aligned}
\sqrt{\frac{6}{5}} \cdot \sqrt{\frac{3}{5}} &= \sqrt{\frac{6}{5} \cdot \frac{3}{5}} \\
&= \sqrt{\frac{18}{25}} \\
&= \frac{\sqrt{18}}{\sqrt{25}} \\
&= \frac{\sqrt{9 \cdot 2}}{5} \\
&= \frac{3\sqrt{2}}{5}
\end{aligned}$$

6.1.7 Adding and Subtracting Square Root Expressions

We learned the Root of a Product Rule previously and applied this to multiplication of square roots, but we cannot apply this property to the operations of addition or subtraction. Here are two examples to demonstrate why not.

$$\sqrt{9} + \sqrt{16} \stackrel{?}{=} \sqrt{9 + 16} \qquad\qquad \sqrt{169} - \sqrt{25} \stackrel{?}{=} \sqrt{169 - 25}$$
$$3 + 4 \stackrel{?}{=} \sqrt{25} \qquad\qquad 13 - 5 \stackrel{?}{=} \sqrt{144}$$
$$7 \stackrel{\text{no}}{=} 5 \qquad\qquad 8 \stackrel{\text{no}}{=} 12$$

We do not get the same result if we combine radical sums and differences in the same way we can combine radical products and quotiens.

To add and subtract radical expressions, we need to recognize that we can only add and subtract like terms. In this case, we will call them **like radicals**. Adding like radicals will work just like adding like terms. In the same way that $x + 3x = 4x$ combines two like terms, $\sqrt{5} + 3\sqrt{5} = 4\sqrt{5}$ combines two like radicals.

Example 6.1.20 Simplify $\sqrt{2} + \sqrt{8}$.

Explanation. First, simplify each radical. Simplifying is the best way to understand whether or not we even have two like radicals that could be combined.

$$\begin{aligned}
\sqrt{2} + \sqrt{8} &= \sqrt{2} + \sqrt{4 \cdot 2} \\
&= \sqrt{2} + 2\sqrt{2}
\end{aligned}$$

$$= 3\sqrt{2}$$

Checkpoint 6.1.21 Simplify $2\sqrt{3} - 3\sqrt{48}$.

Explanation.   First we will simplify the radical term where 48 is the radicand, and we may see that we then have like radicals.

$$\begin{aligned}
2\sqrt{3} - 3\sqrt{48} &= 2\sqrt{3} - 3\sqrt{16 \cdot 3} \\
&= 2\sqrt{3} - 3 \cdot 4\sqrt{3} \\
&= 2\sqrt{3} - 12\sqrt{3} \\
&= -10\sqrt{3}
\end{aligned}$$

Example 6.1.22 Simplify $\sqrt{2} + \sqrt{27}$.

Explanation.

$$\begin{aligned}
\sqrt{2} + \sqrt{27} &= \sqrt{2} + \sqrt{9 \cdot 3} \\
&= \sqrt{2} + 3\sqrt{3}
\end{aligned}$$

We cannot simplify the expression further because $\sqrt{2}$ and $\sqrt{3}$ are not like radicals.

Example 6.1.23 Simplify $\sqrt{6} - \sqrt{18} \cdot \sqrt{12}$.

Explanation.   In this example, we should multiply the latter two square roots first (after simplifying them) and then see if we have like radicals.

$$\begin{aligned}
\sqrt{6} - \sqrt{18} \cdot \sqrt{12} &= \sqrt{6} - \sqrt{9 \cdot 2} \cdot \sqrt{4 \cdot 3} \\
&= \sqrt{6} - 3\sqrt{2} \cdot 2\sqrt{3} \\
&= \sqrt{6} - 6\sqrt{2} \cdot \sqrt{3} \\
&= \sqrt{6} - 6\sqrt{6} \\
&= -5\sqrt{6}
\end{aligned}$$

6.1.8 Distributing with Square Roots

In Section 5.4, we learned how to multiply polynomials like $2(x + 3)$ and $(x + 2)(x + 3)$. All the methods we learned there apply when we multiply square root expressions. We will look at a few examples done with different methods.

Example 6.1.24 Multiply $\sqrt{5}\left(\sqrt{3} - \sqrt{2}\right)$.

Explanation.   We will use the distributive property to do this problem:

$$\begin{aligned}
\sqrt{5}\left(\sqrt{3} - \sqrt{2}\right) &= \sqrt{5} \cdot \sqrt{3} - \sqrt{5} \cdot \sqrt{2} \\
&= \sqrt{15} - \sqrt{10}
\end{aligned}$$

Example 6.1.25 Multiply $\left(\sqrt{6} + \sqrt{12}\right)\left(\sqrt{3} - \sqrt{2}\right)$.

Explanation.   We will use the FOIL Method to expand the product. This time, there is an opportunity to simplify some of the radicals after multiplying.

$$\left(\sqrt{6}+\sqrt{12}\right)\left(\sqrt{3}-\sqrt{2}\right) = \sqrt{6}\cdot\sqrt{3}-\sqrt{6}\cdot\sqrt{2}+\sqrt{12}\cdot\sqrt{3}-\sqrt{12}\cdot\sqrt{2}$$
$$= \sqrt{18}-\sqrt{12}+\sqrt{36}-\sqrt{24}$$
$$= 3\sqrt{2}-2\sqrt{3}+6-2\sqrt{6}$$

Example 6.1.26 Expand $\left(\sqrt{3}-\sqrt{2}\right)^2$.

Explanation. We will use the FOIL method to expand this expression:

$$\left(\sqrt{3}-\sqrt{2}\right)^2 = \left(\sqrt{3}-\sqrt{2}\right)\left(\sqrt{3}-\sqrt{2}\right)$$
$$= \left(\sqrt{3}\right)^2 - \sqrt{3}\cdot\sqrt{2}-\sqrt{2}\cdot\sqrt{3}+\left(\sqrt{2}\right)^2$$
$$= 3-\sqrt{6}-\sqrt{6}+2$$
$$= 5-2\sqrt{6}$$

Example 6.1.27 Multiply $\left(\sqrt{5}-\sqrt{7}\right)\left(\sqrt{5}+\sqrt{7}\right)$.

Explanation. We can once again use the FOIL method to expand this expression. (But it is worth noting that this expression is in the special form $(a-b)(a+b)$ and will simplify to a^2-b^2.)

$$\left(\sqrt{5}-\sqrt{7}\right)\left(\sqrt{5}+\sqrt{7}\right) = \left(\sqrt{5}\right)^2 + \sqrt{5}\cdot\sqrt{7}-\sqrt{7}\cdot\sqrt{5}-\left(\sqrt{7}\right)^2$$
$$= 5+\sqrt{35}-\sqrt{35}-7$$
$$= -2$$

6.1.9 Reading Questions

1. Is there a difference between $\sqrt[3]{2}$ and $3\sqrt{2}$? Explain.

2. Choose one of the radical rules from List 6.1.10. Then find its counterpart in the exponent rules from List 5.6.13.

3. Describe a way you can visualize $\sqrt{81}$ in a geometric shape. Describe a way you can visualize $\sqrt[3]{27}$ in a geometric shape.

6.1.10 Exercises

Review and Warmup Which of the following are square numbers? There may be more than one correct answer.

1.
   ☐ 117   ☐ 54   ☐ 100   ☐ 64   ☐ 49   ☐ 3

2.
   ☐ 1   ☐ 125   ☐ 16   ☐ 115   ☐ 121   ☐ 138

Evaluate the following.

3. a. $\sqrt{144}$
    b. $\sqrt{121}$
    c. $\sqrt{36}$

4. a. $\sqrt{4}$
    b. $\sqrt{64}$
    c. $\sqrt{144}$

5. a. $\sqrt{\dfrac{9}{25}}$
    b. $\sqrt{-\dfrac{36}{49}}$

6. a. $\sqrt{\dfrac{16}{121}}$
    b. $\sqrt{-\dfrac{81}{100}}$

7. Do not use a calculator.
    a. $\sqrt{36}$
    b. $\sqrt{0.36}$
    c. $\sqrt{3600}$

8. Do not use a calculator.
    a. $\sqrt{64}$
    b. $\sqrt{0.64}$
    c. $\sqrt{6400}$

9. Do not use a calculator.
    a. $\sqrt{64}$
    b. $\sqrt{6400}$
    c. $\sqrt{640000}$

10. Do not use a calculator.
    a. $\sqrt{100}$
    b. $\sqrt{10000}$
    c. $\sqrt{1000000}$

11. Do not use a calculator.
    a. $\sqrt{121}$
    b. $\sqrt{1.21}$
    c. $\sqrt{0.0121}$

12. Do not use a calculator.
    a. $\sqrt{144}$
    b. $\sqrt{1.44}$
    c. $\sqrt{0.0144}$

13. Without using a calculator, estimate the value of $\sqrt{18}$:
    ($\square$ 3.76 $\square$ 3.24 $\square$ 4.76 $\square$ 4.24)

14. Without using a calculator, estimate the value of $\sqrt{24}$:
    ($\square$ 4.10 $\square$ 4.90 $\square$ 5.10 $\square$ 5.90)

Simplify Radical Expressions Evaluate the following.

15. $\sqrt{\dfrac{16}{49}}$

16. $\sqrt{\dfrac{25}{36}}$

17. $-\sqrt{64}$

18. $-\sqrt{81}$

19. $\sqrt{-100}$

20. $\sqrt{-121}$

21. $\sqrt{-\dfrac{121}{144}}$

22. $\sqrt{-\dfrac{4}{25}}$

23. $-\sqrt{\dfrac{9}{121}}$

24. $-\sqrt{\dfrac{16}{81}}$

25. a. $\sqrt{100}-\sqrt{36}$
    b. $\sqrt{100-36}$

26. a. $\sqrt{100}-\sqrt{64}$
    b. $\sqrt{100-64}$

Simplify the radical expression or state that it is not a real number.

27. $\dfrac{\sqrt{125}}{\sqrt{5}}$

28. $\dfrac{\sqrt{75}}{\sqrt{3}}$

29. $\dfrac{\sqrt{6}}{\sqrt{216}}$

30. $\dfrac{\sqrt{4}}{\sqrt{144}}$

31. $\sqrt{8}$

32. $\sqrt{147}$

33. $\sqrt{980}$

34. $\sqrt{216}$

35. $\sqrt{231}$ **36.** $\sqrt{70}$

Multiplying Square Root Expressions Simplify the expression.

37. $8\sqrt{3} \cdot 3\sqrt{11}$ **38.** $8\sqrt{7} \cdot 8\sqrt{2}$ **39.** $9\sqrt{7} \cdot 5\sqrt{25}$

40. $2\sqrt{13} \cdot 2\sqrt{121}$ **41.** $2\sqrt{5} \cdot 5\sqrt{40}$ **42.** $3\sqrt{15} \cdot 3\sqrt{30}$

43. $\sqrt{2} \cdot 3\sqrt{32}$ **44.** $\sqrt{4} \cdot 4\sqrt{16}$

45. $\sqrt{\dfrac{2}{7}} \cdot \sqrt{\dfrac{1}{7}}$

46. $\sqrt{\dfrac{1}{8}} \cdot \sqrt{\dfrac{3}{8}}$ **47.** $\sqrt{\dfrac{30}{19}} \cdot \sqrt{\dfrac{6}{19}}$ **48.** $\sqrt{\dfrac{18}{13}} \cdot \sqrt{\dfrac{6}{13}}$

Adding and Subtracting Square Root Expressions Simplify the expression.

49. $10\sqrt{15} - 11\sqrt{15}$ **50.** $12\sqrt{11} - 13\sqrt{11}$

51. $13\sqrt{11} - 13\sqrt{11} + 15\sqrt{11}$ **52.** $14\sqrt{5} - 20\sqrt{5} + 11\sqrt{5}$

53. $\sqrt{80} + \sqrt{45}$ **54.** $\sqrt{45} + \sqrt{125}$

55. $\sqrt{343} - \sqrt{63}$ **56.** $\sqrt{275} - \sqrt{539}$

57. $\sqrt{28} + \sqrt{175} + \sqrt{8} + \sqrt{18}$ **58.** $\sqrt{32} + \sqrt{8} + \sqrt{125} + \sqrt{20}$

59. $\sqrt{98} - \sqrt{8} - \sqrt{12} - \sqrt{27}$ **60.** $\sqrt{75} - \sqrt{27} - \sqrt{8} - \sqrt{50}$

Distributing with Square Roots Expand and simplify the expression.

61. $\sqrt{2}\left(\sqrt{19} + \sqrt{17}\right)$ **62.** $\sqrt{7}\left(\sqrt{11} + \sqrt{5}\right)$

63. $\left(3 + \sqrt{11}\right)\left(7 + \sqrt{11}\right)$ **64.** $\left(9 + \sqrt{11}\right)\left(10 + \sqrt{11}\right)$

65. $\left(6 - \sqrt{7}\right)\left(7 - 3\sqrt{7}\right)$ **66.** $\left(3 - \sqrt{7}\right)\left(4 - 5\sqrt{7}\right)$

67. $\left(1 + \sqrt{6}\right)^2$ **68.** $\left(2 + \sqrt{3}\right)^2$

69. $\left(\sqrt{2} - 3\right)^2$ **70.** $\left(\sqrt{6} - 4\right)^2$

71. $\left(\sqrt{15} - \sqrt{5}\right)^2$ **72.** $\left(\sqrt{35} + \sqrt{5}\right)^2$

73. $\left(8 - 5\sqrt{7}\right)^2$ **74.** $\left(5 - 3\sqrt{7}\right)^2$

75. $\left(10 - \sqrt{13}\right)\left(10 + \sqrt{13}\right)$ **76.** $\left(7 - \sqrt{5}\right)\left(7 + \sqrt{5}\right)$

77. $\left(\sqrt{5} + \sqrt{6}\right)\left(\sqrt{5} - \sqrt{6}\right)$ **78.** $\left(\sqrt{6} + \sqrt{13}\right)\left(\sqrt{6} - \sqrt{13}\right)$

79. $\left(4\sqrt{5} + 5\sqrt{7}\right)\left(4\sqrt{5} - 5\sqrt{7}\right)$ **80.** $\left(5\sqrt{6} + 3\sqrt{11}\right)\left(5\sqrt{6} - 3\sqrt{11}\right)$

Higher Index Roots

81. Simplify $\sqrt[3]{125}$.   **82.** Simplify $\sqrt[3]{27}$.   **83.** Simplify $\sqrt[4]{16}$.

84. Simplify $\sqrt[4]{81}$.   **85.** Simplify $\sqrt[5]{32}$.   **86.** Simplify $\sqrt[3]{8}$.

87. Simplify $\sqrt[5]{-32}$.

88. Simplify $\sqrt[4]{-81}$.

89. Simplify $\sqrt[4]{-16}$.

90. Simplify $\sqrt[4]{-81}$.

91. Simplify $\sqrt[3]{-27}$.

92. Simplify $\sqrt[6]{-64}$.

93. Simplify $\sqrt[3]{16}$.

94. Simplify $\sqrt[3]{162}$.

95. Simplify $\sqrt[3]{192}$.

96. Simplify $\sqrt[3]{54}$.

97. Simplify $\sqrt[3]{80}$.

98. Simplify $\sqrt[4]{192}$.

99. Simplify $\sqrt[3]{\frac{3}{64}}$.

100. Simplify $\sqrt[5]{\frac{11}{32}}$.

101. Simplify $\sqrt[3]{\frac{189}{125}}$.

102. Simplify $\sqrt[3]{\frac{88}{27}}$.

103. Simplify $\sqrt[3]{\frac{54}{125}}$.

104. Simplify $\sqrt[3]{\frac{56}{27}}$.

6.2 Rationalizing the Denominator

A radical expression typically has several equivalent forms. For example, $\frac{\sqrt{2}}{3}$ and $\frac{2}{\sqrt{6}}$ are the same number. Mathematics has a preference for one of these forms over the other, and this section is about how to convert a given radical expression to that form.

6.2.1 Rationalizing the Denominator

To simplify radical expressions, we have seen that it helps to make the radicand as small as possible. Another helpful principle is to not leave any irrational numbers, such as $\sqrt{3}$ or $2\sqrt{5}$, in the denominator of a fraction. In other words, we want the denominator to be rational. The process of dealing with such numbers in the denominator is called **rationalizing the denominator**.

Let's see how we can replace $\frac{1}{\sqrt{5}}$ with an equivalent expression that has no radical expressions in its denominator. If we multiply a radical by itself, the result is the radicand, by Definition 6.1.2. As an example:

$$\sqrt{5} \cdot \sqrt{5} = 5$$

With $\frac{1}{\sqrt{5}}$, we may multiply both the numerator and denominator by the same non-zero number and have an equivalent expression. If we multiply the numerator and denominator by $\sqrt{5}$, we have:

$$\frac{1}{\sqrt{5}} = \frac{1}{\sqrt{5}} \cdot \frac{\sqrt{5}}{\sqrt{5}}$$
$$= \frac{1 \cdot \sqrt{5}}{\sqrt{5} \cdot \sqrt{5}}$$
$$= \frac{\sqrt{5}}{5}$$

And voilà, we have an expression with no radical in its denominator. We can use a calculator to verify that $\frac{1}{\sqrt{5}} \approx 0.4472$, and also $\frac{\sqrt{5}}{5} \approx 0.4472$. They are equal.

Example 6.2.2 Rationalize the denominator of the expressions.

   a. $\frac{3}{\sqrt{6}}$ b. $\frac{\sqrt{5}}{\sqrt{72}}$

Explanation.

   a. To rationalize the denominator of $\frac{3}{\sqrt{6}}$, we multiply both the numerator and denominator by $\frac{\sqrt{6}}{\sqrt{6}}$.

$$\frac{3}{\sqrt{6}} = \frac{3}{\sqrt{6}} \cdot \frac{\sqrt{6}}{\sqrt{6}}$$
$$= \frac{3\sqrt{6}}{6}$$
$$= \frac{\sqrt{6}}{2}$$

Note that we reduced a fraction $\frac{3}{6}$ whose numerator and denominator were no longer inside the radical.

b. To rationalize the denominator of $\frac{\sqrt{5}}{\sqrt{72}}$, we *could* multiply both the numerator and denominator by $\sqrt{72}$, and it would be effective; however, we should note that the $\sqrt{72}$ in the denominator can be *reduced* first. Doing this will simplify the arithmetic because there will be smaller numbers to work with.

$$\frac{\sqrt{5}}{\sqrt{72}} = \frac{\sqrt{5}}{\sqrt{36 \cdot 2}}$$
$$= \frac{\sqrt{5}}{\sqrt{36} \cdot \sqrt{2}}$$
$$= \frac{\sqrt{5}}{6 \cdot \sqrt{2}}$$

Now all that remains is to multiply the numerator and denominator by $\sqrt{2}$.

$$= \frac{\sqrt{5}}{6 \cdot \sqrt{2}} \cdot \frac{\sqrt{2}}{\sqrt{2}}$$
$$= \frac{\sqrt{10}}{6 \cdot 2}$$
$$= \frac{\sqrt{10}}{12}$$

Checkpoint 6.2.3 Rationalize the denominator in $\frac{2}{\sqrt{10}}$.

Explanation.   We will rationalize the denominator by multiplying the numerator and denominator by $\sqrt{10}$:

$$\frac{2}{\sqrt{10}} = \frac{2}{\sqrt{10}} \cdot \frac{\sqrt{10}}{\sqrt{10}}$$
$$= \frac{2 \cdot \sqrt{10}}{\sqrt{10} \cdot \sqrt{10}}$$
$$= \frac{2\sqrt{10}}{10}$$
$$= \frac{\sqrt{10}}{5}$$

Again note that the fraction was simplified in the last step.

Example 6.2.4 Rationalize the denominator in $\sqrt{\frac{2}{7}}$.

Explanation.   This example is slightly different. The entire fraction, including its denominator, is within a radical. Having a denominator within a radical is just as undesirable as having a radical in a denominator. So we want to do something to change the expression.

$$\sqrt{\frac{2}{7}} = \frac{\sqrt{2}}{\sqrt{7}}$$
$$= \frac{\sqrt{2}}{\sqrt{7}} \cdot \frac{\sqrt{7}}{\sqrt{7}}$$

$$= \frac{\sqrt{2} \cdot \sqrt{7}}{\sqrt{7} \cdot \sqrt{7}}$$

$$= \frac{\sqrt{14}}{7}$$

6.2.2 Rationalize the Denominator Using the Difference of Squares Formula

Conside the number $\frac{1}{\sqrt{2}+1}$. Its denominator is irrational, approximately $2.414\ldots$. Can we rewrite this as an equivalent expression where the denominator is rational? Let's try multiplying the numerator and denominator by $\sqrt{2}$:

$$\frac{1}{\sqrt{2}+1} = \frac{1}{\left(\sqrt{2}+1\right)} \cdot \frac{\sqrt{2}}{\sqrt{2}}$$

$$= \frac{\sqrt{2}}{\sqrt{2}\cdot\sqrt{2}+1\cdot\sqrt{2}}$$

$$= \frac{\sqrt{2}}{2+\sqrt{2}}$$

We removed one radical from the denominator, but created another. We need to find another method. The difference of squares formula will help:

$$(a+b)(a-b) = a^2 - b^2$$

Those two squares in $a^2 - b^2$ can be used as a tool to annihilate radicals. Take $\frac{1}{\sqrt{2}+1}$, and multiply both the numerator and denominator by $\sqrt{2}-1$:

$$\frac{1}{\sqrt{2}+1} = \frac{1}{\left(\sqrt{2}+1\right)} \cdot \frac{\left(\sqrt{2}-1\right)}{\left(\sqrt{2}-1\right)}$$

$$= \frac{\sqrt{2}-1}{\left(\sqrt{2}\right)^2 - (1)^2}$$

$$= \frac{\sqrt{2}-1}{2-1}$$

$$= \frac{\sqrt{2}-1}{1}$$

$$= \sqrt{2}-1$$

Example 6.2.5 Rationalize the denominator in $\frac{\sqrt{7}-\sqrt{2}}{\sqrt{5}+\sqrt{3}}$.

Explanation. To address the radicals in the denominator, we multiply both numerator and denominator by $\sqrt{5}-\sqrt{3}$.

$$\frac{\sqrt{7}-\sqrt{2}}{\sqrt{5}+\sqrt{3}} = \frac{\sqrt{7}-\sqrt{2}}{\sqrt{5}+\sqrt{3}} \cdot \frac{\left(\sqrt{5}-\sqrt{3}\right)}{\left(\sqrt{5}-\sqrt{3}\right)}$$

$$= \frac{\sqrt{7} \cdot \sqrt{5} - \sqrt{7} \cdot \sqrt{3} - \sqrt{2} \cdot \sqrt{5} - \sqrt{2} \cdot -\sqrt{3}}{\left(\sqrt{5}\right)^2 - \left(\sqrt{3}\right)^2}$$

$$= \frac{\sqrt{35} - \sqrt{21} - \sqrt{10} + \sqrt{6}}{5 - 3}$$

$$= \frac{\sqrt{35} - \sqrt{21} - \sqrt{10} + \sqrt{6}}{2}$$

Checkpoint 6.2.6 Rationalize the denominator in $\frac{\sqrt{3}}{3 - 2\sqrt{3}}$.

Explanation.   To remove the radical in $3 - 2\sqrt{3}$ with the difference of squares formula, we multiply it with $3 + 2\sqrt{3}$.

$$\frac{\sqrt{3}}{3 - 2\sqrt{3}} = \frac{\sqrt{3}}{(3 - 2\sqrt{3})} \cdot \frac{(3 + 2\sqrt{3})}{(3 + 2\sqrt{3})}$$

$$= \frac{3 \cdot \sqrt{3} + 2\sqrt{3} \cdot \sqrt{3}}{(3)^2 - \left(2\sqrt{3}\right)^2}$$

$$= \frac{3\sqrt{3} + 2 \cdot 3}{9 - 2^2 \left(\sqrt{3}\right)^2}$$

$$= \frac{3\sqrt{3} + 6}{9 - 4(3)}$$

$$= \frac{3\left(\sqrt{3} + 2\right)}{9 - 12}$$

$$= \frac{3\left(\sqrt{3} + 2\right)}{-3}$$

$$= \frac{\sqrt{3} + 2}{-1}$$

$$= -\sqrt{3} - 2$$

6.2.3 Reading Questions

1.   To rationalize a denominator in an expression like $\frac{3}{\sqrt{5}}$, explain the first step you will take.

2.   What is the special pattern from Section 5.5 that helps to rationalize the denominator in an expression like $\frac{3}{2+\sqrt{5}}$?

6.2.4 Exercises

Review and Warmup Rationalize the denominator and simplify the expression.

1. $\dfrac{1}{\sqrt{6}}$ 2. $\dfrac{1}{\sqrt{6}}$ 3. $\dfrac{7}{\sqrt{7}}$ 4. $\dfrac{40}{\sqrt{10}}$

5. $\dfrac{1}{\sqrt{180}}$ **6.** $\dfrac{1}{\sqrt{8}}$ **7.** $\dfrac{2}{\sqrt{252}}$ **8.** $\dfrac{9}{\sqrt{180}}$

Rationalizing the Denominator Evaluate the following.

9. $\dfrac{3}{\sqrt{4}}$ **10.** $\dfrac{5}{\sqrt{64}}$

Rationalize the denominator and simplify the expression.

11. $\dfrac{1}{\sqrt{6}}$ **12.** $\dfrac{1}{\sqrt{7}}$ **13.** $\dfrac{7}{\sqrt{10}}$ **14.** $\dfrac{7}{\sqrt{10}}$

15. $\dfrac{5}{8\sqrt{2}}$ **16.** $\dfrac{7}{3\sqrt{3}}$ **17.** $\dfrac{6}{\sqrt{10}}$ **18.** $\dfrac{20}{\sqrt{14}}$

19. $\dfrac{18}{\sqrt{6}}$ **20.** $\dfrac{12}{\sqrt{6}}$ **21.** $\dfrac{1}{\sqrt{175}}$ **22.** $\dfrac{1}{\sqrt{180}}$

23. $\dfrac{2}{\sqrt{72}}$ **24.** $\dfrac{6}{\sqrt{32}}$ **25.** $\sqrt{\dfrac{7}{9}}$ **26.** $\sqrt{\dfrac{3}{16}}$

27. $\sqrt{\dfrac{9}{2}}$ **28.** $\sqrt{\dfrac{81}{2}}$ **29.** $\sqrt{\dfrac{11}{2}}$ **30.** $\sqrt{\dfrac{13}{15}}$

31. $\sqrt{\dfrac{108}{7}}$ **32.** $\sqrt{\dfrac{72}{5}}$ **33.** $\dfrac{4}{\sqrt{x}}$ **34.** $\dfrac{2}{\sqrt{y}}$

35. $\sqrt{\dfrac{5}{2}}$ **36.** $\sqrt{\dfrac{6}{11}}$ **37.** $\sqrt{\dfrac{11}{48}}$ **38.** $\sqrt{\dfrac{11}{175}}$

Rationalizing the Denominator Using the Difference of Squares Formula Rationalize the denominator and simplify the expression.

39. $\dfrac{7}{\sqrt{15}+7}$ **40.** $\dfrac{2}{\sqrt{22}+5}$ **41.** $\dfrac{8}{\sqrt{22}+9}$ **42.** $\dfrac{2}{\sqrt{14}+9}$

43. $\dfrac{\sqrt{2}-6}{\sqrt{11}+4}$ **44.** $\dfrac{\sqrt{5}-8}{\sqrt{13}+10}$ **45.** $\dfrac{\sqrt{3}-9}{\sqrt{7}+8}$ **46.** $\dfrac{\sqrt{2}-10}{\sqrt{11}+5}$

6.3 Radical Expressions and Rational Exponents

Recall that in Subsection 6.1.3, we learned to evaluate the cube root of a number, say $\sqrt[3]{8}$, we can type 8^(1/3) into a calculator. This suggests that $\sqrt[3]{8} = 8^{1/3}$. In this section, we will learn why this is true, and how to simplify expressions with rational exponents.

Many learners will find a review of exponent rules to be helpful before continuing with the current section. Section 5.2 covers an introduction to exponent rules, and there is more in Section 5.6. The basic rules are summarized in List 5.6.13. These rules are still true and we can use them throughout this section whenever they might help.

6.3.1 Radical Expressions and Rational Exponents

Compare the following calculations:

$$\sqrt{9} \cdot \sqrt{9} = 3 \cdot 3 \qquad\qquad\qquad 9^{1/2} \cdot 9^{1/2} = 9^{1/2 + 1/2}$$
$$= 9 \qquad\qquad\qquad\qquad\qquad = 9^1$$
$$\qquad\qquad\qquad\qquad\qquad\qquad = 9$$

If we rewrite the above calculations with exponents, we have:

$$\left(\sqrt{9}\right)^2 = 9 \qquad\qquad\qquad \left(9^{1/2}\right)^2 = 9$$

Since $\sqrt{9}$ and $9^{1/2}$ are both positive, and squaring either of them generates the same number, we conclude that:

$$\sqrt{9} = 9^{1/2}$$

We can verify this result by entering 9^(1/2) into a calculator, and we get 3. In general for any non-negative real number a, we have:

$$\sqrt{a} = a^{1/2}$$

Similarly, when a is non-negative all of the following are true:

$$\sqrt[2]{a} = a^{1/2} \qquad\quad \sqrt[3]{a} = a^{1/3} \qquad\quad \sqrt[4]{a} = a^{1/4} \qquad\quad \sqrt[5]{a} = a^{1/5} \qquad\quad \cdots$$

For example, when we see $16^{1/4}$, that is equal to $\sqrt[4]{16}$, which we know is 2 because $\overbrace{2 \cdot 2 \cdot 2 \cdot 2}^{\text{four times}} = 16$. How can we relate this to the exponential expression $16^{1/4}$? In a sense, we are cutting up 16 into 4 equal parts. But not parts that you *add* together, rather parts that you *multiply* together.

Let's summarize this information with a new exponent rule.

Fact 6.3.2 Radicals and Rational Exponents Rule. *If m is any natural number, and a is any non-negative real number, then*

$$a^{1/m} = \sqrt[m]{a}.$$

Additionally, if m is an odd *natural number, then even when a is negative, we still have* $a^{1/m} = \sqrt[m]{a}$.

Warning 6.3.3 Exponents on Negative Bases. Some computers and calculators follow different conventions when there is an exponent on a negative base. To see an example of this, visit *WolframAlpha* and try entering cuberoot(-8), and then try (-8)^(1/3), and you will get different results. cuberoot(-8) will come out as

-2, but $(-8)\hat{\ }(1/3)$ will come out as a certain non-real complex number. Most likely, any calculator you are using *does* behave as in Fact 6.3.2, but you should confirm this.

With the Radicals and Rational Exponents Rule, we can re-write radical expressions as expressions with rational exponents.

Example 6.3.4 Write the radical expression $\sqrt[3]{6}$ as an expression with a rational exponent. Then use a calculator to find its decimal approximation.

According to the Radicals and Rational Exponents Rule, $\sqrt[3]{6} = 6^{1/3}$. A calculator tells us that $6\hat{\ }(1/3)$ works out to approximately 1.817.

For many examples that follow, we will not need a calculator. We will, however, need to recognize the roots in Figure 6.3.5.

Square Roots	Cube Roots	4th-Roots	5th-Roots	Roots of Powers of 2
$\sqrt{1} = 1$	$\sqrt[3]{1} = 1$	$\sqrt[4]{1} = 1$	$\sqrt[5]{1} = 1$	
$\sqrt{4} = 2$	$\sqrt[3]{8} = 2$	$\sqrt[4]{16} = 2$	$\sqrt[5]{32} = 2$	$\sqrt{4} = 2$
$\sqrt{9} = 3$	$\sqrt[3]{27} = 3$	$\sqrt[4]{81} = 3$		$\sqrt[3]{8} = 2$
$\sqrt{16} = 4$	$\sqrt[3]{64} = 4$			$\sqrt[4]{16} = 2$
$\sqrt{25} = 5$	$\sqrt[3]{125} = 5$			$\sqrt[5]{32} = 2$
$\sqrt{36} = 6$				$\sqrt[6]{64} = 2$
$\sqrt{49} = 7$				$\sqrt[7]{128} = 2$
$\sqrt{64} = 8$				$\sqrt[8]{256} = 2$
$\sqrt{81} = 9$				$\sqrt[9]{512} = 2$
$\sqrt{100} = 10$				$\sqrt[10]{1024} = 2$
$\sqrt{121} = 11$				
$\sqrt{144} = 12$				

Figure 6.3.5: Small Roots of Appropriate Natural Numbers

Example 6.3.6 Write the expressions in radical form using the Radicals and Rational Exponents Rule and simplify the results.

a. $4^{1/2}$ c. $-16^{1/4}$ e. $(-27)^{1/3}$

b. $(-9)^{1/2}$ d. $64^{-1/3}$ f. $3^{1/2} \cdot 3^{1/2}$

Explanation.

a. $4^{1/2} = \sqrt{4}$
$\phantom{4^{1/2}} = 2$

b. $(-9)^{1/2} = \sqrt{-9}$ This value is non-real.

c. Without parentheses around -16, the negative sign in this problem should be left out of the radical.
$-16^{1/4} = -\sqrt[4]{16}$
$\phantom{-16^{1/4}} = -2$

d. Here we will use the Negative Exponent Rule.

$$64^{-1/3} = \frac{1}{64^{1/3}}$$
$$= \frac{1}{\sqrt[3]{64}}$$
$$= \frac{1}{4}$$

e. $(-27)^{1/3} = \sqrt[3]{-27}$
$$= -3$$

f. $3^{1/2} \cdot 3^{1/2} = \sqrt{3} \cdot \sqrt{3}$
$$= \sqrt{3 \cdot 3}$$
$$= \sqrt{9}$$
$$= 3$$

The Radicals and Rational Exponents Rule applies to variables in expressions just as much as it does to numbers.

Example 6.3.7 Write the expressions as simplified as they can be using radicals.

    a. $2x^{-1/2}$ b. $(5x)^{1/3}$ c. $\left(-27x^{12}\right)^{1/3}$ d. $\left(\frac{16x}{81y^8}\right)^{1/4}$

Explanation.

a. Note that in this example the exponent is only applied to the x. Making this type of observation should be our first step for each of these exercises.

$$2x^{-1/2} = \frac{2}{x^{1/2}} \qquad \text{by the Negative Exponent Rule}$$
$$= \frac{2}{\sqrt{x}} \qquad \text{by the Radicals and Rational Exponents Rule}$$

b. In this exercise, the exponent applies to both the 5 and x.

$$(5x)^{1/3} = \sqrt[3]{5x} \qquad \text{by the Radicals and Rational Exponents Rule}$$

c. We start out as with the previous exercise. As in the previous exercise, we have a choice as to how to simplify this expression. Here we should note that we *do* know what the cube root of -27 is, so we will take the path to splitting up the expression, using the Product to a Power Rule, before applying the root.

$$\left(-27x^{12}\right)^{1/3} = \sqrt[3]{-27x^{12}}$$

Here we notice that -27 has a nice cube root, so it is good to break up the radical.

$$= \sqrt[3]{-27}\sqrt[3]{x^{12}}$$
$$= -3\sqrt[3]{x^{12}}$$

Can this be simplified more? There are two ways to think about that. One way is to focus on the cube root and see that x^4 cubes to make x^{12}, and the other way is to convert the cube root back to a fraction exponent and use exponent rules.

$$= -3\sqrt[3]{x^4 x^4 x^4} \qquad\qquad = -3\left(x^{12}\right)^{1/3}$$
$$= -3x^4 \qquad\qquad = -3x^{12 \cdot 1/3}$$
$$\qquad\qquad\qquad = -3x^4$$

d. We'll use the exponent rule for a fraction raised to a power.

$$\left(\frac{16x}{81y^8}\right)^{1/4} = \frac{(16x)^{1/4}}{\left(81y^8\right)^{1/4}} \qquad \text{by the Quotient to a Power Rule}$$

$$= \frac{16^{1/4} \cdot x^{1/4}}{81^{1/4} \cdot \left(y^8\right)^{1/4}} \qquad \text{by the Product to a Power Rule}$$

$$= \frac{16^{1/4} \cdot x^{1/4}}{81^{1/4} \cdot y^2}$$

$$= \frac{\sqrt[4]{16} \cdot \sqrt[4]{x}}{\sqrt[4]{81} \cdot y^2} \qquad \text{by the Radicals and Rational Exponents Rule}$$

$$= \frac{2\sqrt[4]{x}}{3y^2}$$

Remark 6.3.8 In general, it is easier to do algebra with rational exponents on variables than with radicals of variables. You should use Radicals and Rational Exponents Rule to convert from rational exponents to radicals on variables *only as a last step* in simplifying.

The Radicals and Rational Exponents Rule describes what can be done when there is a fractional exponent and the numerator is a 1. The numerator doesn't have to be a 1 though and we need guidance for that situation.

Fact 6.3.9 Full Radicals and Rational Exponents Rule. *If m and n are natural numbers such that $\frac{m}{n}$ is a reduced fraction, and a is any non-negative real number, then*

$$a^{m/n} = \sqrt[n]{a^m} = \left(\sqrt[n]{a}\right)^m.$$

Additionally, if n is an odd *natural number, then even when a is negative, we still have $a^{m/n} = \sqrt[n]{a^m} = \left(\sqrt[n]{a}\right)^m$.*

Example 6.3.10 Guitar Frets. On a guitar, there are 12 frets separating a note and the same note one octave higher. By moving from one fret to another that is five frets away, the frequency of the note changes by a factor of $2^{5/12}$. Use the Full Radicals and Rational Exponents Rule to write this number as a radical expression. And use a calculator to find this number as a decimal.

Explanation. According to the Full Radicals and Rational Exponents Rule,

$$2^{5/12} = \sqrt[12]{2^5}$$
$$= \sqrt[12]{32}$$

A calculator says $2^{5/12} \approx 1.334\cdots$. The fact that this is very close to $\frac{4}{3} \approx 1.333\ldots$ is important. It is part of the explanation for why two notes that are five frets apart on the same string would sound good to human ears when played together as a chord (known as a "fourth," in music).

Remark 6.3.11 By the Full Radicals and Rational Exponents Rule, there are two ways to express $a^{m/n}$ as a radical expression:

$$a^{m/n} = \sqrt[n]{a^m} \qquad\qquad \text{and} \qquad\qquad a^{m/n} = \left(\sqrt[n]{a}\right)^m$$

There are different times to use each formula. In general, use $a^{m/n} = \sqrt[n]{a^m}$ for variables and $a^{m/n} = \left(\sqrt[n]{a}\right)^m$ for numbers.

Example 6.3.12

a. Consider the expression $27^{4/3}$. Use both versions of the Full Radicals and Rational Exponents Rule to explain why Remark 6.3.11 says that with numbers, $a^{m/n} = \left(\sqrt[n]{a}\right)^m$ is preferred.

b. Consider the expression $x^{4/3}$. Use both versions of the Full Radicals and Rational Exponents Rule to explain why Remark 6.3.11 says that with variables, $a^{m/n} = \sqrt[n]{a^m}$ is preferred.

Explanation.

a. The expression $27^{4/3}$ can be evaluated in the following two ways.

$$\begin{aligned} 27^{4/3} &= \sqrt[3]{27^4} & \text{by the first part of the Full Radicals and Rational Exponents Rule} \\ &= \sqrt[3]{531441} \\ &= 81 \end{aligned}$$

or

$$\begin{aligned} 27^{4/3} &= \left(\sqrt[3]{27}\right)^4 & \text{by the second part of the Full Radicals and Rational Exponents Rule} \\ &= 3^4 \\ &= 81 \end{aligned}$$

The calculation using $a^{m/n} = \left(\sqrt[n]{a}\right)^m$ worked with smaller numbers and can be done without a calculator. This is why we made the general recommendation in Remark 6.3.11.

b. The expression $x^{4/3}$ can be evaluated in the following two ways.

$$x^{4/3} = \sqrt[3]{x^4} \qquad\qquad \text{by the first part of Full Radicals and Rational Exponents Rule}$$

or

$$x^{4/3} = \left(\sqrt[3]{x}\right)^4 \qquad\qquad \text{by the second part of the Full Radicals and Rational Exponents Rule}$$

In this case, the simplification using $a^{m/n} = \sqrt[n]{a^m}$ is just shorter looking and easier to write. This is why we made the general recommendation in Remark 6.3.11.

Example 6.3.13 Simplify the expressions using Fact 6.3.9.

  a. $8^{2/3}$ b. $(64x)^{-2/3}$ c. $\left(-\frac{27}{64}\right)^{2/3}$

Explanation.

a. We will use the second part of the Full Radicals and Rational Exponents Rule, since this expression only involves a number base (not variable).

$$8^{2/3} = \left(\sqrt[3]{8}\right)^2$$
$$= 2^2$$
$$= 4$$

b. $$(64x)^{-2/3} = \frac{1}{(64x)^{2/3}}$$
$$= \frac{1}{64^{2/3}x^{2/3}}$$
$$= \frac{1}{\left(\sqrt[3]{64}\right)^2 \sqrt[3]{x^2}}$$
$$= \frac{1}{4^2 \sqrt[3]{x^2}}$$
$$= \frac{1}{16\sqrt[3]{x^2}}$$

c. In this problem the negative can be associated with either the numerator or the denominator, but not both. We choose the numerator.

$$\left(-\frac{27}{64}\right)^{2/3} = \left(\sqrt[3]{-\frac{27}{64}}\right)^2 \quad \text{by the second part of the Full Radicals and Rational Exponents Rule}$$
$$= \left(\frac{\sqrt[3]{-27}}{\sqrt[3]{64}}\right)^2$$
$$= \left(\frac{-3}{4}\right)^2$$
$$= \frac{(-3)^2}{(4)^2}$$
$$= \frac{9}{16}$$

6.3.2 More Expressions with Rational Exponents

To recap, here is a "complete" list of exponent and radical rules.

List 6.3.14: Complete List of Exponent Rules

Product Rule $a^n \cdot a^m = a^{n+m}$

Power to a Power Rule $(a^n)^m = a^{n \cdot m}$

Product to a Power Rule $(ab)^n = a^n \cdot b^n$

Quotient Rule $\dfrac{a^n}{a^m} = a^{n-m}$, as long as $a \neq 0$

Quotient to a Power Rule $\left(\dfrac{a}{b}\right)^n = \dfrac{a^n}{b^n}$, as long as $b \neq 0$

Zero Exponent Rule $a^0 = 1$ for $a \neq 0$

Negative Exponent Rule $a^{-n} = \dfrac{1}{a^n}$

Negative Exponent Reciprocal Rule $\dfrac{1}{a^{-n}} = a^n$

Negative Exponent on Fraction Rule $\left(\dfrac{x}{y}\right)^{-n} = \left(\dfrac{y}{x}\right)^n$

Radical and Rational Exponent Rule $x^{1/n} = \sqrt[n]{x}$

Radical and Rational Exponent Rule $x^{m/n} = \left(\sqrt[n]{x}\right)^m$, usually for numbers

Radical and Rational Exponent Rule $x^{m/n} = \sqrt[n]{x^m}$, usually for variables

---

Example 6.3.15 Convert the following radical expressions into expressions with rational exponents, and simplify them if possible.

a. $\dfrac{1}{\sqrt{x}}$

b. $\dfrac{1}{\sqrt[3]{25}}$

Explanation.

a.

$$\begin{aligned}
\frac{1}{\sqrt{x}} &= \frac{1}{x^{1/2}} && \text{by the Radicals and Rational Exponents Rule} \\
&= x^{-1/2} && \text{by the Negative Exponent Rule}
\end{aligned}$$

b.

$$\begin{aligned}
\frac{1}{\sqrt[3]{25}} &= \frac{1}{25^{1/3}} && \text{by the Radicals and Rational Exponents Rule} \\
&= \frac{1}{(5^2)^{1/3}}
\end{aligned}$$

$$= \frac{1}{5^{2 \cdot 1/3}} \qquad \text{by the Power to a Power Rule}$$

$$= \frac{1}{5^{2/3}}$$

$$= 5^{-2/3} \qquad \text{by the Negative Exponent Rule}$$

Learners of these simplifications often find it challenging, so we now include a many examples of varying difficulty.

Example 6.3.16 Use exponent properties in List 6.3.14 to simplify the expressions, and write all final versions using radicals.

a. $2w^{7/8}$

b. $\frac{1}{2}y^{-1/2}$

c. $(27b)^{2/3}$

d. $\left(-8p^6\right)^{5/3}$

e. $\sqrt{x^3} \cdot \sqrt[4]{x}$

f. $h^{1/3} + h^{1/3} + h^{1/3}$

g. $\frac{\sqrt{z}}{\sqrt[3]{z}}$

h. $\sqrt{\sqrt[4]{q}}$

i. $3\left(c^{1/2} + d^{1/2}\right)^2$

j. $3\left(4k^{2/3}\right)^{-1/2}$

Explanation.

a.

$$2w^{7/8} = 2\sqrt[8]{w^7} \qquad \text{by the Full Radicals and Rational Exponents Rule}$$

b.

$$\frac{1}{2}y^{-1/2} = \frac{1}{2}\frac{1}{y^{1/2}} \qquad \text{by the Negative Exponent Rule}$$

$$= \frac{1}{2}\frac{1}{\sqrt{y}} \qquad \text{by the Full Radicals and Rational Exponents Rule}$$

$$= \frac{1}{2\sqrt{y}}$$

c.

$$(27b)^{2/3} = (27)^{2/3} \cdot (b)^{2/3} \qquad \text{by the Product to a Power Rule}$$

$$= \left(\sqrt[3]{27}\right)^2 \cdot \sqrt[3]{b^2} \qquad \text{by the Full Radicals and Rational Exponents Rule}$$

$$= 3^2 \cdot \sqrt[3]{b^2}$$

$$= 9\sqrt[3]{b^2}$$

d.

$$\left(-8p^6\right)^{5/3} = (-8)^{5/3} \cdot \left(p^6\right)^{5/3} \qquad \text{by the Product to a Power Rule}$$

$$= (-8)^{5/3} \cdot p^{6 \cdot 5/3} \qquad \text{by the Power to a Power Rule}$$

$$= \left(\sqrt[3]{-8}\right)^5 \cdot p^{10} \qquad \text{by the Full Radicals and Rational Exponents Rule}$$

$$= (-2)^5 \cdot p^{10}$$

$$= -32p^{10}$$

e.

$$\sqrt{x^3} \cdot \sqrt[4]{x} = x^{3/2} \cdot x^{1/4} \qquad \text{by the Full Radicals and Rational Exponents Rule}$$
$$= x^{3/2+1/4} \qquad \text{by the Product Rule}$$
$$= x^{6/4+1/4}$$
$$= x^{7/4}$$
$$= \sqrt[4]{x^7} \qquad \text{by the Full Radicals and Rational Exponents Rule}$$

f.

$$h^{1/3} + h^{1/3} + h^{1/3} = 3h^{1/3}$$
$$= 3\sqrt[3]{h} \qquad \text{by the Radicals and Rational Exponents Rule}$$

g.

$$\frac{\sqrt{z}}{\sqrt[3]{z}} = \frac{z^{1/2}}{z^{1/3}} \qquad \text{by the Radicals and Rational Exponents Rule}$$
$$= z^{1/2-1/3} \qquad \text{by the Quotient Rule}$$
$$= z^{3/6-2/6}$$
$$= z^{1/6}$$
$$= \sqrt[6]{z} \qquad \text{by the Radicals and Rational Exponents Rule}$$

h.

$$\sqrt{\sqrt[4]{q}} = \sqrt{q^{1/4}} \qquad \text{by the Radicals and Rational Exponents Rule}$$
$$= \left(q^{1/4}\right)^{1/2} \qquad \text{by the Radicals and Rational Exponents Rule}$$
$$= q^{1/4 \cdot 1/2} \qquad \text{by the Power to a Power Rule}$$
$$= q^{1/8}$$
$$= \sqrt[8]{q} \qquad \text{by the Radicals and Rational Exponents Rule}$$

i.

$$3\left(c^{1/2} + d^{1/2}\right)^2 = 3\left(c^{1/2} + d^{1/2}\right)\left(c^{1/2} + d^{1/2}\right)$$
$$= 3\left(\left(c^{1/2}\right)^2 + 2c^{1/2} \cdot d^{1/2} + \left(d^{1/2}\right)^2\right)$$
$$= 3\left(c^{1/2 \cdot 2} + 2c^{1/2} \cdot d^{1/2} + d^{1/2 \cdot 2}\right)$$
$$= 3\left(c + 2c^{1/2} \cdot d^{1/2} + d\right)$$
$$= 3\left(c + 2(cd)^{1/2} + d\right) \qquad \text{by the Product to a Power Rule}$$
$$= 3\left(c + 2\sqrt{cd} + d\right) \qquad \text{by the Radicals and Rational Exponents Rule}$$
$$= 3c + 6\sqrt{cd} + 3d$$

j.

$$3\left(4k^{2/3}\right)^{-1/2} = \frac{3}{\left(4k^{2/3}\right)^{1/2}} \qquad \text{by the Negative Exponent Rule}$$

$$= \frac{3}{4^{1/2}\left(k^{2/3}\right)^{1/2}} \qquad \text{by the Product to a Power Rule}$$

$$= \frac{3}{4^{1/2}k^{2/3\cdot 1/2}} \qquad \text{by the Power to a Power Rule}$$

$$= \frac{3}{4^{1/2}k^{1/3}}$$

$$= \frac{3}{\sqrt{4}\cdot\sqrt[3]{k}} \qquad \text{by the Radicals and Rational Exponents Rule}$$

$$= \frac{3}{2\sqrt[3]{k}}$$

We will end a with a short application of rational exponents. Kepler's Laws of Orbital Motion[1] describe how planets orbit stars and how satellites orbit planets. In particular, his third law has a rational exponent, which we will now explore.

Example 6.3.17 Kepler and the Satellite. Kepler's third law of motion says that for objects with a roughly circular orbit that the time (in hours) that it takes to make one full revolution around the planet, T, is proportional to three-halves power of the distance (in kilometers) from the center of the planet to the satellite, r. For the Earth, it looks like this:

$$T = \frac{2\pi}{\sqrt{G\cdot M_E}}r^{3/2}$$

In this case, both G and M_E are constants. G stands for the universal gravitational constant[2] where G is about $8.65\times 10^{-13}\,\frac{km^3}{kg\cdot h^2}$ and M_E stands for the mass of the Earth[3] where M_E is about 5.972×10^{24} kg. Inputting these values into this formula yields a simplified version that looks like this:

$$T \approx 2.76\times 10^{-6}r^{3/2}$$

Most satellites orbit in what is called low Earth orbit[4], including the international space station which orbits at about 340 km above from Earth's surface. The Earth's average radius is about 6380 km. Find the period of the international space station.

Explanation. The formula has already been identified, but the input takes just a little thought. The formula uses r as the distance from the center of the Earth to the satellite, so to find r we need to combine the radius of the Earth and the distance to the satellite above the surface of the Earth.

$$r = 340 + 6380$$
$$= 6720$$

Now we can input this value into the formula and evaluate.

$$T \approx 2.76\cdot 10^{-6}r^{3/2}$$
$$\approx 2.76\cdot 10^{-6}(6720)^{3/2}$$
$$\approx 2.76\cdot 10^{-6}\left(\sqrt{6720}\right)^3$$
$$\approx 1.52$$

The formula tells us that it takes a little more than an hour and a half for the ISS to orbit the Earth! That works out to 15 or 16 sunrises per day.

---

[1]en.wikipedia.org/wiki/Kepler%27s_laws_of_planetary_motion

6.3.3 Reading Questions

1. Raising a number to a reciprocal power (like $\frac{1}{2}$ or $\frac{1}{5}$) is the same as doing what other thing to that number?

2. When the exponent on an expression is a fraction like $\frac{3}{5}$, which part of the fraction is essentially the index of a radical?

6.3.4 Exercises

Review and Warmup Use the properties of exponents to simplify the expression.

1. $x^{13} \cdot x^{17}$ **2.** $y^{15} \cdot y^{11}$ **3.** $\left(t^{11}\right)^3$ **4.** $\left(y^{12}\right)^{10}$

5. $\left(\dfrac{7x^2}{2}\right)^2$ **6.** $\left(\dfrac{3x^3}{8}\right)^2$ **7.** $\left(-6y^4\right)^3$ **8.** $\left(-2x^6\right)^2$

9. $\dfrac{y^{11}}{y}$ **10.** $\dfrac{t^{13}}{t^9}$

Rewrite the expression simplified and using only positive exponents.

11. $r^{-9} \cdot r^3$ **12.** $t^{-3} \cdot t^2$ **13.** $\left(9t^{-14}\right) \cdot \left(10t^2\right)$ **14.** $\left(6x^{-8}\right) \cdot \left(5x^4\right)$

Calculations Without using a calculator, evaluate the expression.

15. a. $9^{\frac{1}{2}}$ **16.** a. $16^{\frac{1}{2}}$ **17.** a. $8^{\frac{1}{3}}$ **18.** a. $27^{\frac{1}{3}}$

     b. $(-9)^{\frac{1}{2}}$ b. $(-16)^{\frac{1}{2}}$ b. $(-8)^{\frac{1}{3}}$ b. $(-27)^{\frac{1}{3}}$

     c. $-9^{\frac{1}{2}}$ c. $-16^{\frac{1}{2}}$ c. $-8^{\frac{1}{3}}$ c. $-27^{\frac{1}{3}}$

19. $9^{-\frac{3}{2}}$ **20.** $125^{-\frac{1}{3}}$ **21.** $\left(\dfrac{1}{81}\right)^{-\frac{3}{4}}$ **22.** $\left(\dfrac{1}{9}\right)^{-\frac{3}{2}}$

23. $\sqrt[2]{9^3}$ **24.** $\sqrt[2]{81^3}$ **25.** $\sqrt[5]{1024}$ **26.** $\sqrt[3]{64}$

27. a. $\sqrt[3]{8}$ **28.** a. $\sqrt[3]{27}$ **29.** a. $\sqrt[4]{16}$ **30.** a. $\sqrt[4]{81}$

     b. $\sqrt[3]{-8}$ b. $\sqrt[3]{-27}$ b. $\sqrt[4]{-16}$ b. $\sqrt[4]{-81}$

     c. $-\sqrt[3]{8}$ c. $-\sqrt[3]{27}$ c. $-\sqrt[4]{16}$ c. $-\sqrt[4]{81}$

31. $\sqrt[3]{-\dfrac{27}{125}}$ **32.** $\sqrt[3]{-\dfrac{27}{125}}$ **33.** $\sqrt[3]{-\dfrac{1}{64}}$ **34.** $\sqrt[3]{-\dfrac{27}{125}}$

Use a calculator to evaluate the expression as a decimal to four significant digits.

35. $\sqrt[3]{9^2}$ **36.** $\sqrt[5]{11^3}$ **37.** $\sqrt[3]{13^2}$ **38.** $\sqrt[5]{18^3}$

---

[2]en.wikipedia.org/wiki/Gravitational_constant
[3]en.wikipedia.org/wiki/Earth_mass
[4]en.wikipedia.org/wiki/Low_Earth_orbit

39. On a guitar, there are 12 frets separating a note and the same note one octave higher. By moving from one fret to another that is seven frets away, the frequency of the note changes by a factor of $2^{7/12}$. Use a calculator to find this number as a decimal. This decimal shows you that $2^{7/12}$ is very close to a "nice" fraction with small numerator and denominator. Notes with this frequency ratio form a "perfect fifth" in music. What is that fraction?

40. On a guitar, there are 12 frets separating a note and the same note one octave higher. By moving from one fret to another that is four frets away, the frequency of the note changes by a factor of $2^{4/12}$. Use a calculator to find this number as a decimal. This decimal shows you that $2^{4/12}$ is very close to a "nice" fraction with small numerator and denominator. Notes with this frequency ratio form a "major third" in music. What is that fraction?

Convert Radicals to Fractional Exponents Use rational exponents to write the expression.

41. $\sqrt[9]{x}$

42. $\sqrt[6]{y}$

43. $\sqrt[3]{4z+6}$

44. $\sqrt{9t+10}$

45. $\sqrt[6]{r}$

46. $\sqrt[3]{m}$

47. $\dfrac{1}{\sqrt[8]{n^3}}$

48. $\dfrac{1}{\sqrt[5]{b^4}}$

Convert Fractional Exponents to Radicals Convert the expression to radical notation.

49. $c^{\frac{2}{3}}$

50. $x^{\frac{5}{6}}$

51. $y^{\frac{5}{9}}$

52. $r^{\frac{2}{3}}$

53. $15^{\frac{1}{6}}t^{\frac{5}{6}}$

54. $4^{\frac{1}{4}}r^{\frac{3}{4}}$

55. Convert $m^{\frac{2}{3}}$ to a radical expression.

56. Convert $n^{\frac{5}{6}}$ to a radical expression.

57. Convert $b^{-\frac{3}{5}}$ to a radical expression.

58. Convert $c^{-\frac{2}{7}}$ to a radical expression.

59. Convert $2^{\frac{1}{5}}x^{\frac{4}{5}}$ to a radical expression.

60. Convert $7^{\frac{1}{7}}y^{\frac{3}{7}}$ to a radical expression.

Simplifying Expressions with Rational Exponents Simplify the expression, answering with rational exponents and not radicals.

61. $\sqrt[11]{z}\,\sqrt[11]{z}$

62. $\sqrt[9]{t}\,\sqrt[9]{t}$

63. $\sqrt[5]{32r^2}$

64. $\sqrt[3]{27m^5}$

65. $\dfrac{\sqrt[3]{27n}}{\sqrt[6]{n^5}}$

66. $\dfrac{\sqrt{36b}}{\sqrt[6]{b^5}}$

67. $\dfrac{\sqrt{4c^3}}{\sqrt[10]{c}}$

68. $\dfrac{\sqrt{49x}}{\sqrt[6]{x^5}}$

69. $\sqrt[5]{y}\cdot\sqrt[10]{y^3}$

70. $\sqrt{z}\cdot\sqrt[6]{z^5}$

71. $\sqrt{\sqrt[3]{t}}$

72. $\sqrt[4]{\sqrt{r}}$

73. $\sqrt{b}\,\sqrt[7]{b}$

74. $\sqrt{r}\,\sqrt[8]{r}$

6.4 Solving Radical Equations

In this section, we will learn how to solve equations involving radicals. The basic strategy to solve radical equations is to isolate the radical on one side of the equation and then raise to a power on both sides to cancel the radical.

6.4.1 Solving Radical Equations

Definition 6.4.2 Radical Equation. A radical equation is an equation in which there is a variable inside at least one radical.   ◊

Examples include the equations $\sqrt{x-2} = 3 + x$ and $1 + \sqrt[3]{2-x} = x$.

Example 6.4.3 The formula $T = 2\pi\sqrt{\frac{L}{g}}$ is used to calculate the period of a pendulum and is attributed to the scientist Christiaan Huygens[1]. In the formula, T stands for the pendulum's period (how long one back-and-forth oscillation takes) in seconds, L stands for the pendulum's length in meters, and g is approximately $9.8 \frac{m}{s^2}$ which is the gravitational acceleration constant on Earth.

An engineer is designing a pendulum. Its period must be 10 seconds. How long should the pendulum's length be?

We will substitute 10 into the formula for T and also the value of g, and then solve for L:

$$10 = 2\pi\sqrt{\frac{L}{9.8}}$$

$$\frac{1}{2\pi} \cdot 10 = \frac{1}{2\pi} \cdot 2\pi\sqrt{\frac{L}{9.8}}$$

$$\frac{5}{\pi} = \sqrt{\frac{L}{9.8}}$$

$$\left(\frac{5}{\pi}\right)^2 = \left(\sqrt{\frac{L}{9.8}}\right)^2 \qquad \text{canceling square root by squaring both sides}$$

$$\frac{25}{\pi^2} = \frac{L}{9.8}$$

$$9.8 \cdot \frac{25}{\pi^2} = 9.8 \cdot \frac{L}{9.8}$$

$$24.82 \approx L$$

To build a pendulum with a period of 10 seconds, its length should be approximately 24.82 meters.

Remark 6.4.4 Squaring both sides of an equation is "dangerous," as it could create **extraneous solutions**, which will not make the equation true. For example, if we square both sides of $1 = -1$, we have:

$$1 = -1 \qquad\qquad \text{false}$$
$$(1)^2 = (-1)^2 \qquad \text{square both sides} \dots$$
$$1 = 1 \qquad\qquad \text{true}$$

By squaring both sides of an equation, we can sometimes turn a false equation into a true one. This is why

---

[1]en.wikipedia.org/wiki/Christiaan_Huygens#Pendulums

we *must check solutions* when we square both sides of an equation.

Example 6.4.5 Solve the equation $1 + \sqrt{y-1} = 4$ for y.

Explanation. We will isolate the radical first, and then square both sides.

$$1 + \sqrt{y-1} = 4$$
$$\sqrt{y-1} = 3$$
$$\left(\sqrt{y-1}\right)^2 = 3^2$$
$$y - 1 = 9$$
$$y = 10$$

Because we squared both sides of an equation, we must check the solution.

$$1 + \sqrt{10-1} \stackrel{?}{=} 4$$
$$1 + \sqrt{9} \stackrel{?}{=} 4$$
$$1 + 3 \stackrel{\checkmark}{=} 4$$

So, 10 is the solution to the equation $1 + \sqrt{y-1} = 4$.

Example 6.4.6 Solve the equation $5 + \sqrt{q} = 3$ for q.

Explanation. First, isolate the radical and square both sides.

$$5 + \sqrt{q} = 3$$
$$\sqrt{q} = -2$$
$$(\sqrt{q})^2 = (-2)^2$$
$$q = 4$$

Because we squared both sides of an equation, we must check the solution.

$$5 + \sqrt{4} \stackrel{?}{=} 3$$
$$5 + 2 \stackrel{?}{=} 3$$
$$7 \stackrel{\text{no}}{=} 3$$

Thus, the potential solution -2 is actually extraneous and we have no real solutions to the equation $5 + \sqrt{q} = 3$. The solution set is the empty set, $\emptyset$.

Remark 6.4.7 In the previous example, it would be legitimate to observe that there are no solutions at earlier stages. From the very beginning, how could 5 plus a positive quantity result in 3? Or at the second step, since square roots are non-negative, how could a square root equal -2?

You do not have to be able to make these observations. If you follow the general steps for solving radical equations *and* you remember to check the possible solutions you find, then that will be enough.

Sometimes, we need to square both sides of an equation *twice* before finding the solutions, like in the next example.

Example 6.4.8 Solve the equation $\sqrt{p-5} = 5 - \sqrt{p}$ for p.

Explanation. We cannot isolate two radicals, so we will simply square both sides, and later try to isolate the remaining radical.

$$\sqrt{p-5} = 5 - \sqrt{p}$$
$$\left(\sqrt{p-5}\right)^2 = (5 - \sqrt{p})^2$$
$$p - 5 = 25 - 10\sqrt{p} + p \qquad \text{after expanding the binomial squared}$$
$$-5 = 25 - 10\sqrt{p}$$
$$-30 = -10\sqrt{p}$$
$$3 = \sqrt{p}$$
$$3^2 = (\sqrt{p})^2$$
$$9 = p$$

Because we squared both sides of an equation, we must check the solution.

$$\sqrt{9-5} \overset{?}{=} 5 - \sqrt{9}$$
$$\sqrt{4} \overset{?}{=} 5 - 3$$
$$2 \overset{\checkmark}{=} 2$$

So 9 is the solution. The solution set is {9}.

Let's look at an example of solving an equation with a cube root. There is very little difference between solving an equation with one cube root and solving an equation with one square root. Instead of *squaring* both sides, you *cube* both sides.

Example 6.4.9 Solve for q in $\sqrt[3]{2-q} + 2 = 5$.
Explanation.

$$\sqrt[3]{2-q} + 2 = 5$$
$$\sqrt[3]{2-q} = 3$$
$$\left(\sqrt[3]{2-q}\right)^3 = 3^3$$
$$2 - q = 27$$
$$-q = 25$$
$$q = -25$$

Unlike squaring both sides of an equation, raising both sides of an equation to the 3rd power will not create extraneous solutions. It's still good practice to check solution, though. This part is left as exercise.

For summary reference, here is the general procedure for solving a radical equation.

Process 6.4.10 Solving Radical Equations. *A basic strategy to solve radical equations is to take the following steps:*

1. *Isolate a radical on one side of the equation.*

2. *Raise both sides of the equation to a power to cancel the radical.*

3. *If there is still a radical in the equation, repeat the isolation and raising to a power.*

4. *Once the remaining equation has no radicals, solve it.*

5. *Check any and all solutions. Be aware that there may be "extraneous solutions".*

6.4.2 Solving a Radical Equation with More Than One Variable

We also need to be able to solve radical equations with other variables, like in the next example. The strategy is the same: isolate the radical, and then raise both sides to a certain power to cancel the radical.

Example 6.4.11 Solve for L in the formula $T = 2\pi\sqrt{\frac{L}{g}}$. (This is the formula for a the period T of a swinging pendulum whose length is L, on earth where the acceleration from earth's gravity is g.)

Explanation.

$$T = 2\pi\sqrt{\frac{L}{g}}$$

$$\frac{1}{2\pi} \cdot T = \frac{1}{2\pi} \cdot 2\pi\sqrt{\frac{L}{g}}$$

$$\frac{T}{2\pi} = \sqrt{\frac{L}{g}}$$

$$\left(\frac{T}{2\pi}\right)^2 = \left(\sqrt{\frac{L}{g}}\right)^2$$

$$\frac{T^2}{4\pi^2} = \frac{L}{g}$$

$$g \cdot \frac{T^2}{4\pi^2} = g \cdot \frac{L}{g}$$

$$\frac{T^2 g}{4\pi^2} = L$$

Example 6.4.12 The study of black holes has resulted in some interesting mathematics. One fundamental concept about black holes is that there is a distance close enough to the black hole that not even light can escape, called the Schwarzschild radius[2] or the event horizon radius. To find the Schwarzschild radius, R_s, we set the formula for the escape velocity equal to the speed of light, c, and we get $c = \sqrt{\frac{2GM}{R_s}}$ which we need to solve for R_s. Note that G is a constant, and M is the mass of the black hole.

Explanation. We will start by taking the equation $c = \sqrt{\frac{2GM}{R_s}}$ and applying our standard radical-equation-solving techniques. Isolate the radical and square both sides:

$$c = \sqrt{\frac{2GM}{R_s}}$$

$$c^2 = \left(\sqrt{\frac{2GM}{R_s}}\right)^2$$

$$c^2 = \frac{2GM}{R_s}$$

$$R_s \cdot c^2 = R_s \cdot \frac{2GM}{R_s}$$

$$R_s c^2 = 2GM$$

$$\frac{R_s c^2}{c^2} = \frac{2GM}{c^2}$$

$$R_s = \frac{2GM}{c^2}$$

So, the Schwarzschild radius can be found using the formula $R_s = \frac{2GM}{c^2}$.

6.4.3 Reading Questions

1. What is the basic approach to solving a radical equation?

2. What is it called when doing algebra leads you to find a number that *could* be a solution to an equation, but is not actually a solution?

6.4.4 Exercises

Review and Warmup Solve the equation.

1.	$-9n + 8 = -n - 8$	**2.**	$-8p + 4 = -p - 24$	**3.**	$18 = -3(8 - 2x)$
4.	$66 = -2(2 - 5y)$	**5.**	$15 = 8 - 7(t - 8)$	**6.**	$144 = 4 - 10(a - 8)$
7.	$(x - 1)^2 = 4$	**8.**	$(x + 2)^2 = 81$	**9.**	$x^2 + x - 20 = 0$
10.	$x^2 + 19x + 84 = 0$	**11.**	$x^2 + 13x + 12 = -18$	**12.**	$x^2 - 17x + 59 = -1$

Solving Radical Equations Solve the equation.

13.	$\sqrt{x} = 12$	**14.**	$\sqrt{x} = 8$	**15.**	$\sqrt{2y} = 8$
16.	$\sqrt{5y} = 10$	**17.**	$4\sqrt{r} = 16$	**18.**	$2\sqrt{r} = 10$
19.	$-5\sqrt{t} = 15$	**20.**	$-4\sqrt{t} = 20$	**21.**	$-5\sqrt{-5 - x} + 2 = -8$
22.	$3\sqrt{3 - x} + 2 = 29$	**23.**	$\sqrt{x - 12} = \sqrt{x} - 2$	**24.**	$\sqrt{y + 3} = \sqrt{y} + 1$
25.	$\sqrt{y + 9} = -1 - \sqrt{y}$	**26.**	$\sqrt{r + 9} = -1 - \sqrt{r}$	**27.**	$\sqrt{2r} = 8$
28.	$\sqrt{8t} = 3$	**29.**	$\sqrt[3]{t - 5} = 7$	**30.**	$\sqrt[3]{x - 2} = 10$
31.	$\sqrt{8x + 5} + 4 = 10$	**32.**	$\sqrt{4x + 9} + 2 = 8$	**33.**	$\sqrt[3]{y - 12} = -5$
34.	$\sqrt[3]{y - 8} = 3$				

[2]en.wikipedia.org/wiki/Schwarzschild_radius

Solving Radical Equations with Variables

35. Solve the equation for R. Assume that R is positive.

$$Z = \sqrt{L^2 + R^2}$$

R

36. According to the Pythagorean Theorem, the length c of the hypothenuse of a rectangular triangle can be found through the following equation:

$$c = \sqrt{a^2 + b^2}$$

Solve the equation for the length a of one of the triangle's legs.

a

37. In an electric circuit, resonance occurs when the frequency f, inductance L, and capacitance C fulfill the following equation:

$$f = \frac{1}{2\pi\sqrt{LC}}$$

Solve the equation for the inductance L. The frequency is measured in Hertz, the inductance in Henry, and the capacitance in Farad.

L

38. A pendulum has the length L. The time period T that it takes to once swing back and forth can be found with the following formula:

$$T = 2\pi\sqrt{\frac{L}{32}}$$

Solve the equation for the length L. The length is measured in feet and the time period in seconds.

L

Radical Equation Applications According to the Pythagorean Theorem, the length c of the hypothenuse of a rectangular triangle can be found through the following equation.

$$c = \sqrt{a^2 + b^2}$$

39. If a rectangular triangle has a hypothenuse of 5 ft and one leg is 4 ft long, how long is the third side of the triangle?
The third side of the triangle is

☐ long.

40. If a rectangular triangle has a hypothenuse of 5 ft and one leg is 4 ft long, how long is the third side of the triangle?
The third side of the triangle is

☐ long.

In a coordinate system, the distance r of a point (x, y) from the origin $(0, 0)$ is given by the following equation.

$$r = \sqrt{x^2 + y^2}$$

41. If a point in a coordinate system is 13 cm away from the origin and its x coordinate is 12 cm, what is its y coordinate? Assume that y is positive.

y

42. If a point in a coordinate system is 13 cm away from the origin and its x coordinate is 12 cm, what is its y coordinate? Assume that y is positive.

y

A pendulum has the length L ft. The time period T that it takes to once swing back and forth is 6 s. Use the following formula to find its length.

$$T = 2\pi\sqrt{\frac{L}{32}}$$

43. The pendulum is [   ] long.   **44.** The pendulum is [   ] long.

Challenge Solve for x.

45.

$$\sqrt{1+\sqrt{7}} = \sqrt{2+\sqrt{\frac{1}{\sqrt{x}}-1}}$$

46.

$$\sqrt{1+\sqrt{8}} = \sqrt{2+\sqrt{\frac{1}{\sqrt{x}}-1}}$$

6.5 Radical Expressions and Equations Chapter Review

6.5.1 Square and nth Root Properties

In Section 6.1 we defined the square root $\sqrt{x}$ and nth root $\sqrt[n]{x}$ radicals. When x is positive, the expression $\sqrt[n]{x}$ means a positive number r, where $\overbrace{r \cdot r \cdots \cdot r}^{n \text{ times}} = x$. The square root $\sqrt{x}$ is just the case where $n = 2$.

When x is negative, $\sqrt[n]{x}$ might not be defined. It depends on whether or not n is an even number. When x is negative and n is odd, $\sqrt[n]{x}$ is a negative number where $\overbrace{r \cdot r \cdots \cdot r}^{n \text{ times}} = x$.

There are two helpful rules for simplifying radicals.

List 6.5.1: Rules of Radicals for Multiplication and Division

> If a and b are positive real numbers, and m is a positive integer , then we have the following rules:
>
> **Root of a Product Rule** $\sqrt[m]{a \cdot b} = \sqrt[m]{a} \cdot \sqrt[m]{b}$
>
> **Root of a Quotient Rule** $\sqrt[m]{\frac{a}{b}} = \frac{\sqrt[m]{a}}{\sqrt[m]{b}}$ as long as $b \neq 0$

Checkpoint 6.5.2

  a. Simplify $\sqrt{72}$.

  b. Simplify $\sqrt[3]{72}$.

  c. Simplify $\sqrt{\frac{72}{25}}$.

Explanation.

a.
$$\begin{aligned}
\sqrt{72} &= \sqrt{4 \cdot 18} \\
&= \sqrt{4} \cdot \sqrt{18} \\
&= 2\sqrt{18} \\
&= 2\sqrt{9 \cdot 2} \\
&= 2\sqrt{9} \cdot \sqrt{2} \\
&= 2 \cdot 3\sqrt{2} \\
&= 6\sqrt{2}
\end{aligned}$$

b.
$$\begin{aligned}
\sqrt[3]{72} &= \sqrt[3]{8 \cdot 9} \\
&= \sqrt[3]{8} \cdot \sqrt[3]{9} \\
&= 2\sqrt[3]{9}
\end{aligned}$$

c.
$$\begin{aligned}
\sqrt{\frac{72}{25}} &= \frac{\sqrt{72}}{\sqrt{25}} \\
&= \frac{6\sqrt{2}}{5}
\end{aligned}$$

6.5.2 Rationalizing the Denominator

In Section 6.2 we covered how to rationalize the denominator when it contains a single square root or a binomial with a square root term.

Example 6.5.3 Rationalize the denominator of the expressions.

  a. $\frac{12}{\sqrt{3}}$

  b. $\frac{\sqrt{5}}{\sqrt{75}}$

Explanation.

a.

$$\frac{12}{\sqrt{3}} = \frac{12}{\sqrt{3}} \cdot \frac{\sqrt{3}}{\sqrt{3}}$$
$$= \frac{12\sqrt{3}}{3}$$
$$= 4\sqrt{3}$$

b. First we will simplify $\sqrt{75}$.

$$\frac{\sqrt{5}}{\sqrt{75}} = \frac{\sqrt{5}}{\sqrt{25 \cdot 3}}$$
$$= \frac{\sqrt{5}}{\sqrt{25} \cdot \sqrt{3}}$$
$$= \frac{\sqrt{5}}{5\sqrt{3}}$$

Now we can rationalize the denominator by multiplying the numerator and denominator by $\sqrt{3}$.

$$= \frac{\sqrt{5}}{5\sqrt{3}} \cdot \frac{\sqrt{3}}{\sqrt{3}}$$
$$= \frac{\sqrt{15}}{5 \cdot 3}$$
$$= \frac{\sqrt{15}}{15}$$

Example 6.5.4 Rationalize Denominator Using the Difference of Squares Formula. Rationalize the denominator in $\frac{\sqrt{6}-\sqrt{5}}{\sqrt{3}+\sqrt{2}}$.

Explanation.   To remove radicals in $\sqrt{3} + \sqrt{2}$ with the difference of squares formula, we multiply it with $\sqrt{3} - \sqrt{2}$.

$$\frac{\sqrt{6}-\sqrt{5}}{\sqrt{3}+\sqrt{2}} = \frac{\sqrt{6}-\sqrt{5}}{\sqrt{3}+\sqrt{2}} \cdot \frac{\left(\sqrt{3}-\sqrt{2}\right)}{\left(\sqrt{3}-\sqrt{2}\right)}$$
$$= \frac{\sqrt{6}\cdot\sqrt{3}-\sqrt{6}\cdot\sqrt{2}-\sqrt{5}\cdot\sqrt{3}-\sqrt{5}\cdot-\sqrt{2}}{\left(\sqrt{3}\right)^2 - \left(\sqrt{2}\right)^2}$$
$$= \frac{\sqrt{18}-\sqrt{12}-\sqrt{15}+\sqrt{10}}{9-4}$$
$$= \frac{3\sqrt{2}-2\sqrt{3}-\sqrt{15}+\sqrt{10}}{5}$$

6.5.3 Radical Expressions and Rational Exponents

In Section 6.3 we learned the rational exponent rule and added it to our list of exponent rules.

Example 6.5.5 Radical Expressions and Rational Exponents. Simplify the expressions using Fact 6.3.2 or Fact 6.3.9.

   a. $100^{1/2}$ b. $(-64)^{-1/3}$ c. $-81^{3/4}$ d. $\left(-\frac{1}{27}\right)^{2/3}$

Explanation.

  a. $100^{1/2} = \left(\sqrt{100}\right)$
$$= 10$$

  b. $(-64)^{-1/3} = \dfrac{1}{(-64)^{1/3}}$
$$= \dfrac{1}{\left(\sqrt[3]{(-64)}\right)}$$
$$= \dfrac{1}{-4}$$

  c. $-81^{3/4} = -\left(\sqrt[4]{81}\right)^3$
$$= -3^3$$
$$= -27$$

  d. In this problem the negative can be associated with either the numerator or the denominator, but not both. We choose the numerator.

$$\left(-\frac{1}{27}\right)^{2/3} = \left(\sqrt[3]{-\frac{1}{27}}\right)^2$$
$$= \left(\frac{\sqrt[3]{-1}}{\sqrt[3]{27}}\right)^2$$
$$= \left(\frac{-1}{3}\right)^2$$
$$= \frac{(-1)^2}{(3)^2}$$
$$= \frac{1}{9}$$

Example 6.5.6 More Expressions with Rational Exponents. Use exponent properties in List 6.3.14 to simplify the expressions, and write all final versions using radicals.

a. $7z^{5/9}$

b. $\frac{5}{4}x^{-2/3}$

c. $\left(-9q^5\right)^{4/5}$

d. $\sqrt{y^5} \cdot \sqrt[4]{y^2}$

e. $\frac{\sqrt{t^3}}{\sqrt[3]{t^2}}$

f. $\sqrt{\sqrt[3]{x}}$

g. $5\left(4 + a^{1/2}\right)^2$

h. $-6\left(2p^{-5/2}\right)^{3/5}$

Explanation.

a. $7z^{5/9} = 7\sqrt[9]{z^5}$

b. $\begin{aligned}\frac{5}{4}x^{-2/3} &= \frac{5}{4} \cdot \frac{1}{x^{2/3}} \\ &= \frac{5}{4} \cdot \frac{1}{\sqrt[3]{x^2}} \\ &= \frac{5}{4\sqrt[3]{x^2}}\end{aligned}$

c. $\begin{aligned}\left(-9q^5\right)^{4/5} &= (-9)^{4/5} \cdot \left(q^5\right)^{4/5} \\ &= (-9)^{4/5} \cdot q^{5 \cdot 4/5} \\ &= \left(\sqrt[5]{-9}\right)^4 \cdot q^4 \\ &= \left(q\sqrt[5]{-9}\right)^4\end{aligned}$

d. $\begin{aligned}\sqrt{y^5} \cdot \sqrt[4]{y^2} &= y^{5/2} \cdot y^{2/4} \\ &= y^{5/2 + 2/4} \\ &= y^{10/4 + 1/4} \\ &= x^{11/4} \\ &= \sqrt[4]{x^{11}}\end{aligned}$

e. $\begin{aligned}\frac{\sqrt{t^3}}{\sqrt[3]{t^2}} &= \frac{t^{3/2}}{t^{2/3}} \\ &= t^{3/2 - 2/3} \\ &= t^{9/6 - 4/6} \\ &= t^{5/6} \\ &= \sqrt[6]{t^5}\end{aligned}$

f. $\begin{aligned}\sqrt{\sqrt[3]{x}} &= \sqrt{x^{1/3}} \\ &= \left(x^{1/3}\right)^{1/2} \\ &= x^{1/3 \cdot 1/2} \\ &= x^{1/6} \\ &= \sqrt[6]{x}\end{aligned}$

g. $\begin{aligned}5\left(4 + a^{1/2}\right)^2 &= 5\left(4 + a^{1/2}\right)\left(4 + a^{1/2}\right) \\ &= 5\left(4^2 + 2 \cdot 4 \cdot a^{1/2} + \left(a^{1/2}\right)^2\right) \\ &= 5\left(16 + 8a^{1/2} + a^{1/2 \cdot 2}\right) \\ &= 5\left(16 + 8a^{1/2} + a\right) \\ &= 5\left(16 + 8\sqrt{a} + a\right) \\ &= 80 + 40\sqrt{a} + 5a\end{aligned}$

h. $\begin{aligned}-6\left(2p^{-5/2}\right)^{3/5} &= -6 \cdot 2^{3/5} \cdot p^{-5/2 \cdot 3/5} \\ &= -6 \cdot 2^{3/5} \cdot p^{-3/2} \\ &= -\frac{6 \cdot 2^{3/5}}{p^{3/2}} \\ &= -\frac{6\sqrt[5]{2^3}}{\sqrt{p^3}} \\ &= -\frac{6\sqrt[5]{8}}{\sqrt{p^3}}\end{aligned}$

6.5.4 Solving Radical Equations

In Section 6.4 we covered solving equations that contain a radical. We learned about extraneous solutions and the need to check our solutions.

Example 6.5.7 Solving Radical Equations. Solve for r in $r = 9 + \sqrt{r + 3}$.

Explanation. We will isolate the radical first, and then square both sides.

$$r = 9 + \sqrt{r + 3}$$
$$r - 9 = \sqrt{r + 3}$$
$$(r - 9)^2 = \left(\sqrt{r + 3}\right)^2$$
$$r^2 - 18r + 81 = r + 3$$
$$r^2 - 19r + 78 = 0$$
$$(r - 6)(r - 13) = 0$$

$$r - 6 = 0 \qquad \text{or } r - 13 \qquad = 0$$
$$r = 6 \qquad \text{or } r \qquad = 13$$

Because we squared both sides of an equation, we must check both solutions.

$$6 \overset{?}{=} 9 + \sqrt{6 + 3} \qquad\qquad 13 \overset{?}{=} 9 + \sqrt{13 + 3}$$
$$6 \overset{?}{=} 9 + \sqrt{9} \qquad\qquad 13 \overset{?}{=} 9 + \sqrt{16}$$
$$6 \overset{\text{no}}{=} 9 + 3 \qquad\qquad 13 \overset{\checkmark}{=} 9 + 4$$

It turns out 6 is an extraneous solution and 13 is a valid solution. So the equation has one solution: 13. The solution set is $\{13\}$.

Example 6.5.8 Solving Radical Equations that Require Squaring Twice. Solve the equation $\sqrt{t + 9} = -1 - \sqrt{t}$ for t.

Explanation. We cannot isolate two radicals, so we will simply square both sides, and later try to isolate the remaining radical.

$$\sqrt{t + 9} = -1 - \sqrt{t}$$
$$\left(\sqrt{t + 9}\right)^2 = \left(-1 - \sqrt{t}\right)^2$$
$$t + 9 = 1 + 2\sqrt{t} + t \qquad\qquad \text{after expanding the binomial squared}$$
$$9 = 1 + 2\sqrt{t}$$
$$8 = 2\sqrt{t}$$
$$4 = \sqrt{t}$$
$$(4)^2 = \left(\sqrt{t}\right)^2$$
$$16 = t$$

Because we squared both sides of an equation, we must check the solution by substituting 16 into $\sqrt{t + 9} = -1 - \sqrt{t}$, and we have:

$$\sqrt{t + 9} = -1 - \sqrt{t}$$

$$\sqrt{16+9} \stackrel{?}{=} -1 - \sqrt{16}$$

$$\sqrt{25} \stackrel{?}{=} -1 - 4$$

$$5 \stackrel{\text{no}}{=} -5$$

Our solution did not check so there is no solution to this equation. The solution set is the empty set, which can be denoted { } or $\emptyset$.

6.5.5 Exercises

Square Root and nth Root Evaluate the following.

1. $\sqrt{\dfrac{1}{100}}$ 2. $\sqrt{\dfrac{4}{121}}$ 3. $-\sqrt{16}$ 4. $-\sqrt{25}$

Simplify the radical expression or state that it is not a real number.

5. $\dfrac{\sqrt{48}}{\sqrt{3}}$ 6. $\dfrac{\sqrt{32}}{\sqrt{2}}$ 7. $\sqrt{250}$ 8. $\sqrt{99}$

Simplify the expression.

9. $9\sqrt{13} \cdot 9\sqrt{121}$ 10. $9\sqrt{3} \cdot 7\sqrt{4}$ 11. $\sqrt{\dfrac{5}{2}} \cdot \sqrt{\dfrac{7}{2}}$ 12. $\sqrt{\dfrac{7}{3}} \cdot \sqrt{\dfrac{1}{3}}$

Simplify the expression.

13. $13\sqrt{10} - 14\sqrt{10}$ 14. $14\sqrt{5} - 15\sqrt{5}$ 15. $\sqrt{180} + \sqrt{45}$ 16. $\sqrt{80} + \sqrt{125}$

17. Simplify $\sqrt[6]{64}$. 18. Simplify $\sqrt[3]{64}$. 19. Simplify $\sqrt[3]{-8}$. 20. Simplify $\sqrt[3]{-8}$.
21. Simplify $\sqrt[4]{-16}$. 22. Simplify $\sqrt[4]{-81}$. 23. Simplify $\sqrt[4]{144}$. 24. Simplify $\sqrt[3]{135}$.
25. Simplify $\sqrt[3]{\dfrac{11}{8}}$. 26. Simplify $\sqrt[6]{\dfrac{9}{64}}$. 27. Simplify $\sqrt[3]{\dfrac{40}{27}}$. 28. Simplify $\sqrt[3]{\dfrac{56}{125}}$.

Rationalizing the Denominator Rationalize the denominator and simplify the expression.

29. $\dfrac{2}{\sqrt{252}}$ 30. $\dfrac{6}{\sqrt{112}}$ 31. $\sqrt{\dfrac{2}{27}}$ 32. $\sqrt{\dfrac{5}{112}}$

33. $\dfrac{6}{\sqrt{15}+8}$ 34. $\dfrac{7}{\sqrt{7}+4}$ 35. $\dfrac{\sqrt{5}-13}{\sqrt{13}+3}$ 36. $\dfrac{\sqrt{3}-14}{\sqrt{7}+10}$

Radical Expressions and Rational Exponents Without using a calculator, evaluate the expression.

37. $125^{-\frac{2}{3}}$ 38. $8^{-\frac{5}{3}}$ 39. $\left(\dfrac{1}{81}\right)^{-\frac{3}{4}}$ 40. $\left(\dfrac{1}{9}\right)^{-\frac{3}{2}}$

41. $\sqrt[3]{125^2}$ 42. $\sqrt[4]{81^3}$ 43. $\sqrt[5]{1024}$ 44. $\sqrt[3]{64}$

Use rational exponents to write the expression.

45. $\sqrt[5]{b}$ **46.** $\sqrt{c}$ **47.** $\sqrt[5]{8x+7}$ **48.** $\sqrt[4]{5z+1}$

Convert the expression to radical notation.

49. $t^{\frac{2}{3}}$ **50.** $r^{\frac{4}{5}}$ **51.** $m^{\frac{5}{4}}$ **52.** $r^{\frac{2}{3}}$ **53.** $5^{\frac{1}{5}}a^{\frac{4}{5}}$ **54.** $13^{\frac{1}{4}}b^{\frac{3}{4}}$

Simplify the expression, answering with rational exponents and not radicals.

55. $\sqrt[11]{c}\ \sqrt[11]{c}$ **56.** $\sqrt[9]{x}\ \sqrt[9]{x}$ **57.** $\sqrt[5]{32z^2}$

58. $\sqrt[3]{125t^5}$ **59.** $\dfrac{\sqrt{16r}}{\sqrt[10]{r^3}}$ **60.** $\dfrac{\sqrt{36m}}{\sqrt[10]{m^3}}$

61. $\sqrt{n}\cdot\sqrt[6]{n^5}$ **62.** $\sqrt{a}\cdot\sqrt[10]{a^3}$

Solving Radical Equations Solve the equation.

63. $t=\sqrt{t-3}+5$ **64.** $t=\sqrt{t-1}+3$ **65.** $\sqrt{x+9}=\sqrt{x}+1$ **66.** $\sqrt{x+8}=\sqrt{x}+2$

67. $\sqrt{y}+110=y$ **68.** $\sqrt{y}+56=y$ **69.** $r=\sqrt{r+4}+16$ **70.** $r=\sqrt{r+2}+88$

71. $\sqrt{52-t}=t+4$ **72.** $\sqrt{17-t}=t+3$

According to the Pythagorean Theorem, the length c of the hypothenuse of a rectangular triangle can be found through the following equation.

$$c=\sqrt{a^2+b^2}$$

73. If a rectangular triangle has a hypothenuse of 41 ft and one leg is 40 ft long, how long is the third side of the triangle?
The third side of the triangle is
[   ] long.

74. If a rectangular triangle has a hypothenuse of 17 ft and one leg is 15 ft long, how long is the third side of the triangle?
The third side of the triangle is
[   ] long.

75. A pendulum has the length L ft. The time period T that it takes to once swing back and forth is 2 s. Use the following formula to find its length.

$$T=2\pi\sqrt{\dfrac{L}{32}}$$

The pendulum is [   ] long.

76. A pendulum has the length L ft. The time period T that it takes to once swing back and forth is 4 s. Use the following formula to find its length.

$$T=2\pi\sqrt{\dfrac{L}{32}}$$

The pendulum is [   ] long.

Chapter 7

Solving Quadratic Equations

7.1 Solving Quadratic Equations by Using a Square Root

In this section, we will learn how to solve some specific types of quadratic equations using the square root property. We will also learn how to use the Pythagorean Theorem to find the length of one side of a right triangle when the other two lengths are known.

7.1.1 Solving Quadratic Equations Using the Square Root Property

When we learned how to solve linear equations, we used inverse operations to isolate the variable. For example, we use subtraction to remove an unwanted term that is added to one side of a linear equation. We can't quite do the same thing with squaring and using square roots, but we can do something very similar. Taking the square root is the inverse of squaring *if you happen to know the original number was positive*. In general, we have to remember that the original number may have been negative, and that usually leads to *two* solutions to a quadratic equation.

For example, if $x^2 = 9$, we can think of undoing the square with a square root, and $\sqrt{9} = 3$. However, there are *two* numbers that we can square to get 9: -3 and 3. So we need to include both solutions. This brings us to the Square Root Property.

Fact 7.1.2 Square Root Property. *If k is positive, and $x^2 = k$ then*

$$x = -\sqrt{k} \qquad or \qquad x = \sqrt{k}.$$

*It is common to write $x = \pm\sqrt{k}$ for short, but it is important to remember that this means x could possibly be one of two things, not that x is two things at the same time. The positive solution, $\sqrt{k}$, is called the **principal root** of k.*

Example 7.1.3 Solve for y in $y^2 = 49$.

Explanation.

$$y^2 = 49$$
$$y = \pm\sqrt{49}$$

$$y = \pm 7$$

$$y = -7 \qquad\qquad \text{or} \qquad\qquad y = 7$$

To check these solutions, we will substitute -7 and 7 for y in the original equation:

$$
\begin{aligned}
y^2 &= 49 \\
(-7)^2 &\overset{?}{=} 49 \\
49 &\overset{\checkmark}{=} 49
\end{aligned}
\qquad\qquad
\begin{aligned}
y^2 &= 49 \\
(7)^2 &\overset{?}{=} 49 \\
49 &\overset{\checkmark}{=} 49
\end{aligned}
$$

The solution set is $\{-7, 7\}$.

Remark 7.1.4 Every solution to a quadratic equation can be checked, as shown in Example 7.1.3. In general, the process of checking is omitted from this section.

Checkpoint 7.1.5 Solve for z in $4z^2 - 81 = 0$.

Explanation.   Before we use the square root property we need to isolate the squared quantity.

$$
\begin{aligned}
4z^2 - 81 &= 0 \\
4z^2 &= 81 \\
z^2 &= \frac{81}{4} \\
z &= \pm\sqrt{\frac{81}{4}} \\
z &= \pm\frac{9}{2}
\end{aligned}
$$

$$z = -\frac{9}{2} \quad \text{or} \quad z = \frac{9}{2}$$

The solution set is $\left\{-\frac{9}{2}, \frac{9}{2}\right\}$.

We can also use the square root property to solve an equation that has a squared expression (as opposed to just having a squared variable).

Example 7.1.6 Solve for p in $50 = 2(p-1)^2$.

Explanation.   It's important here to suppress any urge you may have to expand the squared binomial. We begin by isolating the squared expression.

$$
\begin{aligned}
50 &= 2(p-1)^2 \\
\frac{50}{2} &= \frac{2(p-1)^2}{2} \\
25 &= (p-1)^2
\end{aligned}
$$

Now that we have the squared expression isolated, we can use the square root property.

$$
\begin{aligned}
p - 1 &= \pm\sqrt{25} \\
p - 1 &= \pm 5
\end{aligned}
$$

$$p = \pm 5 + 1$$

$p = -5 + 1$	or	$p = 5 + 1$
$p = -4$	or	$p = 6$

The solution set is $\{-4, 6\}$.

This method of solving quadratic equations is not limited to equations that have rational solutions, or when the radicands are perfect squares. Here are a few examples where the solutions are irrational numbers.

Checkpoint 7.1.7 Solve for q in $(q + 2)^2 - 12 = 0$.

Explanation. It's important here to suppress any urge you may have to expand the squared binomial.

$$(q + 2)^2 - 12 = 0$$
$$(q + 2)^2 = 12$$
$$q + 2 = \pm\sqrt{12}$$
$$q + 2 = \pm\sqrt{4 \cdot 3}$$
$$q + 2 = \pm 2\sqrt{3}$$
$$q = \pm 2\sqrt{3} - 2$$

$$q = -2\sqrt{3} - 2 \quad \text{or} \quad q = 2\sqrt{3} - 2$$

The solution set is $\left\{-2\sqrt{3} - 2, 2\sqrt{3} - 2\right\}$.

To check the solution, we would replace q with each of $-2\sqrt{3} - 2$ and $2\sqrt{3} - 2$ in the original equation, as shown here:

$$\left(\left(-2\sqrt{3} - 2\right) + 2\right)^2 - 12 \stackrel{?}{=} 0 \qquad \left(\left(2\sqrt{3} - 2\right) + 2\right)^2 - 12 \stackrel{?}{=} 0$$
$$\left(-2\sqrt{3}\right)^2 - 12 \stackrel{?}{=} 0 \qquad \left(2\sqrt{3}\right)^2 - 12 \stackrel{?}{=} 0$$
$$(-2)^2 \left(\sqrt{3}\right)^2 - 12 \stackrel{?}{=} 0 \qquad (2)^2 \left(\sqrt{3}\right)^2 - 12 \stackrel{?}{=} 0$$
$$(4)(3) - 12 \stackrel{?}{=} 0 \qquad (4)(3) - 12 \stackrel{?}{=} 0$$
$$12 - 12 \stackrel{\checkmark}{=} 0 \qquad 12 - 12 \stackrel{\checkmark}{=} 0$$

Note that these simplifications relied on exponent rules and the multiplicative property of square roots.

Remember that if a square root is in a denominator then we may be expected to rationalize it as in Section 6.2. We will rationalize the denominator in the next example.

Example 7.1.8 Solve for n in $2n^2 - 3 = 0$.

Explanation.

$$2n^2 - 3 = 0$$
$$2n^2 = 3$$
$$n^2 = \frac{3}{2}$$

$$n = \pm\sqrt{\frac{3}{2}}$$

$$n = \pm\sqrt{\frac{6}{4}}$$

$$n = \pm\frac{\sqrt{6}}{2}$$

$$n = -\frac{\sqrt{6}}{2} \qquad \text{or} \qquad n = \frac{\sqrt{6}}{2}$$

The solution set is $\left\{-\frac{\sqrt{6}}{2}, \frac{\sqrt{6}}{2}\right\}$.

When the radicand is a negative number, there is no real solution. Here is an example of an equation with no real solution.

Example 7.1.9 Solve for x in $x^2 + 49 = 0$.
Explanation.

$$x^2 + 49 = 0$$
$$x^2 = -49$$

Since $\sqrt{-49}$ is not a real number, we say the equation has no real solution.

7.1.2 The Pythagorean Theorem

Right triangles have an important property called the **Pythagorean Theorem**.

Theorem 7.1.10 The Pythagorean Theorem. *For any right triangle, the lengths of the three sides have the following relationship:* $a^2 + b^2 = c^2$. *The sides* a *and* b *are called* ***legs*** *and the longest side* c *is called the* ***hypotenuse***.

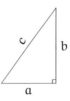

Figure 7.1.11: In a right triangle, the length of its three sides satisfy the equation $a^2 + b^2 = c^2$

Example 7.1.12 Keisha is designing a wooden frame in the shape of a right triangle, as shown in Figure 7.1.13. The legs of the triangle are 3 ft and 4 ft. How long should she make the diagonal side? Use the Pythagorean Theorem to find the length of the hypotenuse.

According to Pythagorean Theorem, we have:

$$c^2 = a^2 + b^2$$
$$c^2 = 3^2 + 4^2$$
$$c^2 = 9 + 16$$
$$c^2 = 25$$

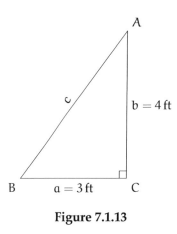

Now we have a quadratic equation that we need to solve. We need to find the number that has a square of 25. That is what the square root operation does.

$$c = \sqrt{25}$$
$$c = 5$$

Figure 7.1.13

The diagonal side Keisha will cut is 5 ft long.

Note that -5 is also a solution of $c^2 = 25$ because $(-5)^2 = 25$ but a length cannot be a negative number. We will need to include both solutions when they are relevant.

Example 7.1.14 A 16.5ft ladder is leaning against a wall. The distance from the base of the ladder to the wall is 4.5 feet. How high on the wall does the ladder reach?
The Pythagorean Theorem says:

$$a^2 + b^2 = c^2$$
$$4.5^2 + b^2 = 16.5^2$$
$$20.25 + b^2 = 272.25$$

Now we need to isolate b^2 in order to solve for b:

$$20.25 + b^2 - 20.25 = 272.25 - 20.25$$
$$b^2 = 252$$

We use the square root property. Because this is a geometric situation we only need to use the principal root:

$$b = \sqrt{252}$$

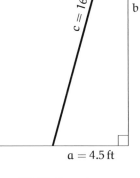

Now simplify this radical and then approximate it:

$$b = \sqrt{36 \cdot 7}$$
$$b = 6\sqrt{7}$$
$$b \approx 15.87$$

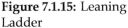

Figure 7.1.15: Leaning Ladder

The ladder reaches about 15.87 feet high on the wall.

Here are some more examples using the Pythagorean Theorem to find sides of triangles. Note that in many contexts, only the principal root will be relevant.

Example 7.1.16 Find the missing length in this right triangle.

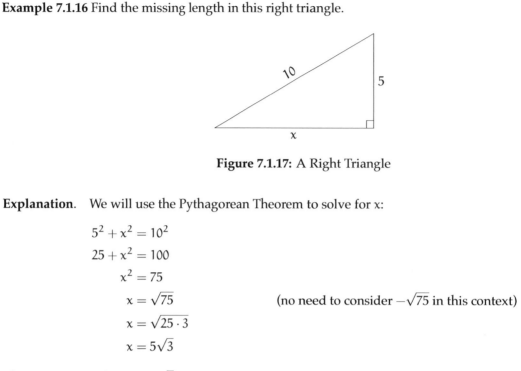

Figure 7.1.17: A Right Triangle

Explanation.   We will use the Pythagorean Theorem to solve for x:

$$5^2 + x^2 = 10^2$$
$$25 + x^2 = 100$$
$$x^2 = 75$$
$$x = \sqrt{75} \qquad \text{(no need to consider } -\sqrt{75} \text{ in this context)}$$
$$x = \sqrt{25 \cdot 3}$$
$$x = 5\sqrt{3}$$

The missing length is $x = 5\sqrt{3}$.

Example 7.1.18 Sergio is designing a 50-inch TV, which implies the diagonal of the TV's screen will be 50 inches long. He needs the screen's width to height ratio to be 4 : 3. Find the TV screen's width and height.

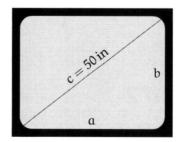

Figure 7.1.19: Pythagorean Theorem Problem

Explanation.   Let's let x represent the height of the screen, in inches. Since the screen's width to height ratio will be 4 : 3, then the width is $\frac{4}{3}$ times as long as the height, or $\frac{4}{3}$x inches. We will draw a diagram.

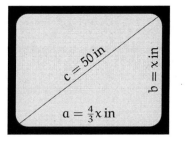

Figure 7.1.20: Pythagorean Theorem Problem

Now we can use the Pythagorean Theorem to write and solve an equation:

$$a^2 + b^2 = c^2$$

$$\left(\frac{4}{3}x\right)^2 + x^2 = 50^2$$

$$\frac{16}{9}x^2 + \frac{9}{9}x^2 = 2500$$

$$\frac{25}{9}x^2 = 2500$$

$$\frac{9}{25} \cdot \frac{25}{9}x^2 = \frac{9}{25} \cdot 2500$$

$$x^2 = 900$$

$$x = 30$$

Since the screen's height is 30 inches, its width is $\frac{4}{3}x = \frac{4}{3}(30) = 40$ inches.

Example 7.1.21 Luca wanted to make a bench.

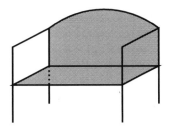

Figure 7.1.22: Sketch of a Bench with Highlighted Back

He wanted the top of the bench back to be a perfect portion of a circle, in the shape of an arc, as in Figure 7.1.23. (Note that this won't be a half-circle, just a small portion of a circular edge.) He started with a rectangular board 6 inches wide and 48 inches long, and a piece of string, like a compass, to draw a circular arc on the board. How long should the string be so that it can be swung round to draw the arc?

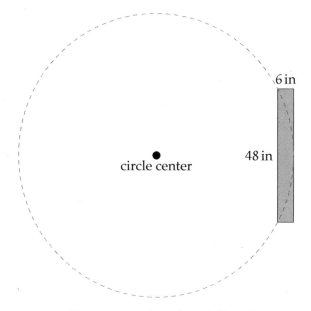

Figure 7.1.23: Bench Back Board

Explanation.   Let's first define x to be the radius of the circle in question, in inches. The circle should go through the bottom corners of the board and just barely touch the top of the board. That means that the line from the middle of the bottom of the board to the center of the circle will be 6 inches shorter than the radius.

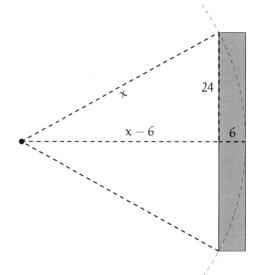

Figure 7.1.24: Bench Back Board Diagram

Now we can set up the Pythagorean Theorem based on the scenario. The equation $a^2 + b^2 = c^2$ turns into…

$$(x - 6)^2 + 24^2 = x^2$$
$$x^2 - 12x + 36 + 576 = x^2$$

$$-12x + 612 = 0$$

Note that at this point the equation is no longer quadratic! Solve the linear equation by isolating x

$$-12x = -612$$
$$x = 51$$

So, the circle radius required is 51 inches. Luca found a friend to stand on the string end and drew a circular segment on the board to great effect.

7.1.3 Reading Questions

1. Typically, how many solutions can there be with a quadratic equation?
2. When you see a $\pm$ sign, as in $x = \pm 2$, is that saying that x is both -2 and 2?
3. Have you memorized the Pythagorean Theorem? State the formula.

7.1.4 Exercises

Solving Quadratic Equations with the Square Root Property Solve the equation.

1. $x^2 = 25$	**2.** $x^2 = 36$	**3.** $x^2 = \frac{1}{64}$
4. $x^2 = \frac{1}{81}$	**5.** $x^2 = 12$	**6.** $x^2 = 20$
7. $x^2 = 67$	**8.** $x^2 = 5$	**9.** $3x^2 = 27$
10. $4x^2 = 100$	**11.** $x^2 = \frac{64}{9}$	**12.** $x^2 = \frac{25}{64}$
13. $4x^2 = 121$	**14.** $36x^2 = 49$	**15.** $7x^2 - 59 = 0$
16. $59x^2 - 67 = 0$	**17.** $2 - 7x^2 = -3$	**18.** $4 - 7x^2 = 2$
19. $53x^2 + 17 = 0$	**20.** $61x^2 + 23 = 0$	**21.** $(x+1)^2 = 9$
22. $(x+3)^2 = 100$	**23.** $(2x+8)^2 = 49$	**24.** $(8x+10)^2 = 9$
25. $9 - 5(t+1)^2 = 4$	**26.** $10 - 3(x+1)^2 = -2$	**27.** $(x-10)^2 = 11$
28. $(x+4)^2 = 17$	**29.** $(y+2)^2 = 45$	**30.** $(r-4)^2 = 98$
31. $-4 = 8 - (r-4)^2$	**32.** $-1 = 62 - (t+5)^2$	

Pythagorean Theorem Applications

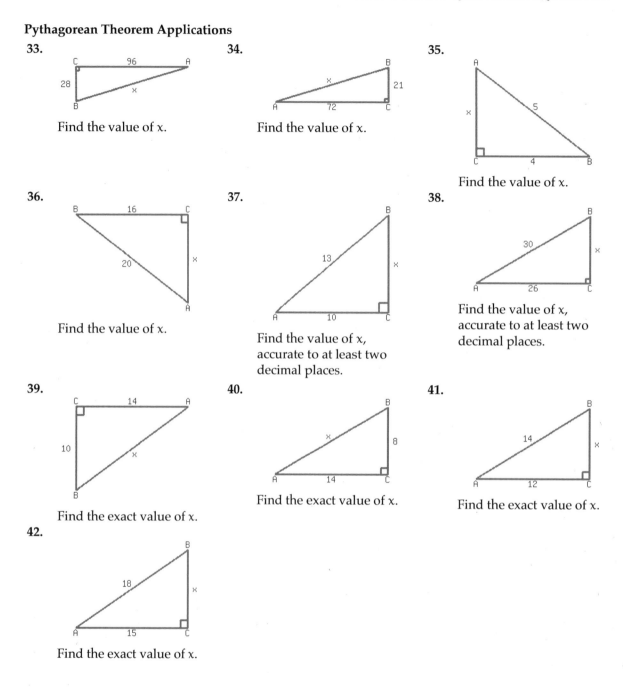

33.

Find the value of x.

34.

Find the value of x.

35.

Find the value of x.

36.

Find the value of x.

37.

Find the value of x,
accurate to at least two
decimal places.

38.

Find the value of x,
accurate to at least two
decimal places.

39.

Find the exact value of x.

40.

Find the exact value of x.

41.

Find the exact value of x.

42.

Find the exact value of x.

43. Kandace is designing a rectangular garden. The garden's diagonal must be 37.7 feet, and the ratio
between the garden's base and height must be 12 : 5. Find the length of the garden's base and
height.

The garden's base is [   ] feet and its height is [   ].

44. Brandon is designing a rectangular garden. The garden's diagonal must be 30.6 feet, and the ratio between the garden's base and height must be 15 : 8. Find the length of the garden's base and height.

The garden's base is [ ] feet and its height is [ ].

45. Peter is designing a rectangular garden. The garden's base must be 8.4 feet, and the ratio between the garden's hypotenuse and height must be 13 : 5. Find the length of the garden's hypotenuse and height.

The garden's hypotenuse is [ ] feet and its height is [ ].

46. Gustav is designing a rectangular garden. The garden's base must be 54 feet, and the ratio between the garden's hypotenuse and height must be 17 : 8. Find the length of the garden's hypotenuse and height.

The garden's hypotenuse is [ ] feet and its height is [ ].

Challenge

47. Imagine that you are in Math Land, where roads are perfectly straight, and Mathlanders can walk along a perfectly straight line between any two points. One day, you bike 4 miles west, 3 miles north, and 6 miles east. Then, your bike gets a flat tire and you have to walk home. How far do you have to walk? You have to walk [ ] miles home.

7.2 The Quadratic Formula

We have learned how to solve certain quadratic equations using the square root property. In this section, we will learn another method, the quadratic formula.

7.2.1 Solving Quadratic Equations with the Quadratic Formula

The standard form for a quadratic equation is

$$ax^2 + bx + c = 0$$

where a is some nonzero number.

When $b = 0$ and the equation's form is $ax^2 + c = 0$, then we can simply use the square root property to solve it. For example, $x^2 - 4 = 0$ leads to $x^2 = 4$, which leads to $x = \pm 2$, a solution set of $\{-2, 2\}$.

But can we solve equations where $b \neq 0$? A general method for solving a quadratic equation is to use what is known as the quadratic formula.

Fact 7.2.2 The Quadratic Formula. *For any quadratic equation* $ax^2 + bx + c = 0$ *where* $a \neq 0$, *the solutions are given by*

$$x = \frac{-b \pm \sqrt{b^2 - 4ac}}{2a}$$

As we have seen from solving quadratic equations, there can be at most two solutions. Both of the solutions are included in the quadratic formula with the $\pm$ symbol. We could write the two solutions separately:

$$x = \frac{-b - \sqrt{b^2 - 4ac}}{2a} \qquad \text{or} \qquad x = \frac{-b + \sqrt{b^2 - 4ac}}{2a}$$

This method for solving quadratic equations will work to solve *every* quadratic equation. It is most helpful when $b \neq 0$.

Example 7.2.3 Linh is in a physics class that launches a tennis ball from a rooftop that is 90.2 feet above the ground. They fire it directly upward at a speed of 14.4 feet per second and measure the time it takes for the ball to hit the ground below. We can model the height of the tennis ball, h, in feet, with the quadratic equation $h = -16x^2 + 14.4x + 90.2$, where x represents the time in seconds after the launch. According to the model, when should the ball hit the ground? Round the time to one decimal place.

The ground has a height of 0 feet. Substituting 0 for h in the equation, we have this quadratic equation:

$$0 = -16x^2 + 14.4x + 90.2$$

We cannot solve this equation with the square root property, so we will use the quadratic formula. First we will identify that $a = -16$, $b = 14.4$ and $c = 90.2$, and substitute them into the formula:

$$x = \frac{-b \pm \sqrt{b^2 - 4ac}}{2a}$$
$$x = \frac{-(14.4) \pm \sqrt{(14.4)^2 - 4(-16)(90.2)}}{2(-16)}$$
$$x = \frac{-14.4 \pm \sqrt{207.36 - (-5772.8)}}{-32}$$

$$x = \frac{-14.4 \pm \sqrt{207.36 + 5772.8}}{-32}$$

$$x = \frac{-14.4 \pm \sqrt{5980.16}}{-32}$$

These are the exact solutions but because we have a context we want to approximate the solutions with decimals.

$$x \approx -1.966 \text{ or } x \approx 2.866$$

We don't use the negative solution because a negative time does not make sense in this context. The ball will hit the ground approximately 2.9 seconds after it is launched.

The quadratic formula can be used to solve any quadratic equation, but it requires that you don't make *any* slip-up with remembering the formula, that you correctly identify a, b, and c, and that you don't make any arithmetic mistakes when you calculate and simplify. We recommend that you always check whether you can use the square root property before using the quadratic formula. Here is another example.

Example 7.2.4 Solve for x in $2x^2 - 9x + 5 = 0$.

Explanation. First, we check and see that we cannot use the square root property (because $b \neq 0$) so we will use the quadratic formula. Next we identify that $a = 2$, $b = -9$ and $c = 5$. We substitute them into the quadratic formula:

$$x = \frac{-b \pm \sqrt{b^2 - 4ac}}{2a}$$

$$x = \frac{-(-9) \pm \sqrt{(-9)^2 - 4(2)(5)}}{2(2)}$$

$$x = \frac{9 \pm \sqrt{81 - 40}}{4}$$

$$x = \frac{9 \pm \sqrt{41}}{4}$$

This is fully simplified because we cannot simplify $\sqrt{41}$ or reduce the fraction. The solution set is $\left\{ \frac{9-\sqrt{22}}{4}, \frac{9+\sqrt{22}}{4} \right\}$. We do not have a context here so we leave the solutions in their exact form.

When a quadratic equation is not in standard form we must convert it before we can identify the values of a, b and c. We will show that in the next example.

Example 7.2.5 Solve for x in $x^2 = -10x - 3$.

Explanation. First, we convert the equation into standard form by adding 10x and 3 to each side of the equation:
$$x^2 + 10x + 3 = 0$$

Next, we check that we cannot use the square root property so we will use the quadratic formula. We identify that $a = 1$, $b = 10$ and $c = 3$. We substitute them into the quadratic formula:

$$x = \frac{-b \pm \sqrt{b^2 - 4ac}}{2a}$$

$$x = \frac{-10 \pm \sqrt{(10)^2 - 4(1)(3)}}{2(1)}$$

$$x = \frac{-10 \pm \sqrt{100 - 12}}{2}$$

$$x = \frac{-10 \pm \sqrt{88}}{2}$$

We notice that the radical can be simplified:

$$x = \frac{-10 \pm 2\sqrt{22}}{2}$$

$$x = \frac{-10}{2} \pm \frac{2\sqrt{22}}{2}$$

$$x = -5 \pm \sqrt{22}$$

The solution set is $\{-5 - \sqrt{22}, -5 + \sqrt{22}\}$.

Remark 7.2.6 The irrational solutions to quadratic equations can be checked, although doing so can sometimes involve a lot of simplification and is not shown throughout this section. As an example, to check the solution of $-5 + \sqrt{22}$ from Example 7.2.5, we would replace x with $-5 + \sqrt{22}$ and check that the two sides of the equation are equal. This check is shown here:

$$x^2 = -10x - 3$$

$$(-5 + \sqrt{22})^2 \stackrel{?}{=} -10(-5 + \sqrt{22}) - 3$$

$$(-5)^2 + 2(-5)(\sqrt{22}) + (\sqrt{22})^2 \stackrel{?}{=} -10(-5 + \sqrt{22}) - 3$$

$$25 - 10\sqrt{22} + 22 \stackrel{?}{=} 50 - 10\sqrt{22} - 3$$

$$47 - 10\sqrt{22} \stackrel{\checkmark}{=} 47 - 10\sqrt{22}$$

When the radicand from the quadratic formula, $b^2 - 4ac$, which is called the **discriminant**, is a negative number, the quadratic equation has no real solution. Example 7.2.7 shows what happens in this case.

Example 7.2.7 Solve for y in $y^2 - 4y + 8 = 0$.

Explanation.   Identify that $a = 1$, $b = -4$ and $c = 8$. We will substitute them into the quadratic formula:

$$y = \frac{-b \pm \sqrt{b^2 - 4ac}}{2a}$$

$$= \frac{-(-4) \pm \sqrt{(-4)^2 - 4(1)(8)}}{2(1)}$$

$$= \frac{4 \pm \sqrt{16 - 32}}{2}$$

$$= \frac{4 \pm \sqrt{-16}}{2}$$

The square root of a negative number is not a real number, so we will simply state that this equation has no real solutions.

Sometimes a radical equation gives rise to a quadratic equation, and the quadratic formula is useful.

Example 7.2.8 Solve for z in $\sqrt{z} + 2 = z$.

Explanation. We will isolate the radical first, and then square both sides.

$$\sqrt{z} + 2 = z$$
$$\sqrt{z} = z - 2$$
$$\left(\sqrt{z}\right)^2 = (z-2)^2$$
$$z = z^2 - 4z + 4$$
$$0 = z^2 - 5z + 4$$
$$z = \frac{5 \pm \sqrt{(-5)^2 - 4(1)(4)}}{2}$$
$$= \frac{5 \pm \sqrt{25 - 16}}{2}$$
$$= \frac{5 \pm \sqrt{9}}{2}$$
$$= \frac{5 \pm 3}{2}$$

$$z = \frac{5-3}{2} \qquad \text{or} \qquad z = \frac{5+3}{2}$$
$$z = 1 \qquad \text{or} \qquad z = 4$$

Because we squared both sides of an equation, we must check both solutions.

$$\sqrt{1} + 2 \overset{?}{=} 1 \qquad\qquad \sqrt{4} + 2 \overset{?}{=} 4$$
$$1 + 2 \overset{\text{no}}{=} 1 \qquad\qquad 2 + 2 \overset{\checkmark}{=} 4$$

It turned out that 1 is an extraneous solution, but 4 is a valid solution. So the equation has one solution: 4. The solution set is $\{4\}$.

Example 7.2.9 Solve the equation $\sqrt{2n - 6} = 1 + \sqrt{n - 2}$ for n.

Explanation. We cannot isolate two radicals, so we will simply square both sides, and later try to isolate the remaining radical.

$$\sqrt{2n - 6} = 1 + \sqrt{n - 2}$$
$$\left(\sqrt{2n-6}\right)^2 = \left(1 + \sqrt{n-2}\right)^2$$
$$2n - 6 = 1^2 + 2\sqrt{n-2} + \left(\sqrt{n-2}\right)^2$$
$$2n - 6 = 1 + 2\sqrt{n-2} + n - 2$$
$$2n - 6 = 2\sqrt{n-2} + n - 1$$
$$n - 5 = 2\sqrt{n-2}$$

Note here that we can leave the factor of 2 next to the radical. We will square the 2 also.

$$(n-5)^2 = \left(2\sqrt{n-2}\right)^2$$
$$n^2 - 10n + 25 = 4(n-2)$$
$$n^2 - 10n + 25 = 4n - 8$$
$$n^2 - 14n + 33 = 0$$

$$n = \frac{14 \pm \sqrt{14^2 - 4(1)(33)}}{2}$$
$$= \frac{14 \pm \sqrt{196 - 132}}{2}$$
$$= \frac{14 \pm \sqrt{64}}{2}$$
$$= \frac{14 \pm 8}{2}$$

$$n = \frac{14 - 8}{2} \qquad \text{or} \qquad n = \frac{14 + 8}{2}$$
$$n = 3 \qquad \text{or} \qquad n = 11$$

So our two potential solutions are 3 and 11. We should now verify that they truly are solutions.

$$\sqrt{2(3) - 6} \overset{?}{=} 1 + \sqrt{3 - 2} \qquad\qquad \sqrt{2(11) - 6} \overset{?}{=} 1 + \sqrt{11 - 2}$$
$$\sqrt{6 - 6} \overset{?}{=} 1 + \sqrt{1} \qquad\qquad \sqrt{22 - 6} \overset{?}{=} 1 + \sqrt{9}$$
$$\sqrt{0} \overset{?}{=} 1 + 1 \qquad\qquad \sqrt{16} \overset{?}{=} 1 + 3$$
$$0 \overset{no}{=} 2 \qquad\qquad 4 \overset{\checkmark}{=} 4$$

So, 11 is the only solution. The solution set is $\{11\}$.

7.2.2 Reading Questions

1.   What is the formula for the discriminant? (The part of the quadratic formula inside the radical.)

2.   Are there any kinds of quadratic equations where the quadratic formula is not the best tool to use?

3.   Given a quadratic euqation, will the quadratic formula always show you two real solutions?

7.2.3 Exercises

Review and Warmup

1.   Evaluate $\dfrac{-5A + 5B + 7}{6A - 9B}$ for $A = 2$ and $B = -4$.

2.   Evaluate $\dfrac{-6C - 5c + 9}{-6C - 3c}$ for $C = -10$ and $c = -9$.

3. Evaluate the expression $\frac{1}{3}(x+4)^2 - 2$ when $x = -7$.

4. Evaluate the expression $\frac{1}{3}(x+4)^2 - 7$ when $x = -7$.

5. Evaluate the expression $-16t^2 + 64t + 128$ when $t = 3$.

6. Evaluate the expression $-16t^2 + 64t + 128$ when $t = -5$.

7. Evaluate the expression x^2:

    a. For $x = 7$.

    b. For $x = -2$.

8. Evaluate the expression y^2:

    a. For $y = 4$.

    b. For $y = -6$.

9. Evaluate each algebraic expression for the given value(s):

$$\frac{\sqrt{x}}{y} - \frac{y}{x}, \text{ for } x = 25 \text{ and } y = 10:$$

10. Evaluate each algebraic expression for the given value(s):

$$\frac{y}{4x} - \frac{\sqrt{x}}{3y}, \text{ for } x = 25 \text{ and } y = -4:$$

Solve Quadratic Equations Using the Quadratic Formula Solve the equation.

11. $x^2 + 7x + 1 = 0$

12. $x^2 + 8x + 11 = 0$

13. $20x^2 + 56x + 15 = 0$

14. $10x^2 + 39x + 35 = 0$

15. $x^2 = x + 1$

16. $x^2 = 5x - 5$

17. $x^2 + 3x - 9 = 0$

18. $x^2 - 9x + 9 = 0$

19. $2x^2 + 3x - 1 = 0$

20. $3x^2 - x - 1 = 0$

21. $4x^2 - 10x - 5 = 0$

22. $7x^2 - 2x - 1 = 0$

23. $5x^2 - 9x + 6 = 0$

24. $3x^2 + 3x + 3 = 0$

Solve Quadratic Equations Using an Appropriate Method Solve the equation.

25. $3x^2 - 27 = 0$

26. $4x^2 - 16 = 0$

27. $25x^2 - 81 = 0$

28. $36x^2 - 25 = 0$

29. $4 - 7r^2 = 1$

30. $0 - 3r^2 = -7$

31. $x^2 + 5x = 24$

32. $x^2 + 4x = 60$

33. $(x - 9)^2 = 64$

34. $(x - 7)^2 = 16$

35. $x^2 = -9x - 16$

36. $x^2 = -3x + 2$

37. $3x^2 = x + 1$

38. $2x^2 = -(5x + 1)$

39. $22 - 4(r + 5)^2 = 6$

40. $23 - 2(t - 8)^2 = 5$

Radical Equations That Give Rise to Quadratic Equations Solve the equation.

41. $\sqrt{t + 72} = t$

42. $\sqrt{2x + 15} = x$

43. $\sqrt{x} + 2 = x$

44. $\sqrt{y} + 56 = y$

45. $y = \sqrt{y + 9} + 3$

46. $r = \sqrt{r + 1} + 5$

47. $\sqrt{r + 90} = r$

48. $\sqrt{r + 42} = r$

49. $t = \sqrt{t + 3} + 9$

50. $t = \sqrt{t + 1} + 89$

51. $\sqrt{51 - x} = x + 5$

52. $\sqrt{148 - x} = x + 8$

Quadratic Formula Applications

53. Two numbers' sum is -1, and their product is -42. Find these two numbers.

These two numbers are [   ].

54. Two numbers' sum is -13, and their product is 42. Find these two numbers.

These two numbers are [   ].

55. Two numbers' sum is 7.7, and their product is −25.5. Find these two numbers.

These two numbers are [ ].
(Use a comma to separate your numbers.)

56. Two numbers' sum is 4.7, and their product is 3.96. Find these two numbers.

These two numbers are [ ].
(Use a comma to separate your numbers.)

57. A rectangle's base is 6 cm longer than its height. The rectangle's area is 112 cm². Find this rectangle's dimensions.

The rectangle's height is [ ].

The rectangle's base is [ ].

58. A rectangle's base is 9 cm longer than its height. The rectangle's area is 162 cm². Find this rectangle's dimensions.

The rectangle's height is [ ].

The rectangle's base is [ ].

59. A rectangle's base is 3 in shorter than four times its height. The rectangle's area is 85 in². Find this rectangle's dimensions.

The rectangle's height is [ ].

The rectangle's base is [ ].

60. A rectangle's base is 1 in shorter than twice its height. The rectangle's area is 15 in². Find this rectangle's dimensions.

The rectangle's height is [ ].

The rectangle's base is [ ].

61. You will build a rectangular sheep pen next to a river. There is no need to build a fence along the river, so you only need to build three sides.

You have a total of 510 feet of fence to use, and the area of the pen must be 31900 square feet. Find the dimensions of the pen. There should be two solutions:When the width is [ ] feet, the length is [ ] feet.

When the width is [ ] feet, the length is [ ] feet.

62. You will build a rectangular sheep pen next to a river. There is no need to build a fence along the river, so you only need to build three sides.

You have a total of 470 feet of fence to use, and the area of the pen must be 27500 square feet. Find the dimensions of the pen. There should be two solutions:When the width is [ ] feet, the length is [ ] feet.

When the width is [ ] feet, the length is [ ] feet.

63. There is a rectangular lot in the garden, with 8 ft in length and 4 ft in width. You plan to expand the lot by an equal length around its four sides, and make the area of the expanded rectangle 140 ft^2. How long should you expand the original lot in four directions?

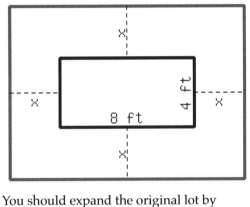

You should expand the original lot by

| |

in four directions.

65. One car started at Town A, and traveled due north at 60 miles per hour. 2 hours later, another car started at the same spot and traveled due east at 55 miles per hour. Assume both cars don't stop, after how many hours since the second car starts would the distance between them be 338 miles? Round your answer to two decimal places if needed.

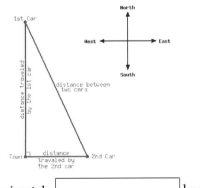

Approximately | | hours since the second car starts, the distance between those two cars would be 338 miles.

64. There is a rectangular lot in the garden, with 9 ft in length and 7 ft in width. You plan to expand the lot by an equal length around its four sides, and make the area of the expanded rectangle 195 ft^2. How long should you expand the original lot in four directions?

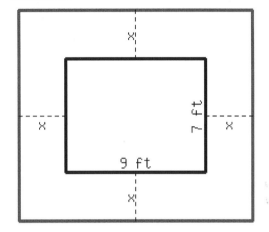

You should expand the original lot by

| |

in four directions.

66. One car started at Town A, and traveled due north at 65 miles per hour. 3 hours later, another car started at the same spot and traveled due east at 40 miles per hour. Assume both cars don't stop, after how many hours since the second car starts would the distance between them be 358 miles? Round your answer to two decimal places if needed.

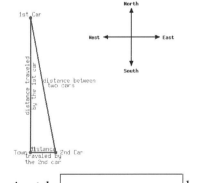

Approximately | | hours since the second car starts, the distance between those two cars would be 358 miles.

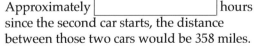

67. An object is launched upward at the height of 370 meters. Its height can be modeled by

$$h = -4.9t^2 + 90t + 370,$$

where h stands for the object's height in meters, and t stands for time passed in seconds since its launch. The object's height will be 380 meters twice before it hits the ground. Find how many seconds since the launch would the object's height be 380 meters. Round your answers to two decimal places if needed.

The object's height would be 380 meters the first time at [＿＿＿＿＿＿＿] seconds, and then the second time at [＿＿＿＿＿＿＿] seconds.

68. An object is launched upward at the height of 400 meters. Its height can be modeled by

$$h = -4.9t^2 + 70t + 400,$$

where h stands for the object's height in meters, and t stands for time passed in seconds since its launch. The object's height will be 430 meters twice before it hits the ground. Find how many seconds since the launch would the object's height be 430 meters. Round your answers to two decimal places if needed.

The object's height would be 430 meters the first time at [＿＿＿＿＿＿＿] seconds, and then the second time at [＿＿＿＿＿＿＿] seconds.

69. Currently, an artist can sell 280 paintings every year at the price of $60.00 per painting. Each time he raises the price per painting by $5.00, he sells 5 fewer paintings every year.

Assume he will raise the price per painting x times, then he will sell $280 - 5x$ paintings every year at the price of $60 + 5x$ dollars. His yearly income can be modeled by the equation:

$$i = (60 + 5x)(280 - 5x)$$

where i stands for his yearly income in dollars. If the artist wants to earn $22,500.00 per year from selling paintings, what new price should he set?

To earn $22,500.00 per year, the artist could sell his paintings at two different prices.

The lower price is [＿＿＿＿＿＿＿] per painting, and the higher price is [＿＿＿＿＿＿＿] per painting.

70. Currently, an artist can sell 210 paintings every year at the price of $130.00 per painting. Each time he raises the price per painting by $10.00, he sells 5 fewer paintings every year.

Assume he will raise the price per painting x times, then he will sell $210 - 5x$ paintings every year at the price of $130 + 10x$ dollars. His yearly income can be modeled by the equation:

$$i = (130 + 10x)(210 - 5x)$$

where i stands for his yearly income in dollars. If the artist wants to earn $33,300.00 per year from selling paintings, what new price should he set?

To earn $33,300.00 per year, the artist could sell his paintings at two different prices.

The lower price is [＿＿＿＿＿＿＿] per painting, and the higher price is [＿＿＿＿＿＿＿] per painting.

71. Solve for x in the equation $mx^2 + nx + p = 0$.

7.3 Complex Solutions to Quadratic Equations

7.3.1 Imaginary Numbers

Let's take a closer look at a square root with a negative radicand. Remember that $\sqrt{16} = 4$ because $4 \cdot 4 = 16$. So what about $\sqrt{-16}$? There is no real number that we can square to get -16, because when you square a real number, the result is either positive or 0. You might think about 4 and -4, but:

$$4 \cdot 4 = 16 \text{ and } (-4)(-4) = 16$$

so neither of those could be $\sqrt{-16}$. To handle this situation, mathematicians separate a factor of $\sqrt{-1}$ and represent it with the letter i.

Definition 7.3.2 Imaginary Numbers. The **imaginary unit**, i, is defined by $i = \sqrt{-1}$. The imaginary unit[1] satisfies the equation $i^2 = -1$. A real number times i, such as 4i, is called an **imaginary number**. ◊

Now we can simplify square roots with negative radicands like $\sqrt{-16}$.

$$\sqrt{-16} = \sqrt{-1 \cdot 16}$$
$$= \sqrt{-1} \cdot \sqrt{16}$$
$$= i \cdot 4$$
$$= 4i$$

Imaginary numbers are used in electrical engineering, physics, computer science, and advanced mathematics. Let's look some more examples.

Example 7.3.3 Simplify $\sqrt{-2}$.
Explanation.

$$\sqrt{-2} = \sqrt{-1 \cdot 2}$$
$$= \sqrt{-1} \cdot \sqrt{2}$$
$$= i\sqrt{2}$$

We write the i in front of the radical because it can be easy to mix up $\sqrt{2}i$ and $\sqrt{2i}$, if you don't draw the radical very carefully.

Example 7.3.4 Simplify $\sqrt{-72}$.
Explanation.

$$\sqrt{-72} = \sqrt{-1 \cdot 36 \cdot 2}$$
$$= \sqrt{-1} \cdot \sqrt{36} \cdot \sqrt{2}$$
$$= 6i\sqrt{2}$$

[1]en.wikipedia.org/wiki/Imaginary_number

7.3.2 Solving Quadratic Equations with Imaginary Solutions

Back in Example 7.1.9, we examined an equation that had no real solution. Let's revisit that example now that we are aware of imaginary numbers.

Example 7.3.5 Solve for x in $x^2 + 49 = 0$, where x might not be a real number.

Explanation.   There is no x term so we will use the square root method.

$$
\begin{aligned}
x^2 + 49 &= 0 \\
x^2 &= -49 \\
x &= \pm\sqrt{-49} \\
x &= \pm\sqrt{-1 \cdot 49} \\
x &= \pm\sqrt{-1} \cdot \sqrt{49} \\
x &= \pm i \cdot 7
\end{aligned}
$$

$$x = -7i \qquad\qquad \text{or} \qquad\qquad x = 7i$$

The solution set is $\{-7i, 7i\}$.

Example 7.3.6 Solve for p in $p^2 + 75 = 0$, where p might not be a real number.

Explanation.   There is no p term so we will use the square root method.

$$
\begin{aligned}
p^2 + 75 &= 0 \\
p^2 &= -75 \\
p &= \pm\sqrt{-75} \\
p &= \pm\sqrt{-1 \cdot 25 \cdot 3} \\
p &= \pm\sqrt{-1} \cdot \sqrt{25} \cdot \sqrt{3} \\
p &= \pm i \cdot 5\sqrt{3}
\end{aligned}
$$

$$p = -5i\sqrt{3} \qquad\qquad \text{or} \qquad\qquad p = 5i\sqrt{3}$$

The solution set is $\left\{-5i\sqrt{3}, 5i\sqrt{3}\right\}$.

7.3.3 Solving Quadratic Equations with Complex Solutions

Sometimes we need to work with a sum of a real number and an imaginary number, like $3 + 2i$ or $-4 - 8i$. These combinations are called "complex numbers".

Definition 7.3.7 Complex Number. A **complex number** is a number that can be expressed in the form $a + bi$, where a and b are real numbers and i is the imaginary unit. In this expression, a is the **real part** and b (not bi) is the **imaginary part** of the complex number[2].   ◊

---

[2]en.wikipedia.org/wiki/Complex_number

Example 7.3.8 In an advanced math course, you might study the relationship between a lynx polulation (or any generic predator) and a hare population (or any generic prey) as time passes. For example, if the predator population is high, they will eat many prey. But then the prey population will become low, so the predators will go hungry and have fewer offspring. With time, the predator population will decline, and that will lead to a rebound in the prey population. Then prey will be plentiful, and the preadator population will rebound, and the whole situaiton starts over. This cycle may take years or even decades to play out.

Strange as it may seem, to understand this phenomenon mathematically, you will need to solve equations similar to:

$$(1 - t)(3 - t) + 10 = 0$$

Let's practice solving this equation.

$$(1 - t)(3 - t) + 10 = 0$$
$$3 - t - 3t + t^2 + 10 = 0$$
$$t^2 - 4t + 13 = 0$$

We can try the quadratic formula.

$$
\begin{aligned}
t &= \frac{4 \pm \sqrt{(-4)^2 - 4(1)(13)}}{2(1)} \\
&= \frac{4 \pm \sqrt{16 - 52}}{2} \\
&= \frac{4 \pm \sqrt{-36}}{2} \\
&= \frac{4 \pm \sqrt{-1} \cdot \sqrt{36}}{2} \\
&= \frac{4 \pm i \cdot 6}{2} \\
&= 2 \pm 3i
\end{aligned}
$$

These two solutions, $2 - 3i$ and $2 + 3i$ have implications for how fast the predator and prey populations rise and fall over time, but an explanation is beyond the scope of basic algebra.

Here are some more examples of equations that have complex number solutions.

Example 7.3.9 Solve for m in $(m - 1)^2 + 18 = 0$, where m might not be a real number.

Explanation. This equation has a squared expression so we will use the square root method.

$$
\begin{aligned}
(m - 1)^2 + 18 &= 0 \\
(m - 1)^2 &= -18 \\
m - 1 &= \pm\sqrt{-18} \\
m - 1 &= \pm\sqrt{-1 \cdot 9 \cdot 2} \\
m - 1 &= \pm\sqrt{-1} \cdot \sqrt{9} \cdot \sqrt{2} \\
m - 1 &= \pm i \cdot 3\sqrt{2} \\
m &= 1 \pm i \cdot 3\sqrt{2}
\end{aligned}
$$

$$m = 1 - 3i\sqrt{2} \qquad\qquad \text{or} \qquad\qquad m = 1 + 3i\sqrt{2}$$

The solution set is $\left\{1 - 3i\sqrt{2}, 1 + 3i\sqrt{2}\right\}$.

Example 7.3.10 Solve for y in $y^2 - 4y + 13 = 0$, where y might not be a real number.

Explanation. Note that there is a y term, so the square root method is not available. We will use the quadratic formula. We identify that $a = 1$, $b = -4$ and $c = 13$ and substitute them into the quadratic formula.

$$\begin{aligned}
y &= \frac{-b \pm \sqrt{b^2 - 4ac}}{2a} \\
&= \frac{-(-4) \pm \sqrt{(-4)^2 - 4(1)(13)}}{2(1)} \\
&= \frac{4 \pm \sqrt{16 - 52}}{2} \\
&= \frac{4 \pm \sqrt{-36}}{2} \\
&= \frac{4 \pm \sqrt{-1} \cdot \sqrt{36}}{2} \\
&= \frac{4 \pm 6i}{2} \\
&= 2 \pm 3i
\end{aligned}$$

The solution set is $\{2 - 3i, 2 + 3i\}$.

Note that in Example 7.3.10, the expressions $2 + 3i$ and $2 - 3i$ are fully simplified. In the same way that the terms 2 and $3x$ cannot be combined, the terms 2 and $3i$ can not be combined.

Remark 7.3.11 Each complex solution can be checked, just as every real solution can be checked. For example, to check the solution of $2 + 3i$ from Example 7.3.10, we would replace y with $2 + 3i$ and check that the two sides of the equation are equal. In doing so, we will need to use the fact that $i^2 = -1$. This check is shown here:

$$\begin{aligned}
y^2 - 4y + 13 &= 0 \\
(2 + 3i)^2 - 4(2 + 3i) + 13 &\overset{?}{=} 0 \\
(2^2 + 2(3i) + 2(3i) + (3i)^2) - 4 \cdot 2 - 4 \cdot (3i) + 13 &\overset{?}{=} 0 \\
4 + 6i + 6i + 9i^2 - 8 - 12i + 13 &\overset{?}{=} 0 \\
4 + 9(-1) - 8 + 13 &\overset{?}{=} 0 \\
4 - 9 - 8 + 13 &\overset{?}{=} 0 \\
0 &\overset{\checkmark}{=} 0
\end{aligned}$$

7.3.4 Reading Questions

1. What is $\left(i^2\right)^2$?

2. A number like $4i$ is called a ⬚ number. A number like $3 + 4i$ is called a ⬚ number.

7.3.5 Exercises

Simplifying Square Roots with Negative Radicands Simplify the radical and write it as a complex number using i.

1. $\sqrt{-30}$	2. $\sqrt{-30}$	3. $\sqrt{-24}$
4. $\sqrt{-56}$	5. $\sqrt{-270}$	6. $\sqrt{-240}$

Quadratic Equations with Imaginary and Complex Solutions Solve the quadratic equation. Solutions could be complex numbers.

7. $x^2 = -100$	8. $x^2 = -49$	9. $5y^2 - 6 = -86$
10. $3y^2 - 6 = -306$	11. $-2r^2 - 9 = 3$	12. $-5r^2 - 7 = 8$
13. $-3r^2 - 10 = 140$	14. $-3t^2 - 4 = 131$	15. $-8(t - 10)^2 - 8 = 64$
16. $-6(x + 5)^2 - 8 = 478$	17. $x^2 + 2x + 5 = 0$	18. $y^2 + 4y + 5 = 0$
19. $y^2 + 4y + 11 = 0$	20. $r^2 - 8r + 19 = 0$	

7.4 Solving Equations in General

In your algebra studies, you have learned how to solve linear equations, quadratic equations, and radical equations. In this section, we examine some similarities among the processes for solving these equations. Understanding these similarities can improve your general equation solving ability, even into the future with new equations that are not of these three types.

7.4.1 Equations Where the Variable Appears Once

Here are some examples of equations that all have something in common: the variable only appears once.

$$2x + 1 = 7 \qquad\qquad (x + 4)^2 = 36 \qquad\qquad \sqrt{2x - 3} = 3$$

For equations like this, there is a strategy for solving them that will keep you from overcomplicating things. In each case, according to the order of operations, the variable is having some things "done" to it in a specific order.

With $2x + 1 = 7$,

1. x is multiplied by 2

2. then that result is added to 1

3. and this result is a number, 7

With $(x + 4)^2 = 36$,

1. x is added to 4

2. then that result is squared

3. and this result is a number, 36

With $\sqrt{2x - 3} = 3$,

1. x is multiplied by 2

2. then that result has 3 subtracted from it

3. then that result has a square root applied

4. and this result is a number, 3

Because there is just one instance of the variable, and then things happen to that value in a specific order according to the order of operations, then there is a good strategy to solve these equations. We can just *undo each step in the opposite order*.

Example 7.4.2 Solve the equation $2x + 1 = 7$.

Explanation. The actions that happen to x are *multiply* by 2, and then *add* 1. So we will do the opposite actions in the opposite order to each side of the equation. We will *subtract* 1 and then *divide* by 2.

$$\begin{aligned} 2x + 1 &= 7 & &\text{now subtract 1 from each side} \\ 2x + 1 - 1 &= 7 - 1 \\ 2x &= 6 & &\text{now divide by 2 on each side} \\ \frac{2x}{2} &= \frac{6}{2} \\ x &= 3 \end{aligned}$$

You should check this solution by substituting it into the original equation.

Example 7.4.3 Solve the equation $(x + 4)^2 = 36$.

Explanation. The actions that happen to x are *add* 4, and then *square*. So we will do the opposite actions in the opposite order to each side of the equation. We will apply the Square Root Property and then *subtract* 4.

$$(x+4)^2 = 36 \qquad \text{now apply the Square Root Property}$$
$$x+4 = \pm\sqrt{36}$$
$$x+4 = \pm 6 \qquad \text{now subtract 4 on each side}$$
$$x+4-4 = \pm 6 - 4$$
$$x = \pm 6 - 4$$

$$x = -6-4 \qquad \text{or} \qquad x = 6-4$$
$$x = -10 \qquad \text{or} \qquad x = 2$$

You should check these solutions by substituting them into the original equation.

Example 7.4.4 Solve the equation $\sqrt{2x-3} = 3$.

Explanation. The actions that happen to x are *multiply* by 2, and then *subtract* 3, and then apply the square root. So we will do the opposite actions in the opposite order to each side of the equation. We will *square* both sides, *add* 3 and then *divide* by 2.

$$\sqrt{2x-3} = 3 \qquad \text{now square both sides}$$
$$2x - 3 = 9 \qquad \text{now add 3 to each side}$$
$$2x - 3 + 3 = 9 + 3$$
$$2x = 12 \qquad \text{now divide by 2 on each side}$$
$$\frac{2x}{2} = \frac{12}{2}$$
$$x = 6$$

You should check this solution by substituting it into the original equation.

7.4.2 Equations With More Than One Instance of the Variable

Now consider equations like

$$5\overset{\downarrow}{x} + 1 = 3\overset{\downarrow}{x} + 2 \qquad \overset{\downarrow}{x}^2 + 6\overset{\downarrow}{x} = -8 \qquad \sqrt{\overset{\downarrow}{x} - 3} = \sqrt{\overset{\downarrow}{x} - 1}$$

In these examples, the variable appears more than once. We can't exactly dive in to the strategy of undoing each step in the opposite order. For each of these equations, remind yourself that you can apply any operation you want, as long as you apply it to both sides of the equation. In many cases, you will find that there is some basic algebra move you can take that will turn the equation into something more "standard" that you know how to work with.

With $5x + 1 = 3x + 2$, we have a linear equation. If we can simply reorganize the terms to combine like terms, a solution will be apparent.

With $x^2 + 6x = -8$, adding 8 to both sides would give us a quadratic equation in standard form. And then the quadratic formula can be used.

With $\sqrt{x - 3} = \sqrt{x} - 1$, the complication is those two radicals. We can take any action we like as long as we apply it to both sides, and *squaring* both sides would remove at least one radical. Maybe after that we will have a simpler equation.

Example 7.4.5 Solve the equation $5x + 1 = 3x + 2$.

Explanation.   We'll use basic algebra to rearrange the terms.

$$
\begin{aligned}
5x + 1 &= 3x + 2 &&\text{now subtract 1 from each side} \\
5x &= 3x + 1 &&\text{now subtract } 3x \text{ from each side} \\
2x &= 1 &&\text{now divide by 2 on each side} \\
x &= \frac{1}{2}
\end{aligned}
$$

You should check this solution by substituting it into the original equation.

Example 7.4.6 Solve the equation $x^2 + 6x = -8$.

Explanation.   Adding 8 to each side will give us a quadratic equation in standard form, and then we may apply The Quadratic Formula.

$$
\begin{aligned}
x^2 + 6x &= -8 &&\text{now add 8 to each side} \\
x^2 + 6x + 8 &= 0 &&\text{now apply The Quadratic Formula}
\end{aligned}
$$

$$
\begin{aligned}
x &= \frac{-6 \pm \sqrt{6^2 - 4(1)(8)}}{2(1)} \\
&= \frac{-6 \pm \sqrt{36 - 32}}{2} \\
&= \frac{-6 \pm \sqrt{4}}{2} \\
&= \frac{-6 \pm 2}{2}
\end{aligned}
$$

$$
\begin{aligned}
x &= \frac{-6 - 2}{2} &&\text{or} &&& x = \frac{-6 + 2}{2} \\
x &= \frac{-8}{2} &&\text{or} &&& x = \frac{-4}{2} \\
x &= -4 &&\text{or} &&& x = -2
\end{aligned}
$$

You should check these solutions by substituting them into the original equation.

Example 7.4.7 Solve the equation $\sqrt{x - 3} = \sqrt{x} - 1$.

Explanation. Hoping to obtain a simpler equation, we will square each side. This will eliminate at least one radical, which may help.

$$\sqrt{x-3} = \sqrt{x} - 1 \qquad \text{now square both sides}$$
$$\left(\sqrt{x-3}\right)^2 = \left(\sqrt{x} - 1\right)^2$$
$$x - 3 = \left(\sqrt{x}\right)^2 - 2\sqrt{x} + 1$$
$$x - 3 = x - 2\sqrt{x} + 1 \qquad \text{now note that there are some like terms}$$
$$-3 = -2\sqrt{x} + 1 \qquad \text{now we have an equation with only one instance of the variable}$$
$$-4 = -2\sqrt{x}$$
$$2 = \sqrt{x}$$
$$2^2 = x$$
$$x = 4$$

You should check this solution by substituting it into the original equation. It is *especially* important to do this when the equation was a radical equation. At one point, we squared both sides, and this can introduce extraneous solutions (see Remark 6.4.4).

7.4.3 Solving For a Variable in Terms of Other Variables

In the examples so far in this section, there has been one variable (but possibly more than one instance of that variable). This leaves out important situations in science applications where you have a formula with *multiple* variables, and you need to isolate *one* of them. Fortunately these situations are not more difficult than what we have explored so far, as long as you can keep track of which variable you are trying to solve for.

Example 7.4.8 In physics, there is a formula for converting a Celsius temperature to Fahrenheit:

$$F = \frac{9}{5}C + 32$$

Solve this equation for C in terms of F.

Explanation. The variable we are after is C, and that variable only appears once. So we will apply the strategy of undoing the things that are happening to C. First C is multiplied by $\frac{9}{5}$, and then it is added to 32. So we will undo these actions in the opposite order: *subtract* 32 and then multiply by $\frac{5}{9}$ (or *divide* by $\frac{9}{5}$ if you prefer).

$$F = \frac{9}{5}\overset{\downarrow}{C} + 32$$
$$F - 32 = \frac{9}{5}\overset{\downarrow}{C} + 32 - 32$$
$$F - 32 = \frac{9}{5}\overset{\downarrow}{C}$$
$$\frac{5}{9} \cdot (F - 32) = \frac{5}{9} \cdot \frac{9}{5}\overset{\downarrow}{C}$$
$$\frac{5}{9}(F - 32) = \overset{\downarrow}{C}$$

$$C = \frac{5}{9}(F - 32)$$

We are satisfied, because we have isolated C in terms of F.

Example 7.4.9 In physics, when an object of mass m is moving with a speed v, its "kinetic energy" E is given by:

$$E = \frac{1}{2}mv^2$$

Solve this equation for v in terms of the other variables.

Explanation. The variable we are after is v, and that variable only appears once. So we will apply the strategy of undoing the things that are happening to v. First v is squared, then it is multiplied by m and by $\frac{1}{2}$. So we will undo these actions in the opposite order: *multiply* by 2, *divide* by m, and apply the square root.

$$E = \frac{1}{2}mv^{\overset{\downarrow}{2}}$$

$$2 \cdot E = 2 \cdot \frac{1}{2}mv^{\overset{\downarrow}{2}}$$

$$2E = mv^{\overset{\downarrow}{2}}$$

$$\frac{2E}{m} = \frac{mv^{\overset{\downarrow}{2}}}{m}$$

$$\frac{2E}{m} = v^{\overset{\downarrow}{2}}$$

$$\pm\sqrt{\frac{2E}{m}} = \overset{\downarrow}{v}$$

$$v = \sqrt{\frac{2E}{m}}$$

At the very end, we chose the positive square root, since a speed v cannot be negative. We are satisfied, because we have isolated v in terms of E and m.

7.4.4 Reading Questions

1.   When there is only one instance of a variable in an equation, describe a strategy for solving the equation.

2.   You can do whatever algebra you like to the sides of an equation, as long as you do what?

7.4.5 Exercises

Solve the equation.

1.	$x + 3 = -8$	**2.**	$9x + 5 = 4$	**3.**	$7x - 2 = -4x$
4.	$9x + 6 = -9x$	**5.**	$-9x - 6 = 5x - 9$	**6.**	$-7x + 4 = -3x + 5$
7.	$-8x^2 = -200$	**8.**	$3x^2 = 108$	**9.**	$6(x - 8)^2 = 294$

10. $-3(x+19)^2 = -192$

11. $2x^2 - 162 = 0$

12. $-4x^2 + 484 = 0$

13. $49x^2 = 144$

14. $x^2 = 4$

15. $3x^2 = 2$

16. $13x^2 = 5$

17. $6(x+5)^2 = 5$

18. $5(x-3)^2 = 2$

19. $2x^2 + 6x - 9 = 0$

20. $-x^2 + 3x + 3 = 0$

21. $6x^2 + 8x + 7 = 9$

22. $8x^2 + 6x + 3 = 4$

23. $x^2 + 4x + 1 = 7x + 8$

24. $2x^2 + x + 7 = 3x + 8$

25. $x^2 + 9x + 6 = 6x^2 + 8x + 5$

26. $4x^2 + 9x + 7 = 5x^2 + 2x + 4$

27. $\sqrt{-9x - 2} = 8$

28. $\sqrt{2x + 4} = 6$

29. $\sqrt[3]{4x - 3} = -5$

30. $\sqrt[3]{6x - 9} = 3$

31. $\sqrt[4]{8x + 3} = -9$

32. $\sqrt[4]{-9x - 4} = -1$

33. $\sqrt{x - 7} = \sqrt{x + 9} + 7$

34. $\sqrt{x - 4} = \sqrt{x + 2} - 4$

35. $\sqrt{9x + 8} = \sqrt{6x - 8} + 4$

36. $\sqrt{7x - 4} = \sqrt{8x + 6} - 3$

Solve an Equation for a Variable

37. Solve the equation $A = bh$ for b.

38. Solve the equation $A = bh$ for h.

39. Solve the equation $P = 2(\ell + w)$ for l.

40. Solve the equation $P = 2(\ell + w)$ for w.

41. Solve the equation $A = \frac{1}{2}bh$ for b.

42. Solve the equation $A = \frac{1}{2}bh$ for h.

43. Solve the equation $y = mx + b$ for m.

44. Solve the equation $y = mx + b$ for x.

45. Solve the equation $y = mx + b$ for b.

46. Solve the equation $y = m(x - h) + k$ for k.

47. Solve the equation $y = m(x - h) + k$ for h.

48. Solve the equation $y = m(x - h) + k$ for x.

49. Solve the equation $c = 2\pi r$ for r.

50. Solve the equation $c = \pi d$ for d.

51. Solve the equation $A = s^2$ for s. Assume $s > 0$.

52. Solve the equation $A = \pi r^2$ for r. Assume $r > 0$.

53. Solve the equation $V = \pi r^2 h$ for r. Assume $r > 0$.

54. Solve the equation $V = \frac{1}{3}s^2h$ for s. Assume $s > 0$.

55. Solve the equation $V = \pi r^2 h$ for h.

56. Solve the equation $V = \frac{1}{3}s^2h$ for h.

57. Solve the equation $V = s^3$ for s.

58. Solve the equation $V = \frac{4}{3}\pi r^3$ for r.

59. Solve the equation $S = 6s^2$ for s. Assume $s > 0$.

60. Solve the equation $S = 4\pi r^2$ for r. Assume $r > 0$.

61. Solve the equation $v = \frac{d}{t}$ for d.

62. Solve the equation $v = \frac{d}{t}$ for t.

63. Solve the equation $p = \frac{1}{2}gt^2 + vt + d$ for t.

64. Solve the equation $y = ax^2 + bx + c$ for x.

65. Solve the equation $F = ma$ for m.

66. Solve the equation $F = ma$ for a.

67. Solve the equation $a = \frac{v^2}{r}$ for v. Assume $v > 0$.

68. Solve the equation $K = \frac{1}{2}mv^2$ for v. Assume $v > 0$.

69. Solve the equation $T = 2\pi\sqrt{\frac{\ell}{g}}$ for l.

70. Solve the equation $T = 2\pi\sqrt{\frac{\ell}{g}}$ for g.

7.5 Solving Quadratic Equations Chapter Review

7.5.1 Solving Quadratic Equations by Using a Square Root

In Section 7.1 we covered how to solve quadratic equations using the square root property and how to use the Pythagorean Theorem.

Example 7.5.1 Solving Quadratic Equations Using the Square Root Property. Solve for w in $3(2-w)^2-24 = 0$.

Explanation. It's important here to suppress any urge you may have to expand the squared binomial. We begin by isolating the squared expression.

$$3(2-w)^2 - 24 = 0$$
$$3(2-w)^2 = 24$$
$$(2-w)^2 = 8$$

Now that we have the squared expression isolated, we can use the square root property.

$2-w = -\sqrt{8}$	or	$2-w = \sqrt{8}$
$2-w = -\sqrt{4\cdot 2}$	or	$2-w = \sqrt{4\cdot 2}$
$2-w = -\sqrt{4}\cdot\sqrt{2}$	or	$2-w = \sqrt{4}\cdot\sqrt{2}$
$2-w = -2\sqrt{2}$	or	$2-w = 2\sqrt{2}$
$-w = -2\sqrt{2}-2$	or	$-w = 2\sqrt{2}-2$
$w = 2\sqrt{2}+2$	or	$w = -2\sqrt{2}+2$

The solution set is $\left\{2\sqrt{2}+2, -2\sqrt{2}+2\right\}$.

Example 7.5.2 The Pythagorean Theorem. Faven was doing some wood working in her garage. She needed to cut a triangular piece of wood for her project that had a hypotenuse of 16 inches, and the sides of the triangle should be equal in length. How long should she make her sides?

Explanation. Let's start by representing the length of the triangle, measured in inches, by the letter x. That would also make the other side x inches long.

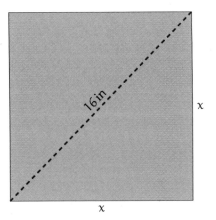

Figure 7.5.3: Piece of wood with labels for Faven

Faven should now set up the Pythagorean theorem regarding the picture. That would be

$$x^2 + x^2 = 16^2$$

Solving this equation, we have:

$$x^2 + x^2 = 16^2$$
$$2x^2 = 256$$
$$x^2 = 128$$
$$\sqrt{x^2} = \sqrt{128}$$
$$x = \sqrt{64 \cdot 2}$$
$$x = \sqrt{64} \cdot \sqrt{2}$$
$$x = 8\sqrt{2}$$
$$x \approx 11.3$$

Faven should make the sides of her triangle about 11.3 inches long to force the hypotenuse to be 16 inches long.

7.5.2 The Quadratic Formula

In Section 7.2 we covered how to use the quadratic formula to solve any quadratic equation.

Example 7.5.4 Solving Quadratic Equations with the Quadratic Formula. Solve the equations using the quadratic formula.

    a. $x^2 + 4x = 6$ b. $5x^2 - 2x + 1 = 0$

Explanation.

    a. First we should change the equation into standard form.

$$x^2 + 4x = 6$$

$$x^2 + 4x - 6 = 0$$

Next, we check and see that we cannot factor the left side or use the square root property so we must use the quadratic formula. We identify that $a = 1$, $b = 4$, and $c = -6$. We will substitute them into the quadratic formula:

$$x = \frac{-b \pm \sqrt{b^2 - 4ac}}{2a}$$

$$x = \frac{-4 \pm \sqrt{(4)^2 - 4(1)(-6)}}{2(1)}$$

$$= \frac{-4 \pm \sqrt{16 + 24}}{2}$$

$$= \frac{-4 \pm \sqrt{40}}{2}$$

$$= \frac{-4 \pm \sqrt{4 \cdot 10}}{2}$$

$$= \frac{-4 \pm \sqrt{4} \cdot \sqrt{10}}{2}$$

$$= \frac{-4 \pm 2\sqrt{10}}{2}$$

$$= -\frac{4}{2} \pm \frac{2\sqrt{10}}{2}$$

$$= -2 \pm \sqrt{10}$$

So the solution set is $\left\{ -2 + \sqrt{10}, -2 - \sqrt{10} \right\}$.

b. Since the equation $5x^2 - 2x + 1 = 0$ is already in standard form, we check and see that we cannot factor the left side or use the square root property so we must use the quadratic formula. We identify that $a = 5$, $b = -2$, and $c = 1$. We will substitute them into the quadratic formula:

$$x = \frac{-b \pm \sqrt{b^2 - 4ac}}{2a}$$

$$x = \frac{-(-2) \pm \sqrt{(-2)^2 - 4(5)(1)}}{2(5)}$$

$$= \frac{2 \pm \sqrt{4 - 20}}{10}$$

$$= \frac{2 \pm \sqrt{-16}}{10}$$

Since the solutions have square roots of negative numbers, we must conclude that there are no real solutions.

7.5.3 Complex Solutions to Quadratic Equations

In Section 7.3 we covered what both imaginary numbers and complex numbers are, as well as how to solve quadratic equations where the solutions are imaginary numbers or complex numbers.

Example 7.5.5 Imaginary Numbers. Simplify the expression $\sqrt{-12}$ using the imaginary number, i.

Explanation. Start by splitting the -1 from the 12 and by looking for the largest perfect-square factor of -12, which happens to be 4.

$$\begin{aligned}
\sqrt{-12} &= \sqrt{4 \cdot -1 \cdot 3} \\
&= \sqrt{4} \cdot \sqrt{-1} \cdot \sqrt{3} \\
&= 2i\sqrt{3}
\end{aligned}$$

Example 7.5.6 Solving Quadratic Equations with Imaginary Solutions. Solve for m in $2m^2 + 16 = 0$, where p is an imaginary number.

Explanation. There is no m term so we will use the square root method.

$$\begin{aligned}
2m^2 + 16 &= 0 \\
2m^2 &= -16 \\
m^2 &= -8
\end{aligned}$$

$$\begin{array}{ccc}
m = -\sqrt{-8} & \text{or} & m = \sqrt{-8} \\
m = -\sqrt{4} \cdot \sqrt{-1} \cdot \sqrt{2} & \text{or} & m = \sqrt{4} \cdot \sqrt{-1} \cdot \sqrt{2} \\
m = -2i\sqrt{2} & \text{or} & m = 2i\sqrt{2}
\end{array}$$

The solution set is $\left\{ -2i\sqrt{2}, 2i\sqrt{2} \right\}$.

Example 7.5.7 Solving Quadratic Equations with Complex Solutions. Solve the equation $3(v-2)^2 + 54 = 0$, where v is a complex number.

Explanation.

$$\begin{aligned}
3(v-2)^2 + 54 &= 0 \\
3(v-2)^2 &= -54 \\
(v-2)^2 &= -18
\end{aligned}$$

$$\begin{array}{ccc}
v - 2 = -\sqrt{-18} & \text{or} & v - 2 = \sqrt{-18} \\
v - 2 = -\sqrt{9 \cdot -1 \cdot 2} & \text{or} & v - 2 = \sqrt{9 \cdot -1 \cdot 2} \\
v - 2 = -\sqrt{9} \cdot \sqrt{-1} \cdot \sqrt{2} & \text{or} & v - 2 = \sqrt{9} \cdot \sqrt{-1} \cdot \sqrt{2} \\
v - 2 = -3i\sqrt{2} & \text{or} & v - 2 = 3i\sqrt{2} \\
v = 2 - 3i\sqrt{2} & \text{or} & v = 2 + 3i\sqrt{2}
\end{array}$$

So, the solution set is $\left\{ 2 + 3i\sqrt{2}, 2 - 3i\sqrt{2} \right\}$.

7.5.4 Solving Equations in General

In Section 2.1 we learned how to solve linear equations. In Section 6.4 we learned how to solve radical equations. In Section 7.1 and Section, we learned how to solve quadratic equations.

Then in Section 7.4 we looked at a few strategies to solve equations in general, often relying on those earlier specific techniques.

Example 7.5.8 Equations where the Variable Appears Once. Solve the equations using an effective method.

   a. $(x-4)^2 - 2 = 0$ b. $\sqrt{3x+2} - 2 = 5$ c. $3(5x-6) - 7 = 2$

Explanation.

  a. Since the variable x only appears once, we can apply steps one at a time to undo all of the operations that are done to x and eventually isolate it.

$$(x-4)^2 - 2 = 0$$
$$(x-4)^2 = 2$$
$$x - 4 = \pm\sqrt{2}$$
$$x = 4 \pm \sqrt{2}$$

So the solution set is $\left\{4 + \sqrt{2}, 4 - \sqrt{2}\right\}$

  b. Since the variable x only appears once, we can apply steps one at a time to undo all of the operations that are done to x and eventually isolate it.

$$\sqrt{3x+2} - 2 = 5$$
$$\sqrt{3x+2} = 7$$
$$\left(\sqrt{3x+2}\right)^2 = 7^2$$
$$3x + 2 = 49$$
$$3x = 47$$
$$x = \frac{47}{3}$$

At this point $\frac{47}{3}$ is only a potential solution. We may have introduced an extraneous solution at the point where we squared both sides. So we should check it.

$$\sqrt{3 \cdot \frac{47}{3} + 2} - 2 \overset{?}{=} 5$$
$$\sqrt{47 + 2} \overset{?}{=} 7$$
$$\sqrt{49} \overset{\checkmark}{=} 7$$

So, the solution set is $\left\{\frac{47}{3}\right\}$.

  c. Since the variable x only appears once, we can apply steps one at a time to undo all of the operations that are done to x and eventually isolate it.

$$3(5x-6) - 7 = 2$$

$$3(5x - 6) = 9$$
$$5x - 6 = 3$$
$$5x = 9$$
$$x = \frac{9}{5}$$

The solution set is $\left\{\frac{9}{5}\right\}$.

Example 7.5.9 Equations With More Than One Instance of the Variable. Recognize that these equations have more than one instance of the variable, so it is not immediately possible to isolate the variable by undoing the operations that are done to it. Instead, call upon a special technique to solve the equation.

    a. $(x - 4)^2 + 2x = 0$ b. $16x - 2(3x - 1) = 7$ c. $\sqrt{x + 2} = x - 4$

Explanation.

    a. To solve the equation $(x - 4)^2 + 2x = 0$, note that it is a quadratic equation, and we can write it in standard form.

$$(x - 4)^2 + 2x = 0$$
$$x^2 - 8x + 16 + 2x = 0$$
$$x^2 - 6x + 16 = 0$$

Now we may use the quadratic formula 7.2.2.

$$x = \frac{-b \pm \sqrt{b^2 - 4ac}}{2a}$$
$$x = \frac{-(-6) \pm \sqrt{(-6)^2 - 4(1)(16)}}{2(1)}$$
$$= \frac{6 \pm \sqrt{36 - 48}}{2}$$
$$= \frac{6 \pm \sqrt{-12}}{2}$$

At this point, we notice that the solutions are complex. Continue to simplify until they are completely reduced.

$$x = \frac{6 \pm \sqrt{4 \cdot -1 \cdot 3}}{2}$$
$$= \frac{6 \pm \sqrt{4} \cdot \sqrt{-1} \cdot \sqrt{3}}{2}$$
$$= \frac{6 \pm 2i\sqrt{3}}{2}$$
$$= \frac{6}{2} \pm \frac{2i\sqrt{3}}{2}$$
$$= 3 \pm i\sqrt{3}$$

So the solution set is $\left\{3 - i\sqrt{3}, 3 + i\sqrt{3}\right\}$.

b. To solve the equation $16x - 2(3x - 1) = 3$ we first we first note that it is linear. Since it is linear, we just need to follow the steps outlined in Process 2.1.4.

$$16x - 2(3x - 1) = 7$$
$$16x - 6x + 3 = 7$$
$$10x + 3 = 7$$
$$10x = 4$$
$$x = \frac{4}{10}$$
$$x = \frac{2}{5}$$

So, the solution set is $\left\{ \frac{2}{5} \right\}$.

c. Since the equation $\sqrt{x + 2} = x - 4$ is a radical equation, we should isolate the radical (which it already is) and square both sides of the equation.

$$\sqrt{x + 2} = x - 4$$
$$\left(\sqrt{x + 2} \right)^2 = (x - 4)^2$$
$$x + 2 = x^2 - 8x + 16$$
$$0 = x^2 - 9x + 14$$

Since the equation is now quadratic, we may use the quadratic formula 7.2.2 to solve it.

$$x = \frac{-b \pm \sqrt{b^2 - 4ac}}{2a}$$
$$x = \frac{-(-9) \pm \sqrt{(-9)^2 - 4(1)(14)}}{2(1)}$$
$$= \frac{9 \pm \sqrt{81 - 56}}{2}$$
$$= \frac{9 \pm \sqrt{25}}{2}$$
$$= \frac{9 \pm 5}{2}$$

$$x = \frac{9 - 5}{2} \qquad \text{or} \qquad x = \frac{9 + 5}{2}$$
$$x = \frac{4}{2} \qquad \text{or} \qquad x = \frac{14}{2}$$
$$x = 2 \qquad \text{or} \qquad x = 7$$

Since this is a radical equation, we should verify our solutions and look out for "extraneous solutions".

$$\sqrt{2 + 2} \overset{?}{=} 2 - 4 \qquad \text{or} \qquad \sqrt{7 + 2} \overset{?}{=} 7 - 4$$
$$\sqrt{4} \overset{no}{=} -2 \qquad \text{or} \qquad \sqrt{9} \overset{\checkmark}{=} 3$$

So the solution set is $\{7\}$.

Example 7.5.10 Solving For a Variable in Terms of Other Variables. Often in science classes, you are given a formula that needs to be rearranged to be useful to a situation. Below are a few equations from physics that describe the natural world.

  a. Solve the equation $v^2 = v_0^2 + 2ax$ for x. (This equation describes the motion of objects that are accelerating.)

  b. Solve the equation $c\ell = \ell_0 \sqrt{c^2 - v^2}$ for v. (This equation describes the size of things moving at very fast speeds.)

  c. Solve the equation $y = \frac{\alpha t^2}{2} + vt$ for t. (This is another equation that describes the motion of objects that are accelerating.)

Explanation.

  a. Since x only appears once in the euqation, we only need to undo the operations that are done to it.

$$v^2 = v_0^2 + 2ax$$
$$v^2 - v_0^2 = 2ax$$
$$\frac{v^2 - v_0^2}{2a} = x$$

So we find $x = \frac{v^2 - v_0^2}{2a}$.

  b. Since v only appears once in the euqation, we only need to undo the operations that are done to it. According to the order of operations, on the right side of the equation,

  (a) v is squared.

  (b) The result is negated.

  (c) The result is added to c^2.

  (d) The result has a square root applied.

  (e) The result is multiplied by ℓ_0.

So we do all of the opposite things in the opposite order.

$$c\ell = \ell_0 \sqrt{c^2 - v^2}$$
$$\frac{c \cdot \ell}{\ell_0} = \sqrt{c^2 - v^2}$$
$$\left(\frac{c \cdot \ell}{\ell_0}\right)^2 = \left(\sqrt{c^2 - v^2}\right)^2$$
$$\left(\frac{c \cdot \ell}{\ell_0}\right)^2 = c^2 - v^2$$
$$\left(\frac{c \cdot \ell}{\ell_0}\right)^2 - c^2 = -v^2$$
$$-\left(\frac{c \cdot \ell}{\ell_0}\right)^2 + c^2 = v^2$$

$$\pm\sqrt{-\left(\frac{c\cdot\ell}{\ell_0}\right)^2 + c^2} = v$$

$$\pm\sqrt{c^2 - \left(\frac{c\cdot\ell}{\ell_0}\right)^2} = v$$

So, we find $v = \pm\sqrt{c^2 - \left(\frac{c\cdot\ell}{\ell_0}\right)^2}$.

c. This is a quadratic equtaion when we view t as the variable. First, we should rearrange the equation to standard form.

$$y = \frac{\alpha t^2}{2} + vt$$

$$0 = \frac{\alpha}{2}t^2 + vt - y$$

It is helpful with many equations to "clear denominators". In this case, that means multiplying each side of the equation by 2.

$$0 = \alpha t^2 + 2vt - 2y$$

Now, we may apply the quadratic formula 7.2.2.

$$t = \frac{-b \pm \sqrt{b^2 - 4ac}}{2a}$$

$$t = \frac{-2v \pm \sqrt{(2v)^2 - 4\alpha(-2y)}}{2\alpha}$$

$$t = \frac{-2v \pm \sqrt{4v^2 + 8\alpha y}}{2\alpha}$$

$$t = \frac{-2v \pm \sqrt{4\left(v^2 + 2\alpha y\right)}}{2\alpha}$$

$$t = \frac{-2v \pm 2\sqrt{v^2 + 2\alpha y}}{2\alpha}$$

$$t = \frac{-v \pm \sqrt{v^2 + 2\alpha y}}{\alpha}$$

So we find $t = \frac{-v \pm \sqrt{v^2 + 2\alpha y}}{\alpha}$.

7.5.5 Exercises

Solving Quadratic Equations by Using a Square Root Solve the equation.

1. $x^2 = 27$
2. $x^2 = 63$
3. $64x^2 = 9$
4. $4x^2 = 81$
5. $(x+6)^2 = 36$
6. $(x+9)^2 = 4$
7. $-4 - 5(x-9)^2 = -9$
8. $18 - 3(x-9)^2 = 6$

9.

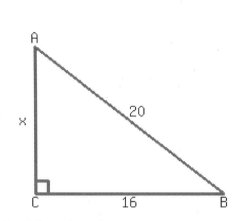

Find the value of x.

10.

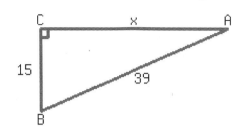

Find the value of x.

11. Devon is designing a rectangular garden. The garden's diagonal must be 64.6 feet, and the ratio between the garden's base and height must be 15 : 8. Find the length of the garden's base and height.

The garden's base is [   ]

feet and its height is [   ].

12. Tammy is designing a rectangular garden. The garden's diagonal must be 13.5 feet, and the ratio between the garden's base and height must be 4 : 3. Find the length of the garden's base and height.

The garden's base is [   ]

feet and its height is [   ].

The Quadratic Formula Solve the equation.

13. $28x^2 + 29x + 6 = 0$ **14.** $24x^2 + 29x - 4 = 0$ **15.** $x^2 = -7x - 11$

16. $x^2 = 7x - 11$ **17.** $4x^2 + 4x + 6 = 0$ **18.** $2x^2 + 7x + 7 = 0$

19. $x^2 - 26x = 0$ **20.** $x^2 - 6x = 0$ **21.** $x^2 - 7x = 18$

22. $x^2 - x = 20$ **23.** $x^2 = 9x - 19$ **24.** $x^2 = -5x - 5$

25. An object is launched upward at the height of 200 meters. Its height can be modeled by

$$h = -4.9t^2 + 70t + 200,$$

where h stands for the object's height in meters, and t stands for time passed in seconds since its launch. The object's height will be 240 meters twice before it hits the ground. Find how many seconds since the launch would the object's height be 240 meters. Round your answers to two decimal places if needed.
The object's height would be 240 meters the

first time at [   ] seconds,
and then the second time at
[   ] seconds.

26. An object is launched upward at the height of 220 meters. Its height can be modeled by

$$h = -4.9t^2 + 50t + 220,$$

where h stands for the object's height in meters, and t stands for time passed in seconds since its launch. The object's height will be 230 meters twice before it hits the ground. Find how many seconds since the launch would the object's height be 230 meters. Round your answers to two decimal places if needed.
The object's height would be 230 meters the

first time at [   ] seconds,
and then the second time at
[   ] seconds.

Complex Solutions to Quadratic Equations Simplify the radical and write it as a complex number using i.

27. $\sqrt{-40}$

28. $\sqrt{-56}$

Solve the quadratic equation. Solutions could be complex numbers.

29. $-2y^2 - 5 = 1$

30. $3r^2 + 8 = 2$

31. $-5(r+4)^2 + 5 = 85$

32. $3(t-6)^2 + 5 = -295$

Solving Equations in General Solve the equation.

33. $\sqrt{t} + 72 = t$

34. $\sqrt{x} + 30 = x$

35. $5 + 10(y-5) = -6 - (7-2y)$

36. $3 + 8(t-3) = 1 - (2-3t)$

37. $x^2 + 5x = 24$

38. $x^2 + 8x = 9$

39. $-8 - 8A + 2 = -A + 12 - 7A$

40. $-6 - 10C + 6 = -C + 13$

41. $9x^2 + 8x + 3 = 0$

42. $x^2 - 6x - 9 = 0$

43. $-7 - 2(x+2)^2 = -9$

44. $30 - 6(x+2)^2 = 6$

45. $14 = \dfrac{t}{5} + \dfrac{t}{2}$

46. $3 = \dfrac{a}{3} + \dfrac{a}{6}$

47. $y = \sqrt{y+4} + 86$

48. $r = \sqrt{r+2} + 40$

49. $3x^2 + 41 = 0$

50. $43x^2 + 47 = 0$

51. $5x^2 = -42x - 49$

52. $2x^2 = -21x - 10$

53. $x = \sqrt{x-1} + 7$

54. $x = \sqrt{x+7} - 1$

Chapter 8

Quantities in the Physical World

8.1 Scientific Notation

Very large and very small numbers can be awkward to write and calculate with. These kinds of numbers can show in the sciences. For example in biology, a human hair might be as thick as 0.000181 meters. And the closest that Mars gets to the sun is 206620000 meters. Keeping track of the decimal places and extra zeros raises the potential for mistakes to be made. In this section, we discuss a format used for very large and very small numbers called **scientific notation** that helps alleviate the issues with these numbers.

8.1.1 The Basics of Scientific Notation

An October 3, 2016 CBS News headline[1] read:

> Federal Debt in FY 2016 Jumped $1,422,827,047,452.46—that's $12,036 Per Household.

The article also later states:

> By the close of business on Sept. 30, 2016, the last day of fiscal 2016, it had climbed to $19,573,444,713,936.79.

When presented in this format, trying to comprehend the value of these numbers can be overwhelming. More commonly, such numbers would be presented in a descriptive manner:

- The federal debt climbed by 1.42 trillion dollars in 2016.

- The federal debt was 19.6 trillion dollars at the close of business on Sept. 30, 2016.

In science, government, business, and many other disciplines, it's not uncommon to deal with very large numbers like these. When numbers get this large, it can be hard to discern when a number has eleven digits and when it has twelve.

We have descriptive language for all numbers based on the place value of the different digits: ones, tens, thousands, ten thousands, etc. We tend to rely upon this language more when we start dealing with larger numbers. Here's a chart for some of the most common numbers we see and use in the world around us:

---
[1]http://www.cnsnews.com/news/article/terence-p-jeffrey/federal-debt-fy-2016-jumped-142282704745246

Number	US English Name	Power of 10
1	one	10^0
10	ten	10^1
100	hundred	10^2
1,000	one thousand	10^3
10,000	ten thousand	10^4
100,000	one hundred thousand	10^5
1,000,000	one million	10^6
1,000,000,000	one billion	10^9

Figure 8.1.2: Whole Number Powers of 10

Each number above has a corresponding power of ten and this power of ten will be important as we start to work with the content in this section. This descriptive language also covers even larger numbers: trillion, quadrillion, quintillion, sextillion, septillion, and so on. There's also corresponding language to describe very small numbers, such as thousandth, millionth, billionth, trillionth, etc.

Through centuries of scientific progress, humanity became increasingly aware of very large numbers and very small measurements. As one example, the star that is nearest to our sun is Proxima Centauri[2]. Proxima Centauri is about 25,000,000,000,000 miles from our sun. Again, many will find the descriptive language easier to read: Proxima Centauri is about 25 trillion miles from our sun.

To make computations involving such numbers more manageable, a standardized notation called "scientific notation" was established. The foundation of scientific notation is the fact that multiplying or dividing by a power of 10 will move the decimal point of a number so many places to the right or left, respectively. So first, let's take a moment to review that level of basic arithmetic.

Checkpoint 8.1.3 Perform the following operations:

    a. Multiply 5.7 by 10.   b. Multiply 3.1 by 10000.

Explanation.

    a. $5.7 \times 10 = 57$

       $10 = 10^1$ and multiplying by 10^1 moved the decimal point one place to the right.

    b. $3.1 \times 10000 = 31000$

       $10000 = 10^4$ and multiplying by 10^4 moved the decimal point four places to the right.

Multiplying a number by 10^n where n is a positive integer had the effect of moving the decimal point n places to the right.

Every number can be written as a product of a number between 1 and 10 and a power of 10. For example, $650 = 6.5 \times 100$. Since $100 = 10^2$, we can also write

$$650 = 6.5 \times 10^2$$

and this is our first example of writing a number in scientific notation.

Definition 8.1.4 A positive number is written in **scientific notation** when it has the form $a \times 10^n$ where n is an integer and $1 \le a < 10$. In other words, a has precisely one non-zero digit to the left of the decimal place. The exponent n used here is called the number's **order of magnitude**. The number a is sometimes

---

[2]imagine.gsfc.nasa.gov/features/cosmic/nearest_star_info.html

called the **significand** or the **mantissa**.

Some conventions do not require a to be between 1 and 10, excluding both values, but that is the convention used in this book.

Some calculators and computer readouts cannot display exponents in superscript. In some cases, these devices will display scientific notation in the form 6.5E2 instead of 6.5×10^2. ◇

8.1.2 Scientific Notation for Large Numbers

To write a number larger than 10 in scientific notation, like 89412, first write the number with the decimal point right after its first digit, like 8.9412. Now count how many places there are between where the decimal point originally was and where it is now.

$$8.\overbrace{9412}^{4}$$

Use that count as the power of 10. In this example, we have

$$89412 = 8.9412 \times 10^4$$

Scientific notation communicates the "essence" of the number (8.9412) and then its size, or order of magnitude (10^4).

Example 8.1.5 To get a sense of how scientific notation works, let's consider familiar lengths of time converted to seconds.

Length of Time	Length in Seconds	Scientific Notation
one second	1 second	1×10^0 second
one minute	60 seconds	6×10^1 seconds
one hour	3600 seconds	3.6×10^3 seconds
one month	2,628,000 seconds	2.628×10^6 seconds
ten years	315,400,000 seconds	3.154×10^8 seconds
79 years (about a lifetime)	2,491,000,000 seconds	2.491×10^9 seconds

Note that roughly 2.6 *million* seconds is one month, while roughly 2.5 *billion* seconds is an entire lifetime.

Checkpoint 8.1.6 Write each of the following in scientific notation.

a. The federal debt at the close of business on Sept. 30, 2016: about 19,600,000,000,000 dollars.

b. The world's population in 2016: about 7,418,000,000 people.

Explanation.

a. To convert the federal debt to scientific notation, we will count the number of digits after the first non-zero digit (which happens to be a 1 here). Since there are 13 places after the first non-zero digit, we write:

$$1\overbrace{9,600,000,000,000}^{13 \text{ places}} \text{ dollars} = 1.96 \times 10^{13} \text{ dollars}$$

b. Since there are nine places after the first non-zero digit of 7, the world's population in 2016 was about

$$7,\overbrace{418,000,000}^{9 \text{ places}} \text{ people} = 7.418 \times 10^9 \text{ people}$$

Checkpoint 8.1.7 Convert each of the following from scientific notation to decimal notation (without any exponents).

    a. The earth's diameter is about 1.27×10^7 meters.

    b. As of 2019, there are 3.14×10^{13} known digits of π.

Explanation.

    a. To convert this number to decimal notation we will move the decimal point after the digit 1 seven places to the right, including zeros where necessary. The earth's diameter is:

$$1.27 \times 10^7 \text{ meters} = 1\overbrace{2,700,000}^{7 \text{ places}} \text{ meters.}$$

    b. As of 2019 there are

$$3.14 \times 10^{13} = 3\overbrace{1,400,000,000,000}^{13 \text{ places}}$$

known digits of π.

8.1.3 Scientific Notation for Small Numbers

Scientific notation can also be useful when working with numbers smaller than 1. As we saw in Figure 8.1.2, we can represent thousands, millions, billions, trillions, etc., with positive integer exponents on 10. We can similarly represent numbers smaller than 1 (which are written as tenths, hundredths, thousandths, millionths, billionths, trillionths, etc.), with *negative* integer exponents on 10. This relationship is outlined in Figure 8.1.8.

Number	English Name	Power of 10
1	one	10^0
0.1	one tenth	$\frac{1}{10} = 10^{-1}$
0.01	one hundredth	$\frac{1}{100} = 10^{-2}$
0.001	one thousandth	$\frac{1}{1,000} = 10^{-3}$
0.0001	one ten thousandth	$\frac{1}{10,000} = 10^{-4}$
0.00001	one hundred thousandth	$\frac{1}{100,000} = 10^{-5}$
0.000001	one millionth	$\frac{1}{1,000,000} = 10^{-6}$
0.000000001	one billionth	$\frac{1}{1,000,000,000} = 10^{-9}$

Figure 8.1.8: Negative Integer Powers of 10

To see how this works with a digit other than 1, let's look at 0.005. When we state 0.005 as a number, we say "5 thousandths." Thus $0.005 = 5 \times \frac{1}{1000}$. The fraction $\frac{1}{1000}$ can be written as $\frac{1}{10^3}$, which we know is equivalent to 10^{-3}. Using negative exponents, we can then rewrite 0.005 as 5×10^{-3}. This is the scientific notation for 0.005.

In practice, we won't generally do that much computation. To write a small number in scientific notation we start as we did before and place the decimal point behind the first non-zero digit. We then count the number of decimal places between where the decimal had originally been and where it now is. Keep in mind that negative powers of ten are used to help represent very small numbers (smaller than 1) and positive powers of ten are used to represent very large numbers (larger than 1). So to convert 0.005 to scientific notation, we have:

$$0.\overbrace{005}^{3} = 5 \times 10^{-3}$$

Example 8.1.9 In quantum mechanics, there is an important value called Planck's Constant[3]. Written as a decimal, the value of Planck's constant (rounded to six significant digits) is

$$0.000\,000\,000\,000\,000\,000\,000\,000\,000\,000\,000\,000\,662\,607.$$

In scientific notation, this number will be $6.62607 \times 10^{?}$. To determine the exponent, we need to count the number of places from where the decimal originally is to where we will move it (following the first "6"):

$$0.\overbrace{000\,000\,000\,000\,000\,000\,000\,000\,000\,000\,000\,6}^{34 \text{ places}}62\,607$$

So in scientific notation, Planck's Constant is 6.62607×10^{-34}. It will be much easier to use 6.62607×10^{-34} in a calculation, and an added benefit is that scientific notation quickly communicates both the value and the order of magnitude of Planck's Constant.

Checkpoint 8.1.10 Write each of the following in scientific notation.

    a. The weight of a single grain of long grain rice is about 0.029 grams.

    b. The gate pitch of a microprocessor is 0.000 000 014 meters

Explanation.

    a. To convert this weight to scientific notation, we must first move the decimal behind the first non-zero digit to obtain 2.9, which requires that we move the decimal point 2 places. Thus we have:

$$0.\overbrace{02}^{2}9 \text{ grams} = 2.9 \times 10^{-2} \text{ grams}$$

    b. The gate pitch of a microprocessor is:

$$0.\overbrace{000\,000\,01}^{8 \text{ places}}4 \text{ meters} = 1.4 \times 10^{-8} \text{ meters}$$

Checkpoint 8.1.11 Convert each of the following from scientific notation to decimal notation (without any exponents).

    a. A download speed of 7.53×10^{-3} Gigabyte per second.

    b. The weight of a poppy seed is about 3×10^{-7} kilograms

Explanation.

    a. To convert a download speed of 7.53×10^{-3} Gigabyte per second to decimal notation, we will move

---

[3]en.wikipedia.org/wiki/Planck_constant

the decimal point 3 places to the left and include the appropriate number of zeros:

$$7.53 \times 10^{-3} \text{ Gigabyte per second} = 0\overset{3}{\overbrace{.007}}53 \text{ Gigabyte per second}$$

b. The weight of a poppy seed is about:

$$3 \times 10^{-7} \text{ kilograms} = 0\overset{7 \text{ places}}{\overbrace{.0000003}} \text{ kilograms}$$

Checkpoint 8.1.12 Decide if the numbers are written in scientific notation or not. Use Definition 8.1.4.

a. The number $7 \times 10^{1.9}$ (□ is   □ is not)   in scientific notation.

b. The number 2.6×10^{-31} (□ is   □ is not)   in scientific notation.

c. The number 10×7^4 (□ is   □ is not)   in scientific notation.

d. The number 0.93×10^3 (□ is   □ is not)   in scientific notation.

e. The number 4.2×10^0 (□ is   □ is not)   in scientific notation.

f. The number 12.5×10^{-6} (□ is   □ is not)   in scientific notation.

Explanation.

a. The number $7 \times 10^{1.9}$ *is not* in scientific notation. The exponent on the 10 is required to be an integer and 1.9 is not.

b. The number 2.6×10^{-31} *is* in scientific notation.

c. The number 10×7^4 *is not* in scientific notation. The base must be 10, not 7.

d. The number 0.93×10^3 *is not* in scientific notation. The coefficient of the 10 must be between 1 (inclusive) and 10.

e. The number 4.2×10^0 *is* in scientific notation.

f. The number 12.5×10^{-6} *is not* in scientific notation. The coefficient of the 10 must be between 1 (inclusive) and 10.

8.1.4 Multiplying and Dividing Using Scientific Notation

One main reason for having scientific notation is to make calculations involving immensely large or small numbers easier to perform. By having the order of magnitude separated out in scientific notation, we can separate any calculation into two components.

Example 8.1.13 On Sept. 30th, 2016, the US federal debt was about \$19,600,000,000,000 and the US population was about 323,000,000. What was the average debt per person that day?

a. Calculate the answer using the numbers provided, which are not in scientific notation.

b. First, confirm that the given values in scientific notation are 1.96×10^{13} and 3.23×10^8. Then calculate the answer using scientific notation.

Explanation. We've been asked to answer the same question, but to perform the calculation using two different approaches. In both cases, we'll need to divide the debt by the population.

a. We may need to use a calculator to handle such large numbers and we have to be careful that we type the correct number of 0s.

$$\frac{19600000000000}{323000000} \approx 60681.11$$

b. To perform this calculation using scientific notation, our work would begin by setting up the quotient as $\frac{1.96 \times 10^{13}}{3.23 \times 10^8}$. Dividing this quotient follows the same process we did with variable expressions of the same format, such as $\frac{1.96w^{13}}{3.23w^8}$. In both situations, we'll divide the coefficients and then use exponent rules to simplify the powers.

$$\frac{1.96 \times 10^{13}}{3.23 \times 10^8} = \frac{1.96}{3.23} \times \frac{10^{13}}{10^8}$$
$$\approx 0.6068111 \times 10^5$$
$$\approx 60681.11$$

The federal debt per capita in the US on September 30th, 2016 was about $60,681.11 per person. Both calculations give us the same answer, but the calculation relying upon scientific notation has less room for error and allows us to perform the calculation as two smaller steps.

Whenever we multiply or divide numbers that are written in scientific notation, we must separate the calculation for the coefficients from the calculation for the powers of ten, just as we simplified earlier expressions using variables and the exponent rules.

Example 8.1.14

a. Multiply $\left(2 \times 10^5\right)\left(3 \times 10^4\right)$.

b. Divide $\frac{8 \times 10^{17}}{4 \times 10^2}$.

Explanation. We will simplify the significand/mantissa parts as one step and then simplify the powers of 10 as a separate step.

a. $\left(2 \times 10^5\right)\left(3 \times 10^4\right) = (2 \times 3) \times \left(10^5 \times 10^4\right)$
$$= 6 \times 10^9$$

b. $\frac{8 \times 10^{17}}{4 \times 10^2} = \frac{8}{4} \times \frac{10^{17}}{10^2}$
$$= 2 \times 10^{15}$$

Often when we multiply or divide numbers in scientific notation, the resulting value will not be in scientific notation. Suppose we were multiplying $\left(9.3 \times 10^{17}\right)\left(8.2 \times 10^{-6}\right)$ and need to state our answer using scientific notation. We would start as we have previously:

$$\left(9.3 \times 10^{17}\right)\left(8.2 \times 10^{-6}\right) = (9.3 \times 8.2) \times \left(10^{17} \times 10^{-6}\right)$$
$$= 76.26 \times 10^{11}$$

While this is a correct value, it is not written using scientific notation. One way to convert this answer into scientific notation is to turn just the coefficient into scientific notation and momentarily ignore the power of ten:

$$= 76.26 \times 10^{11}$$
$$= 7.626 \times 10^{1} \times 10^{11}$$

Now that the coefficient fits into the proper format, we can combine the powers of ten and have our answer written using scientific notation.

$$= 7.626 \times 10^{1} \times 10^{11}$$
$$= 7.626 \times 10^{12}$$

Example 8.1.15 Multiply or divide as indicated. Write your answer using scientific notation.

a. $\left(8 \times 10^{21}\right)\left(2 \times 10^{-7}\right)$

b. $\dfrac{2 \times 10^{-6}}{8 \times 10^{-19}}$

Explanation.   Again, we'll separate out the work for the significand/mantissa from the work for the powers of ten. If the resulting coefficient is not between 1 and 10, we'll need to adjust that coefficient to put it into scientific notation.

a. $\left(8 \times 10^{21}\right)\left(2 \times 10^{-7}\right) = (8 \times 2) \times \left(10^{21} \times 10^{-7}\right)$
$$= 16 \times 10^{14}$$
$$= 1.6 \times 10^{1} \times 10^{14}$$
$$= 1.6 \times 10^{15}$$

We need to remember to apply the product rule for exponents to the powers of ten.

b. $\dfrac{2 \times 10^{-6}}{8 \times 10^{-19}} = \dfrac{2}{8} \times \dfrac{10^{-6}}{10^{-19}}$
$$= 0.25 \times 10^{13}$$
$$= 2.5 \times 10^{-1} \times 10^{13}$$
$$= 2.5 \times 10^{12}$$

There are times where we will have to raise numbers written in scientific notation to a power. For example, suppose we have to find the area of a square whose radius is 3×10^{7} feet. To perform this calculation, we first remember the formula for the area of a square, $A = s^2$ and then substitute 3×10^{7} for s: $A = \left(3 \times 10^{7}\right)^2$. To perform this calculation, we'll need to remember to use the product to a power rule and the power to a power rule:

$$A = \left(3 \times 10^{7}\right)^2$$
$$= (3)^2 \times \left(10^{7}\right)^2$$
$$= 9 \times 10^{14}$$

8.1.5 Reading Questions

1. Which number is very large and which number is very small?

$$9.99 \times 10^{-47} \qquad 1.01 \times 10^{23}$$

2. Since some computer/calculator screens can't display an exponent, how might a computer/calculator display the number 2.318×10^{13}?

3. Why do we bother having scientific notation for numbers?

8.1.6 Exercises

Converting To and From Scientific Notation Write the following number in scientific notation.

1.	100000	**2.**	20000	**3.**	300	**4.**	400000
5.	0.005	**6.**	0.0006	**7.**	0.07	**8.**	0.008

Write the following number in decimal notation without using exponents.

9. 9×10^2 **10.** 1.1×10^5 **11.** 2.02×10^3

12. 3.02×10^2 **13.** 4.01×10^0 **14.** 5.01×10^0

15. 6×10^{-4} **16.** 7×10^{-2} **17.** 8×10^{-4}

18. 8.99×10^{-2}

Arithmetic with Scientific Notation Multiply the following numbers, writing your answer in scientific notation.

19. $(9 \times 10^2)(7 \times 10^2)$ **20.** $(2 \times 10^4)(4 \times 10^5)$ **21.** $(3 \times 10^2)(9 \times 10^4)$

22. $(4 \times 10^3)(6 \times 10^3)$ **23.** $(5 \times 10^5)(3 \times 10^5)$ **24.** $(6 \times 10^3)(9 \times 10^4)$

Divide the following numbers, writing your answer in scientific notation.

25. $\dfrac{4.2 \times 10^5}{7 \times 10^3}$ **26.** $\dfrac{2.4 \times 10^3}{8 \times 10^2}$ **27.** $\dfrac{7.2 \times 10^5}{9 \times 10^2}$

28. $\dfrac{5.4 \times 10^6}{9 \times 10^4}$ **29.** $\dfrac{6 \times 10^3}{2 \times 10^{-4}}$ **30.** $\dfrac{2.4 \times 10^5}{3 \times 10^{-2}}$

31. $\dfrac{2 \times 10^2}{4 \times 10^{-3}}$ **32.** $\dfrac{1 \times 10^4}{5 \times 10^{-2}}$ **33.** $\dfrac{4.8 \times 10^{-5}}{6 \times 10^2}$

34. $\dfrac{3.5 \times 10^{-3}}{7 \times 10^5}$ **35.** $\dfrac{1.6 \times 10^{-2}}{8 \times 10^4}$ **36.** $\dfrac{6.3 \times 10^{-4}}{9 \times 10^3}$

Simplify the following expression, writing your answer in scientific notation.

37. $(5 \times 10^5)^4$ **38.** $(2 \times 10^2)^2$ **39.** $(2 \times 10^8)^3$

40. $(3 \times 10^5)^2$ **41.** $(3 \times 10^{10})^3$ **42.** $(4 \times 10^7)^4$

8.2 Unit Conversion

Unit Conversion References.   This textbook provides unit conversions in Appendix B for your convenience. But you may also find unit conversion facts in many other places, including the internet.

Unit conversion is a systematic method for converting from one kind of unit of measurement to another. It is used extensively in chemistry and other health- or science-related fields. It is a valuable skill to learn, and necessary for success in many applications.

8.2.1 Unit Ratios

Example 8.2.1
When building a staircase, a step typically has a rise of 7 inches (7 in). An inch is a unit of length in the imperial unit system, used in the United States, Canada, the United Kingdom, and a few other places. Many parts of the world do not use this unit of measurement, and the people there do not have a sense of how long 7 inches is. Instead, much of the world would measure a length like this using centimeters (cm). How many centimeters is 7 inches?

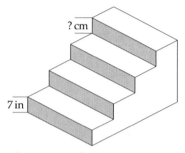

To convert from one unit of measurement to another (like inches to centimeters), we use what are called unit ratios. A **unit ratio** is a ratio (or fraction) where the numerator and denominator are quantities *with units* that equal each other. They equal each other as measurements, but they are measured with different units. For example, Appendix B tells us that 1 inch is equal to 2.54 centimeters. Knowing that, we can build the unit ratios $\frac{1\,\text{in}}{2.54\,\text{cm}}$ and $\frac{2.54\,\text{cm}}{1\,\text{in}}$. Each of these unit ratios are equivalent to 1, because their numerator equals their denominator.

With a unit ratio, we can work out a conversion by taking what we would like to convert (7 in) and multiplying by a unit ratio in such a way that the "old" units cancel and the "new" units remain.

$$
\begin{aligned}
7\,\text{in} &= \frac{7\,\text{in}}{1} && \text{We are about to do fraction-like multiplication.}\\
&= \frac{7\,\text{in}}{1}\cdot\frac{2.54\,\text{cm}}{1\,\text{in}} && 1\text{ in equals }2.54\text{ cm.}\\
&= \frac{7\,\cancel{\text{in}}}{1}\cdot\frac{2.54\,\text{cm}}{1\,\cancel{\text{in}}} && \text{Units may now cancel.}\\
&= \frac{7}{1}\cdot\frac{2.54\,\text{cm}}{1}\\
&= 7\cdot 2.54\,\text{cm}\\
&= 17.78\,\text{cm}
\end{aligned}
$$

So 7 inches is equal to 17.78 centimeters. In practice, anyone talking about the rise of a stair might simply round to 18 cm.

Note there was another unit ratio, $\frac{1\,\text{in}}{2.54\,\text{cm}}$, but using that would not have been helpful, since it would not have arranged units such that the inches canceled.

Remark 8.2.2 When you are comfortable, you might do the steps from Example 8.2.1 on one line, like:

$$
7\,\text{in} = \frac{7\,\cancel{\text{in}}}{1}\cdot\frac{2.54\,\text{cm}}{1\,\cancel{\text{in}}} = \frac{7}{1}\cdot\frac{2.54}{1}\,\text{cm} = 17.78\,\text{cm}
$$

The examples in this section will continue to show the steps completely drawn out, to give a better sense of what you would write first, second, and so on.

Example 8.2.3 A canned beverage typically contains 12 fluid ounces (12 fl oz). A fluid ounce is a unit of volume used in the United States. (The United Kingdom also has a fluid ounce, but it is a slightly different amount.) In the rest of the world, people do not have a sense of how much 12 fluid ounces is. Most of the world would measure a canned beverage's volume using milliliters (mL). How many milliliters is 12 fluid ounces?

Appendix B tells us that 1 fl oz is (almost) equal to 29.57 mL. Knowing that, we can build the unit ratios $\frac{1 \text{ fl oz}}{29.57 \text{ mL}}$ and $\frac{29.57 \text{ mL}}{1 \text{ fl oz}}$. Each of these unit ratios are (almost) equivalent to 1, because their numerator (almost) equals their denominator.

Using the appropriate unit ratio to enable cancellation of fluid ounces:

$$12 \text{ fl oz} = \frac{12 \text{ fl oz}}{1} \qquad \text{We are about to do fraction-like multiplication.}$$

$$\approx \frac{12 \text{ fl oz}}{1} \cdot \frac{29.57 \text{ mL}}{1 \text{ fl oz}} \qquad \text{1 fl oz approximately equals 29.57 mL.}$$

$$= \frac{12 \,\cancel{\text{fl oz}}}{1} \cdot \frac{29.57 \text{ mL}}{1 \,\cancel{\text{fl oz}}} \qquad \text{Units may now cancel.}$$

$$= \frac{12}{1} \cdot \frac{29.57 \text{ mL}}{1}$$

$$= 12 \cdot 29.57 \text{ mL}$$

$$\approx 354.8 \text{ mL}$$

So 12 fluid ounces is *approximately* equal to 354.8 milliliters. In practice, you might round to 355 mL.

Notice that each conversion fact from Appendix B gives two possible unit ratios. Deciding which one to use will depend on where units need to be placed in order to cancel the appropriate units. In unit conversion, we multiply ratios together and cancel common units the same way we can cancel common factors when multiplying fractions.

Example 8.2.4 It's 1760 feet (1760 ft) to walk from Jonah's house to where he works. How many miles is that?

Explanation. Since we are converting feet to miles, we use the conversion fact that there are 5280 feet in 1 mile. In this conversion, we need to use a unit ratio that will allow the feet units to cancel. So we need to use $\frac{1 \text{ mi}}{5280 \text{ ft}}$. This is different from previous examples in that the 1 is in the numerator this time. But the process is not all that different.

$$1760 \text{ ft} = \frac{1760 \text{ ft}}{1} \qquad \text{We are about to do fraction-like multiplication.}$$

$$= \frac{1760 \text{ ft}}{1} \cdot \frac{1 \text{ mi}}{5280 \text{ ft}} \qquad \text{1 mi equals 5280 ft.}$$

$$= \frac{1760 \,\cancel{\text{ft}}}{1} \cdot \frac{1 \text{ mi}}{5280 \,\cancel{\text{ft}}} \qquad \text{Units may now cancel.}$$

$$= \frac{1760}{1} \cdot \frac{1 \text{ mi}}{5280}$$

$$= \frac{1760}{5280} \text{ mi}$$

$$= \frac{1}{3} \, \text{mi} \approx 0.3333 \, \text{mi}$$

So Jonah walks $\frac{1}{3}$ of a mile, or about $0.3333 \, \text{mi}$, to get from his house to where he works.

Checkpoint 8.2.5 Convert 60 inches to feet.

Explanation.   We start by writing what it is that we are converting as a ratio, by placing it over a 1. This is similar to writing a whole number as a fraction when we want to multiply it by a fraction. Next we multiply that ratio by a unit ratio, one that will have inches in the denominator so that inches will cancel. Multiply what's left just as we multiply fractions (multiply the numerators together and multiply the denominators together), including the units, and simplify by dividing.

$$60 \, \text{in} = \frac{60 \, \text{in}}{1} \qquad \text{We are about to do fraction-like multiplication.}$$

$$= \frac{60 \, \text{in}}{1} \cdot \frac{1 \, \text{ft}}{12 \, \text{in}} \qquad \text{1 ft equals 12 in.}$$

$$= \frac{60 \, \cancel{\text{in}}}{1} \cdot \frac{1 \, \text{ft}}{12 \, \cancel{\text{in}}} \qquad \text{Units may now cancel.}$$

$$= \frac{60}{1} \cdot \frac{1 \, \text{ft}}{12}$$

$$= \frac{60}{12} \, \text{ft}$$

$$= 5 \, \text{ft}$$

We find that 60 inches is equivalent to 5 feet.

Example 8.2.6 Why Do We Convert Units? Converting from one unit to another can be necessary when you are given information where the units don't quite match. Cassidy was driving at a speed of 32 mph for seven minutes. How far did they travel in that time span?

Normally, to find a distance traveled, you would multiply speed by how much time passed. For example if Cassidy had been driving 50 mph for two hours, we would find $50 \cdot 2 = 100$, and conclude they had driven 100 miles.

But in this example, Cassidy's speed is 32 miles per *hour*, but the time elapsed is seven *minutes*. The time units do not match. It will help to convert the 7 min into hours. So let's do that.

$$7 \, \text{min} = \frac{7 \, \text{min}}{1} \qquad \text{We are about to do fraction-like multiplication.}$$

$$= \frac{7 \, \text{min}}{1} \cdot \frac{1 \, \text{h}}{60 \, \text{min}} \qquad \text{1 h equals 60 min.}$$

$$= \frac{7 \, \cancel{\text{min}}}{1} \cdot \frac{1 \, \text{h}}{60 \, \cancel{\text{min}}} \qquad \text{Units may now cancel.}$$

$$= \frac{7}{1} \cdot \frac{1 \, \text{h}}{60}$$

$$= \frac{7}{60} \, \text{h}$$

$$\approx 0.1167 \, \text{h}$$

Now we can multiply Cassidy's speed (32 mph) by their elapsed time ($\frac{7}{60}$ h). We find $32 \cdot \frac{7}{60} \approx 3.733$, so Cassidy has traveled about 3.733 miles.

Actually we can do this multiplication *with units* and the units will cancel appropriately:

$$32\frac{\text{mi}}{\text{h}} \cdot \frac{7}{60}\text{h} = \frac{32\,\text{mi}}{1\,\text{h}} \cdot \frac{7\,\text{h}}{60}$$

$$= \frac{32\,\text{mi}}{1\,\cancel{\text{h}}} \cdot \frac{7\,\cancel{\text{h}}}{60}$$

$$= \frac{32 \cdot 7}{60}\,\text{mi}$$

$$\approx 3.733\,\text{mi}$$

Checkpoint 8.2.7 The density of oil is 6.9 pounds per gallon. You have a 2.5-liter bottle of oil. How much does this much oil weigh? (To find weight, multiply density with volume when the units match.)

Explanation. The density is in pounds per *gallon*, but the volume is in *liters*. So first let's convert the 2.5 L to gallons.

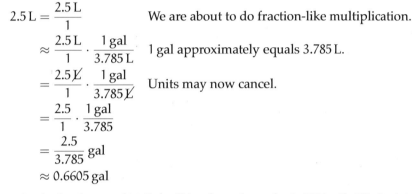

$$2.5\,\text{L} = \frac{2.5\,\text{L}}{1} \qquad \text{We are about to do fraction-like multiplication.}$$

$$\approx \frac{2.5\,\text{L}}{1} \cdot \frac{1\,\text{gal}}{3.785\,\text{L}} \qquad 1\,\text{gal approximately equals }3.785\,\text{L}.$$

$$= \frac{2.5\,\cancel{\text{L}}}{1} \cdot \frac{1\,\text{gal}}{3.785\,\cancel{\text{L}}} \qquad \text{Units may now cancel.}$$

$$= \frac{2.5}{1} \cdot \frac{1\,\text{gal}}{3.785}$$

$$= \frac{2.5}{3.785}\,\text{gal}$$

$$\approx 0.6605\,\text{gal}$$

Now we can multiply the density (6.9 lb/gal) by the volume (≈ 0.6605 gal). We find $6.9 \cdot 0.6605 \approx 4.557$, so the oil weighs about 4.557 pounds.

With units:

$$6.9\frac{\text{lb}}{\text{gal}} \cdot 0.6605\,\text{gal} = \frac{6.9\,\text{lb}}{1\,\text{gal}} \cdot \frac{0.6605\,\text{gal}}{1}$$

$$= \frac{6.9\,\text{lb}}{1\,\cancel{\text{gal}}} \cdot \frac{0.6605\,\cancel{\text{gal}}}{1}$$

$$= 6.9 \cdot 0.6605\,\text{lb}$$

$$\approx 4.557\,\text{lb}$$

8.2.2 Using Multiple Unit Ratios

In previous examples, we used only one unit ratio to make a conversion. However, sometimes there is a need to use more than one unit ratio in a conversion. This may happen when your reference guide for conversions does not directly tell you how to convert from one unit to another. In those situations, we'll have to consider the conversion facts that are available and then make a plan.

Example 8.2.8 Convert 350 yards to miles.

Explanation. In Appendix B, there is not a conversion that relates yards to miles. But notice that we can convert yards to feet (using the fact that one yard is three feet) and then we can convert feet to miles (using the fact that one mile is 5280 feet). So we will use two unit ratios. The unit ratio $\frac{3\,\text{ft}}{1\,\text{yd}}$ can be used to cancel the yards in 350 yd. Then the unit ratio $\frac{1\,\text{mi}}{5280\,\text{ft}}$ can be used to cancel the feet that are left over from the first conversion.

$$350\,\text{yd} = \frac{350\,\text{yd}}{1}$$

We are about to do fraction-like multiplication.

$$= \frac{350\,\text{yd}}{1} \cdot \frac{3\,\text{ft}}{1\,\text{yd}} \cdot \frac{1\,\text{mi}}{5280\,\text{ft}}$$

Both unit ratios are needed.

$$= \frac{350\,\cancel{\text{yd}}}{1} \cdot \frac{3\,\cancel{\text{ft}}}{1\,\cancel{\text{yd}}} \cdot \frac{1\,\text{mi}}{5280\,\cancel{\text{ft}}}$$

Units may now cancel.

$$= \frac{350}{1} \cdot \frac{3}{1} \cdot \frac{1\,\text{mi}}{5280}$$

$$= \frac{350 \cdot 3}{5280}\,\text{mi}$$

$$\approx 0.1989\,\text{mi}$$

So 350 yards is about 0.1989 miles.

Checkpoint 8.2.9 Convert 4.5 months into hours.

Explanation.   Notice that we can convert months to days (using the fact that one month is approximately 30 days) and then we can convert days to hours (using the fact that one day is 24 hours).

$$4.5\,\text{mo} = \frac{4.5\,\text{mo}}{1}$$

We are about to do fraction-like multiplication.

$$\approx \frac{4.5\,\text{mo}}{1} \cdot \frac{30\,\text{d}}{1\,\text{mo}} \cdot \frac{24\,\text{h}}{1\,\text{d}}$$

Two unit ratios are needed.

$$= \frac{4.5\,\cancel{\text{mo}}}{1} \cdot \frac{30\,\cancel{\text{d}}}{1\,\cancel{\text{mo}}} \cdot \frac{24\,\text{h}}{1\,\cancel{\text{d}}}$$

Units may now cancel.

$$= \frac{4.5}{1} \cdot \frac{30}{1} \cdot \frac{24\,\text{h}}{1}$$

$$= 4.5 \cdot 30 \cdot 24\,\text{h}$$

$$= 3240\,\text{h}$$

So 4.5 months is about 3240 hours.

8.2.3 Converting Squared or Cubed Units

When calculating the area or volume of a geometric figure, units of measurement are multiplied together, resulting in squared units (when calculating area) or cubed units (when calculating volume). Thus, there may be circumstances where you may need to convert either squared or cubed units. For example, suppose you are carpeting a room in your home and you know the square footage of the room, but the carpet is sold in square yards. In that case, you would need to convert the square feet of the room into square yards.

Example 8.2.10 Jin's bedroom is 153 square feet (153 ft^2). How many square yards is that?
    We start the process the same as in the previous examples. That is, we write what we are converting in

ratio form with a denominator of 1.

$$153\,\text{ft}^2 = \frac{153\,\text{ft}^2}{1} \qquad \text{We are about to do fraction-like multiplication.}$$

Now, we do want feet to be replaced with yards, so the unit ratio $\frac{1\,\text{yd}}{3\,\text{ft}}$ will be useful. But using it once is not enough:

$$153\,\text{ft}^2 = \frac{153\,\text{ft}^2}{1}$$
$$= \frac{153\,\text{ft}^2}{1} \cdot \frac{1\,\text{yd}}{3\,\text{ft}} \qquad \text{1 yd equals 3 feet.}$$

The ft^2 in the first numerator do not fully cancel with the ft in the second denominator. We need to use this unit ratio *twice*.

$$153\,\text{ft}^2 = \frac{153\,\text{ft}^2}{1}$$
$$= \frac{153\,\text{ft}^2}{1} \cdot \frac{1\,\text{yd}}{3\,\text{ft}} \cdot \frac{1\,\text{yd}}{3\,\text{ft}} \qquad \text{1 yd equals 3 feet.}$$

Now there is ft^2 in the overall numerator, and ft $\cdot$ ft in the overall denominator. They will fully cancel.

Here is the complete process from the beginning.

$$153\,\text{ft}^2 = \frac{153\,\text{ft}^2}{1}$$
$$= \frac{153\,\text{ft}^2}{1} \cdot \frac{1\,\text{yd}}{3\,\text{ft}} \cdot \frac{1\,\text{yd}}{3\,\text{ft}}$$
$$= \frac{153\,\cancel{\text{ft}^2}}{1} \cdot \frac{1\,\text{yd}}{3\,\cancel{\text{ft}}} \cdot \frac{1\,\text{yd}}{3\,\cancel{\text{ft}}} \qquad \text{Units may now cancel.}$$
$$= \frac{153}{1} \cdot \frac{1\,\text{yd}}{3} \cdot \frac{1\,\text{yd}}{3}$$
$$= \frac{153}{9}\,\text{yd} \cdot \text{yd}$$
$$= 17\,\text{yd}^2$$

So Jin's bedroom has 17 square yards of area.

Alternatively, we can set up conversions with squared or cubed units this way:

$$153\,\text{ft}^2 = \frac{153\,\text{ft}^2}{1}$$
$$= \frac{153\,\text{ft}^2}{1} \cdot \left(\frac{1\,\text{yd}}{3\,\text{ft}}\right)^2 \qquad \text{The ft in the denominator will be squared.}$$
$$= \frac{153\,\text{ft}^2}{1} \cdot \frac{1\,\text{yd}^2}{9\,\text{ft}^2} \qquad \text{Using Fact 5.6.5.}$$
$$= \frac{153\,\cancel{\text{ft}^2}}{1} \cdot \frac{1\,\text{yd}^2}{9\,\cancel{\text{ft}^2}} \qquad \text{Units may now cancel.}$$

$$= \frac{153}{1} \cdot \frac{1\,\text{yd}^2}{9}$$

$$= \frac{153}{9}\,\text{yd}^2$$

$$= 17\,\text{yd}^2$$

When using this setup where the unit ratio is raised to a power, you must be careful to remember that *everything* inside the parentheses is raised to that power: the units and the numbers alike.

Checkpoint 8.2.11 Convert 85 cubic inches into cubic centimeters.

Explanation.

$$85\,\text{in}^3 = \frac{85\,\text{in}^3}{1}$$

$$= \frac{85\,\text{in}^3}{1} \cdot \left(\frac{2.54\,\text{cm}}{1\,\text{in}}\right)^3 \qquad \text{The inches in the denominator will be cubed.}$$

$$= \frac{85\,\text{in}^3}{1} \cdot \frac{2.54^3\,\text{cm}^3}{1\,\text{in}^3} \qquad \text{Using the quotient to a power rule.}$$

$$= \frac{85\,\cancel{\text{in}^3}}{1} \cdot \frac{2.54^3\,\text{cm}^3}{1\,\cancel{\text{in}^3}} \qquad \text{Units may now cancel.}$$

$$= \frac{85}{1}\cdot\frac{2.54^3\,\text{cm}^3}{1}$$

$$= 85 \cdot 2.54^3\,\text{cm}^3$$

$$\approx 1393\,\text{cm}^3$$

So 85 cubic inches is about 1393 cubic centimeters.

8.2.4 Converting Rates

A rate unit has a numerator and a denominator. For example, speed is a rate, and speed can be measured in $\frac{\text{mi}}{\text{h}}$. The numerator unit is a mile and the denominator unit is an hour.

Suppose we wanted to convert a speed rate, such as $65\,\frac{\text{mi}}{\text{h}}$, into $\frac{\text{m}}{\text{s}}$. Or a concentration rate, such as $180\,\frac{\text{mg}}{\text{L}}$, into $\frac{\text{g}}{\text{dL}}$. We can use the same process that we've used before to do these conversions. That is, we start by writing what we want to convert as a ratio, which will have units in both the numerator and denominator, and then we multiply by unit ratios until both units have been converted into the units we want. It helps to focus on converting one unit at a time and to make sure that the units in our unit ratios are placed so that the proper units will cancel.

Example 8.2.12 Convert $65\,\frac{\text{mi}}{\text{h}}$ into $\frac{\text{m}}{\text{min}}$.

Explanation. We start by writing what we are converting, which is $65\,\frac{\text{mi}}{\text{h}}$, as a ratio. Then, our job is to convert the miles to meters and the hours to minutes, one at a time. It doesn't matter which unit ratio we use first, as long as the units line up to cancel appropriately.

$$65\,\frac{\text{mi}}{\text{h}} = \frac{65\,\text{mi}}{1\,\text{h}} \qquad\qquad \text{Write the rate as a ratio.}$$

$$\approx \frac{65\,\text{mi}}{1\,\text{h}} \cdot \frac{1.609\,\text{km}}{1\,\text{mi}} \cdot \frac{1000\,\text{m}}{1\,\text{km}} \cdot \frac{1\,\text{h}}{60\,\text{min}}$$

Use unit ratios to make cancellations.

$$= \frac{65\,\cancel{\text{mi}}}{1\,\cancel{\text{h}}} \cdot \frac{1.609\,\cancel{\text{km}}}{1\,\cancel{\text{mi}}} \cdot \frac{1000\,\text{m}}{1\,\cancel{\text{km}}} \cdot \frac{1\,\cancel{\text{h}}}{60\,\text{min}}$$

Units may now cancel.

$$= \frac{65}{1} \cdot \frac{1.609}{1} \cdot \frac{1000\,\text{m}}{1} \cdot \frac{1}{60\,\text{min}}$$

$$= \frac{65 \cdot 1.609 \cdot 1000}{60} \frac{\text{m}}{\text{min}}$$

$$\approx 1743\,\frac{\text{m}}{\text{min}}$$

Notice that the last unit ratio is used to convert the hours to minutes and the hour must be placed in the numerator to cancel the hour in the original rate that was in the denominator. Also, note that this will automatically cause minutes to end up in the denominator, which is where this unit should end up so that we end up with meters *per minute* for our final unit.

An important thing to keep in mind, as demonstrated in the previous example, as well as the next example, is that we avoid multiplying or dividing any numbers until the end, after the final units that we want have been obtained. Stopping partway through to multiply or divide some numbers could lead to confusion and mistakes.

Checkpoint 8.2.13 Convert 180 mg/L into g/dL, given that there are 10 deciliters in a liter.

Explanation. We start by writing what we are converting, which is 180 mg/L, as a ratio. Then, we need to convert the milligrams into grams and the liters into deciliters, converting one unit at a time. We will start by converting the milligrams into grams. Then, we will convert the liters to deciliters.

$$180\,\frac{\text{mg}}{\text{L}} = \frac{180\,\text{mg}}{1\,\text{L}}$$

Write the rate as a ratio.

$$= \frac{180\,\text{mg}}{1\,\text{L}} \cdot \frac{1\,\text{g}}{1000\,\text{mg}} \cdot \frac{1\,\text{L}}{10\,\text{dL}}$$

Use unit ratios to make cancellations.

$$= \frac{180\,\cancel{\text{mg}}}{1\,\cancel{\text{L}}} \cdot \frac{1\,\text{g}}{1000\,\cancel{\text{mg}}} \cdot \frac{1\,\cancel{\text{L}}}{10\,\text{dL}}$$

Units may now cancel.

$$= \frac{180}{1} \cdot \frac{1\,\text{g}}{1000} \cdot \frac{1}{10\,\text{dL}}$$

$$= \frac{180}{1000 \cdot 10} \frac{\text{g}}{\text{dL}}$$

$$\approx 0.018\,\frac{\text{g}}{\text{dL}}$$

So for example if salt is mixed into water with a concentration of 180 mg/L, the concentration can also be described as 0.018 g/dL.

8.2.5 Reading Questions

1.   Unit conversion is a lot like multiplying ⬚ .

2.   If you are using a unit ratio to convert inches to feet, how do you decide whether to use $\frac{1\,\text{ft}}{12\,\text{in}}$ or to use $\frac{12\,\text{in}}{1\,\text{ft}}$?

3.   If you use a power of a unit ratio to make a unit conversion, what do you need to remember?

8.2.6 Exercises

Review and Warmup

1.   Multiply: $\dfrac{5}{9} \cdot \dfrac{5}{8}$

2.   Multiply: $\dfrac{4}{9} \cdot \dfrac{4}{7}$

3.   Multiply: $\dfrac{14}{11} \cdot \dfrac{13}{6}$

4.   Multiply: $\dfrac{15}{7} \cdot \dfrac{4}{15}$

5.   Multiply: $10 \cdot \dfrac{1}{7}$

6.   Multiply: $3 \cdot \dfrac{2}{5}$

Unit Conversions

7.   Convert 7.8 min to seconds.

8.   Convert 2.6 mi^2 to acres.

9.   Convert 633 mi^2 to acres.

10.   Convert 1.11 mi to feet.

11.   Convert 49.7 mg to grams.

12.   Convert 865 mg to grams.

13.   Convert 3.42 m^2 to hectares.

14.   Convert 7.9 mL to cubic centimeters.

15.   Convert 16 mL to gallons.

16.   Convert 5.4 B to kilobits.

17.   Convert 91 T to ounces.

18.   Convert 418 ns to milliseconds.

19.   Convert 7.95 mm to hectometers.

20.   Convert 26.3 km to hectometers.

21.   Convert 649 ft^2 to square miles.

22.   Convert 1.17 kg to milligrams.

23.   Convert 45 m^3 to cubic yards.

24.   Convert 25 hm^2 to square meters.

25.   Convert 8.5 yd^3 to cubic feet.

26.   Convert 65 dm^2 to square meters.

27.   Convert 3.85 in^3 to cubic centimeters.

28.   Convert 13.5 mm^2 to square meters.

29.   Convert 785 km^3 to cubic meters.

30.   Convert 5.35 mi^2 to square feet.

31.   Convert 40.5 $\frac{\text{yd}}{\text{ms}}$ to meters per second.

32.   Convert 29 $\frac{\text{m}}{\text{s}}$ to decimeters per millisecond.

33.   Convert 64 $\frac{\text{acre}}{\text{wk}}$ to square miles per day.

34.   Convert 1.4 $\frac{\text{mi}^2}{\text{ms}}$ to acres per second.

35.   Convert 84 $\frac{\text{mL}}{\text{d}}$ to liters per hour.

36.   Convert 8.78 $\frac{\text{cc}}{\text{wk}}$ to liters per day.

37.   Convert 34.5 $\frac{\text{T}}{\text{wk}}$ to pounds per day.

38.   Convert 77.3 $\frac{\text{g}}{\text{wk}}$ to kilograms per day.

39.   Convert 1.99 $\frac{\text{kb}}{\text{h}}$ to bits per day.

40.   Convert 57.7 $\frac{\text{kb}}{\text{h}}$ to megabits per minute.

41.   Convert 94 $\frac{\text{oz}}{\text{in}^3}$ to pounds per gallon.

42.   Convert 4.2 $\frac{\text{oz}}{\text{cc}}$ to pounds per milliliter.

Applications

43.   Renee's bedroom has 124 ft^2 of floor. She would like to carpet the floor, but carpeting is sold by the square yard. How many square yards of carpeting will she need to get?

44.   Charlotte's bedroom has 137 ft^2 of floor. She would like to carpet the floor, but carpeting is sold by the square yard. How many square yards of carpeting will she need to get?

45.   Kenji is traveling in Europe and renting a car. He is used to thinking of gasoline amounts in gallons, but in Europe it is sold in liters. After filling the gas tank, he notices it took 39 L of gas. How many gallons is that?

46. Alisa is traveling in Europe and renting a car. She is used to thinking of gasoline amounts in gallons, but in Europe it is sold in liters. After filling the gas tank, she notices it took 42 L of gas. How many gallons is that?

47. Kara found a family recipe from the old country that uses 330 mL of soup stock. The recipe serves four, but Kara wants to scale it up to serve fourteen. And none of Kara's measuring devices use the metric system. How many cups of soup stock should she use?

48. Scot found a family recipe from the old country that uses 360 mL of soup stock. The recipe serves four, but Scot wants to scale it up to serve ten. And none of Scot's measuring devices use the metric system. How many cups of soup stock should he use?

49. Dawn was driving at a steady speed of 67 mph for 10 minutes. How far did she travel in that time?

50. Tien was driving at a steady speed of 25 mph for 23 minutes. How far did he travel in that time?

51. The algae in a pond is growing at a rate of $0.18 \frac{kg}{d}$. How much algae is in the poind after 16 weeks?

52. The algae in a pond is growing at a rate of $0.22 \frac{kg}{d}$. How much algae is in the poind after 9 weeks?

53. Brandon is downloading content at an average rate of 48 Mbps (megabits per second). After 189 minutes, how much has he downloaded? It is appropriate to express an amount of data like this in bytes, kilobytes, megabytes, gigabytes, or terabytes.

54. Sarah is downloading content at an average rate of 58 Mbps (megabits per second). After 124 minutes, how much has she downloaded? It is appropriate to express an amount of data like this in bytes, kilobytes, megabytes, gigabytes, or terabytes.

This section is adapted from *Dimensional Analysis*[1], *Converting Between Two Systems of Measurements*[2], and *Converting Rates*[3] by Wendy Lightheart, OpenStax CNX, which is licensed under CC BY 4.0[4]

[1]https://cnx.org/contents/hAiMlVjM@8.4:caPlSDX_@6/Dimensional-Analysis
[2]https://cnx.org/contents/hAiMlVjM@8.4:8DuPvYyV@7/Converting-Between-the-Two-Systems-of-Measurement
[3]https://cnx.org/contents/hAiMlVjM@8.5:jRv6NP4J@7/Converting-Rates
[4]http://creativecommons.org/licenses/by/4.0

8.3 Geometry Formulas

In this section we will evaluate some formulas related to the geometry of two- and three-dimensional shapes.

8.3.1 Evaluating Perimeter and Area Formulas

Rectangles.   The rectangle in Figure 8.3.2 has a length (as measured by the edges on the top and bottom) and a width (as measured by the edges on the left and right).

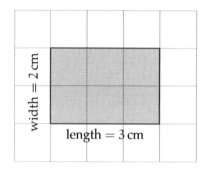

Figure 8.3.2: A Rectangle

Perimeter is the distance around the edge(s) of a two-dimensional shape. To calculate perimeter, start from a point on the shape (usually a corner), travel around the shape, and add up the total distance traveled. For the rectangle in Figure 8.3.2, if we travel around it, the total distance would be:

$$\text{rectangle perimeter} = 3\,\text{cm} + 2\,\text{cm} + 3\,\text{cm} + 2\,\text{cm}$$
$$= 10\,\text{cm}.$$

Another way to compute a rectangle's perimeter would be to start at one corner, add up the edge length half-way around, and then double that. So we could have calculated the perimeter this way:

$$\text{rectangle perimeter} = 2(3\,\text{cm} + 2\,\text{cm})$$
$$= 2(5\,\text{cm})$$
$$= 10\,\text{cm}.$$

There is nothing special about this rectangle having length 3 cm and width 2 cm. With a generic rectangle, it has some length we can represent with the variable ℓ and some width we can represent with the variable w. We can use P to represent its perimeter, and then the perimeter of the rectangle will be given by:

$$P = 2(\ell + w).$$

Area is the number of 1×1 squares that fit inside a two-dimensional shape (possibly after morphing them into non-square shapes). If the edges of the squares are, say, 1 cm long, then the area is measured in "square cm," written cm^2. In Figure 8.3.2, the rectangle has six $1\,\text{cm} \times 1\,\text{cm}$ squares, so its area is 6 square centimeters.

Note that we can find that area by multiplying the length and the width:

$$\text{rectangle area} = (3\,\text{cm}) \cdot (2\,\text{cm})$$

$$= 6\,\text{cm}^2$$

Again, there is nothing special about this rectangle having length 3 cm and width 2 cm. With a generic rectangle, it has some length we can represent with the variable ℓ and some width we can represent with the variable w. We can represent its area with the variable A, and then the area of the rectangle will be given by:

$$A = \ell \cdot w.$$

Checkpoint 8.3.3 Find the perimeter and area of the rectangle.

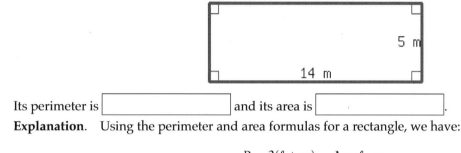

Its perimeter is [   ] and its area is [   ].

Explanation. Using the perimeter and area formulas for a rectangle, we have:

$$
\begin{aligned}
P &= 2(\ell + w) & A &= \ell \cdot w \\
&= 2(14 + 5) & &= 14 \cdot 5 \\
&= 2(19) & &= 70 \\
&= 38
\end{aligned}
$$

Since length and width were measured in meters, we find that the perimeter is 38 meters and the area is 70 square meters.

Example 8.3.4
Imagine a rectangle with width 7.5 in and height 11.43 cm as in Figure 8.3.5.

a. Find the perimeter (in inches) of the rectangle.

b. Find the area (in square centimeters) of the rectangle.

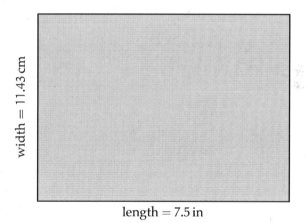

Figure 8.3.5: A Rectangle

Explanation.

a. To find the perimeter (in inches) of the rectangle, we should first convert all lengths into inches. By Appendix B, we know that 1 in = 2.54 cm. So, we have

$$11.43\,\text{cm} = \frac{11.43\,\text{cm}}{1} \cdot \frac{1\,\text{in}}{2.54\,\text{cm}}$$

$$= \frac{11.43}{2.54} \, \text{in}$$
$$= 4.5 \, \text{in}$$

So, the total perimeter is $2 \cdot 4.5 \, \text{in} + 2 \cdot 7.5 \, \text{in} = 24 \, \text{in}$.

b. To find the area (in square centimeters) of the rectangle, we should first convert all lengths into centimeters. So, we have

$$7.5 \, \text{in} = \frac{7.5 \, \text{in}}{1} \cdot \frac{2.54 \, \text{cm}}{1 \, \text{in}}$$
$$= \frac{7.5}{2.54} \, \text{cm}$$
$$= 19.05 \, \text{cm}$$

So, the total area is $19.05 \, \text{cm} \cdot 11.43 \, \text{cm} = 85.725 \, \text{cm}^2$.

Triangles.   The perimeter of a general triangle has no special formula—all that is needed is to add the lengths of its three sides. The *area* of a triangle is a bit more interesting. In Figure 8.3.6, there are three triangles. From left to right, there is an acute triangle, a right triangle, and an obtuse triangle. Each triangle is drawn so that there is a "bottom" horizontal edge. This edge is referred to as the "base" of the triangle. With each triangle, a "height" that is perpendicular to the base is also illustrated.

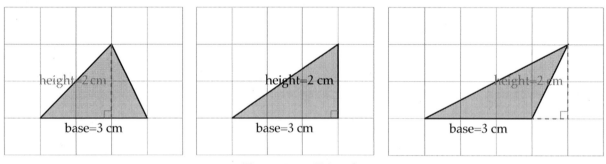

Figure 8.3.6: Triangles

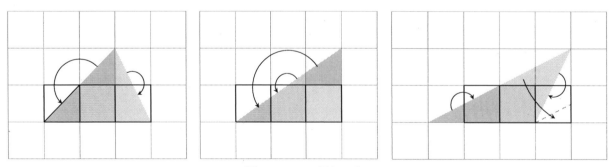

Figure 8.3.7: Triangles

Each of these triangles has the same base width, 3 cm, and the same height, 2 cm. Note that they each have the same area as well. Figure 8.3.7 illustrates how they each have an area of 3 cm².

As with the triangles in Figure 8.3.7, you can always rearrange little pieces of a triangle so that the resulting shape is a rectangle with the same base width, but with a height that's one-half of the triangle's height. With a generic rectangle, it has some base width we can represent with the variable b and some height we can represent with the variable h. We can represent its area with the variable A, and then the area of the triangle will be given by $A = b \cdot \left(\frac{1}{2}h\right)$, or more conventionally:

$$A = \frac{1}{2}bh.$$

Checkpoint 8.3.8 Find the perimeter and area of the triangle.

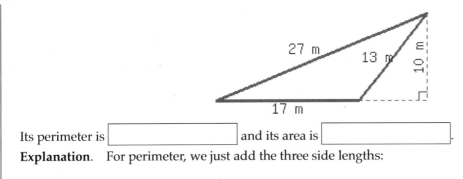

Its perimeter is ⬚ and its area is ⬚.

Explanation. For perimeter, we just add the three side lengths:

$$P = 13 + 27 + 17$$
$$= 57$$

For area, we use the triangle area formula:

$$A = \frac{1}{2}bh$$
$$= \frac{1}{2}(17)(10)$$
$$= 5(17)$$
$$= 85$$

Since length and width were measured in meters, we find that the perimeter is 57 meters and the area is 85 square meters.

Circles. To find formulas for the perimeter and area of a circle, it helps to first know that there is a special number called π (spelled "pi" and pronounced like "pie") that appears in many places in mathematics. The decimal value of π is about 3.14159265..., and it helps to memorize some of these digits. It also helps to understand that π is a little larger than 3. There are many definitions for π that can explain where it comes from and how you can find all its decimal places, but here we are just going to accept that it is a special number, and it is roughly 3.14159265....

The perimeter of a circle is the distance around its edge. For circles, the perimeter has a special name: the **circumference**. Imagine wrapping a string around the circle and cutting it so that it makes one complete loop. If we straighten out that piece of string, we have a length that is just as long as the circle's circumference.

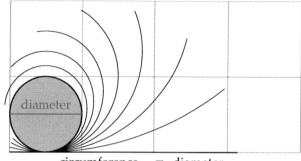

circumference = $\pi \cdot$ diameter

Figure 8.3.9: Circle Diameter and Circumference

As we can see in Figure 8.3.9, the circumference of a circle is a little more than three times as long as its diameter. (The diameter of a circle is the length of a straight line running from a point on the edge through the center to the opposite edge.) In fact, the circumference is actually exactly π times the length of the diameter. With a generic circle, it has some diameter we can represent with the variable d. We can represent its circumference with the variable c, and then the circumference of the circle will be given by:

$$c = \pi d.$$

Alternatively, we often prefer to work with a circle's **radius** instead of its diameter. The radius is the distance from any point on the circle's edge to its center. (Note that the radius is half the diameter.) From this perspective, we can see in Figure 8.3.10 that the circumference is a little more than 6 times the radius.

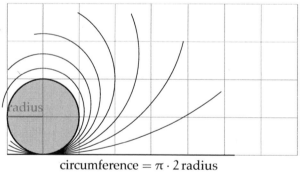

circumference = $\pi \cdot 2$ radius

Figure 8.3.10: Circle Diameter and Circumference

This gives us another formula for a circle's circumerence that uses the variable r for its radius: $c = \pi \cdot 2r$. Or more conventionally,

$$c = 2\pi r.$$

There is also a formula for the *area* of a circle based on its radius. Figure 8.3.11 shows how three squares can be cut up and rearranged to fit inside a circle. This shows how the area of a circle of radius r is just a little larger than $3r^2$. Since π is just a little larger than 3, could it be that the area of a circle is given by πr^2?

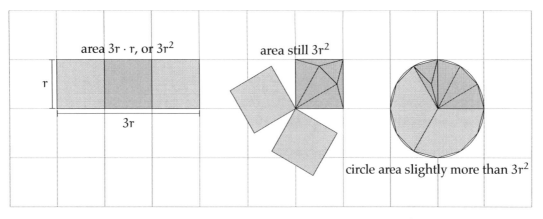

Figure 8.3.11: Circle area is slightly larger than $3r^2$.

One way to establish this formula is to imagine slicing up the circle into many pie slices as in Figure 8.3.12. Then you can rearrange the slices into a strange shape that is *almost* a rectangle with height equal to the radius of the original circle, and width equal to half the circumference of the original circle.

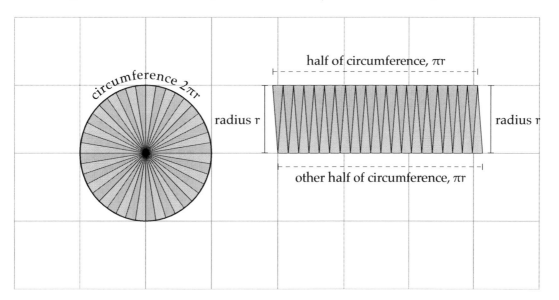

Figure 8.3.12: Reasoning the circle area formula.

Since the area of the circle is equal to the area of the almost-rectangular shape in Figure 8.3.12, we have the circle area formula:

$$A = \pi r^2.$$

Checkpoint 8.3.13 A circle's diameter is 6 m.

a. This circle's circumference, in terms of π, is [⎵].

b. This circle's circumference, rounded to the hundredth place, is [⎵].

  c. This circle's area, in terms of π, is $\boxed{}$.

  d. This circle's area, rounded to the hundredth place, is $\boxed{}$.

Explanation. We use r to represent radius and d to represent diameter. In this problem, it's given that the diameter is 6 m. A circle's radius is half as long as its diameter, so the radius is 3 m.

 Throughout these computations, all quantities have units attached, but we only show them in the final step.

a. $c = \pi d$
$$= \pi \cdot 6$$
$$= 6\pi \text{ m}$$

c. $A = \pi r^2$
$$= \pi \cdot 3^2$$
$$= \pi \cdot 9$$
$$= 9\pi \text{ m}^2$$

d. $A = \pi r^2$
$$\approx 3.1415926 \cdot 3^2$$
$$\approx 3.1415926 \cdot 9$$
$$\approx 28.27 \text{ m}^2$$

b. $c = \pi d$
$$\approx 3.1415926 \cdot 6$$
$$\approx 18.85 \text{ m}$$

8.3.2 Volume

The **volume** of a three-dimensional object is the number of $1 \times 1 \times 1$ cubes that fit inside the object (possibly after morphing them into non-cube shapes). If the edges of the cubes are, say, 1 cm long, then the volume is measured in "cubic centimeters ," written cm^3.

Rectangular Prisms. The 3D shape in Figure 8.3.14 is called a rectangular prism.

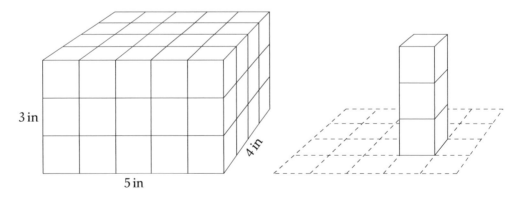

Figure 8.3.14: Volume of a Rectangular Prism

The rectangular prism in Figure 8.3.14 is composed of $1 \text{ in} \times 1 \text{ in} \times 1 \text{ in}$ unit cubes, with each cube's volume being 1 cubic inch (or in^3). The shape's volume is the number of such unit cubes. The bottom face has $5 \cdot 4 = 20$ unit squares. Since there are 3 layers of cubes, the shape has a total of $3 \cdot 20 = 60$ unit cubes. In other words, the shape's volume is 60 in^3 because it has sixty $1 \text{ in} \times 1 \text{ in} \times 1 \text{ in}$ cubes inside it.

We found the number of unit squares in the bottom face by multiplying $5 \cdot 4 = 20$. Then to find the volume, we multiplied by 3 because there are three layers of cubes. So one formula for a prism's volume is

$$V = wdh$$

where V stands for volume, w for width, d for depth, and h for height.

Checkpoint 8.3.15 A masonry brick is in the shape of a rectangular prism and is 8 inches wide, 3.5 inches deep, and 2.25 inches high. What is its volume?

Explanation. Using the formula for the volume of a rectangular prism:

$$
\begin{aligned}
V &= wdh \\
&= 8(3.5)(2.25) \\
&= 63
\end{aligned}
$$

So the brick's volume is 63 cubic inches.

Example 8.3.16
Imagine a rectangular prism with width 40 in, depth 4 ft, and height 2 yd as in Figure 8.3.17.

1. Find the volume (in cubic feet) of the prism.

2. Find the surface area (in square inches) of the prism.

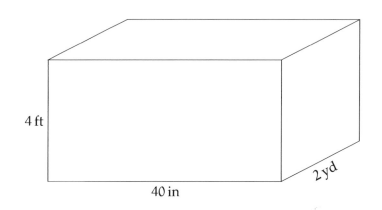

Figure 8.3.17: A Prism

Explanation.

1. To find the volume (in cubic feet) of the prism, we should first convert all lengths into feet. By Appendix B, we know that 1 ft = 12 in and that 1 yd = 3 ft. So, we have

$$
\begin{aligned}
40\,\text{in} &= \frac{40\,\text{in}}{1} \cdot \frac{1\,\text{ft}}{12\,\text{in}} \\
&= \frac{40}{12}\,\text{ft} \\
&= \frac{10}{3}\,\text{ft}
\end{aligned}
$$

and

$$
\begin{aligned}
2\,\text{yd} &= \frac{2\,\text{yd}}{1} \cdot \frac{3\,\text{ft}}{1\,\text{yd}} \\
&= 2 \cdot 3\,\text{ft} \\
&= 6\,\text{ft}
\end{aligned}
$$

So, the total volume is $4\,\text{ft} \cdot \frac{10}{3}\,\text{ft} \cdot 6\,\text{ft} = 80\,\text{ft}^3$.

2. To find the surface area (in square inches) of the prism, we should first convert all lengths into inches. So, we have

$$4\,\text{ft} = \frac{4\,\text{ft}}{1} \cdot \frac{12\,\text{in}}{1\,\text{ft}}$$
$$= 4 \cdot 12\,\text{in}$$
$$= 48\,\text{in}$$

and

$$2\,\text{yd} = \frac{2\,\text{yd}}{1} \cdot \frac{36\,\text{in}}{1\,\text{yd}}$$
$$= 2 \cdot 36\,\text{in}$$
$$= 72\,\text{in}$$

To find the surface area, we should add up the six areas of the faces of the prism, each of which is a rectangle. Note that each face has a corresponding symmetrical face on the other side of the prism.

$$\text{Surface Area} = \overbrace{2(40\,\text{in} \cdot 36\,\text{in})}^{\text{top and bottom}} + \overbrace{2(48\,\text{in} \cdot 36\,\text{in})}^{\text{left and right}} + \overbrace{2(40\,\text{in} \cdot 48\,\text{in})}^{\text{front and back}}$$
$$= 10176\,\text{in}^2$$

Cylinders.   A cylinder is not a prism, but it has some similarities. Instead of a square base, the base is a circle. Its volume can also be calculated in a similar way to how prism volume is calculated. Let's look at an example.

Example 8.3.18 Find the volume of a cylinder with a radius of 3 meters and a height of 2 meters.

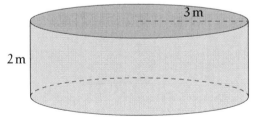

Figure 8.3.19: A Cylinder

Explanation.   The base of the cylinder is a circle. We know the area of a circle is given by the formula $A = \pi r^2$, so the base area is $9\pi\,\text{m}^2$, or about $28.27\,\text{m}^2$. That means about 28.27 unit squares can fit into the base. One of them is drawn in Figure 8.3.20 along with two unit cubes above it.

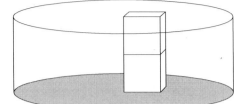

Figure 8.3.20: Finding Cylinder Volume

For each unit square in the base circle, there are two unit cubes of volume. So the volume is the base area times the height: $9\pi\,\text{m}^2 \cdot 2\,\text{m}$, which equals $18\pi\,\text{m}^3$. Approximating π with a decimal value, this is about $56.55\,\text{m}^3$.

Example 8.3.18 demonstrates that the volume of a cylinder can be calculated with the formula

$$V = \pi r^2 h$$

where r is the radius and h is the height.

Checkpoint 8.3.21 A soda can is basically in the shape of a cylinder with radius 1.3 inches and height 4.8 inches. What is its volume?

Its exact volume in terms of π is: ☐ .

As a decimal approximation rounded to four significant digits, its volume is: ☐ .

Explanation. Using the formula for the volume of a cylinder:

$$\begin{aligned}
V &= \pi r^2 h \\
&= \pi (1.3)^2 (4.8) \\
&= 8.112\pi \\
&\approx 25.48
\end{aligned}$$

So the can's volume is 8.112π cubic inches, which is about 25.48 cubic inches.

Note that the volume formulas for a rectangular prism and a cylinder have something in common: both formulas first find the area of the base (which is a rectangle for a prism and a circle for a cylinder) and then multiply by the height. So there is another formula

$$V = Bh$$

that works for both shapes. Here, B stands for the base area (which is wd for a prism and πr^2 for a cylinder.)

8.3.3 Summary

Here is a list of all the formulas we've learned in this section.

List 8.3.22: Geometry Formulas

Perimeter of a Rectangle $P = 2(\ell + w)$

Area of a Rectangle $A = \ell w$

Area of a Triangle $A = \frac{1}{2}bh$

Circumference of a Circle $c = 2\pi r$

Area of a Circle $A = \pi r^2$

Volume of a Rectangular Prism $V = wdh$

Volume of a Cylinder $V = \pi r^2 h$

Volume of a Rectangular Prism or Cylinder $V = Bh$

8.3.4 Exercises

Perimeter and Area

1. Find the perimeter and area of the rectangle.

8 m

16 m

Its perimeter is ⬚ and its area is ⬚.

2. Find the perimeter and area of the rectangle.

8 m

18 m

Its perimeter is ⬚ and its area is ⬚.

3. Find the perimeter of the rectangle below.

1/10 m

3/8 m

4. Find the perimeter of the rectangle below.

1/9 m

3/10 m

5. Find the area of the rectangle below.

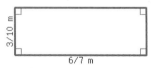

3/10 m

6/7 m

6. Find the area of the rectangle below.

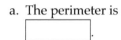

3/8 m

5/6 m

7. Find the perimeter and area of a rectangular table top with a length of 5.8 ft and a width of 29 in.

Its perimeter is ☐

and its area is ☐.

8. Find the perimeter and area of a rectangular table top with a length of 6 ft and a width of 25 in.

Its perimeter is ☐

and its area is ☐.

9. Find the perimeter and area of the square.

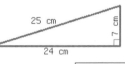

5 cm

a. The perimeter is

☐.

b. The area is ☐.

10. Find the perimeter and area of the square.

7 cm

a. The perimeter is

☐.

b. The area is ☐.

11. Find the perimeter and area of the triangle.

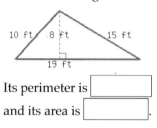

10 ft · 8 ft 15 ft

19 ft

Its perimeter is ☐

and its area is ☐.

12. Find the perimeter and area of the triangle.

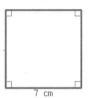

13 ft 10 ft 17 ft

22 ft

Its perimeter is ☐

and its area is ☐.

13. Find the perimeter and area of the right triangle.

25 cm · 7 cm

24 cm

Its perimeter is ☐

and its area is ☐.

14. Find the perimeter and area of the right triangle.

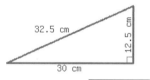

32.5 cm · 12.5 cm

30 cm

Its perimeter is ☐

and its area is ☐.

15. Find the perimeter and area of the triangle.

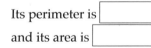

31 m 19 m 15 m

15 m

Its perimeter is ☐

and its area is ☐.

16. Find the perimeter and area of the triangle.

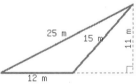

25 m 15 m 11 m

12 m

Its perimeter is ☐

and its area is ☐.

17. The area of the triangle below is ☐ square feet.

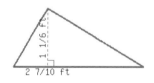

1 1/6 ft

2 7/10 ft

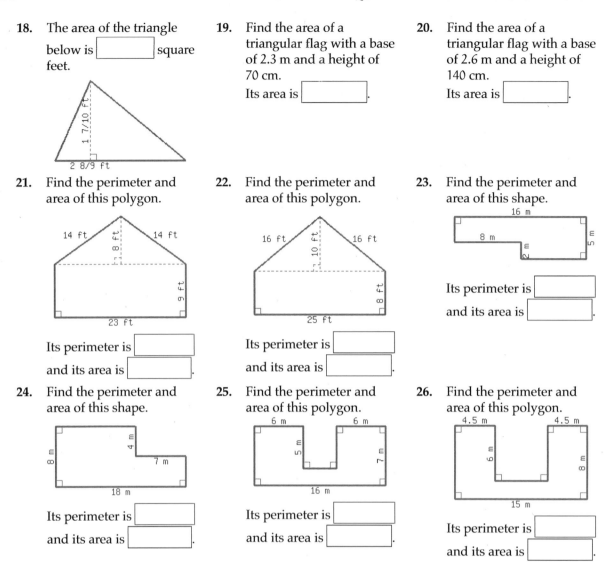

18. The area of the triangle below is ⬚ square feet.

19. Find the area of a triangular flag with a base of 2.3 m and a height of 70 cm.

Its area is ⬚.

20. Find the area of a triangular flag with a base of 2.6 m and a height of 140 cm.

Its area is ⬚.

21. Find the perimeter and area of this polygon.

Its perimeter is ⬚

and its area is ⬚.

22. Find the perimeter and area of this polygon.

Its perimeter is ⬚

and its area is ⬚.

23. Find the perimeter and area of this shape.

Its perimeter is ⬚

and its area is ⬚.

24. Find the perimeter and area of this shape.

Its perimeter is ⬚

and its area is ⬚.

25. Find the perimeter and area of this polygon.

Its perimeter is ⬚

and its area is ⬚.

26. Find the perimeter and area of this polygon.

Its perimeter is ⬚

and its area is ⬚.

A trapezoid's area can be calculated by the formula $A = \frac{1}{2}(b_1 + b_2)h$, where A stands for area, b_1 for the first base's length, b_2 for the second base's length, and h for height.

27. Find the area of the trapezoid below.

28. Find the area of the trapezoid below.

The formula $A = \frac{1}{2} r \, n \, s$ gives the area of a regular polygon with side length s, number of sides n and, apothem r. (The *apothem* is the distance from the center of the polygon to one of its sides.)

29. What is the area of a regular pentagon with s = 30 in and r = 54 in?

30. What is the area of a regular 94-gon with s = 42 in and r = 43 in?

31. A circle's radius is 6 m.

a. The circumference, in terms of π, is [   ].

b. This circle's circumference, rounded to the hundredths place, is [   ].

c. This circle's area, in terms of π, is [   ].

d. This circle's area, rounded to the hundredths place, is [   ].

32. A circle's radius is 7 m.

a. The circumference, in terms of π, is [   ].

b. This circle's circumference, rounded to the hundredths place, is [   ].

c. This circle's area, in terms of π, is [   ].

d. This circle's area, rounded to the hundredths place, is [   ].

33. A circle's diameter is 16 m.

a. This circle's circumference, in terms of π, is [   ].

b. This circle's circumference, rounded to the hundredths place, is [   ].

c. This circle's area, in terms of π, is [   ].

d. This circle's area, rounded to the hundredths place, is [   ].

34. A circle's diameter is 18 m.

a. This circle's circumference, in terms of π, is [   ].

b. This circle's circumference, rounded to the hundredths place, is [   ].

c. This circle's area, in terms of π, is [   ].

d. This circle's area, rounded to the hundredths place, is [   ].

Find the perimeter and area of this shape, which is a semicircle on top of a rectangle.

35.

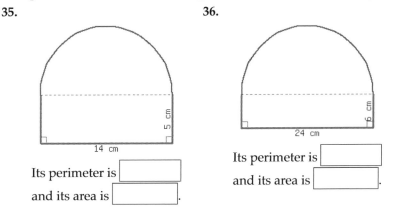

5 cm

14 cm

Its perimeter is [   ]
and its area is [   ].

36.

24 cm

6 cm

Its perimeter is [   ]
and its area is [   ].

Volume

37. Find the volume of this rectangular prism.

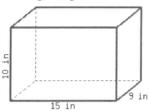

38. Find the volume of this rectangular prism.

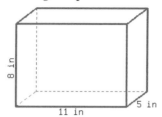

39. Find the volume of this rectangular prism.

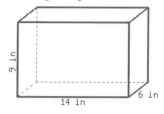

40. Find the volume of this rectangular prism.

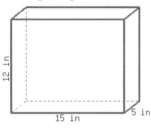

41. A cube's side length is 7 cm. Its volume is

.

42. A cube's side length is 8 cm. Its volume is

.

43. Find the volume of this cylinder.

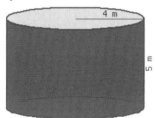

a. This cylinder's volume, in terms of π, is <br>.

b. This cylinder's volume, rounded to the hundredths place, is <br>.

44. Find the volume of this cylinder.

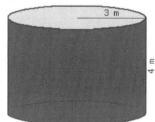

a. This cylinder's volume, in terms of π, is <br>.

b. This cylinder's volume, rounded to the hundredths place, is <br>.

45. Find the volume of this cylinder.

a. This cylinder's volume, in terms of π, is <br>.

b. This cylinder's volume, rounded to the hundredths place, is <br>.

46. Find the volume of this cylinder.

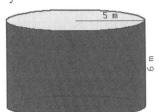

5 m

6 m

   a. This cylinder's volume, in terms of π, is [   ].

   b. This cylinder's volume, rounded to the hundredths place, is [   ].

47. A cylinder's base's diameter is 12 ft, and its height is 4 ft.

   a. This cylinder's volume, in terms of π, is [   ].

   b. This cylinder's volume, rounded to the hundredths place, is [   ].

48. A cylinder's base's diameter is 6 ft, and its height is 5 ft.

   a. This cylinder's volume, in terms of π, is [   ].

   b. This cylinder's volume, rounded to the hundredths place, is [   ].

The formula $V = \frac{1}{3} \cdot s^2 \cdot h$ gives the volume of a right square pyramid.

49. What is the volume of a right square pyramid with $s = 51$ in and $h = 82$ in?

50. What is the volume of a right square pyramid with $s = 63$ in and $h = 48$ in?

51. Fill out the table with various formulas as they were given in this section.

Rectangle Perimeter   _____

Rectangle Area   _____

Triangle Area   _____

Circle Circumference   _____

Circle Area   _____

Rectangular Prism Volume   _____

Cylinder Volume   _____

Volume of either Rectangular Prism or Cylinder   _____

8.4 Geometry Applications

8.4.1 Solving Equations for Geometry Problems

With geometry problems in algebra, it is really helpful to draw a picture to understand the scenario better. After drawing the shape and labeling the given information, we will choose the formula to use from the list in Subsection 8.3.3.

Example 8.4.1 An Olympic-size swimming pool is rectangular and 50 m in length. We don't know its width, but we do know that it required 150 m of painter's tape to outline the edge of the pool during recent renovations. Use this information to set up an equation and find the width of the pool.

Explanation.

The pool's shape is a rectangle, so it helps to sketch a rectangle representing the pool as in Figure 8.4.2. Since we know its length is 50 m, it is a good idea to label that in the sketch. The width is our unknown quantity, so we can use w as a variable to represent the pool's width in meters and label that too.

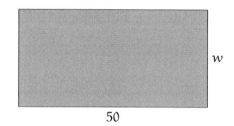

Figure 8.4.2: An Olympic-size pool

Since it required 150 m of painter's tape to outline the pool, we know the perimeter of the pool is 150 m. This suggests using the perimeter formula for a rectangle: $P = 2(\ell + w)$. (This formula was discussed in Subsection 8.3.1).

With this formula, we can substitute 150 in for P and 50 in for ℓ:

$$150 = 2(50 + w).$$

Now we can solve the equation for the width of the pool.

First, we will distribute on the right side, and then isolate w.

$$150 = 100 + 2w$$
$$150 - 100 = 100 - 100 + 2w$$
$$50 = 2w$$
$$\frac{50}{2} = \frac{2w}{2}$$
$$25 = w.$$

Checking the solution $w = 25$ meters:

$$150 = 2(50 + w)$$
$$150 \stackrel{?}{=} 2(50 + 25)$$
$$150 \stackrel{?}{=} 2(75)$$
$$150 \stackrel{\checkmark}{=} 150.$$

We found that the width of the pool is 25 meters.

Checkpoint 8.4.3 One sail on a sail boat is approximately shaped like a triangle. If the base length is 10 feet and the total sail area is 125 square feet, we can wonder how tall is the sail. Set up an equation to model the sail's height.

Explanation.   Since the sail's shape is (approximately) a triangle, it helps to sketch a triangle representing the sail. Since we know its base width is 10 feet, it is a good idea to label that in the sketch. The heigth is our unknown quantity, so we can use h as a variable to represent the sail's height in feet and label that too.

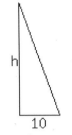

Since the total area is known to be 125 square feet, this suggests using the area formula for a triangle: $A = \frac{1}{2}bh$.

With this formula, we can substitute 125 in for A and 100 in for b:

$$125 = \frac{1}{2}(10)h$$

and this equation models the height of the pool.

Let's look at another example. In this one we need to use an algebraic expression for one of the sides of a rectangle.

Example 8.4.4 Azul is designing a rectangular garden and they have 40 meters of wood planking for the border. Their garden's length is 4 meters less than three times the width, and the perimeter must be 40 meters. Find the garden's length and width.

Explanation. Let Azul's garden width be w meters. We can then represent the length as $3w - 4$ meters since we are told that it is 4 meters less than three times the width. It's given that the perimeter is 40 meters. Substituting those values into the formula, we have:

$$P = 2(\ell + w)$$
$$40 = 2(3w - 4 + w)$$
$$40 = 2(4w - 4) \qquad\qquad \text{Like terms were combined.}$$

The next step to solve this equation is to remove the parentheses by distribution.

Checking the solution $w = 6$:

$$40 = 2(4w - 4)$$
$$40 = 8w - 8$$
$$40 + 8 = 8w - 8 + 8$$
$$48 = 8w$$
$$\frac{48}{8} = \frac{8w}{8}$$
$$6 = w.$$

$$40 = 2(4w - 4)$$
$$40 \stackrel{?}{=} 2(4(6) - 4)$$
$$40 \stackrel{\checkmark}{=} 2(20).$$

To determine the length, recall that this was represented by $3w - 4$, which is:

$$3w - 4 = 3(6) - 4$$
$$= 14.$$

Thus, the width of Azul's garden is 6 meters and the length is 14 meters.

Checkpoint 8.4.5 A rectangle's perimeter is 56 m. Its width is 10 m. Use an equation to solve for the rectangle's length.

Its length is ⬚.

Explanation. When we deal with a geometric figure, it's always a good idea to sketch it to help us think. Let the length be x meters.

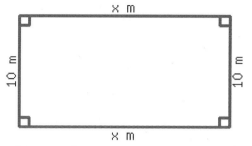

The perimeter is given as 56 m. Adding up the rectangle's 4 sides gives the perimeter. The equation is:

$$x + x + 10 + 10 = 56$$
$$2x + 20 = 56$$
$$2x + 20 - \mathbf{20} = 56 - \mathbf{20}$$
$$2x = 36$$
$$\frac{2x}{2} = \frac{36}{2}$$
$$x = 18$$

So the rectangle's length is 18 m. Don't forget the unit m.

For triangle problems, we may need to use the Pythagorean Theorem that we learned in Subsection 7.1.2. If we know the lengths of two sides of a right triangle then we can find the length of the third side.

Example 8.4.6 Tan owns a road sign manufacturing company and he is producing triangular yield signs for the State of Oregon. The signs are equilateral triangles measuring 36 inches on each side as shown in Figure 8.4.7. Find the area of one sign in square feet to help Tan estimate the amount of material he needs to produce the signs.

Explanation. We will start by converting 36 inches to 3 feet, because the area needs to be in square feet. The area of a triangle is found using $A = \frac{1}{2}bh$, where A is the area, b is the width of the base, and h is the height. In this case the base is at the top of the triangle.

We know the width of the triangle is 3 feet, but we don't know the height. By drawing in the height we form two right triangles so we can use the Pythagorean Theorem to find the height. Half of the width is 1.5 feet, so we will substitute for b and c in the pythagorean theorem.

According to Pythagorean Theorem, we have:

$$c^2 = a^2 + b^2$$
$$3^2 = a^2 + 1.5^2$$
$$9 = a^2 + 2.25$$
$$9 - 2.25 = a^2 + 2.25 - 2.25$$
$$6.75 = a^2$$
$$\sqrt{6.75} = a$$
$$2.598 \approx a$$

The height of the triangle is approximately 2.598 feet.

Now we can calculate the area of one sign.

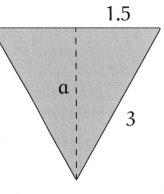

$$A = \frac{1}{2}bh$$
$$\approx \frac{1}{2}(3)(2.598)$$
$$= 3.897$$

Figure 8.4.7

The area of one sign is approximately 3.897 ft^2.

Now we will look at an example that involves a circle. It can be difficult to measure the radius of a circle or cylinder. But if we can measure the circumference, then we can find the radius.

Example 8.4.8 Batula wants to order a custom replacement column for the front of her house and she needs to know the radius. She takes a string and wraps it around the old column. She measures the string and finds the circumference is 3 feet, 2.5 inches. What is the radius of the column?

Explanation.   The formula for the circumference of a circle is $C = 2\pi r$, where C stands for the circumference and r stands for the radius.

We will let the radius of Batula's column be r inches. It's given that the circumference is 3 feet, 2.5 inches, so let's convert 3 feet into inches.

$$3\,\text{ft} = \frac{3\,\text{ft}}{1} \cdot \frac{12\,\text{in}}{1\,\text{ft}}$$
$$= \frac{3\,\cancel{\text{ft}}}{1} \cdot \frac{12\,\text{in}}{1\,\cancel{\text{ft}}}$$
$$= 3 \cdot 12\,\text{in}$$
$$= 36\,\text{in}$$

Since 3 feet is 36 inches, we can add the 2.5 inches for a total of 38.5 inches. Substituting the circumference into the formula, we have:

$$C = 2\pi r$$
$$38.5 = 2\pi r$$

The next step is to divide both sides by 2π.   Checking the solution $r \approx 6.13$ inches:

$$38.5 = 2\pi r$$

$$\frac{38.5}{2\pi} = \frac{2\pi r}{2\pi}$$

$$6.127 \approx r.$$

$$38.5 = 2\pi r$$

$$38.5 \overset{?}{\approx} 2\pi(6.127)$$

$$38.5 \overset{\checkmark}{\approx} 38.5.$$

Therefore, Batula should order a column with a radius of 6.127 inches. A specific measurement like that may not be possible, but Batula could round to something like $6\frac{1}{8}$ inches, which is very close. If the manufacturer wanted the diameter instead, we would multiply that by 2 to get 12.25 or $6\frac{1}{4}$ inches.

Here is an example using volume.

Example 8.4.9 Mark is designing a cylindrical container for his ice cream business. He wants each container to be 15 centimeters tall and hold 1 gallon of ice cream. What dimension should Mark use for the radius of the container?

Explanation.   The formula for the volume of a cylinder is $V = \pi r^2 h$, where V stands for the volume, r stands for the radius and h is the height.

Since the volume is in gallons and the dimensions are in centimeters, we need to convert 1 gallon to cubic centimeters.

$$1\,\text{gal} = \frac{1\,\text{gal}}{1} \cdot \frac{231\,\text{in}^3}{1\,\text{gal}} \cdot \frac{2.54^3\,\text{cm}^3}{1\,\text{in}^3}$$

$$= \frac{1\,\cancel{\text{gal}}}{1} \cdot \frac{231\,\cancel{\text{in}^3}}{1\,\cancel{\text{gal}}} \cdot \frac{2.54^3\,\text{cm}^3}{1\,\cancel{\text{in}^3}}$$

$$= 1 \cdot 231 \cdot 2.54^3\,\text{cm}^3$$

$$= 3785.41\,\text{cm}^3$$

Now we can substitute the volume and height into the formula:

$$V = \pi r^2 h$$

$$3785.41 = \pi r^2 (15)$$

The next step is to divide both sides by 15π.   Checking the solution $r \approx 8.963$ centimeters:

$$3785.41 = 15\pi r^2$$

$$\frac{3785.41}{15\pi} = \frac{15\pi r^2}{15\pi}$$

$$\frac{3785.41}{15\pi} = r^2$$

$$\sqrt{\frac{3785.41}{15\pi}} = r$$

$$8.963 \approx r.$$

$$3785.41 = \pi r^2 h$$

$$3785.41 \overset{?}{\approx} \pi(8.963^2)(15)$$

$$3785.41 \overset{\checkmark}{\approx} 3783.18.$$

Note that our check is approximate because we rounded our answer. Mark will want to make the radius of his container at least 8.963 centimeters. He should make it a little larger to have space at the top of the container.

8.4.2 Proportionality in Similar Triangles

Another appliction of geometry involves similar triangles. Two triangles are considered **similar** if they have the same angles and their side lengths are proportional, as shown in Figure 8.4.10:

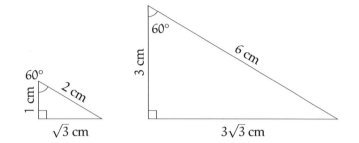

Figure 8.4.10: Similar Triangles

In the first triangle in Figure 8.4.10, the ratio of the left side length to the hypotenuse length is $\frac{1\,\text{cm}}{2\,\text{cm}}$; in the second triangle, the ratio of the left side length to the hypotenuse length is $\frac{3\,\text{cm}}{6\,\text{cm}}$. Since both reduce to $\frac{1}{2}$, we can write the following proportion:

$$\frac{1\,\text{cm}}{2\,\text{cm}} = \frac{3\,\text{cm}}{6\,\text{cm}}$$

If we extend this concept, we can use it to solve for an unknown side length. Consider the two similar triangles in the next example.

Example 8.4.11

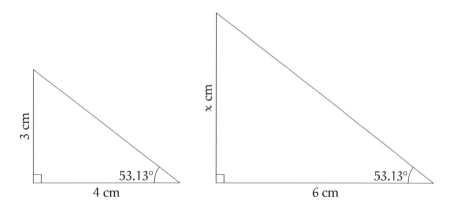

Figure 8.4.12: Similar Triangles

Since the two triangles are similar, we know that their side length should be proportional. To determine the unknown length, we can set up a proportion and solve for x:

$$\frac{\text{bigger triangle's left side length in cm}}{\text{bigger triangle's bottom side length in cm}} = \frac{\text{smaller triangle's left side length in cm}}{\text{smaller triangle's bottom side length in cm}}$$

$$\frac{x\,\text{cm}}{6\,\text{cm}} = \frac{3\,\text{cm}}{4\,\text{cm}}$$

$$\frac{x}{6} = \frac{3}{4}$$

$$6 \cdot \frac{x}{6} = 6 \cdot \frac{3}{4}$$

$$x = \frac{18}{4}$$

$$x = \frac{9}{2} = 4.5$$

The unknown side length is then 4.5 cm.

Remark 8.4.13 Looking at the triangles in Figure 8.4.10, you may notice that there are many different proportions you could set up, such as:

$$\frac{2\,\text{cm}}{1\,\text{cm}} = \frac{6\,\text{cm}}{3\,\text{cm}}$$

$$\frac{2\,\text{cm}}{6\,\text{cm}} = \frac{1\,\text{cm}}{3\,\text{cm}}$$

$$\frac{6\,\text{cm}}{2\,\text{cm}} = \frac{3\,\text{cm}}{1\,\text{cm}}$$

$$\frac{3\sqrt{3}\,\text{cm}}{\sqrt{3}\,\text{cm}} = \frac{3\,\text{cm}}{1\,\text{cm}}$$

This is often the case when we set up ratios and proportions.

If we take a second look at Figure 8.4.12, there are also several other proportions we could have used to find the value of x.

$$\frac{\text{bigger triangle's left side length}}{\text{smaller triangle's left side length}} = \frac{\text{bigger triangle's bottom side length}}{\text{smaller triangle's bottom side length}}$$

$$\frac{\text{smaller triangle's bottom side length}}{\text{bigger triangle's bottom side length}} = \frac{\text{smaller triangle's left side length}}{\text{bigger triangle's left side length}}$$

$$\frac{\text{bigger triangle's bottom side length}}{\text{smaller triangle's bottom side length}} = \frac{\text{bigger triangle's left side length}}{\text{smaller triangle's left side length}}$$

Written as algebraic proportions, these three equations would, respectively, be

$$\frac{x\,\text{cm}}{3\,\text{cm}} = \frac{6\,\text{cm}}{4\,\text{cm}}, \qquad \frac{4\,\text{cm}}{6\,\text{cm}} = \frac{3\,\text{cm}}{x\,\text{cm}}, \qquad \frac{6\,\text{cm}}{4\,\text{cm}} = \frac{x\,\text{cm}}{3\,\text{cm}}$$

While these are only a few of the possibilities, if we clear the denominators from any properly designed proportion, every one is equivalent to x = 4.5.

8.4.3 Exercises

1. A circle's circumference is 4π mm.

    a. This circle's diameter is

        [   ].

    b. This circle's radius is

        [   ].

2. A circle's circumference is 6π mm.

    a. This circle's diameter is

        [   ].

    b. This circle's radius is

        [   ].

3. A circle's circumference is 36 cm. Find the following values. Round your answer to at least 2 decimal places.

    a. This circle's diameter is

        [   ].

    b. This circle's radius is

        [   ].

4. A circle's circumference is 38 cm. Find the following values. Round your answer to at least 2 decimal places.

    a. This circle's diameter is

        [   ].

    b. This circle's radius is

        [   ].

5. A circle's circumference is 12π mm.

    a. This circle's diameter is

        [   ].

    b. This circle's radius is

        [   ].

6. A circle's circumference is 14π mm.

    a. This circle's diameter is

        [   ].

    b. This circle's radius is

        [   ].

7. A circle's circumference is 45 cm. Find the following values. Round your answer to at least 2 decimal places.

    a. This circle's diameter is

        [   ].

    b. This circle's radius is

        [   ].

8. A circle's circumference is 47 cm. Find the following values. Round your answer to at least 2 decimal places.

    a. This circle's diameter is

        [   ].

    b. This circle's radius is

        [   ].

9. A cylinder's base's radius is 4 m, and its volume is 160π m^3.

This cylinder's height is [   ].

10. A cylinder's base's radius is 10 m, and its volume is 200π m^3.

This cylinder's height is [   ].

11. A rectangle's area is 336 mm^2. Its height is 16 mm.

Its base is [   ].

12. A rectangle's area is 276 mm^2. Its height is 12 mm.

Its base is [   ].

13. A rectangular prism's volume is 13224 ft^3. The prism's base is a rectangle. The rectangle's length is 24 ft and the rectangle's width is 19 ft.

This prism's height is [   ].

14. A rectangular prism's volume is 5600 ft^3. The prism's base is a rectangle. The rectangle's length is 25 ft and the rectangle's width is 16 ft.

This prism's height is [   ].

15. A triangle's area is 175.5 m². Its base is 27 m.

Its height is [＿＿＿＿＿＿＿＿＿＿].

16. A triangle's area is 275.5 m². Its base is 29 m.

Its height is [＿＿＿＿＿＿＿＿＿＿].

17. The following two triangles are similar to each other. Find the length of the missing side.

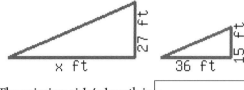

The missing side's length is [＿＿＿＿＿＿＿].

18. The following two triangles are similar to each other. Find the length of the missing side.

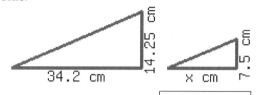

The missing side's length is [＿＿＿＿＿＿＿].

19. The following two triangles are similar to each other. Find the length of the missing side.

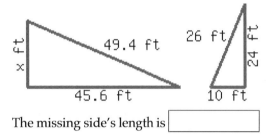

The missing side's length is [＿＿＿＿＿＿＿].

20. The following two triangles are similar to each other. Find the length of the missing side.

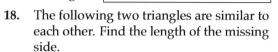
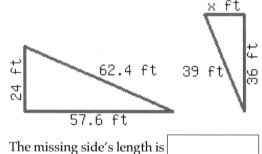

The missing side's length is [＿＿＿＿＿＿＿].

8.5 Quantities in the Physical World Chapter Review

8.5.1 Scientific Notation

In Section 8.1 we covered the definition of scientific notation, how to convert to and from scientific notation, and how to do some calculations in scientific notation.

Example 8.5.1 Scientific Notation for Large Numbers.

a. The distance to the star Betelgeuse is about 3,780,000,000,000,000 miles. Write this number in scientific notation.

b. The gross domestic product (GDP) of California in the year 2017 was about $\$2.746 \times 10^{13}$. Write this number in standard notation.

Explanation.

a. $3{,}780{,}000{,}000{,}000{,}000 = 3.78 \times 10^{15}$.

b. $\$2.746 \times 10^{13} = \$2{,}746{,}000{,}000{,}000$.

Example 8.5.2 Scientific Notation for Small Numbers.

a. Human DNA forms a double helix with diameter 2×10^{-9} meters. Write this number in standard notation.

b. A single grain of Forget-me-not (Myosotis) pollen is about 0.00024 inches in diameter. Write this number in scientific notation.

Explanation.

a. $2 \times 10^{-9} = 0.000000002$.
b. $0.00024 = 2.4 \times 10^{-4}$.

Example 8.5.3 Multiplying and Dividing Using Scientific Notation. The fastest spacecraft so far have traveled about 5×10^{6} miles per day.

a. If that spacecraft traveled at that same speed for 2×10^{4} days (which is about 55 years), how far would it have gone? Write your answer in scientific notation.

b. The nearest star to Earth, besides the Sun, is Proxima Centauri, about 2.5×10^{13} miles from Earth. How many days would you have to fly in that spacecraft at top speed to reach Proxima Centauri

Explanation.

a. Remember that you can find the distance traveled by multiplying the rate of travel times the time traveled: $d = r \cdot t$. So this problem turns into

$$d = r \cdot t$$
$$d = \left(5 \times 10^{6}\right) \cdot \left(2 \times 10^{4}\right)$$

Multiply coefficient with coefficient and power of 10 with power of 10.

$$= (5 \cdot 2)\left(10^{6} \times 10^{4}\right)$$

$$= 10 \times 10^{10}$$

Remember that this still isn't in scientific notation. So we convert like this:

$$= 1.0 \times 10^1 \times 10^{10}$$
$$= 1.0 \times 10^{11}$$

So, after traveling for 2×10^4 days (55 years), we will have traveled about 1.0×10^{11} miles. That's one-hundred million miles. I hope someone remembered the snacks.

b. Since we are looking for time, let's solve the equation $d = r \cdot t$ for t by dividing by r on both sides: $t = \frac{d}{r}$. So we have:

$$t = \frac{d}{r}$$
$$t = \frac{2.5 \times 10^{13}}{5 \times 10^6}$$

Now we can divide coefficient by coefficient and power of 10 with power of 10.

$$t = \frac{2.5}{5} \times \frac{10^{13}}{10^6}$$
$$t = 0.5 \times 10^7$$
$$t = 5 \times 10^{-1} \times 10^7$$
$$t = 5 \times 10^6$$

This means that to get to Proxima Centauri, even in our fastest spacecraft, would take 5×10^6 years. Converting to standard form, this is 5,000,000 years. I think we're going to need a faster ship.

8.5.2 Unit Conversion

Unit conversion is a particular process that uses unit ratios to convert units. You may refer to Appendix B to find unit conversion facts needed to do these conversions.

Example 8.5.4 Using Multiple Unit Ratios. How many grams are in 5 pounds?

$$5\,\text{lb} = \frac{5\,\text{lb}}{1} \qquad\qquad \text{Rewrite as a ratio.}$$

$$= \frac{5\,\text{lb}}{1} \cdot \frac{1\,\text{kg}}{2.205\,\text{lb}} \cdot \frac{1000\,\text{g}}{1\,\text{kg}} \qquad\qquad \text{Two unit ratios are needed.}$$

$$= \frac{5\,\cancel{\text{lb}}}{1} \cdot \frac{1\,\cancel{\text{kg}}}{2.205\,\cancel{\text{lb}}} \cdot \frac{1000\,\text{g}}{1\,\cancel{\text{kg}}} \qquad\qquad \text{Units may now cancel.}$$

$$= \frac{5}{1} \cdot \frac{1}{2.205} \cdot \frac{1000\,\text{g}}{1} \qquad\qquad \text{Only units of g remain.}$$

$$= \frac{5 \cdot 1000}{2.205}\,\text{g} \qquad\qquad \text{Multiply what's left and then divide.}$$

$$\approx 2268\,\text{g}$$

So 5 pounds is about 2268 grams.

Example 8.5.5 Converting Squared or Cubed Units. Convert 240 square inches into square centimeters.

$$240\,\text{in}^2 = \frac{240\,\text{in}^2}{1} \qquad\qquad \text{Rewrite as a ratio.}$$

$$= \frac{240\,\text{in}^2}{1} \cdot \left(\frac{2.54\,\text{cm}}{1\,\text{in}}\right)^2 \qquad \text{The unit ratio needs to be squared.}$$

$$= \frac{240\,\text{in}^2}{1} \cdot \frac{2.54^2\,\text{cm}^2}{1\,\text{in}^2} \qquad \text{Everything inside the parentheses is squared.}$$

$$= \frac{240\,\cancel{\text{in}^2}}{1} \cdot \frac{2.54^2\,\text{cm}^2}{1\,\cancel{\text{in}^2}} \qquad \text{Units may now cancel.}$$

$$= \frac{240}{1} \cdot \frac{2.54^2\,\text{cm}^2}{1} \qquad\quad \text{Only units of sq cm remain.}$$

$$= 240 \cdot 2.54^2\,\text{cm}^2 \qquad\qquad \text{Multiply.}$$

$$\approx 1548\,\text{cm}^2$$

So 240 square inches is approximately 1548 square centimeters.

Example 8.5.6 Converting Rates. Gold has a density of $19.3\,\frac{\text{g}}{\text{mL}}$. What is this density in ounces per cubic inch?

$$19.3\,\frac{\text{g}}{\text{mL}} = \frac{19.3\,\text{g}}{1\,\text{mL}} \qquad\qquad \text{Write the rate as a ratio.}$$

$$\approx \frac{19.3\,\text{g}}{1\,\text{mL}} \cdot \frac{16.39\,\text{mL}}{1\,\text{in}^3} \cdot \frac{1\,\text{oz}}{28.35\,\text{g}} \qquad \text{Use unit ratios to make cancellations.}$$

$$= \frac{19.3\,\cancel{\text{g}}}{1\,\cancel{\text{mL}}} \cdot \frac{16.39\,\cancel{\text{mL}}}{1\,\text{in}^3} \cdot \frac{1\,\text{oz}}{28.35\,\cancel{\text{g}}} \qquad \text{Units may now cancel.}$$

$$= \frac{19.3}{1} \cdot \frac{16.39}{1\,\text{in}^3} \cdot \frac{1\,\text{oz}}{28.35} \qquad \text{Only oz per cubic inch remain.}$$

$$= \frac{19.3 \cdot 16.39}{28.35} \frac{\text{oz}}{\text{in}^3} \qquad\qquad \text{Multiply what's left and then divide.}$$

$$\approx 11.16\,\frac{\text{oz}}{\text{in}^3}$$

Notice that we did not need to raise any unit ratios to a power since there is a conversion fact that tells us that $1\,\text{in}^3 \approx 16.39\,\text{mL}$.

Thus, the density of gold is about $11.16\,\frac{\text{oz}}{\text{in}^3}$.

8.5.3 Geometry Formulas

In Section 8.3 we established the following formulas.

Perimeter of a Rectangle $P = 2(\ell + w)$

Area of a Rectangle $A = \ell w$

Area of a Triangle $A = \frac{1}{2} bh$

Circumference of a Circle $c = 2\pi r$

Area of a Circle $A = \pi r^2$

Volume of a Rectangular Prism $V = wdh$

Volume of a Cylinder $V = \pi r^2 h$

Volume of a Rectangular Prism or Cylinder $V = Bh$

8.5.4 Exercises

Scientific Notation Write the following number in scientific notation.

1. 350   2. 450000
3. 0.0055   4. 0.00065

Write the following number in decimal notation without using exponents.

5. 7.51×10^4 6. 8.51×10^3 7. 9.5×10^0
8. 1.49×10^0 9. 2.5×10^{-3} 10. 3.49×10^{-4}

Multiply the following numbers, writing your answer in scientific notation.

11. $(5 \times 10^3)(7 \times 10^2)$ 12. $(5 \times 10^5)(4 \times 10^5)$

Divide the following numbers, writing your answer in scientific notation.

13. $\dfrac{5.4 \times 10^3}{6 \times 10^{-2}}$ 14. $\dfrac{4.2 \times 10^4}{7 \times 10^{-2}}$

Unit Conversion

15. Convert 211 tbsp to teaspoons.   16. Convert 5.98 t to kilograms.
17. Convert 9.5 s to milliseconds.   18. Convert 43 hm to feet.
19. Convert 8.9 yd to centimeters.   20. Convert 2.7 pt to gallons.
21. Convert 48 cm^2 to square inches.   22. Convert 2.08 ft^3 to cubic miles.
23. Convert 52.8 $\frac{\text{dam}}{\text{s}}$ to meters per millisecond.   24. Convert 226 $\frac{\text{mi}^2}{\text{wk}}$ to acres per day.
25. Convert 7.6 $\frac{\text{T}}{\text{s}}$ to pounds per nanosecond.   26. Convert 46 $\frac{\text{B}}{\text{d}}$ to kilobytes per week.

27. Carly's bedroom has 107 ft² of floor. She would like to carpet the floor, but carpeting is sold by the square yard. How many square yards of carpeting will she need to get?

28. Jon is traveling in Europe and renting a car. He is used to thinking of gasoline amounts in gallons, but in Europe it is sold in liters. After filling the gas tank, he notices it took 32 L of gas. How many gallons is that?

29. Cody was driving at a steady speed of 39 mph for 11 minutes. How far did he travel in that time?

30. The algae in a pond is growing at a rate of 0.3 $\frac{kg}{d}$. How much algae is in the poind after 4 weeks?

Geometry

31. Find the perimeter and area of the rectangle.

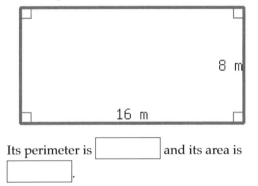

Its perimeter is [   ] and its area is [   ].

32. Find the perimeter and area of the rectangle.

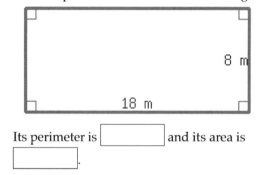

Its perimeter is [   ] and its area is [   ].

33. Find the area of the rectangle below.

34. Find the perimeter and area of a rectangular table top with a length of 5.9 ft and a width of 32 in.
Its perimeter is [   ] and its area is [   ].

35. Find the perimeter and area of the triangle.

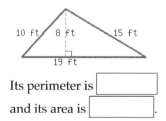

Its perimeter is [   ] and its area is [   ].

36. Find the perimeter and area of the right triangle.

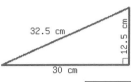

Its perimeter is [   ]

and its area is [   ].

37. The area of the triangle below is [   ] square feet.

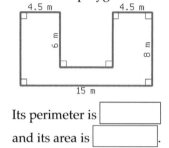

38. Find the area of a triangular flag with a base of 2.7 m and a height of 70 cm.

Its area is [   ].

39. Find the perimeter and area of this shape.

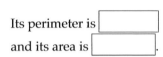

Its perimeter is [   ]

and its area is [   ].

40. Find the perimeter and area of this polygon.

Its perimeter is [   ]

and its area is [   ].

41. The formula $A = \frac{1}{2} r n s$ gives the area of a regular polygon with side length s, number of sides n and, apothem r. (The *apothem* is the distance from the center of the polygon to one of its sides.)
What is the area of a regular pentagon with $s = 72$ in and $r = 96$ in?

42. A circle's radius is 9 m.

   a. The circumference, in terms of π, is [   ].

   b. This circle's circumference, rounded to the hundredths place, is [   ].

   c. This circle's area, in terms of π, is [   ].

   d. This circle's area, rounded to the hundredths place, is [   ].

43. Find the perimeter and area of this shape, which is a semicircle on top of a rectangle.

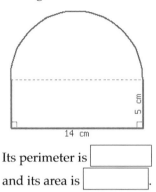

14 cm

Its perimeter is [ ]

and its area is [ ].

44. Find the volume of this rectangular prism.

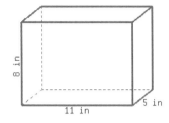

11 in   5 in   8 in

45. A cube's side length is 3 cm. Its volume is [ ].

46. Find the volume of this cylinder.

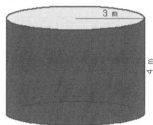

3 m   4 m

a. This cylinder's volume, in terms of π, is [ ].

b. This cylinder's volume, rounded to the hundredths place, is [ ].

47. A cylinder's base's diameter is 6 ft, and its height is 5 ft.

a. This cylinder's volume, in terms of π, is [ ].

b. This cylinder's volume, rounded to the hundredths place, is [ ].

48. A cylinder's base's diameter is 18 ft, and its height is 6 ft.

a. This cylinder's volume, in terms of π, is [ ].

b. This cylinder's volume, rounded to the hundredths place, is [ ].

49. Fill out the table with various formulas as they were given in this section.

Rectangle Perimeter	_____
Rectangle Area	_____
Triangle Area	_____
Circle Circumference	_____
Circle Area	_____
Rectangular Prism Volume	_____
Cylinder Volume	_____
Volume of either Rectangular Prism or Cylinder	_____

50. A circle's circumference is 16π mm.

   a. This circle's diameter is

   _____.

   b. This circle's radius is

   _____.

51. A circle's circumference is 47 cm. Find the following values. Round your answer to at least 2 decimal places.

   a. This circle's diameter is

   _____.

   b. This circle's radius is

   _____.

52. A circle's circumference is 49 cm. Find the following values. Round your answer to at least 2 decimal places.

   a. This circle's diameter is

   _____.

   b. This circle's radius is

   _____.

53. A cylinder's base's radius is 2 m, and its volume is 8π m^3.
This cylinder's height is _____.

54. A rectangular prism's volume is 5355 ft^3. The prism's base is a rectangle. The rectangle's length is 21 ft and the rectangle's width is 17 ft.
This prism's height is _____.

55. A triangle's area is 149.5 m^2. Its base is 23 m.
Its height is _____.

56. The following two triangles are similar to each other. Find the length of the missing side.

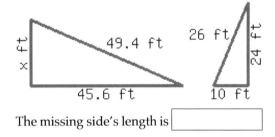

The missing side's length is _____.

57. The following two triangles are similar to each other. Find the length of the missing side.

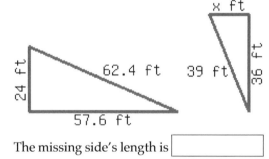

The missing side's length is _____.

Chapter 9

Topics in Graphing

9.1 Review of Graphing

This section is a short review of the basics of graphing. The topics here are introduced in Sections 3.1 and 3.2 from Part I. Here we only briefly remind readers of the basics to warm up for the graphing topics in the rest of this chapter. Some readers may benefit from turning to those earlier sections instead of reviewing from this section.

9.1.1 Cartesian Coordinates

A Cartesian coordinate system is usually represented as a graph where there are two "axes" (straight lines extending infinitely), one horizontal and one vertical. The horizontal axis is usually labeled "x", and the vertical axis is usually labeled "y". The scale marks on the axes are used to define locations on the plane that they span. An address is a pair of "coordinates" written as in this example: $(3, 2)$. The first coordinate tells you where the location is with respect to the horizontal axis, and the second coordinate tells you a location with respect to the vertical axis. The point $(3, 2)$ is marked in Figure 9.1.2.

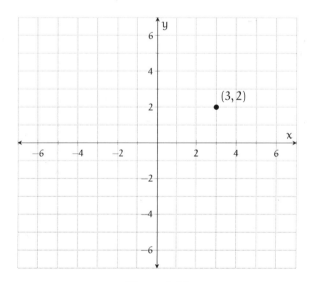

Figure 9.1.2

Example 9.1.3 On paper, sketch a Cartesian coordinate system with the axes scaled using regularly spaced ticks and labels, and then plot the following points: $(2, 3), (-5, 1), (0, -3), (4, 0)$.

Explanation.

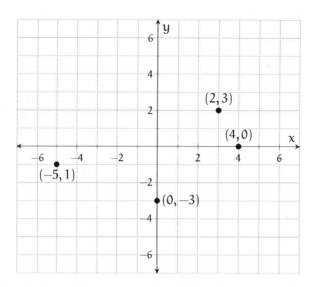

Figure 9.1.4: A Cartesian grid with the four points plotted.

Note that negative numbers in the first coordinate mean that a point is left of the y-axis. And similarly, negative numbers in the second coordinate mean that a point is below the x-axis.

9.1.2 Graphing Equations by Plotting Points

When you have an equation in the form

$$y = \text{expression in } x$$

it suggests that we could substitute in different values for x and get back different values for y. Pairing these x- and y-values together, we can plot points and create a "graph" of the equation. Creating a graph of a given equation in x and y is the basic objective of this section. Sometimes the equation has special features that give you a shortcut for creating a graph, for example as discussed in Section 3.5. However, here we want to focus on the universal approach of just substituting in values for x and seeing what comes out.

Example 9.1.5 Rheema helped plant a lovely Douglas Fir in a local park volunteering with Portland's Friends of Trees [1]. The tree they planted was 4 ft tall when they planted it. Rheema watched the tree grow over the next few years and noticed that every year, the tree grew about 1.5 ft. So, the height of the tree can be found by using the formula $y = 1.5x + 4$, where x-values represent the number of years since the tree was planted. Let's make a graph of this equation by making a table of values. The most straightforward method to graph any equation is to build a table of x- and y-values, and then plot the points.

x	$y = 1.5x + 4$	Point	Interpretation
0	$1.5(0) + 4$ $= 4$	$(0, 4)$	When the tree was planted, the tree was 4 ft tall.
2	$1.5(2) + 4$ $= 7$	$(2, 7)$	Two years after tree was planted, the tree was 7 ft tall.
4	$1.5(4) + 4$ $= 10$	$(4, 10)$	Four years after tree was planted, the tree was 10 ft tall.
6	$1.5(6) + 4$ $= 13$	$(6, 13)$	Six years after tree was planted, the tree was 13 ft tall.
8	$1.5(8) + 4$ $= 16$	$(8, 16)$	Eight years after tree was planted, the tree was 16 ft tall.

Figure 9.1.6: A table of values for $y = 1.5x + 4$

Figure 9.1.7: A graph of $y = 1.5x + 4$

Example 9.1.8 Make a graph of the linear equation $y = \frac{5}{2}x - 3$ by building a table of x- and y-values and plotting the points.

Explanation. To create an easy-to-graph table of values, we should examine the formula and notice that if all of the x-values were multiples of 2, then the fraction in the equation would cancel nicely and leave us with integer y-values.

x	$y = \frac{5}{2}x - 3$	Point
-4	$\frac{5}{2}(-4) - 3$ $= -13$	$(-4, -13)$
-2	$\frac{5}{2}(-2) - 3$ $= -8$	$(-2, -8)$
0	$\frac{5}{2}(0) - 3$ $= -3$	$(0, -3)$
2	$\frac{5}{2}(2) - 3$ $= 2$	$(2, 2)$
4	$\frac{5}{2}(4) - 3$ $= 7$	$(4, 7)$
6	$\frac{5}{2}(6) - 3$ $= 12$	$(6, 12)$

Figure 9.1.9: A table of values for $y = \frac{5}{2}x - 3$

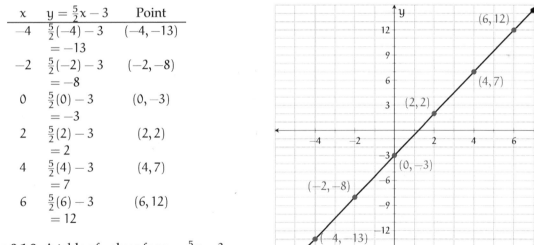

Figure 9.1.10: A graph of $y = \frac{5}{2}x - 3$

Example 9.1.11 Create a table of ordered pairs and then make a plot of the equation $y = -\frac{2}{5}x - 3$. Note that this equation is a linear equation, and we can see that the slope is negative. Therefore we should *expect* to see a downward sloping line as we view it from left to right. If we don't see that in the end, it suggests some

[1]friendsoftrees.org/

mistake was made.

Explanation.   This time, with the slope having denominator 5, it is wise to use multiples of 5 as the x-values.

x	$y = -\frac{2}{5}x - 3$	Point
−5	$-\frac{2}{5}(-5) - 3$ $= -5$	$(-5, -5)$
0	$-\frac{2}{5}(0) - 3$ $= -3$	$(0, -3)$
5	$-\frac{2}{5}(5) - 3$ $= -1$	$(5, -1)$

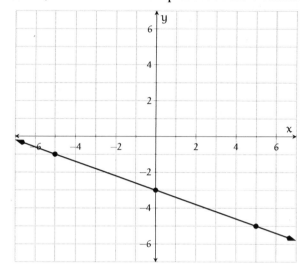

Checkpoint 9.1.12 Make a table for the equation.

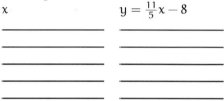

$$x \qquad\qquad\qquad y = \tfrac{11}{5}x - 8$$

Explanation.   Since this equation has a fractional coefficient for x with denominator 5, it would be wise to choose our own x-values that are multiples of 5. Then when we use them to solve for y, the denominator will be cleared, and we will not need to continue with fraction arithmetic.

This solution will use the x-values −5, 0, 5, 10 and 15. The choice to use these x-values is arbitrary, but they are small multiples of 5, which will make computation easier.

One at a time, we substitute these x-values into the equation $y = \frac{11}{5}x - 8$, and solve for y:

$$y = \frac{11}{5}(-5) - 8 \implies y = -19$$

$$y = \frac{11}{5}(0) - 8 \implies y = -8$$

$$y = \frac{11}{5}(5) - 8 \implies y = 3$$

$$y = \frac{11}{5}(10) - 8 \implies y = 14$$

$$y = \frac{11}{5}(15) - 8 \implies y = 25$$

So the table may be completed as:

x	y
−5	−19
0	−8
5	3
10	14
15	25

Even when the equation is not a linear equation, this method (making a table of points) will work to help create a graph.

Example 9.1.13 Create a table of ordered pairs and then make a plot of the equation $y = \frac{6}{x^2-2x+2}$.

Explanation. The form of this equation is not one that we recognize yet. But the general approach for making a graph is still going to work out.

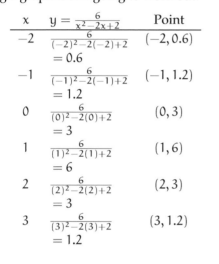

x	$y = \frac{6}{x^2-2x+2}$	Point
−2	$\frac{6}{(-2)^2-2(-2)+2}$ $= 0.6$	$(-2, 0.6)$
−1	$\frac{6}{(-1)^2-2(-1)+2}$ $= 1.2$	$(-1, 1.2)$
0	$\frac{6}{(0)^2-2(0)+2}$ $= 3$	$(0, 3)$
1	$\frac{6}{(1)^2-2(1)+2}$ $= 6$	$(1, 6)$
2	$\frac{6}{(2)^2-2(2)+2}$ $= 3$	$(2, 3)$
3	$\frac{6}{(3)^2-2(3)+2}$ $= 1.2$	$(3, 1.2)$

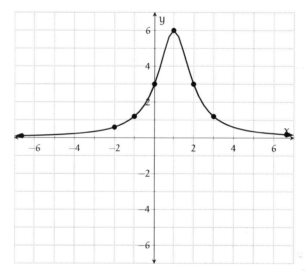

9.1.3 Graphing Lines Using Intercepts

As noted earlier, sometimes the form of an equation suggests an alternative way that we could graph it. In the case of a linear equation, an alternative to making a table is to find the line's "intercepts". These are the locations where the line crosses either the x-axis or the y-axis. In the case of a straight line, that is theoretically all you need to graph the complete line. Here, we review this approach. We also hope this example simply serves as a reminder of what intercepts are.

Recall that the standard form (3.7.1) of a line equation is $Ax + By = C$ where where A, B, and C are three numbers (each of which might be 0, although at least one of A and B must be nonzero). If a linear equation is given in standard form, we can relative easily find the line's x- and y-intercepts by substituting in $y = 0$ and $x = 0$, respectively.

Example 9.1.14 Find the intercepts of $3x + 5y = 60$, and then graph the equation given those intercepts.

To find the x-intercept, set $y = 0$ and solve for x.

$$3x + 5(0) = 60$$
$$3x = 60$$
$$x = 20$$

So the x-intercept is the point $(20, 0)$.

Next, we just plot these points and draw the line that runs through them.

To find the y-intercept, set $x = 0$ and solve for y.

$$3(0) + 5y = 60$$
$$5y = 60$$
$$y = 12$$

So, the y-intercept is the point $(0, 12)$.

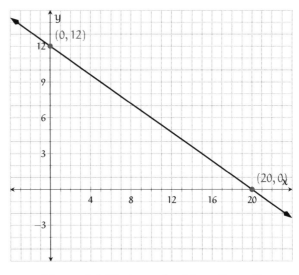

Figure 9.1.15: A graph of $3x + 5y = 60$

Checkpoint 9.1.16 Find the y-intercept and x-intercept of the line given by the equation. If a particular intercept does not exist, enter none into all the answer blanks for that row.

$$2x + 5y = -20$$

	x-value	y-value	Location (as an ordered pair)
y-intercept	_____	_____	_____
x-intercept	_____	_____	_____

Explanation. A line's y-intercept is on the y-axis, implying that its x-value must be 0. To find a line's y-intercept, we substitute in $x = 0$. In this problem we have:

$$2x + 5y = -20$$
$$2(0) + 5y = -20$$
$$5y = -20$$
$$\frac{5y}{5} = \frac{-20}{5}$$
$$y = -4$$

This line's y-intercept is $(0, -4)$.

Next, a line's x-intercept is on the x-axis, implying that its y-value must be 0. To find a line's x-intercept, we substitute in $y = 0$. In this problem we have:

$$2x + 5y = -20$$
$$2x + 5(0) = -20$$
$$2x = -20$$
$$\frac{2x}{2} = \frac{-20}{2}$$
$$x = -10$$

The line's x-intercept is $(-10, 0)$.
The entries for the table are:

	x-value	y-value	Location
y-intercept	0	−4	$(0, -4)$
x-intercept	−10	0	$(-10, 0)$

9.1.4 Exercises

Identifying Coordinates Locate each point in the graph:

1.

Write each point's position as an ordered pair, like $(1, 2)$.

$A = $ _____ $B = $ _____
$C = $ _____ $D = $ _____

2.

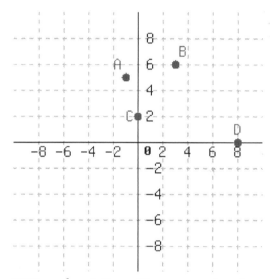

Write each point's position as an ordered pair, like $(1, 2)$.

$A = $ _____ $B = $ _____
$C = $ _____ $D = $ _____

Plotting Points

3. Sketch the points $(8, 2)$, $(5, 5)$, $(-3, 0)$, and $(2, -6)$ on a Cartesian plane.

4. Sketch the points $(1, -4)$, $(-3, 5)$, $(0, 4)$, and $(-2, -6)$ on a Cartesian plane.

Tables for Equations Make a table for the equation.

5.

x	$y = 4x$

6.

x	$y = 8x$

7.

x	$y = 6x + 3$

8.

x	$y = 8x - 3$

9.

x	$y = \frac{10}{3}x + 10$

10.

x	$y = \frac{13}{10}x - 8$

11.

x	$y = -\frac{9}{8}x - 6$

12.

x	$y = \frac{9}{8}x - 4$

Graphs of Equations

13. Create a table of ordered pairs and then make a plot of the equation $y = 2x + 3$.

14. Create a table of ordered pairs and then make a plot of the equation $y = -x - 4$.

15. Create a table of ordered pairs and then make a plot of the equation $y = \frac{4}{3}x$.

16. Create a table of ordered pairs and then make a plot of the equation $y = -\frac{3}{4}x + 2$.

17. Create a table of ordered pairs and then make a plot of the equation $y = x^2 + 1$.

18. Create a table of ordered pairs and then make a plot of the equation $y = (x - 2)^2$. Use x-values from 0 to 4.

Lines and Intercepts

19. Find the y-intercept and x-intercept of the line given by the equation. If a particular intercept does not exist, enter none into all the answer blanks for that row.

$$5x + 6y = 30$$

	x-value	y-value	Location (as an ordered pair)
y-intercept	_____	_____	_____
x-intercept	_____	_____	_____

20. Find the y-intercept and x-intercept of the line given by the equation. If a particular intercept does not exist, enter none into all the answer blanks for that row.

$$6x + 3y = -36$$

	x-value	y-value	Location (as an ordered pair)
y-intercept	_____	_____	_____
x-intercept	_____	_____	_____

21. Find the y-intercept and x-intercept of the line given by the equation. If a particular intercept does not exist, enter none into all the answer blanks for that row.

$$6x - 7y = -42$$

	x-value	y-value	Location (as an ordered pair)
y-intercept	_____	_____	_____
x-intercept	_____	_____	_____

22. Find the y-intercept and x-intercept of the line given by the equation. If a particular intercept does not exist, enter none into all the answer blanks for that row.

$$x - 7y = -14$$

	x-value	y-value	Location (as an ordered pair)
y-intercept	_____	_____	_____
x-intercept	_____	_____	_____

23. Find the x- and y-intercepts of the line with equation $5x - 2y = 10$. Then find one other point on the line. Use your results to graph the line.

24. Find the x- and y-intercepts of the line with equation $5x - 6y = -90$. Then find one other point on the line. Use your results to graph the line.

25. Find the x- and y-intercepts of the line with equation $x + 5y = -15$. Then find one other point on the line. Use your results to graph the line.

26. Find the x- and y-intercepts of the line with equation $6x + y = -18$. Then find one other point on the line. Use your results to graph the line.

27. Make a graph of the line $-5x - y = -3$.   28. Make a graph of the line $x + 5y = 5$.

29. Make a graph of the line $20x - 4y = 8$.   30. Make a graph of the line $3x + 5y = 10$.

9.2 Key Features of Quadratic Graphs

In this section we will learn about quadratic graphs and their key features, including vertex, axis of symmetry and intercepts.

9.2.1 Properties of Quadratic Graphs

Hannah fired a toy rocket from the ground, which launched into the air with an initial speed of 64 feet per second. The height of the rocket can be modeled by the equation $y = -16t^2 + 64t$, where t is how many seconds had passed since the launch. To see the shape of the graph made by this equation, we make a table of values and plot the points.

t	$y = -16t^2 + 64t$	Point
0	$-16(0)^2 + 64(0)$ $= 0$	$(0, 0)$
1	$-16(1)^2 + 64(1)$ $= 48$	$(1, 48)$
2	$-16(2)^2 + 64(2)$ $= 64$	$(2, 64)$
3	$-16(3)^2 + 64(3)$ $= 48$	$(3, 48)$
4	$-16(4)^2 + 64(4)$ $= 0$	$(4, 0)$

Figure 9.2.2: Points for $y = -16t^2 + 64t$

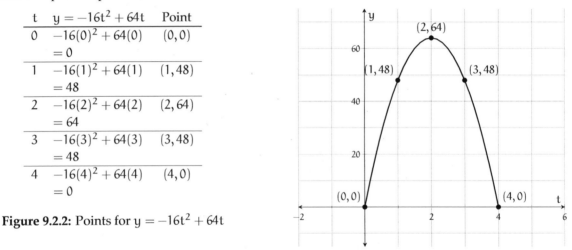

Figure 9.2.3: Graph of $y = -16t^2 + 64t$

A curve with the shape that we see in Figure 9.2.3 is called a **parabola**. Notice the symmetry in Figure 9.2.2, how the y-values in rows above the middle row match those below the middle row. Also notice the symmetry in the shape of the graph, how its left side is a mirror image of its right side.

The first feature that we will talk about is the *direction* that a parabola opens. All parabolas open either upward or downward. This parabola in the rocket example opens downward because a is negative. That means that for large values of t, the at^2 term will be large and negative, and the resulting y-value will be low on the y-axis. So the negative leading coefficient causes the arms of the parabola to point downward.

Here are some more quadratic graphs so we can see which way they open.

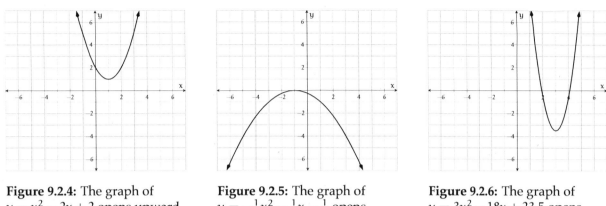

Figure 9.2.4: The graph of $y = x^2 - 2x + 2$ opens upward. Its leading coefficient is positive.

Figure 9.2.5: The graph of $y = -\frac{1}{4}x^2 - \frac{1}{2}x - \frac{1}{4}$ opens downward. Its leading coefficient is negative.

Figure 9.2.6: The graph of $y = 3x^2 - 18x + 23.5$ opens upward. Its leading coefficient is positive.

Fact 9.2.7 *The graph of a quadratic equation $y = ax^2 + bx + c$ opens upward or downward according to the sign of the leading coefficient a. If the leading coefficient is positive, the parabola opens upward. If the leading coefficient is negative, the parabola opens downward.*

Checkpoint 9.2.8 Determine whether each quadratic graph opens upward or downward.

   a. The graph of $y = 3x^2 - 4x - 7$ opens   (□ upward   □ downward) .

   b. The graph of $y = -5x^2 + x$ opens   (□ upward   □ downward) .

   c. The graph of $y = 2 + 3x - x^2$ opens   (□ upward   □ downward) .

   d. The graph of $y = \frac{1}{3}x^2 - \frac{2}{5}x + \frac{1}{4}$ opens   (□ upward   □ downward) .

Explanation.

   a. The graph of $y = 3x^2 - 4x - 7$ opens upward as the leading coefficient is the positive number 3.

   b. The graph of $y = -5x^2 + x$ opens downward as the leading coefficient is the negative number -5.

   c. The graph of $y = 2 + 3x - x^2$ opens downward as the leading coefficient is -1. (Note that the leading coefficient is the coefficient on x^2.)

   d. The graph of $y = \frac{1}{3}x^2 - \frac{2}{5}x + \frac{1}{4}$ opens upward as the leading coefficient is the positive number $\frac{1}{3}$.

The **vertex** of a quadratic graph is the highest or lowest point on the graph, depending on whether the graph opens downward or upward. In Figure 9.2.3, the vertex is $(2, 64)$. This tells us that Hannah's rocket reached its maximum height of 64 feet after 2 seconds. If the parabola opens downward, as in the rocket example, then the y-value of the vertex is the **maximum** y-value. If the parabola opens upward then the y-value of the vertex is the **minimum** y-value.

   The **axis of symmetry** is a vertical line that passes through the vertex, cutting the quadratic graph into two symmetric halves. We write the axis of symmetry as an equation of a vertical line so it always starts with "$x =$." In Figure 9.2.3, the equation for the axis of symmetry is $x = 2$.

   The **vertical intercept** is the point where the parabola crosses the vertical axis. The vertical intercept is the y-intercept if the vertical axis is labeled y. In Figure 9.2.3, the point $(0, 0)$ is the starting point of the rocket, and it is where the graph crosses the y-axis, so it is the vertical intercept. The y-value of 0 means the rocket was on the ground when the t-value was 0, which was when the rocket launched.

The **horizontal intercept(s)** are the points where the parabola crosses the horizontal axis. They are the x-intercepts if the horizontal axis is labeled x. The point $(0, 0)$ on the path of the rocket is also a horizontal intercept. The t-value of 0 indicates the time when the rocket was launched from the ground. There is another horizontal intercept at the point $(4, 0)$, which means the rocket came back to hit the ground after 4 seconds.

It is possible for a quadratic graph to have zero, one, or two horizontal intercepts. The figures below show an example of each.

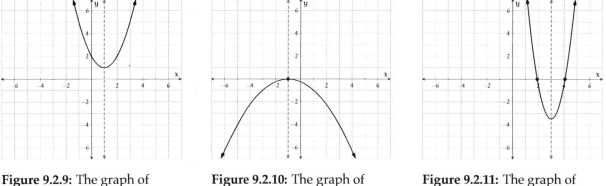

Figure 9.2.9: The graph of $y = x^2 - 2x + 2$ has no horizontal intercepts

Figure 9.2.10: The graph of $y = -\frac{1}{4}x^2 - \frac{1}{2}x - \frac{1}{4}$ has one horizontal intercept

Figure 9.2.11: The graph of $y = 3x^2 - 18x + 23.5$ has two horizontal intercepts

Here is a summary of the key features of quadratic graphs.

List 9.2.12: Summary of Key Features of Quadratic Graphs

Consider a quadratic equation in the form $y = ax^2 + bx + c$ and the parabola that it makes when graphed.

Direction The parabola opens upward if a is positive and opens downward of a is negative.

Vertex The vertex of the parabola is the maximum or minimum point on the graph.

Axis of Symmetry The axis of symmetry is the vertical line that passes through the vertex.

Vertical Intercept The vertical intercept is the point where the graph intersects the vertical axis. There is exactly one vertical intercept.

Horizontal Intercept(s) The horizontal intercept(s) are the point(s) where a graph intersects the horizontal axis. The graph of a parabola can have zero, one, or two horizontal intercepts.

Example 9.2.13 Identify the key features of the quadratic graph of $y = x^2 - 2x - 8$ shown in Figure 9.2.14.

Explanation.

First, we see that this parabola opens upward because the leading coefficient is positive.

Then we locate the vertex which is the point $(1, -9)$. The axis of symmetry is the vertical line $x = 1$.

The vertical intercept or y-intercept is the point $(0, -8)$.

The horizontal intercepts are the points $(-2, 0)$ and $(4, 0)$.

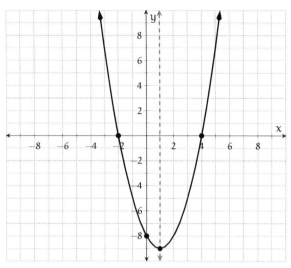

Figure 9.2.14: Graph of $y = x^2 - 2x - 8$

Checkpoint 9.2.15 Use the graph to answer the following questions.

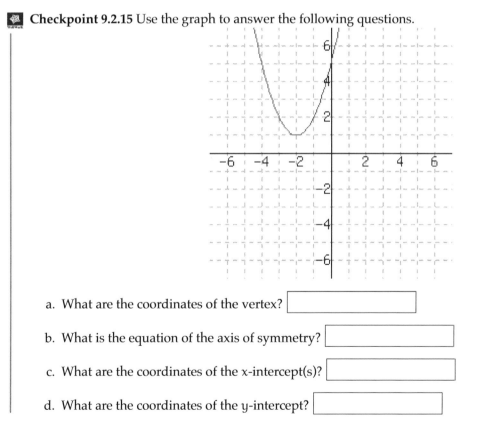

a. What are the coordinates of the vertex?

b. What is the equation of the axis of symmetry?

c. What are the coordinates of the x-intercept(s)?

d. What are the coordinates of the y-intercept?

Explanation.

    a. The vertex is at $(-2, 1)$.

    b. The equation of the axis of symmetry is $x = -2$.

    c. There are no x-intercepts. (Answer None.)

    d. The y-intercept is at $(0, 5)$.

9.2.2 Finding the Vertex and Axis of Symmetry Algebraically

The coordinates of the vertex are not easy to identify on a graph if they are not integers . Another way to find the coordinates of the vertex is by using a formula.

Fact 9.2.16 *If we denote* (h, k) *as the coordinates of the vertex of a quadratic graph defined by* $y = ax^2 + bx + c$, *then* $h = -\frac{b}{2a}$. *Then we can find* k *by substituting* h *in for* x.

    To understand why, we can look at the quadratic formula 7.2.2. The vertex is on the axis of symmetry, so it will always occur halfway between the two x-intercepts (if there are any). The quadratic formula shows that the x-intercepts happen at $-\frac{b}{2a}$ minus some number and at $-\frac{b}{2a}$ plus that same number. So $-\frac{b}{2a}$ is right in the middle, and it must be the horizontal coordinate of the vertex, h. If we have already memorized the quadratic formula, this new formula for h is not hard to remember:

$$\frac{-b \pm \sqrt{b^2 - 4ac}}{2a}$$

Example 9.2.17 Determine the vertex and axis of symmetry of the parabola $y = x^2 - 4x - 12$.
    We find the first coordinate of the vertex using the formula $h = -\frac{b}{2a}$, for $a = 1$ and $b = -4$.

$$\begin{aligned} h &= -\frac{b}{2a} \\ &= -\frac{(-4)}{2(1)} \\ &= 2 \end{aligned}$$

    Now we know the first coordinate of the vertex is 2, so we may substitute $x = 2$ to determine the second coordinate of the vertex:

$$\begin{aligned} k &= (2)^2 - 4(2) - 12 \\ &= 4 - 8 - 12 \\ &= -16 \end{aligned}$$

The vertex is the point $(2, -16)$ and the axis of symmetry is the line $x = 2$.

Example 9.2.18 Determine the vertex and axis of symmetry of the parabola $y = -3x^2 - 3x + 7$.
Explanation.   Using the formula $h = -\frac{b}{2a}$ with $a = -3$ and $b = -3$, we have :

$$h = -\frac{b}{2a}$$

$$= -\frac{(-3)}{2(-3)}$$

$$= -\frac{1}{2}$$

Now that we've determined $h = -\frac{1}{2}$, we can substitute it for x to find the y-value of the vertex:

$$k = -3x^2 - 3x + 7$$

$$= -3\left(-\frac{1}{2}\right)^2 - 3\left(-\frac{1}{2}\right) + 7$$

$$= -3\left(\frac{1}{4}\right) + \frac{3}{2} + 7$$

$$= -\frac{3}{4} + \frac{3}{2} + 7$$

$$= -\frac{3}{4} + \frac{6}{4} + \frac{28}{4}$$

$$= \frac{31}{4}$$

The vertex is the point $\left(-\frac{1}{2}, \frac{31}{4}\right)$ and the axis of symmetry is the line $x = -\frac{1}{2}$.

9.2.3 Graphing Quadratic Equations by Making a Table

When we learned how to graph lines, we could choose any x-values to build a table of values. For quadratic equations, we want to make sure the vertex is present in the table, since it is such a special point. So we find the vertex first and then choose our x-values surrounding it. We can use the property of symmetry to speed things up.

Example 9.2.19 Determine the vertex and axis of symmetry for the parabola $y = -x^2 - 2x + 3$. Then make a table of values and sketch the graph.

Explanation. To determine the vertex of $y = -x^2 - 2x + 3$, we want to find the x-value of the vertex first. We use $h = -\frac{b}{2a}$ with $a = -1$ and $b = -2$:

$$h = -\frac{(-2)}{2(-1)}$$

$$= \frac{2}{-2}$$

$$= -1$$

To find the y-coordinate of the vertex, we substitute $x = -1$ into the equation for our parabola.

$$k = -x^2 - 2x + 3$$

$$= -(-1)^2 - 2(-1) + 3$$

$$= -1 + 2 + 3$$

$$= 4$$

Now we know that our axis of symmetry is the line $x = -1$ and the vertex is the point $(-1, 4)$. We set up our table with two values on each side of $x = -1$. We choose $x = -3, -2, -1, 0$, and 1 as shown in Figure 9.2.20.

Next, we determine the y-coordinates by replacing x with each value and we have the complete table as shown in Figure 9.2.21. Notice that each pair of y-values on either side of the vertex match. This helps us to check that our vertex and y-values are correct.

x	$y = -x^2 - 2x + 3$	Point
-3		
-2		
-1		
0		
1		

x	$y = -x^2 - 2x + 3$		Point
-3	$-(-3)^2 - 2(-3) + 3$	$= 0$	$(-3, 0)$
-2	$-(-2)^2 - 2(-2) + 3$	$= 3$	$(-2, 3)$
-1	$-(-1)^2 - 2(-1) + 3$	$= 4$	$(-1, 4)$
0	$-(0)^2 - 2(0) + 3$	$= 3$	$(0, 3)$
1	$-(1)^2 - 2(1) + 3$	$= 0$	$(1, 0)$

Figure 9.2.20: Setting up the table   **Figure 9.2.21:** Values and points for $y = -x^2 - 2x + 3$

Now that we have our table, we plot the points and draw in the axis of symmetry as shown in Figure 9.2.22. We complete the graph by drawing a smooth curve through the points and drawing an arrow on each end as shown in Figure 9.2.23.

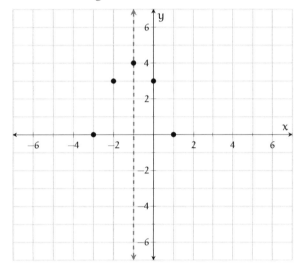

Figure 9.2.22: Plot of the points and axis of symmetry

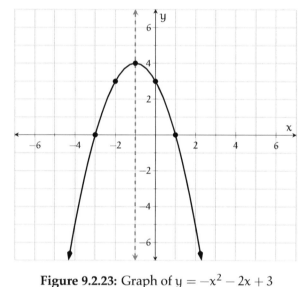

Figure 9.2.23: Graph of $y = -x^2 - 2x + 3$

The method we used works best when the x-value of the vertex is an integer. We can still make a graph if that is not the case as we will demonstrate in the next example.

Example 9.2.24 Determine the vertex and axis of symmetry for the parabola $y = 2x^2 - 3x - 4$. Use this to create a table of values and sketch the graph.

Explanation.   To determine the vertex of $y = 2x^2 - 3x - 4$, we find $h = -\frac{b}{2a}$ with $a = 2$ and $b = -3$:

$$h = -\frac{(-3)}{2(2)}$$
$$= \frac{3}{4}$$

Next, we determine the y-coordinate by replacing x with $\frac{3}{4}$ in $y = 2x^2 - 3x - 4$:

$$k = 2\left(\frac{3}{4}\right)^2 - 3\left(\frac{3}{4}\right) - 4$$
$$= 2\left(\frac{9}{16}\right) - \frac{9}{4} - 4$$
$$= \frac{9}{8} - \frac{18}{8} - \frac{32}{8}$$
$$= -\frac{41}{8}$$

Thus the vertex occurs at $\left(\frac{3}{4}, -\frac{41}{8}\right)$, or at $(0.75, -5.125)$. The axis of symmetry is then the line $x = \frac{3}{4}$, or $x = 0.75$. Now that we know the x-value of the vertex, we create a table. We choose x-values on both sides of $x = 0.75$, but we choose integers because it will be easier to find the y-values.

x	$y = 2x^2 - 3x - 4$	Point
-1	$2(-1)^2 - 3(-1) - 4$ $= 1$	$(-1, 1)$
0	$2(0)^2 - 3(0) - 4$ $= -4$	$(0, -4)$
0.75	$2(0.75)^2 - 3(-0.75) - 4$ $= -5.125$	$(0.75, -5.125)$
1	$2(1)^2 - 3(1) - 4$ $= -5$	$(1, -5)$
2	$2(2)^2 - 3(2) - 4$ $= -2$	$(2, -2)$

Figure 9.2.25: Values and points for $y = 2x^2 - 3x - 4$

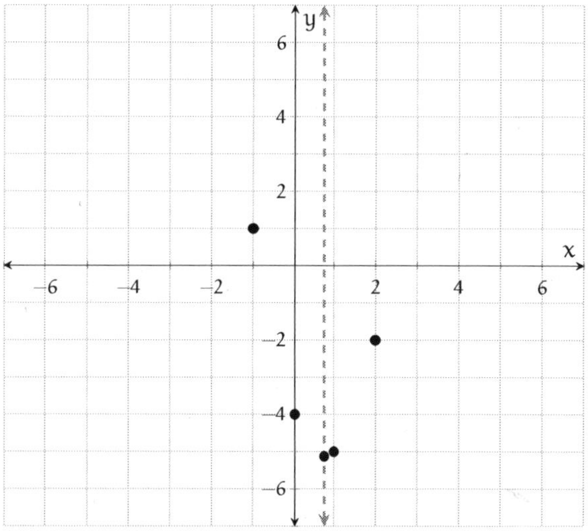

Figure 9.2.26: Plot of initial points

The points graphed in Figure 9.2.26 don't have the symmetry we'd expect from a parabola. This is because the vertex occurs at an x-value that is not an integer, and all of the chosen values in the table are integers. We can use the axis of symmetry to determine more points on the graph (as shown in Figure 9.2.27), which will give it the symmetry we expect. From there, we can complete the sketch of this graph.

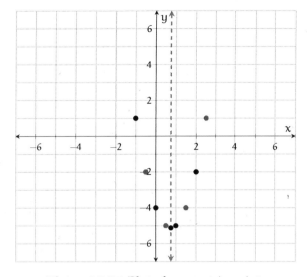

Figure 9.2.27: Plot of symmetric points

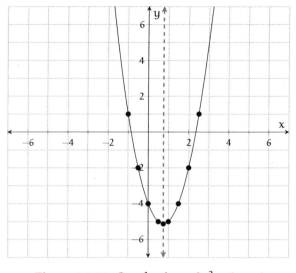

Figure 9.2.28: Graph of $y = 2x^2 - 3x - 4$

9.2.4 Applications of Quadratic Graphs Involving the Vertex.

We looked at the height of Hannah's toy rocket with respect to time at the beginning of this section and saw that it reached a maximum height of 64 feet after 2 seconds. Let's look at some more applications that involve finding the minimum or maximum y-value on a quadratic graph.

Example 9.2.29 Jae got a new air rifle for target practice. The first thing they did with it was some testing to find out how accurate the targeting cross-hairs were. In Olympic 10-meter air rifle shooting[1], the bulls-eye is a 0.5 mm diameter dot, about the size of the head of a pin, so accuracy is key. To test the accuracy, Jae stood at certain specific distances from a bullseye target, aimed the cross-hairs on the bullseye, and fired. Jae recorded how far above or how far below the pellet hit relative to the bullseye.

Distance to Target in Yards	5	10	20	30	35	40	50
Above/Below Bulls-eye	↓	↑	↑	↑	⊙	↓	↓
Distance Above/Below in Inches	0.1	0.6	1.1	0.6	0	0.8	3.2

Figure 9.2.30: Shooting Distance vs Pellet Rise/Fall

Make a graph of the height of the pellet relative to the bulls-eye at the shooting distances Jae used in Figure 9.2.30 and find the vertex. What does the vertex mean in this context?

Explanation.

Note that values measured below the bulls-eye should be graphed as negative y-values. Keep in mind that the units on the axes are different: along the x-axis, the units are yards, whereas on the y-axis, the units are inches.

Since the input values seem to be increasing by 5s or 10s, we scale the x-axis by 10s. The y-axis needs to be scaled by 1s.

From the graph we can see that the point $(20, 1.1)$ is our best guess for the vertex. This means the highest above the cross-hairs Jae hit was 1.1 inches when the target was 20 yards away.

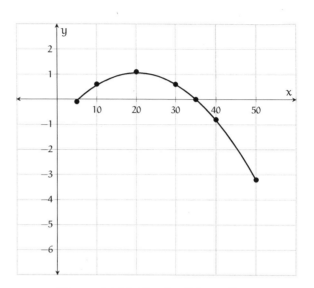

Figure 9.2.31: Graph of Target Data

Example 9.2.32 We looked at the quadratic equation $R = (13 + 0.25x)(1500 - 50x)$ in Example 5.4.2 of Section 5.4, where R was the revenue (in dollars) for x 25-cent price increases from an initial price of \$13. The expression simplified to

$$R = -12.5x^2 - 275x + 19500.$$

Find the vertex of this quadratic expression and explain what it means in the context of this model.

Explanation. Note that if we tried to use $R = (13 + 0.25x)(1500 - 50x)$, we would not be able to immediately identify the values of a and b needed to determine the vertex. Using the expanded form of $R = -12.5x^2 - 275x + 19500$, we see that $a = -12.5$ and $b = -275$, so the vertex occurs at:

$$h = -\frac{b}{2a}$$
$$= -\frac{-275}{2(-12.5)}$$
$$= -11$$

And the second coordinate for the vertex is at:

$$k = -12.5(-11)^2 - 275(-11) + 19500$$
$$= 21012.5$$

So the vertex occurs at $(-11, 21012.5)$.

Literally interpreting this, we can state that -11 of the 25-cent price increases result in a maximum revenue of \$21,012.50.

We can calculate "-11 of the 25-cent price increases" to be a decrease of \$2.75. The price was set at \$13 per jar, so the maximum revenue of \$21,012.50 would occur when Avery sets the price at \$10.25 per jar.

---

[1]en.wikipedia.org/wiki/ISSF_10_meter_air_rifle

Example 9.2.33 Kali has 500 feet of fencing and she needs to build a rectangular pen for her goats. What are the dimensions of the rectangle that would give her goats the largest area?

Explanation.   We use ℓ for the length of the pen and w for the width, in feet. We know that the perimeter must be 500 feet so that gives us

$$2\ell + 2w = 500$$

First we solve for the length:

$$2\ell + 2w = 500$$
$$2\ell = 500 - 2w$$
$$\ell = 250 - w$$

Now we can write a formula for the rectangle's area:

$$A = \ell \cdot w$$
$$A = (250 - w) \cdot w$$
$$A = 250w - w^2$$
$$A = -w^2 + 250w$$

The area is a quadratic expression so we can identify $a = -1$ and $b = 250$ and find the vertex:

$$h = -\frac{(250)}{2(-1)}$$
$$= \frac{250}{2}$$
$$= 125$$

Since the width of the rectangle that will maximize area is 125 ft, we can find the length using our expression:

$$\ell = 250 - w$$
$$= 250 - 125$$
$$= 125$$

To find the maximum area we can either substitute the width into the area formula or multiply the length by the width:

$$A = \ell \cdot w$$
$$A = 125 \cdot 125$$
$$A = 15{,}625$$

The maximum area that Kali can get is 15,625 square feet if she builds her pen to be a square with a length and width of 125 feet.

9.2.5 Reading Questions

1. There are four key features of a quadratic graph discussed in this section. What are they?

2. Explain how the formula for the first coordinate of a parabola's vertex is similar to the quadratic formula.

3. If a parabola's vertex is at $(4, 6)$, and you know the coordinates of some points on the parabola where $x = 1, 2, 3$, at what other x-values do you know coordinates on the parabola?

9.2.6 Exercises

Review and Warmup Make a table for the equation.

1. The first row is an example.

x	$y = -x + 2$	Points
-3	5	$(-3, 5)$
-2	_____	_____
-1	_____	_____
0	_____	_____
1	_____	_____
2	_____	_____

2. The first row is an example.

x	$y = -x + 3$	Points
-3	6	$(-3, 6)$
-2	_____	_____
-1	_____	_____
0	_____	_____
1	_____	_____
2	_____	_____

3. The first row is an example.

x	$y = \frac{3}{10}x - 3$	Points
-30	-12	$(-30, -12)$
-20	_____	_____
-10	_____	_____
0	_____	_____
10	_____	_____
20	_____	_____

4. The first row is an example.

x	$y = \frac{5}{6}x + 9$	Points
-18	-6	$(-18, -6)$
-12	_____	_____
-6	_____	_____
0	_____	_____
6	_____	_____
12	_____	_____

5. Evaluate the expression $\frac{1}{5}(x + 3)^2 - 2$ when $x = -8$.

6. Evaluate the expression $\frac{1}{3}(x + 3)^2 - 8$ when $x = -6$.

7. Evaluate the expression $-16t^2 + 64t + 128$ when $t = 3$.

8. Evaluate the expression $-16t^2 + 64t + 128$ when $t = 2$.

Algebraically Determining the Vertex and Axis of Symmetry of Quadratic Equations Find the axis of symmetry and vertex of the quadratic function.

9. $y = 5x^2 + 20x - 5$

10. $y = -4x^2 + 8x - 1$

11. $y = 4 + 40x - 4x^2$

12. $y = -3 - 16x - 4x^2$

13. $y = -2 - x^2 + 2x$

14. $y = -4 - x^2 - 10x$

15. $y = 2x^2 + 8x$

16. $y = 3x^2 - 12x$

17. $y = 5 + 4x^2$

18. $y = 1 + 5x^2$

19. $y = -4x^2 + 12x - 3$

20. $y = -3x^2 - 15x + 1$

21. $y = -4x^2 - 4x - 5$

22. $y = -2x^2 + 6x - 1$

23. $y = 2x^2$

24. $y = 3x^2$

25. $y = 0.4x^2 + 2$

26. $y = 4x^2 - 4$

27. $y = 0.5(x + 2)^2 - 2$

28. $y = -0.5(x + 5)^2 - 1$

Graphing Quadratic Equations Using the Vertex and a Table For the given quadratic equation, find the vertex. Then create a table of ordered pairs centered around the vertex and make a graph.

29. $y = x^2 + 2$

30. $y = x^2 + 1$

31. $y = x^2 - 5$

32. $y = x^2 - 3$

33. $y = (x - 2)^2$

34. $y = (x - 4)^2$

35. $y = (x + 3)^2$

36. $y = (x + 2)^2$

Graphing Quadratic Equations Using the Vertex and a Table

37. For $y = 4x^2 - 8x + 5$, determine the vertex, create a table of ordered pairs, and then make a graph.

38. For $y = 2x^2 + 4x + 7$, determine the vertex, create a table of ordered pairs, and then make a graph.

39. For $y = -x^2 + 4x + 2$, determine the vertex, create a table of ordered pairs, and then make a graph.

40. For $y = -x^2 + 2x - 5$, determine the vertex, create a table of ordered pairs, and then make a graph.

41. For $y = x^2 - 5x + 3$, determine the vertex, create a table of ordered pairs, and then make a graph.

42. For $y = x^2 + 7x - 1$, determine the vertex, create a table of ordered pairs, and then make a graph.

43. For $y = -2x^2 - 5x + 6$, determine the vertex, create a table of ordered pairs, and then make a graph.

44. For $y = 2x^2 - 9x$, determine the vertex, create a table of ordered pairs, and then make a graph.

Finding Maximum and Minimum Values for Applications of Quadratic Equations

45. Consider two numbers where one number is 5 less than a second number. Find a pair of such numbers that has the least product possible. One approach is to let x represent the smaller number, and write a formula for a function of x that outputs the product of the two numbers. Then find its vertex and interpret it.

    These two numbers are [   ] and the least possible product is [   ].

46. Consider two numbers where one number is 6 less than a second number. Find a pair of such numbers that has the least product possible. One approach is to let x represent the smaller number, and write a formula for a function of x that outputs the product of the two numbers. Then find its vertex and interpret it.

    These two numbers are [   ] and the least possible product is [   ].

47. Consider two numbers where one number is 4 less than 4 times a second number. Find a pair of such numbers that has the least product possible. One approach is to let x represent the smaller number, and write a formula for a function of x that outputs the product of the two numbers. Then find its vertex and interpret it.

    These two numbers are [   ] and the least possible product is [   ].

48. Consider two numbers where one number is 9 less than 4 times a second number. Find a pair of such numbers that has the least product possible. One approach is to let x represent the smaller number, and write a formula for a function of x that outputs the product of the two numbers. Then find its vertex and interpret it.

    These two numbers are [   ] and the least possible product is [   ].

49. You will build a rectangular sheep enclosure next to a river. There is no need to build a fence along the river, so you only need to build on three sides. You have a total of 470 feet of fence to use. Find the dimensions of the pen such that you can enclose the maximum possible area. One approach is to let x represent the length of fencing that runs perpendicular to the river, and write a formula for a function of x that outputs the area of the enclosure. Then find its vertex and interpret it.

    The length of the pen (parallel to the river) should be [   ], the width (perpendicular to the river) should be [   ], and the maximum possible area is [   ].

50. You will build a rectangular sheep enclosure next to a river. There is no need to build a fence along the river, so you only need to build on three sides. You have a total of 480 feet of fence to use. Find the dimensions of the pen such that you can enclose the maximum possible area. One approach is to let x represent the length of fencing that runs perpendicular to the river, and write a formula for a function of x that outputs the area of the enclosure. Then find its vertex and interpret it.

    The length of the pen (parallel to the river) should be [   ], the width (perpendicular to the river) should be [   ], and the maximum possible area is [   ].

51. You will build a rectangular sheep enclosure next to a river. There is no need to build a fence along the river, so you only need to build on three sides. You have a total of 490 feet of fence to use. Find the dimensions of the pen such that you can enclose the maximum possible area. One approach is to let x represent the length of fencing that runs perpendicular to the river, and write a formula for a function of x that outputs the area of the enclosure. Then find its vertex and interpret it.

    The length of the pen (parallel to the river) should be [   ], the width (perpendicular to the river) should be [   ], and the maximum possible area is [   ].

52. You will build a rectangular sheep enclosure next to a river. There is no need to build a fence along the river, so you only need to build on three sides. You have a total of 500 feet of fence to use. Find the dimensions of the pen such that you can enclose the maximum possible area. One approach is to let x represent the length of fencing that runs perpendicular to the river, and write a formula for a function of x that outputs the area of the enclosure. Then find its vertex and interpret it.

    The length of the pen (parallel to the river) should be [   ], the width (perpendicular to the river) should be [   ], and the maximum possible area is [   ].

53. You will build two identical rectangular enclosures next to a each other, sharing a side. You have a total of 300 feet of fence to use. Find the dimensions of each pen such that you can enclose the maximum possible area. One approach is to let x represent the length of fencing that the two pens share, and write a formula for a function of x that outputs the total area of the enclosures. Then find its vertex and interpret it.

    The length of each (along the wall that they share) should be [   ], the width should be [   ], and the maximum possible area of each pen is [   ].

54. You will build two identical rectangular enclosures next to a each other, sharing a side. You have a total of 324 feet of fence to use. Find the dimensions of each pen such that you can enclose the maximum possible area. One approach is to let x represent the length of fencing that the two pens share, and write a formula for a function of x that outputs the total area of the enclosures. Then find its vertex and interpret it.

    The length of each (along the wall that they share) should be [   ], the width should be [　　　　　], and the maximum possible area of each pen is [　　　　　].

55. You plan to build four identical rectangular animal enclosures in a row. Each adjacent pair of pens share a fence between them. You have a total of 336 feet of fence to use. Find the dimensions of each pen such that you can enclose the maximum possible area. One approach is to let x represent the length of fencing that adjacent pens share, and write a formula for a function of x that outputs the total area. Then find its vertex and interpret it.

The length of each pen (along the walls that they share) should be [　　　　　], the width (perpendicular to the river) should be [　　　　　], and the maximum possible area of each pen is [　　　　　].

56. You plan to build four identical rectangular animal enclosures in a row. Each adjacent pair of pens share a fence between them. You have a total of 352 feet of fence to use. Find the dimensions of each pen such that you can enclose the maximum possible area. One approach is to let x represent the length of fencing that adjacent pens share, and write a formula for a function of x that outputs the total area. Then find its vertex and interpret it.

The length of each pen (along the walls that they share) should be [　　　　　], the width (perpendicular to the river) should be [　　　　　], and the maximum possible area of each pen is [　　　　　].

57. Currently, an artist can sell 240 paintings every year at the price of $90.00 per painting. Each time he raises the price per painting by $15.00, he sells 5 fewer paintings every year.

    a. To obtain maximum income of [　　　　　], the artist should set the price per painting at [　　　　　].

    b. To earn $43,875.00 per year, the artist could sell his paintings at two different prices. The lower price is [　　　　　] per painting, and the higher price is [　　　　　] per painting.

58. Currently, an artist can sell 270 paintings every year at the price of $150.00 per painting. Each time he raises the price per painting by $5.00, he sells 5 fewer paintings every year.

    a. To obtain maximum income of [　　　　　], the artist should set the price per painting at [　　　　　].

    b. To earn $43,700.00 per year, the artist could sell his paintings at two different prices. The lower price is [　　　　　] per painting, and the higher price is [　　　　　] per painting.

9.3 Graphing Quadratic Expressions

We have learned how to visually locate the key features of quadratic graphs and how to find the vertex algebraically. In this section we'll explore how to find the intercepts algebraically and use their coordinates to more precisely graph a quadratic equation. Then we will see how to interpret the key features in context and distinguish between quadratic and other graphs.

Let's start by looking at a quadratic equation that models the path of a baseball after it is hit by Ignacio, the batter. The height of the baseball, H, measured in feet, after t seconds is given by $H = -16t^2 + 75t + 4.7$. We know the graph will have the shape of a parabola and we want to know the initial height, the maximum height, and the amount of time it takes for the ball to hit the ground if it is not caught. These important ideas correspond to the vertical intercept, the vertex, and one of the horizontal intercepts.

The graph of this equation is shown in Figure 9.3.2. We cannot easily read where the intercepts occur from the graph because they are not integers. We previously covered how to determine the vertex algebraically. In this section, we'll learn how to find the intercepts algebraically. Then we'll come back to this example and find the intercepts for the path of the baseball.

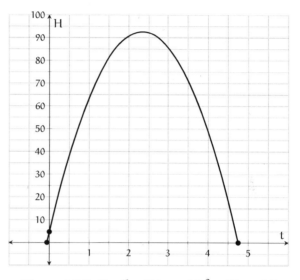

Figure 9.3.2: Graph of $H = -16t^2 + 75t + 4.7$

9.3.1 Finding the Vertical and Horizontal Intercepts Algebraically

In List 9.2.12, we identified that the **vertical intercept** occurs where the graph intersects the vertical axis. If we're using x and y as our variables, the x-value on the vertical axis is $x = 0$. We can substitute 0 for x to find the value of y.

The **horizontal intercepts** occur where the graph intersects the horizontal axis. If we're using x and y as our variables, the y-value on the horizontal axis is $y = 0$, so we can substitute 0 for y and find the value(s) of x.

Example 9.3.3 Find the intercepts for the quadratic equation $y = x^2 - 4x - 12$ using algebra.

To determine the y-intercept, we substitute $x = 0$ and find $y = 0^2 - 4(0) - 12 = -12$. So the y-intercept occurs where $y = -12$. On a graph, this is the point $(0, -12)$.

To determine the x-intercept(s), we set $y = 0$ and solve for x:

$$0 = x^2 - 4x - 12$$
$$x = \frac{-(-4) \pm \sqrt{(-4)^2 - 4(1)(-12)}}{2(1)}$$
$$= \frac{4 \pm \sqrt{16 + 48}}{2}$$
$$= \frac{4 \pm \sqrt{64}}{2}$$

$$= \frac{4 \pm 8}{2}$$

$$x = \frac{4-8}{2} \qquad \text{or} \qquad x = \frac{4+8}{2}$$

$$x = \frac{-4}{2} \qquad \text{or} \qquad x = \frac{12}{2}$$

$$x = -2 \qquad \text{or} \qquad x = 6$$

The x-intercepts occur where $x = -2$ and where $x = 6$. On a graph, these are the points $(-2, 0)$ and $(6, 0)$.

Notice in Example 9.3.3 that the y-intercept was $(0, -12)$ and the value of c was -12. When we substitute 0 for x we will always get the value of c.

Fact 9.3.4 *The vertical intercept of a quadratic equation occurs at the point* $(0, c)$ *where c is the constant term, because substituting* $x = 0$ *leaves only the constant term.*

Example 9.3.5 Algebraically determine any horizontal and vertical intercepts of the quadratic equation $y = -x^2 + 5x - 7$.

Explanation. To determine the vertical intercept, take the constant term -7, and recognize that the y-intercept is at the point $(0, -7)$.

To determine the horizontal intercepts, we'll set $y = 0$ and solve for x:

$$0 = -x^2 + 5x - 7$$

$$x = \frac{-5 \pm \sqrt{5^2 - 4(-1)(-7)}}{2(-1)}$$

$$x = \frac{-5 \pm \sqrt{-3}}{-2}$$

The radicand is negative so there are no real solutions to the equation. This means there are no horizontal intercepts.

9.3.2 Graphing Quadratic Equations Using Their Key Features

To graph a quadratic equation using its key features, we can use algebra to determine the following: whether the parabola opens upward or downward, the vertical intercept, the horizontal intercepts and the vertex. Then we can graph the points and connect them with a smooth curve.

Example 9.3.6 Graph the quadratic equation $y = 2x^2 + 10x + 8$ by algebraically determining its key features.

To start, we'll note that this parabola will open upward, since the leading coefficient is positive.

To find the y-intercept, we substitute $x = 0$ to find $2(0)^2 + 10(0) + 8 = 8$. The y-intercept is $(0, 8)$.

Next, we'll find the horizontal intercepts by setting $y = 0$ and solving for x:

$$2x^2 + 10x + 8 = 0$$

$$x = \frac{-10 \pm \sqrt{10^2 - 4(2)(8)}}{2(2)}$$

$$= \frac{-10 \pm \sqrt{100 - 64}}{4}$$
$$= \frac{-10 \pm \sqrt{36}}{4}$$
$$= \frac{-10 \pm 6}{4}$$

$$x = \frac{-10 - 6}{4} \qquad \text{or} \qquad x = \frac{-10 + 6}{4}$$
$$x = \frac{-16}{4} \qquad \text{or} \qquad x = \frac{-4}{4}$$
$$x = -4 \qquad \text{or} \qquad x = -1$$

The x-intercepts are $(-4, 0)$ and $(-1, 0)$.

Lastly, we'll determine the vertex. Noting that $a = 2$ and $b = 10$, we have:

$$h = -\frac{b}{2a}$$
$$= -\frac{10}{2(2)}$$
$$= -2.5$$

Using this x-value to find the y-coordinate, we have:

$$k = 2(-2.5)^2 + 10(-2.5) + 8$$
$$= 12.5 - 25 + 8$$
$$= -4.5$$

The vertex is the point $(-2.5, -4.5)$, and the axis of symmetry is the line $x = -2.5$.

We're now ready to graph this curve. We'll start by drawing and scaling the axes so all of our key features will be displayed as shown in Figure 9.3.7. Next, we'll plot these key points as shown in Figure 9.3.8. Finally, we'll note that this parabola opens upward and connect these points with a smooth curve, as shown in Figure 9.3.9.

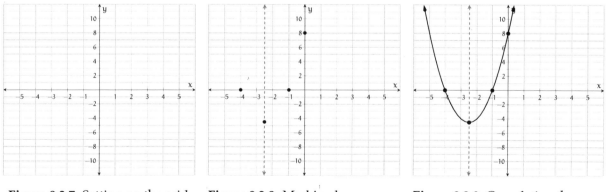

Figure 9.3.7: Setting up the grid.

Figure 9.3.8: Marking key features.

Figure 9.3.9: Completing the graph.

Example 9.3.10 Graph the quadratic equation $y = -x^2 + 4x - 5$ by algebraically determining its key features.

To start, we'll note that this parabola will open downward, as the leading coefficient is negative.

To find the y-intercept, we'll substitute x with 0:

$$y = -(0)^2 + 4(0) - 5$$
$$= -5$$

The y-intercept is $(0, -5)$.

Next, we'll find the horizontal intercepts by setting $y = 0$ and solving for x.

$$-x^2 + 4x - 5 = 0$$

$$x = \frac{-4 \pm \sqrt{(4)^2 - 4(-1)(-5)}}{2(-1)}$$

$$= \frac{-4 \pm \sqrt{16 - 20}}{-2}$$

$$= \frac{-4 \pm \sqrt{-8}}{-2}$$

The radicand is negative, so there are no real solutions to the equation. This is a parabola that does not have any horizontal intercepts.

To determine the vertex, we'll use $a = -1$ and $b = 4$:

$$h = -\frac{4}{2(-1)}$$

$$= 2$$

Using this x-value to find the y-coordinate, we have:

$$k = -(2)^2 + 4(2) - 5$$
$$= -4 + 8 - 5$$
$$= -1$$

The vertex is the point $(2, -1)$, and the axis of symmetry is the line $x = 2$.

Plotting this information in an appropriate grid, we have:

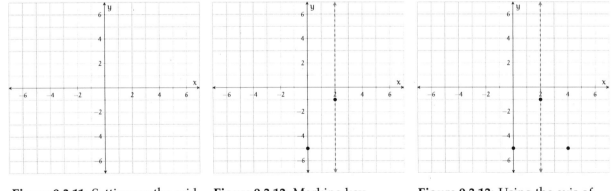

Figure 9.3.11: Setting up the grid.

Figure 9.3.12: Marking key features.

Figure 9.3.13: Using the axis of symmetry to determine one additional point.

Since we don't have any x-intercepts, we would like to have a few more points to graph. We make a table with a few more values around the vertex, plot these, and then draw a smooth curve. This is shown in Figure 9.3.14 and Figure 9.3.15.

x	$y = -x^2 + 4x - 5$	Point
0	$-(0)^2 + 4(0) - 5$ $= -5$	$(0, -5)$
1	$-(1)^2 + 4(1) - 5$ $= -2$	$(1, -2)$
2	$-(2)^2 + 4(2) - 5$ $= -1$	$(2, -1)$
3	$-(3)^2 + 4(3) - 5$ $= -2$	$(3, -2)$
4	$-(4)^2 + 4(4) - 5$ $= -5$	$(4, -5)$

Figure 9.3.14: Determine additional points to plot.

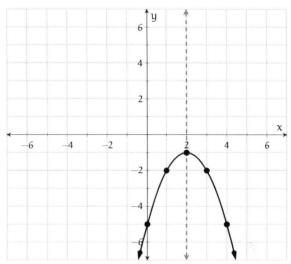

Figure 9.3.15: Completing the graph.

9.3.3 Applications of Quadratic Equations

Now we have learned how to find all the key features of a quadratic equation algebraically. Here are some applications of quadratic equations so we can learn how to identify and interpret the vertex, intercepts and additional points in context.

Example 9.3.16 Returning to the path of the baseball in Figure 9.3.2, the equation that represents the height of the baseball after Ignacio hit it, is $H = -16t^2 + 75t + 4.7$. The height is in feet and the time, t, is in seconds. Find and interpret the following, in context.

    a. The vertical intercept.

    b. The horizontal intercept(s).

    c. The vertex.

    d. The height of the baseball 1 second after it was hit.

    e. The time(s) when the baseball is 80 feet above the ground.

Explanation.

    a. To determine the vertical intercept, we'll substitute $t = 0$ to find $-16(0)^2 + 75(0) + 4.7 = 4.7$. The vertical intercept occurs at $(0, 4.7)$. This is the height of the baseball at time $t = 0$, so the initial height of the baseball was 4.7 feet.

b. To determine the horizontal intercepts, we'll solve H = 0.

$$H = 0$$
$$-16t^2 + 75t + 4.7 = 0$$

$$t = \frac{-75 \pm \sqrt{75^2 - 4(-16)(4.7)}}{2(-16)}$$
$$= \frac{-75 \pm \sqrt{5925.8}}{-32}$$

Rounding these two values with a calculator, we obtain:

$$\approx -0.06185, 4.749$$

The horizontal intercepts occur at approximately $(-0.06185, 0)$ and $(4.749, 0)$. If we assume that the ball was hit when $t = 0$, a negative time does not make sense. The second horizontal intercept tells us that the ball hit the ground after approximately 4.75 seconds.

c. The vertex occurs at $t = h = -\frac{b}{2a}$, and for this equation $a = -16$ and $b = 75$. So we have:

$$h = -\frac{75}{2(-16)}$$
$$= 2.34375$$

And then we can find the vertex's second coordinate:

$$k = -16(2.34375)^2 + 75(2.34375) + 4.7$$
$$\approx 92.59$$

Thus the vertex is about $(2.344, 92.59)$.

The vertex tells us that the baseball reached a maximum height of approximately 92.6 feet about 2.3 seconds after Ignacio hit it.

d. To find the height of the baseball after 1 second, we can compute H when $t = 1$:

$$-16(1)^2 + 75(1) + 4.7 = 63.7$$

The height of the baseball was 63.7 feet after 1 second.

e. If we want to know when the baseball was 80 feet in the air, then we set H = 80 and we have:

$$H = 80$$
$$-16t^2 + 75t + 4.7 = 80$$
$$-16t^2 + 75t - 75.3 = 0$$

$$t = \frac{-75 \pm \sqrt{75^2 - 4(-16)(-75.3)}}{2(-16)}$$

$$= \frac{-75 \pm \sqrt{805.8}}{-32}$$

Rounding these two values with a calculator, we obtain:

$$\approx 1.457, 3.231$$

The baseball was 80 feet above the ground at two times, at about 1.5 seconds on the way up and about 3.2 seconds on the way down.

Example 9.3.17 The profit that Keenan's manufacturing company makes for producing n refrigerators is given by $P = -0.01n^2 + 520n - 54000$, for $0 \leq n \leq 51{,}896$.

   a. Determine the profit the company will make when they produce 1000 refrigerators.

   b. Determine the maximum profit and the number of refrigerators produced that yields this profit.

   c. How many refrigerators need to be produced in order for the company to "break even?" (In other words, for their profit to be $0.)

   d. How many refrigerators need to be produced in order for the company to make a profit of $1,000,000?

Explanation.

   a. This question is giving us an input value and asking for the output value. We substitute 1000 for n and we have:

$$P = -0.01(1000)^2 + 520(1000) - 54000$$
$$= 366000$$

If Keenan's company sells 1000 refrigerators it will make a profit of $366,000.

   b. This question is asking for the maximum, so we need to find the vertex. This parabola opens downward so the vertex will tell us the maximum profit and the corresponding number of refrigerators that need to be produced. Using $a = -0.01$ and $b = 520$, we have:

$$h = -\frac{b}{2a}$$
$$= -\frac{520}{2(-0.01)}$$
$$= 26000$$

Now we find the value of P when $n = 26000$:

$$k = -0.01(26000)^2 + 520(26000) - 54000$$
$$= 6706000$$

The maximum profit is $6,706,000, which occurs if 26,000 units are produced.

   c. This question is giving a height of 0 and asking us to find the time(s). So we will be finding the horizontal intercept(s). We set $P = 0$ and solve for n using the quadratic formula:

$$0 = -0.01n^2 + 520n - 54000$$

$$n = \frac{-520 \pm \sqrt{520^2 - 4(-0.01)(-54000)}}{2(-0.01)}$$

$$= \frac{-520 \pm \sqrt{268240}}{-0.02}$$

$$\approx 104, 51896$$

The company will break even if they produce about 104 refrigerators or 51,896 refrigerators. If the company produces more refrigerators than it can sell its profit will go down.

d. This question is giving us the profit value. We set $P = 1000000$ and solve for n using the quadratic formula:

$$1000000 = -0.01n^2 + 520n - 54000$$

$$0 = -0.01n^2 + 520n - 1054000$$

$$n = \frac{-520 \pm \sqrt{520^2 - 4(-0.01)(-1054000)}}{2(-0.01)}$$

$$= \frac{-520 \pm \sqrt{228240}}{-0.02}$$

$$\approx 2113, 49887$$

The company will make $1,000,000 in profit if they produce about 2113 refrigerators or 49,887 refrigerators.

Example 9.3.18 Maia has a remote-controlled airplane and she is going to do a stunt dive where the plane dives toward the ground and back up along a parabolic path. The height of the plane after t seconds is given by $H = 0.7t^2 - 23t + 200$, for $0 \leq t \leq 30$. The height is measured in feet.

   a. Determine the starting height of the plane as the dive begins.

   b. Determine the height of the plane after 5 seconds.

   c. Will the plane hit the ground, and if so, at what time?

   d. If the plane does not hit the ground, what is the closest it gets to the ground, and at what time?

   e. At what time(s) will the plane have a height of 50 feet?

Explanation.

   a. This question is asking for the starting height which is the vertical intercept. So we find H when $t = 0$:

$$0.7(0)^2 - 23(0) + 200 = 200$$

When Maia begins the stunt, the plane has a height of 200 feet. Recall that we can also look at the value of $c = 200$ to determine the vertical intercept.

   b. This question is telling us to use $t = 5$ and find H:

$$0.7(5)^2 - 23(5) + 200 = 102.5$$

After 5 seconds, the plane is 102.5 feet above the ground.

c. The ground has a height of 0 feet, so it is asking us to find the horizontal intercept(s) if there are any. We set $H = 0$ and solve for t using the quadratic formula:

$$H = 0.7t^2 - 23t + 200$$
$$0 = 0.7t^2 - 23t + 200$$
$$t = \frac{23 \pm \sqrt{(-23)^2 - 4(0.7)(200)}}{2(0.7)}$$
$$t = \frac{23 \pm \sqrt{-31}}{1.4}$$

The radicand is negative so there are no real solutions to the equation $H = 0$. That means the plane did not hit the ground.

d. This question is asking for the lowest point of the airplane so we should find the vertex. Using $a = 0.7$ and $b = -23$, we have:

$$h = -\frac{b}{2a}$$
$$= -\frac{(-23)}{2(0.7)}$$
$$\approx 16.43$$

Now we can find the value of H when $t \approx 16.43$:

$$k = 0.7(16.43)^2 - 23(16.43) + 200$$
$$\approx 11.07$$

The minimum height of the plane is about 11 feet, which occurs after about 16 seconds.

e. This question is giving us a height and asking for the corresponding time(s) so we set $H = 50$ and solve for t using the quadratic formula:

$$H = 0.7t^2 - 23t + 200$$
$$50 = 0.7t^2 - 23t + 200$$
$$0 = 0.7t^2 - 23t + 150$$
$$t = \frac{23 \pm \sqrt{(-23)^2 - 4(0.7)(150)}}{2(0.7)}$$
$$= \frac{23 \pm \sqrt{109}}{1.4}$$
$$\approx 8.971, 23.89$$

Maia's plane will be 50 feet above the ground about 9 seconds and 24 seconds after the plane begins the stunt.

9.3.4 Distinguishing Quadratic Equations from Other Equations

So far, we've seen that the graphs of quadratic equations are parabolas and have a specific curved with a vertex. We've also seen that they have the algebraic form of $y = ax^2 + bx + c$. Here, we practice recognizing a quadratic equation so that we can call to mind that the equation has these features, which may be useful in some application.

Example 9.3.19 Determine if each equation is a quadratic equation.

    a. $y + 5x^2 - 4 = 0$ c. $y = -5x + 1$ e. $y = \sqrt{x + 1} + 5$

    b. $x^2 + y^2 = 9$ d. $y = (x - 6)^2 + 3$

Explanation.

    a. As $y + 5x^2 - 4 = 0$ can be re-written as $y = -5x^2 + 4$, this equation is a quadratic equation.

    b. The equation $x^2 + y^2 = 9$ cannot be re-written in the form $y = ax^2 + bx + c$ (due to the y^2 term), so this equation is not a quadratic equation.

    c. The equation $y = -5x + 1$ is a linear equation, not a quadratic equation.

    d. The equation $y = (x - 6)^2 + 3$ can be re-written as $y = x^2 - 12x + 39$, so this is a quadratic equation.

    e. The equation $y = \sqrt{x + 1} + 5$ is not a quadratic equation as x is inside a radical, not squared.

Example 9.3.20 Determine if each graph *could* be the graph of a quadratic equation.

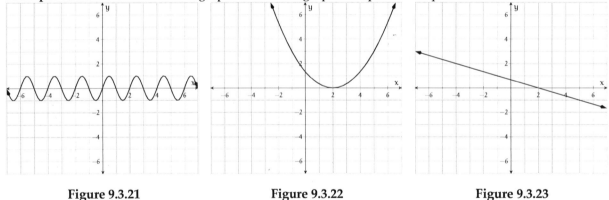

       Figure 9.3.21   **Figure 9.3.22**   **Figure 9.3.23**

Explanation.

    a. Since this graph has multiple maximum points and minimum points, it is not a parabola and it is not possible that it represents a quadratic equation.

    b. This graph looks like a parabola, and it's possible that it represents a quadratic equation.

    c. This graph does not appear to be a parabola, but looks like a straight line. It's not likely that it represents a quadratic equation.

9.3.5 Reading Questions

1.   Explain how to find a parabola's y-intercept when you have the equation for the parabola.

2.   Why does a parabola sometimes have zero x-intercepts, sometimes have one, and sometimes have two?

3.   When you have the equation for a quadratic graph, what can you always try to use to find any horizontal intercepts?

9.3.6 Exercises

Review and Warmup Solve the equation.

1. $x^2 + 10x + 16 = 0$	**2.** $x^2 + 8x + 15 = 0$	**3.** $x^2 - 8x + 16 = 0$
4. $x^2 - 12x + 36 = 0$	**5.** $x^2 - 1 = 0$	**6.** $x^2 - 9 = 0$
7. $41x^2 - 47 = 0$	**8.** $17x^2 - 59 = 0$	**9.** $3x^2 - 8x - 4 = 0$
10. $7x^2 + 4x - 2 = 0$	**11.** $2x^2 + 3x + 6 = 0$	**12.** $5x^2 + 5x + 7 = 0$

Finding the Intercepts of Quadratic Equations Algebraically Find the y-intercept and any x-intercept(s) of the quadratic curve.

13. $y = x^2 + 4x + 3$	**14.** $y = -x^2 - 2x + 3$	**15.** $y = x^2 - 4$
16. $y = -x^2 + 9$	**17.** $y = x^2 - 4x$	**18.** $y = -x^2 + 5x$
19. $y = x^2 + 8x + 16$	**20.** $y = x^2 + x + 3$	**21.** $y = x^2 + 3x + 4$
22. $y = x^2 + 2x + 5$	**23.** $y = x^2 + x + 6$	**24.** $y = x^2 + 8x + 3$
25. $y = x^2 + 8x + 6$	**26.** $y = x^2 + 7x + 8$	**27.** $y = x^2 + 8x + 10$
28. $y = 2x^2 - 9x + 10$	**29.** $y = 4x^2 + 4x + 1$	**30.** $y = 4x^2 - 49$
31. $y = -11x - 7 - 4x^2$	**32.** $y = 5x - 4x^2$	

Sketching Graphs of Quadratic Equations Graph each curve by algebraically determining its key features.

33. $y = x^2 - 7x + 12$	**34.** $y = x^2 + 5x - 14$	**35.** $y = -x^2 - x + 20$
36. $y = -x^2 + 4x + 21$	**37.** $y = x^2 - 8x + 16$	**38.** $y = x^2 + 6x + 9$
39. $y = x^2 - 4$	**40.** $y = x^2 - 9$	**41.** $y = x^2 + 6x$
42. $y = x^2 - 8x$	**43.** $y = -x^2 + 5x$	**44.** $y = -x^2 + 16$
45. $y = x^2 + 4x + 7$	**46.** $y = x^2 - 2x + 6$	**47.** $y = x^2 + 2x - 5$
48. $y = x^2 - 6x + 2$	**49.** $y = -x^2 + 4x - 1$	**50.** $y = -x^2 - x + 3$
51. $y = 2x^2 - 4x - 30$	**52.** $y = 3x^2 + 21x + 36$	

Applications of Quadratic Equations

53.   An object was shot up into the air with an initial vertical speed of 544 feet per second. Its height as time passes can be modeled by the quadratic equation $y = -16t^2 + 544t$. Here t represents the number of seconds since the object's release, and y represents the object's height in feet.

   a. After [ ], this object reached its maximum height of [ ].

b. This object flew for [   ] before it landed on the ground.

c. This object was [   ] in the air 22 s after its release.

d. This object was 3600 ft high at two times: once [   ] after its release, and again later [   ] after its release.

54. An object was shot up into the air with an initial vertical speed of 576 feet per second. Its height as time passes can be modeled by the quadratic equation $y = -16t^2 + 576t$. Here t represents the number of seconds since the object's release, and y represents the object's height in feet.

a. After [   ], this object reached its maximum height of [   ].

b. This object flew for [   ] before it landed on the ground.

c. This object was [   ] in the air 11 s after its release.

d. This object was 5120 ft high at two times: once [   ] after its release, and again later [   ] after its release.

55. From an oceanside clifftop 200 m above sea level, an object was shot into the air with an initial vertical speed of 274.4 $\frac{m}{s}$. It fell into the ocean. Its height (above sea level) as time passes can be modeled by the quadratic equation $y = -4.9t^2 + 274.4t + 200$. Here t represents the number of seconds since the object's release, and y represents the object's height (above sea level) in meters.

a. After [   ], this object reached its maximum height of [   ].

b. This object flew for [   ] before it landed in the ocean.

c. This object was [   ] above sea level 20 s after its release.

d. This object was 3081.2 m above sea level twice: once [   ] after its release, and again later [   ] after its release.

56. From an oceanside clifftop 160 m above sea level, an object was shot into the air with an initial vertical speed of 294 $\frac{m}{s}$. It fell into the ocean. Its height (above sea level) as time passes can be modeled by the quadratic equation $y = -4.9t^2 + 294t + 160$. Here t represents the number of seconds since the object's release, and y represents the object's height (above sea level) in meters.

a. After [   ], this object reached its maximum height of [   ].

b. This object flew for [   ] before it landed in the ocean.

c. This object was [   ] above sea level 46 s after its release.

d. This object was 1747.6 m above sea level twice: once [   ] after its release, and again later [   ] after its release.

57. A remote control aircraft will perform a stunt by flying toward the ground and then up. Its height, in feet, can be modeled by the equation $h = 0.4t^2 - 2.4t + 0.6$, where t is in seconds. The plane (☐ will ☐ will not) hit the ground during this stunt.

58. A remote control aircraft will perform a stunt by flying toward the ground and then up. Its height, in feet, can be modeled by the equation $h = 1.1t^2 - 8.8t + 21.6$, where t is in seconds. The plane (☐ will ☐ will not) hit the ground during this stunt.

59. A submarine is traveling in the sea. Its depth, in meters, can be modeled by $d = -0.1t^2 + t - 1.5$, where t stands for time in seconds. The submarine (☐ will ☐ will not) hit the sea surface along this route.

60. A submarine is traveling in the sea. Its depth, in meters, can be modeled by $d = -0.8t^2 + 9.6t - 31.8$, where t stands for time in seconds. The submarine (☐ will ☐ will not) hit the sea surface along this route.

61. An object is launched upward at the height of 310 meters. Its height can be modeled by

$$h = -4.9t^2 + 100t + 310,$$

where h stands for the object's height in meters, and t stands for time passed in seconds since its launch. The object's height will be 360 meters twice before it hits the ground. Find how many seconds since the launch would the object's height be 360 meters. Round your answers to two decimal places if needed.

The object's height would be 360 meters the first time at ☐ seconds, and then the second time at ☐ seconds.

62. An object is launched upward at the height of 330 meters. Its height can be modeled by

$$h = -4.9t^2 + 80t + 330,$$

where h stands for the object's height in meters, and t stands for time passed in seconds since its launch. The object's height will be 350 meters twice before it hits the ground. Find how many seconds since the launch would the object's height be 350 meters. Round your answers to two decimal places if needed.

The object's height would be 350 meters the first time at ☐ seconds, and then the second time at ☐ seconds.

63. Currently, an artist can sell 280 paintings every year at the price of $60.00 per painting. Each time he raises the price per painting by $15.00, he sells 10 fewer paintings every year.

Assume he will raise the price per painting x times, then he will sell $280 - 10x$ paintings every year at the price of $60 + 15x$ dollars. His yearly income can be modeled by the equation:

$$i = (60 + 15x)(280 - 10x)$$

where i stands for his yearly income in dollars. If the artist wants to earn $28,800.00 per year from selling paintings, what new price should he set?

To earn $28,800.00 per year, the artist could sell his paintings at two different prices. The lower price is ☐ per painting, and the higher price is ☐ per painting.

64. Currently, an artist can sell 280 paintings every year at the price of \$80.00 per painting. Each time he raises the price per painting by \$10.00, he sells 5 fewer paintings every year.

    Assume he will raise the price per painting x times, then he will sell $280 - 5x$ paintings every year at the price of $80 + 10x$ dollars. His yearly income can be modeled by the equation:

    $$i = (80 + 10x)(280 - 5x)$$

    where i stands for his yearly income in dollars. If the artist wants to earn \$29,150.00 per year from selling paintings, what new price should he set?

    To earn \$29,150.00 per year, the artist could sell his paintings at two different prices. The lower price is [_____] per painting, and the higher price is [_____] per painting.

Challenge

65. Consider the equation $y = x^2 + nx + p$. Let n and p be real numbers. Give your answers as points.

    a. Suppose the graph has two real x-intercepts. What are they?

    b. What is its y-intercept?

    c. What is its vertex?

9.4 Graphically Solving Equations and Inequalities

It is possible to solve equations and inequalities simply by reading a graph well. In this section, we take that approach to solving equations.

9.4.1 Solving Equations Using a Graph

To *algebraically* solve an equation like $-0.01x^2 + 0.7x - 18 = -0.04x^2 - 3.6x + 32$, we'd start by rearranging terms so that we could apply the quadratic formula. That would be a lot of pencil-and-paper work, and a lot of opportunity to make human errors. An alternative is to *graphically* solve this equation. We start by graphing both

$$y = -0.01x^2 + 0.7x - 18 \qquad \text{and} \qquad y = -0.04x^2 - 3.6x + 32.$$

It happens that we learned how to graph equations like these by hand in Section 9.3, but we will "cheat" in this section and use graphing technology to just make the graphs for us.

Example 9.4.2 Solve the equation $-0.01x^2 + 0.7x - 18 = -0.04x^2 - 3.6x + 32$ graphically.

Explanation.

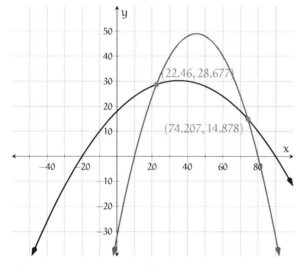

There are two points of intersection where the curves cross each other: $(22.46, 28.677)$ and $(74.207, 14.878)$. Each one of them tells you a solution to the equation we started with. The point $(22.46, 28.677)$ means that when x is about 22.46, both $-0.01x^2 + 0.7x - 18$ and $-0.04x^2 - 3.6x + 32$ work out to the same result. That result is about 28.677, but that really doesn't matter right now. Its the x-value, about 22.46, that matters. That is one solution to the equation.

The second point of intersection similarly shows us that 74.207 is another approximate solution. We can conclude that the solution set to the equation is approximately $\{22.46, 74.207\}$.

Figure 9.4.3: $y = -0.01x^2 + 0.7x - 18$ and $y = -0.04x^2 - 3.6x + 32$

Example 9.4.4 Graphically solve the equation $-0.01(x - 90)(x + 20) = 25$.

Explanation. Start by graphing two curves on the same plot: $y = $ left and $y = $ right. Specifically for this example, $y = -0.01(x - 90)(x + 20)$ and $y = 25$.

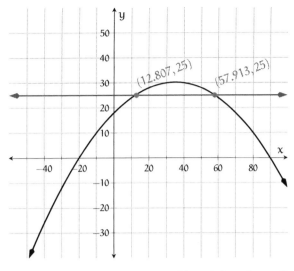

The points of intersection are $(12.807, 25)$ and $(57.913, 25)$, which tells us that the solutions are approximately 12.807 and 57.913. The solution set is approximately $\{12.807, 57.913\}$.

Figure 9.4.5: $y = -0.01(x - 90)(x + 20)$ and $y = 25$

One excellent thing about solving equations graphically is that it doesn't really matter what "kind" of equation it is. The equation can have mathematics in it that you haven't specifically studied, but as long as something (like a computer or your teacher) provides you with the graphs, you can still solve the equation.

Example 9.4.6 Graphically solve the equation $|x + 5| = \frac{1}{x+1}$.

Explanation. If you've only been learning algebra from this textbook, this equation has some unfamiliar bits and pieces. The vertical bars in $|x+5|$ represent the basic math concept of absolute value, which you can brush up on in Appendix A.3. On the other side of the equation there is the expression $\frac{1}{x+1}$, with a variable in the denominator. This textbook hasn't discussed such things yet.

Even though we don't yet have general knowledge for these kinds of math expressions and their graphs, we can still trust some source to provide the graphs for us.

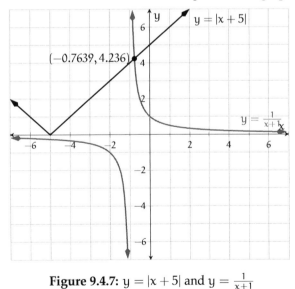

It appears there is only one point of intersection at about $(-0.7639, 4.236)$. So the solution set is approximately $\{-0.7639\}$.

Figure 9.4.7: $y = |x + 5|$ and $y = \frac{1}{x+1}$

If we are solving graphically and something is already providing you with the graph, it's not even necessary to have math expressions for the two curves.

Example 9.4.8
In Figure 9.4.9, there are two curves plotted. The horizontal axis represents years, one curve represents the population of California, and the other curve represents the population of New York. In what year did the population of California equal the population of New York?

It appears there is only one point of intersection at about (1963, 17.5). So the solution set is approximately {1963}. But in context, this says that 1963 is the year when California's population equaled New York's.

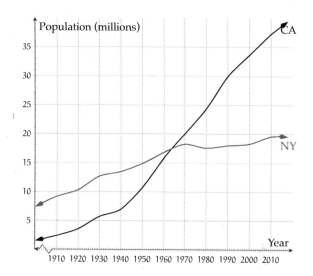

Figure 9.4.9: Populations of California and New York

9.4.2 Solving Inequalities Using a Graph

In Part I of this book, we learn how to solve linear inequalities such as $2x + 1 < 5$ using algebra. By using graphs instead of symbolic algebra, we can solve inequalities with more complicated math expressions, as well as inequalities in context that may not even have math expressions.

Example 9.4.10
In Figure 9.4.11, there are two curves plotted. The horizontal axis represents years, one curve represents the percent of US women ages 25–34 years old participating in the workforce, and the other curve represents the percent of US women ages 45–54 years old participating in the workforce. When was the percent from the 25–34 group more than the percent from the 45–54 group?

The curve for women 25–34 appears to rise above the other curve between the years 1975 and 1997. So the solution set is the interval (1975, 1997). But in context, this means that in between 1975 and 1997, the percentage of women 25–34 in the workforce was greater than the percentage of women 45–54 in the workforce.

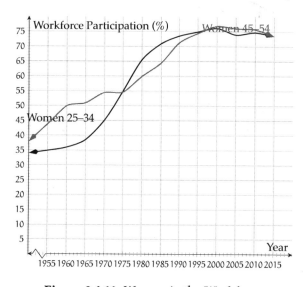

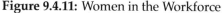

Figure 9.4.11: Women in the Workforce

It is helpful to take another look at this graph, with some annotations. We wanted the 25–34 curve to be greater than the 45–54 curve. Visually, we lock sights onto the indicated region. The solution set we are looking for is the *years* that this happened, which are down on the horizontal axis. So we have to project the region we've identified down onto the horizontal axis. After we've done this, the interval we see on the horizontal axis is the solution set.

Figure 9.4.12: Women in the Workforce

Example 9.4.13 Graphically solve the following inequalities.

a. $-20t^2 - 70t + 300 \geq -5t + 300$

b. $-20t^2 - 70t + 300 < -5t + 300$

Explanation.

For both parts of this example, we start by graphing the equations $y = -20t^2 - 70t + 300$ and $y = -5t + 300$ and determining the points of intersection. You may use some piece of technology to do this, or perhaps you find yourself provided with these graphs, with the intersection points clearly marked or easy to determine.

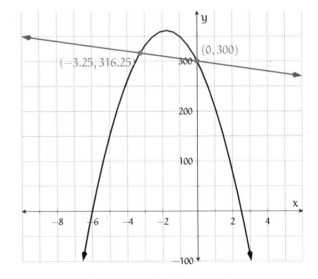

Figure 9.4.14: Points of intersection for $y = -20t^2 - 70t + 300$ and $y = -5t + 300$

a.

To solve $-20t^2 - 70t + 300 \geq -5t + 300$, we need to determine where the y-values of the parabola are higher than (or equal to) those of the line. This region is highlighted in Figure 9.4.15.

We can see that this region includes all values of t between, and including, $t = -3.25$ and $t = 0$. So the solutions to this inequality include all values of t for which $-3.25 \leq t \leq 0$. We can write this solution set in interval notation as $[-3.25, 0]$ or in set-builder notation as $\{t \mid -3.25 \leq t \leq 0\}$.

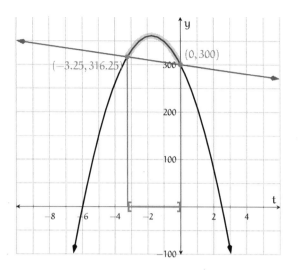

Figure 9.4.15

b.

To now solve $-20t^2 - 70t + 300 < -5t + 300$, we will need to determine where the y-values of the parabola are *less* than those of the line. This region is highlighted in Figure 9.4.16.

We can see that $-20t^2 - 70t + 300 < -5t + 300$ for all values of t where $t < -3.25$ or $t > 0$. We can write this solution set in interval notation as $(-\infty, -3.25) \cup (0, \infty)$ or in set-builder notation as $\{t \mid t < -3.25$ or $t > 0\}$.

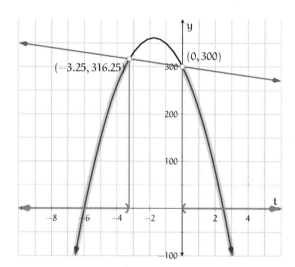

Figure 9.4.16

Occasionally, a curve abruptly "stops", and we need to recognize this in a solution to an inequality.

Example 9.4.17 Solve the inequality $1 - x > \sqrt{x + 5}$ using a graph.

Explanation.

We plot $y = 1 - x$ and $y = \sqrt{x + 5}$, and then look for the intersection(s) of the graphs. The two curves intersect at $(-1, 2)$.

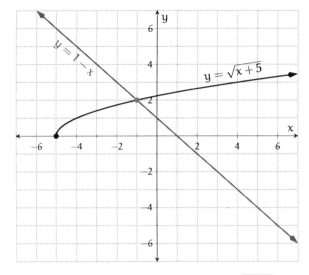

Figure 9.4.18: $y = 1 - x$ and $y = \sqrt{x + 5}$

Since the inequality is $\overbrace{1 - x}^{\text{line}} > \overbrace{\sqrt{x + 5}}^{\text{half-parabola}}$, we want to identify the region where the line is higher than the half-parabola. While the line extends higher and higher off to the left, the half-parabola abruptly stops at $(-5, 0)$. So the solution set needs to stop at the corresponding place. As illustrated, the solution set is the interval $[-5, -1)$.

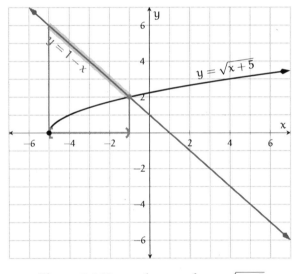

Figure 9.4.19: $y = 1 - x$ and $y = \sqrt{x + 5}$

9.4.3 Reading Questions

1.   Suppose you have an equation where x is the only variable. In order to solve that equation, explain how you could use a graph. Assume that some technology can provide you with any graph you would like to see.

2. The curves $y = x^4 - 3x^2 + x$ and $y = 1 - \sqrt{x-1}$ cross at three locations. How many solutions are there to $x^4 - 3x^2 + x = 1 - \sqrt{x-1}$?

3. The solution set to an inequality is generally not a single number or a small collection of numbers. In general, the solution set to an inequality is a ⬚ .

9.4.4 Exercises

Points of Intersection Use technology to make some graphs and determine how many times the graphs of the following curves cross each other.

1. $y = (441 - 17x)(-67 - 16x)$ and $y = -8000$ intersect (☐ zero times ☐ one time ☐ two times ☐ three times) .

2. $y = (-143 - 12x)(-344 + 11x)$ and $y = -9000$ intersect (☐ zero times ☐ one time ☐ two times ☐ three times) .

3. $y = -4x^3 - x^2 + 5x$ and $y = 7x - 4$ intersect (☐ zero times ☐ one time ☐ two times ☐ three times) .

4. $y = -x^3 - 3x^2 - 6x$ and $y = 2x - 4$ intersect (☐ zero times ☐ one time ☐ two times ☐ three times) .

5. $y = -0.5(5x^2 + 2)$ and $y = 0.45(7x - 3)$ intersect (☐ zero times ☐ one time ☐ two times ☐ three times) .

6. $y = -0.5(6x^2 - 9)$ and $y = -0.46(4x - 9)$ intersect (☐ zero times ☐ one time ☐ two times ☐ three times) .

7. $y = 1.05(x + 9)^2 - 1.05$ and $y = 1.1x - 1$ intersect (☐ zero times ☐ one time ☐ two times ☐ three times) .

8. $y = 1.5(x - 4)^2 + 6.45$ and $y = -0.05x - 1$ intersect (☐ zero times ☐ one time ☐ two times ☐ three times) .

Solving Equations and Inequalities Graphically

9. The equations $y = \frac{1}{2}x^2 + 2x - 1$ and $y = 5$ are plotted.

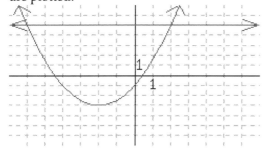

a. What are the points of intersection?

b. Solve $\frac{1}{2}x^2 + 2x - 1 = 5$.

c. Solve $\frac{1}{2}x^2 + 2x - 1 > 5$.

10. The equations $y = \frac{1}{3}x^2 - 3x + 3$ and $y = -3$ are plotted.

a. What are the points of intersection?

b. Solve $\frac{1}{3}x^2 - 3x + 3 = -3$.

c. Solve $\frac{1}{3}x^2 - 3x + 3 > -3$.

11. The equations $y = -x^2 + 1.5x + 5$ and $y = -5$ are plotted.

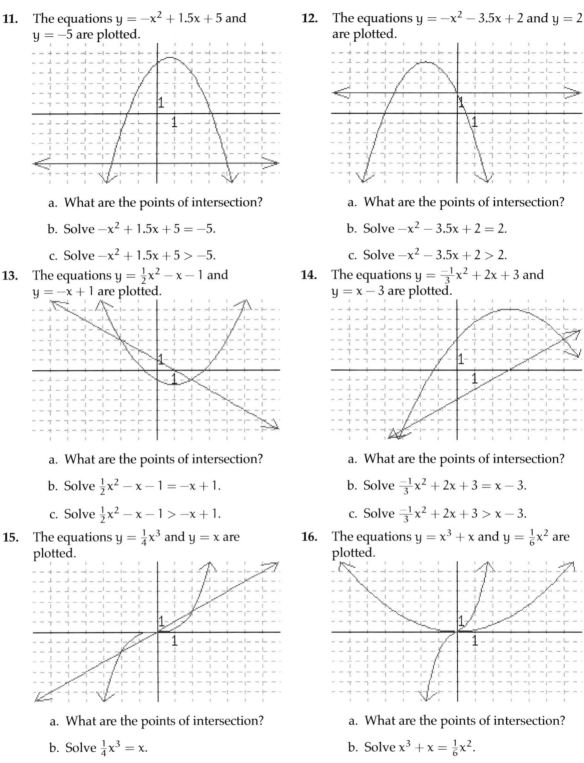

    a. What are the points of intersection?

    b. Solve $-x^2 + 1.5x + 5 = -5$.

    c. Solve $-x^2 + 1.5x + 5 > -5$.

12. The equations $y = -x^2 - 3.5x + 2$ and $y = 2$ are plotted.

    a. What are the points of intersection?

    b. Solve $-x^2 - 3.5x + 2 = 2$.

    c. Solve $-x^2 - 3.5x + 2 > 2$.

13. The equations $y = \frac{1}{2}x^2 - x - 1$ and $y = -x + 1$ are plotted.

    a. What are the points of intersection?

    b. Solve $\frac{1}{2}x^2 - x - 1 = -x + 1$.

    c. Solve $\frac{1}{2}x^2 - x - 1 > -x + 1$.

14. The equations $y = \frac{-1}{3}x^2 + 2x + 3$ and $y = x - 3$ are plotted.

    a. What are the points of intersection?

    b. Solve $\frac{-1}{3}x^2 + 2x + 3 = x - 3$.

    c. Solve $\frac{-1}{3}x^2 + 2x + 3 > x - 3$.

15. The equations $y = \frac{1}{4}x^3$ and $y = x$ are plotted.

    a. What are the points of intersection?

    b. Solve $\frac{1}{4}x^3 = x$.

    c. Solve $\frac{1}{4}x^3 > x$.

16. The equations $y = x^3 + x$ and $y = \frac{1}{6}x^2$ are plotted.

    a. What are the points of intersection?

    b. Solve $x^3 + x = \frac{1}{6}x^2$.

    c. Solve $x^3 + x > \frac{1}{6}x^2$.

17. The equations $y = \sqrt{x+4}$ and $y = \frac{4x^2+x+3}{36}$ are plotted.

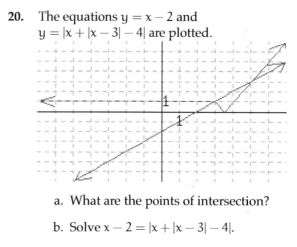

    a. What are the points of intersection?

    b. Solve $\sqrt{x+4} = \frac{4x^2+x+3}{36}$.

    c. Solve $\sqrt{x+4} > \frac{4x^2+x+3}{36}$.

18. The equations $y = \sqrt{4-x}$ and $y = -2-x$ are plotted.

    a. What are the points of intersection?

    b. Solve $\sqrt{4-x} = -2-x$.

    c. Solve $\sqrt{4-x} > -2-x$.

19. The equations $y = \frac{1}{2}x^2 + 2x$ and $y = \sqrt[3]{9-2x^2} + \frac{23}{50}x - \frac{52}{25}$ are plotted.

    a. What are the points of intersection?

    b. Solve
$$\frac{1}{2}x^2 + 2x = \sqrt[3]{9-2x^2} + \frac{23}{50}x - \frac{52}{25}.$$

    c. Solve
$$\frac{1}{2}x^2 + 2x > \sqrt[3]{9-2x^2} + \frac{23}{50}x - \frac{52}{25}.$$

20. The equations $y = x - 2$ and $y = |x + |x - 3| - 4|$ are plotted.

    a. What are the points of intersection?

    b. Solve $x - 2 = |x + |x - 3| - 4|$.

    c. Solve $x - 2 > |x + |x - 3| - 4|$.

9.5 Topics in Graphing Chapter Review

9.5.1 Review of Graphing

In Section 9.1, we reviewed the fundamentals of graph-making. In particular, given an equation of the form y = expression in x, the fundamental approach to making a graph is to make a table of points to plot.

We also looked back at the notions of "intercepts" on a graph. In the case of a linear equation in x and y, finding the x- and y-intercepts can be a way to create a graph.

9.5.2 Key Features of Quadratic Graphs

In Section 9.2, we identified the key features of a quadratic graph (which takes the shape of a parabola). The key features are the direction that it opens, the vertex, the axis of symmetry, the vertical intercept, and the horizontal intercepts (if there are any).

If the equation for a quadratic curve is $y = ax^2 + bx + c$, then the formula $h = -\frac{b}{2a}$ gives the first coordinate of the vertex. So you can find the location of the vertex with that coordinate and subbing that number into the equation to find the second coordinate.

If we know the location of a parabola's vertex and the direction that it opens, we can sketch the parabola. It helps to make a table finding a few points the the left and to the right of the vertex. The symmetry of a parabola means you only need to find points on one side to automatically get corresponding points on the other side.

9.5.3 Graphing Quadratic Equations

In Section 9.3, we practiced finding the exact locations of the vertical and horizontal intercepts for a quadratic equation curve. The vertical intercept can be found by lettting x = 0. The result is a number on the y-axis.

The horizontal intercepts can be found by setting y equal to 0. This leaves you with a quadratic equation in one variable, x, and the quadratic formula can be used to solve for x. There might be no solutions, as is the case when the parabola doesn't touch the x-axis. There might be one solution, when the vertex is on the x-axis. Or there might be two solutions, and therefore two horizontal intercepts.

When we know the exact locations of the intercepts (as well as the location of the vertex as found in Section 9.2) then we can plot accurate graphs of quadratic equations.

9.5.4 Graphically Solving Equations and Inequalities

In Section 9.4, we see how a graph can be used to solve an equation or inequality. Each side of an equation gives you a curve, and where the two curves cross tells you where there are solutions to the equation.

For example, to solve the equation $x^2 + x - 1 = 2x + 1$, we could plot two curves: $y = x^2 + x - 1$ and $y = 2x + 1$. We might use a computer to make the graphs for us, as in Figure 9.5.1.

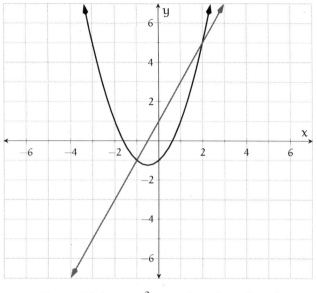

Figure 9.5.1: $y = x^2 + x - 1$ and $y = 2x + 1$

Since the curves cross at $(-1, -1)$ and $(2, 5)$, the solutions are $x = -1$ and $x = 2$. This means the solution set is $\{-1, 2\}$.

9.5.5 Exercises

Review of Graphing Make a table for the equation.

1.

x	$y = -9x$

2.

x	$y = -3x + 5$

3.

x	$y = \frac{10}{3}x + 1$

4.

x	$y = -\frac{5}{4}x + 3$

5.   Create a table of ordered pairs and then make a plot of the equation $y = 2x + 3$.

6.   Create a table of ordered pairs and then make a plot of the equation $y = -\frac{3}{4}x + 2$.

7. Find the y-intercept and x-intercept of the line given by the equation. If a particular intercept does not exist, enter *none* into all the answer blanks for that row.

$$8x + 7y = -168$$

	x-value	y-value	Location (as an ordered pair)
y-intercept	_____	_____	_____
x-intercept	_____	_____	_____

8. Find the y-intercept and x-intercept of the line given by the equation. If a particular intercept does not exist, enter *none* into all the answer blanks for that row.

$$8x - 5y = -80$$

	x-value	y-value	Location (as an ordered pair)
y-intercept	_____	_____	_____
x-intercept	_____	_____	_____

9. Find the x- and y-intercepts of the line with equation $5x - 6y = -90$. Then find one other point on the line. Use your results to graph the line.

10. Find the x- and y-intercepts of the line with equation $x + 5y = -15$. Then find one other point on the line. Use your results to graph the line.

Key Features of Quadratic Graphs Find the axis of symmetry and vertex of the quadratic function.

11. $y = 5x^2 - 50x + 3$ 　　　　　 12. $y = -3 - 30x - 5x^2$ 　　　　　 13. $y = -1 - x^2 + 6x$

14. $y = -2x^2 + 20x$ 　　　　　 15. $y = 2 - x^2$ 　　　　　 16. $y = -2x^2 - 10x + 4$

17. $y = 2x^2 + 10x - 2$ 　　　　　 18. $y = 3x^2$ 　　　　　 19. $y = 0.4x^2 - 4$

20. $y = 5(x + 3)^2 + 4$

For the given quadratic equation, find the vertex. Then create a table of ordered pairs centered around the vertex and make a graph.

21. $y = x^2 + 2$ 　　　　 22. $y = x^2 - 5$ 　　　　 23. $y = (x - 2)^2$ 　　　　 24. $y = (x + 3)^2$

25. For $y = 4x^2 - 8x + 5$, determine the vertex, create a table of ordered pairs, and then make a graph.

26. For $y = -x^2 + 4x + 2$, determine the vertex, create a table of ordered pairs, and then make a graph.

27. For $y = x^2 - 5x + 3$, determine the vertex, create a table of ordered pairs, and then make a graph.

28. For $y = -2x^2 - 5x + 6$, determine the vertex, create a table of ordered pairs, and then make a graph.

29. Consider two numbers where one number is 4 less than a second number. Find a pair of such numbers that has the least product possible. One approach is to let x represent the smaller number, and write a formula for a function of x that outputs the product of the two numbers. Then find its vertex and interpret it.

These two numbers are [blank] and the least possible product is [blank].

30. You will build a rectangular sheep enclosure next to a river. There is no need to build a fence along the river, so you only need to build on three sides. You have a total of 420 feet of fence to use. Find the dimensions of the pen such that you can enclose the maximum possible area. One approach is to let x represent the length of fencing that runs perpendicular to the river, and write a formula for a function of x that outputs the area of the enclosure. Then find its vertex and interpret it.

The length of the pen (parallel to the river) should be [blank], the width (perpendicular to the river) should be [blank], and the maximum possible area is [blank].

Graphing Quadratic Equations Find the y-intercept and any x-intercept(s) of the quadratic curve.

31. $y = x^2 - 2x - 8$
32. $y = -x^2 + 1$
33. $y = x^2 + 6x + 9$
34. $y = x^2 + 4x + 7$
35. $y = x^2 + 8x + 5$
36. $y = 5x^2 - 8x - 4$
37. $y = -x + 18 - 5x^2$
38. $y = 5x - 2x^2$

Graph each curve by algebraically determining its key features.

39. $y = x^2 - 7x + 12$
40. $y = -x^2 - x + 20$
41. $y = x^2 - 8x + 16$
42. $y = x^2 - 4$
43. $y = x^2 + 6x$
44. $y = -x^2 + 5x$
45. $y = x^2 + 4x + 7$
46. $y = x^2 + 2x - 5$
47. $y = -x^2 + 4x - 1$
48. $y = 2x^2 - 4x - 30$

49. An object was shot up into the air with an initial vertical speed of 384 feet per second. Its height as time passes can be modeled by the quadratic equation $y = -16t^2 + 384t$. Here t represents the number of seconds since the object's release, and y represents the object's height in feet.

   a. After [blank], this object reached its maximum height of [blank].

   b. This object flew for [blank] before it landed on the ground.

   c. This object was [blank] in the air 3 s after its release.

   d. This object was 704 ft high at two times: once [blank] after its release, and again later [blank] after its release.

50. A remote control aircraft will perform a stunt by flying toward the ground and then up. Its height, in feet, can be modeled by the equation $h = t^2 - 10t + 28$, where t is in seconds. The plane (☐ will ☐ will not) hit the ground during this stunt.

51. An object is launched upward at the height of 280 meters. Its height can be modeled by

$$h = -4.9t^2 + 70t + 280,$$

where h stands for the object's height in meters, and t stands for time passed in seconds since its launch. The object's height will be 330 meters twice before it hits the ground. Find how many seconds since the launch would the object's height be 330 meters. Round your answers to two decimal places if needed.

The object's height would be 330 meters the first time at ⬚ seconds, and then the second time at ⬚ seconds.

52. Currently, an artist can sell 230 paintings every year at the price of $70.00 per painting. Each time he raises the price per painting by $10.00, he sells 10 fewer paintings every year.

Assume he will raise the price per painting x times, then he will sell $230 - 10x$ paintings every year at the price of $70 + 10x$ dollars. His yearly income can be modeled by the equation:

$$i = (70 + 10x)(230 - 10x)$$

where i stands for his yearly income in dollars. If the artist wants to earn $21,600.00 per year from selling paintings, what new price should he set?

To earn $21,600.00 per year, the artist could sell his paintings at two different prices. The lower price is ⬚ per painting, and the higher price is ⬚ per painting.

Graphically Solving Equations and Inequalities Use technology to make some graphs and determine how many times the graphs of the following curves cross each other.

53. $y = (286 + 5x)(78 + 10x)$ and $y = 6000$ intersect (☐ zero times ☐ one time ☐ two times ☐ three times) .

54. $y = 5x^3 - x^2 - 6x$ and $y = -4x + 3$ intersect (☐ zero times ☐ one time ☐ two times ☐ three times) .

55. $y = 0.2(8x^2 + 2)$ and $y = 0.2(x - 9)$ intersect (☐ zero times ☐ one time ☐ two times ☐ three times) .

56. $y = 1.85(x - 4)^2 - 8.4$ and $y = x + 1$ intersect (☐ zero times ☐ one time ☐ two times ☐ three times) .

57. The equations $y = \frac{1}{2}x^2 + 2x - 1$ and $y = 5$ are plotted.

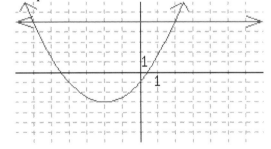

a. What are the points of intersection?

b. Solve $\frac{1}{2}x^2 + 2x - 1 = 5$.

c. Solve $\frac{1}{2}x^2 + 2x - 1 > 5$.

58. The equations $y = -x^2 + 1.5x + 5$ and $y = -5$ are plotted.

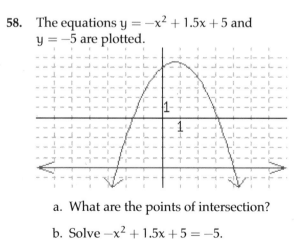

a. What are the points of intersection?

b. Solve $-x^2 + 1.5x + 5 = -5$.

c. Solve $-x^2 + 1.5x + 5 > -5$.

59. The equations $y = \frac{1}{2}x^2 - x - 1$ and $y = -x + 1$ are plotted.

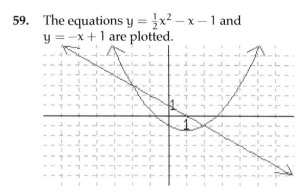

    a. What are the points of intersection?

    b. Solve $\frac{1}{2}x^2 - x - 1 = -x + 1$.

    c. Solve $\frac{1}{2}x^2 - x - 1 > -x + 1$.

60. The equations $y = \frac{1}{4}x^3$ and $y = x$ are plotted.

    a. What are the points of intersection?

    b. Solve $\frac{1}{4}x^3 = x$.

    c. Solve $\frac{1}{4}x^3 > x$.

61. The equations $y = \sqrt{x + 4}$ and $y = \frac{4x^2 + x + 3}{36}$ are plotted.

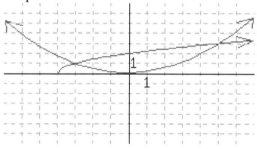

    a. What are the points of intersection?

    b. Solve $\sqrt{x + 4} = \frac{4x^2 + x + 3}{36}$.

    c. Solve $\sqrt{x + 4} > \frac{4x^2 + x + 3}{36}$.

62. The equations $y = \frac{1}{2}x^2 + 2x$ and $y = \sqrt[3]{9 - 2x^2} + \frac{23}{50}x - \frac{52}{25}$ are plotted.

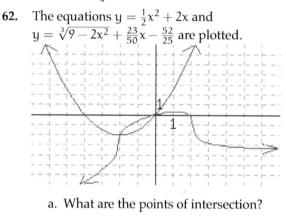

    a. What are the points of intersection?

    b. Solve
$$\frac{1}{2}x^2 + 2x = \sqrt[3]{9 - 2x^2} + \frac{23}{50}x - \frac{52}{25}.$$

    c. Solve
$$\frac{1}{2}x^2 + 2x > \sqrt[3]{9 - 2x^2} + \frac{23}{50}x - \frac{52}{25}.$$

Appendix B

Unit Conversions

Units of Length in the US/Imperial System	Units of Length in the Metric System	System to System Length Conversions
1 foot (ft) = 12 inches (in)	1 meter (m) = 1000 millimeters (mm)	1 inch (in) = 2.54 centimeters (cm)
1 yard (yd) = 3 feet (ft)	1 meter (m) = 100 centimeters (cm)	1 meter (m) $\approx$ 3.281 feet (ft)
1 yard (yd) = 36 inches (in)	1 meter (m) = 10 decimeters (dm)	1 meter (m) $\approx$ 1.094 yard (yd)
1 mile (mi) = 5280 feet (ft)	1 dekameter (dam) = 10 meters (m)	1 mile (mi) $\approx$ 1.609 kilometer (km)
	1 hectometer (hm) = 100 meters (m)	
	1 kilometer (km) = 1000 meters (m)	

Table B.0.1: Length Unit Conversion Factors

Units of Area in the US/Imperial System	Units of Area in the Metric System	System to System Area Conversions
1 acre = 43560 square feet (ft^2)	1 hectare (ha) = 10000 square meters (m^2)	1 hectare (ha) $\approx$ 2.471 acres
640 acres = 1 square mile (mi^2)	100 hectares (ha) = 1 square kilometer (km^2)	

Table B.0.2: Area Unit Conversion Factors

Units of Volume in the US/Imperial System	Units of Volume in the Metric System	System to System Volume Conversions
1 tablespoon (tbsp) = 3 teaspoon (tsp)	1 cubic centimeter (cc) = 1 cubic centimeter (cm^3)	1 cubic inch (in^3) $\approx$ 16.39 milliliters (mL)
1 fluid ounce (fl oz) = 2 tablespoons (tbsp)	1 milliliter (mL) = 1 cubic centimeter (cm^3)	1 fluid ounce (fl oz) $\approx$ 29.57 milliliters (mL)
1 cup (c) = 8 fluid ounces (fl oz)	1 liter (L) = 1000 milliliters (mL)	1 liter (L) $\approx$ 1.057 quarts (qt)
1 pint (pt) = 2 cups (c)	1 liter (L) = 1000 cubic centimeters (cm^3)	1 gallon (gal) $\approx$ 3.785 liters (L)
1 quart (qt) = 2 pints (pt)		
1 gallon (gal) = 4 quarts (qt)		
1 gallon (gal) = 231 cubic inches (in^3)		

Table B.0.3: Volume Unit Conversion Factors

Units of Mass/Weight in the US/Imperial System	Units of Mass/Weight in the Metric System	System to System Mass/Weight Conversions
1 pound (lb) = 16 ounces (oz)	1 gram (g) = 1000 milligrams (mg)	1 ounce (oz) $\approx$ 28.35 grams (g)
1 ton (T) = 2000 pounds (lb)	1 gram (g) = 1000 kilograms (kg)	1 kilogram (kg) $\approx$ 2.205 pounds (lb)
	1 metric ton (t) = 1000 kilograms (kg)	

Table B.0.4: Weight/Mass Unit Conversion Factors

Precise Units of Time	Imprecise Units of Time	Units of Time in the Metric System
1 week (wk) = 7 days (d)	1 year (yr) ≈ 12 months (mo)	1 second (s) = 1000 milliseconds (ms)
1 day (d) = 24 hours (h)	1 year (yr) ≈ 52 weeks (wk)	1 second (s) = 10^6 microseconds (μs)
1 hour (h) = 60 minutes (min)	1 year (yr) ≈ 365 days (d)	1 second (s) = 10^9 nanoseconds (ns)
1 minute (min) = 60 seconds (s)	1 month (mo) ≈ 30 days (d)	

Table B.0.5: Time Unit Conversion Factors

1 byte (B) = 8 bits (b)	1 kilobit (kb) = 1024 bits (b)
1 kilobyte (kB) = 1024 bytes (B)	1 megabit (Mb) = 1024 kilobits (kb)
1 megabyte (MB) = 1024 kilobytes (kB)	
1 gigabyte (GB) = 1024 megabytes (MB)	
1 terabyte (TB) = 1024 gigabytes (GB)	

Table B.0.6: Computer Storage/Memory Conversion Factors

Index

Made in the USA
Las Vegas, NV
03 September 2021